The Language of the Inka since the European Invasion

The Language of the Inka since the European Invasion

by Bruce Mannheim

University of Texas Press, Austin

Printed in the United States of America

First paperback edition, 2011

♾ The paper used in this publication meets the minimum requirements of American National Standard for Information Sciences—Permanence of Paper for Printed Library Materials, ANSI Z39.48-1984.

This book has been supported by a grant from the National Endowment for the Humanities, an independent federal agency.

Library of Congress Cataloging-in-Publication Data
Mannheim, Bruce.
The language of the Inka since the European invasion / by Bruce Mannheim. — 1st ed.
p. cm. — (Texas linguistics series)
Includes bibliographical references (p.) and index.
ISBN: 978-0-292-72926-1
1. Quechua language—Peru—History. 2. Incas—History. 3. Peru—History—Conquest, 1522–1548. 4. Peru—Languages. I. Title. II. Title: Language of the Inca since the European invasion. III. Series.
PM602.M36 1991
498'.323'0985—dc20 90-12634
CIP

In memory of
Stephen Herman
and Antonio Cusihuamán Gutiérrez

Contents

Foreword

by Paul Friedrich
University of Chicago

In this book, Bruce Mannheim, drawing on his lengthy bibliography, gives us a wide-ranging review and synthesis of the relevant linguistic, sociocultural/linguistic, and sociopolitical scholarship of the half-millennial history of Southern Peruvian Quechua, one of the major high culture languages of Native America. He also forges a precedent for a truly historical and diachronic sociocultural linguistics that saliently interconnects language change with the "social ecology of language"; he shows, for example, why and how regular sound change must be combined with an interpretation in terms of less regular variables such as sound imagery. He gives us intimations of a future sociocultural linguistics that will work synergistically between synchrony and diachrony, language and culture, speech and society, and, as defined below, a comprehensive macrolinguistics and a primal, dialogical linguistics. Given the author's sustained and encompassing vision of language and society/culture as continuously interacting—reminiscent of a Möbius strip where one side continuously shades into another—the most effective or representative way to sketch his contributions would be to follow his own argument while dwelling briefly on the major bends and turns of its theoretical import.

The overall arch of linguistic and sociopolitical history starts in medias res with the Inka empire where, for example, surplus was extracted via labor and services (with obvious linguistic consequences) in the context of an organizing "template" of 328 "sacred places" arranged in forty-one lines that ran "like spokes on a bicycle wheel" out of Cuzco. The extraordinary multilingualism of those times was gradually replaced after the conquest in 1532 by an agonizing "double bind" situation where Southern Peruvian Quechua, the language of Cuzco and the imperial lingua franca, was retained as the favored speech form of the Spanish colonials and their descendants while at the same time it devolved into the stigmatized language of a majority that was as huge as it was powerless. Mannheim cogently analyzes the antagonistic ideologies and political sociologies of this "dual society." There is a suggestive review of the literary and linguistic history of postconquest Southern Peruvian Quechua, including the "Quechua Renaissance" of the eighteenth century (which ended with the failed revolt of 1781), as well as the tension-ridden contemporary situation in the southern highlands of Peru where the urban Spanish-speaking minority opposes the great majority (over ninety percent Quechua-speaking). Particularly revealing are the pages where Mannheim characterizes the Quechua value of reciprocity that bonds Quechua speakers to each other and sets them off from the Hispanic "other society." Similarly revealing is the way he shows the long-term continuity of linguistic and cultural ideologies (including softhearted "assimilationism") that keep validating the same political oppression. Chapter 3 on "Language and Colonialism" should be read by all Andeanists, particularly those outside language studies proper, and by all those interested in issues of linguistic colonization.

Mannheim summarizes a whole series of themes or interconnected problems and concerns: for example, the four themes of diachronic sociocultural linguistics (e.g., the noncontiguous territorial organization) or the four themes in the social ecology of "endogenous variation" (e.g., the *ethnocentric* character of linguistic features "above the threshold of awareness"); his discussion of "the dimensions of language variation" (i.e., covertness, equivalence, ethnocentrism, nonsystematicity—giving one term of each dimension); his definition of hegemony at a level of both New Gramscian theory and his own no-nonsense lingo ("When I say that Spanish is 'hegemonic,' I mean . . . the gnawing closure that it places on the lives of Quechua monolinguals . . . the silence of Quechua-speaking children in a Spanish-speaking classroom . . . the pride with which a Quechua peasant *writes* his name . . . the shame of a military draftee who cannot understand the Spanish spoken around him . . . bilingual puns used in the marketplace . . . the insults shouted at a monolingual Spanish speaker . . ."). A final example of these sets of themes is Mannheim's creative adaptation and utilization of the idea of the "social ecology of language" that was launched by Haugen, the Voegelins, and others. "The social ecology of language consists of the ways in which linguistic differences are organized and set into a social landscape; of the ways in which language and dialect differences are institutionally channeled and used; of the degree to which diversity is encouraged or, conversely, restricted by language standardization; of the particular contexts of written attestations; of the social evaluation of linguistic differences; and of the cultural and psychological resonances of linguistic differences for their speakers." Mannheim's project is to operationalize this master concept and to show how Southern Peruvian Quechua data can be informed by it.

The bulk of this study deals with "Linguistic Change," with topics that run from "The Sound Pattern of Common Southern Peruvian Quechua," to the chapter on the sibilants (Mannheim agreeing with Landerman's two-sibilant solution), to a long discussion of the author's chief concern: the complementary relation between syllable-final weakenings and the flourishing of ejective and aspirate stops (at the beginning of lexical roots only). The inadequacy of standard phonological theory and the notion of "exceptionless sound laws" and recent homologues to it leads the author to a brilliantly formulated hypothesis of the spread of ejective and aspirate stops throughout the Quechua sound system through the workings of "sound imagery and associative lexical influences" (in a model derived mainly from Peirce). When Mannheim moves bridgingly between specific, conventional linguistic sets (e.g., an array of cognate sets) to the dynamic, structuring force of lexical sets (illustrated, for example, by the connotations of the *yll* root as formulated by the poet Arguedas), we have a (highly anthologizable) demonstration of the creative interaction between structure and process in historical linguistics.

Just as striking as the sorts of crossovers just described is the solid instantiation of what might be called (unjargoning a bit of jargon) "thick philology." Mannheim's inferences and hypotheses are massively cross-referenced and buttressed by texts, dictionaries, historical grammars, and the like. One would think that he had been trained in Indo-European linguistics and philology by Emile Benveniste! An entire chapter is devoted to "Reading Colonial Texts," where a close reading of many texts is discussed in terms of Becker's (Emersonian) idea of "exuberances" and "deficiencies" in translation and interpretation. But perhaps the most original part of Mannheim's linguistic analysis comes in the tenth chapter when he discusses "The Word as Diagram, Diagrams of the Word"; using a Peircean and Jakobsonian sort of conceptualization, and implicational hierarchies à la Jakobson and Greenberg, and morphophonological analysis à la Sapir and Kuryłowicz, Mannheim shows that, in his own words, "there is a definite hierarchical and sequential order among the changes . . . the erosion of syllable endings follows a predictable course that reflects the internal grammatical structure of the Quechua word, from suffixes into stems. . . . Paradoxically, [these patterns] emerge only when language change is viewed in a perspective that is both more fine-grained and more holistic; more fine-grained, in that a variety of evidence—especially philological and dialectological—is used to reconstruct the precise course followed by the erosions of syllable endings over five hundred years; more holistic in that the course of these changes has been constant from change to change over the entire period."

A final linguistic contribution of *The Language of the Inka since the European Invasion* with great cultural and archaeological implications, which space prevents me from elaborating here, is phylogenetic. Mannheim concludes that, despite many shared features and spatial/temporal association, Quechua is not related to the contiguous Aymara language—an example of "splitting" that contrasts with the current trend to "long-range comparison" that lumps together all New World languages as "Amerind" except Na-Dene and Eskimo!

Mannheim's masterful synthesis of Quechua scholarship and avant-garde sociocultural linguistics suggests two contrastive, complementary approaches. On the one hand, we can interrelate the social patterns of dyads such as two friends, or small groups such as the household, to the relatively empirical patterning in the use of words, conversational regularities—or poetry in immediate, even intimate social contexts. Such sociolinguistics is relatively close to native experience, requires comparatively few moves between language/speech and sociocultural process, and could perhaps be dubbed immediate, intimate, primal, or *dialogical* sociocultural linguistics (good examples are the work of Abu-Lughod or Tannen). The second approach, on the other hand, goes further from the native model and stretches into the analytical recesses of the variables whose interrelation is our object of inquiry and tends to embrace larger entities such as the city, nation-state, or a linguistic-cultural region such as Southern Peruvian Quechua. This might be called extended or *encompassing* sociocultural linguistics (good examples include the work of Errington and Haugen). This book, by synthesizing a fully realized encompassing (or macro-) sociolinguistics with the elements of a primal (or micro-) sociolinguistics, creates or at least suggests an essentially new model for sociocultural linguistics, one that will be pursued for many decades by scholars with the talent, skills, and open-mindedness for the requisite inferences from fieldwork and historical evidence.

Acknowledgments

I flirted with this book for the better part of ten years, since my fieldwork in Cuzco, Peru, during the later 1970s. It is the product of a long personal and professional itinerary, which I could not have followed without the gracious advice, lessons, and support of friends, colleagues, and students, Peruvian and North American. My list of debts is long; I beg the indulgence of anyone who was inadvertently omitted.

I am indebted intellectually to my teachers and first colleagues, whose insights into language and life shaped my own, especially the late Antonio Cusihuamán Gutiérrez, Paul Friedrich, Billie Jean Isbell, James D. McCawley, Sally McConnell-Ginet, Michael Silverstein, Linda R. Waugh, and R. T. Zuidema.

Diane E. Hopkins shared the emotional tribulations of field research and the tedium of the archive with me; I am certain that I would not have lasted through it without her support and counsel. Antoinette Molinié Fioravanti was an outstanding collaborator in the archives, whose impatience was the match of my own. My friends, colleagues, and collaborators during the years in Cuzco were a vital source of intellectual and moral support, including Miguel Ayala, Rosalía Puma Escalante vda. de Cusihuamán, Rosa Chillca Huallpa, Florencio Menzala Quispe, Matilde Farfán, Rondi Ericksen, and Dario León.

A photocopy of the manuscript of Molina's *Ritos* . . . and a microfilm of Santa Cruz Pachacuti Yamqui's holographic manuscript were kindly sent to me by R. T. Zuidema. Diane E. Hopkins allowed me to consult her transcription of an episcopal inquest into church economy in Andahuaylillas held after Pérez Bocanegra's death. Antoinette Molinié Fioravanti filmed a copy of Pérez Bocanegra's *Ritual formulario* with me at the library of the University of Cuzco. Graciela Sánchez-Cerro of the Sala de Investigaciones of the Biblioteca Nacional del Perú facilitated the use of the *Ollanta* and *Usca Paucar* manuscripts, the badly charred manuscript by Diego de Molina, and several rare colonial Quechua books. The late Msgr. Luís Vallejos Santoni, the archbishop of Cuzco, graciously allowed me to consult the Archives of the Archdiocese. Horacio Villanueva Urteaga and Manual J. Aparicio Vega, the directors of the Departmental Archives of Cuzco, facilitated my work there; I would have been lost without the assistance of the workers at the archives.

Theresa May, the executive editor of the University of Texas Press, has been exemplary as an editor and made the publication of my first book an enjoyable experience, from the first draft to the final proofs. Kathleen Lewis edited the manuscript for the press. I am grateful to Abdullah Dashti, Susan A. Gelman, Jane Hill, Billie Jean Isbell, Barry Lyons, Rosario Montoya, Janis Nuckolls, Deborah A. Poole, Marla Schwaller, Marilyn Shatz, and Dennis Tedlock for their comments on an earlier version of the manuscript. In addition, I would like to thank the colleagues who commented on earlier versions of specific chapters: for chapter 2, Lyle Campbell, Rodolfo Cerrón-Palomino, Harriet E. Manelis Klein, and Louisa R. Stark; for chapter 3, Rolena Adorno, Roswith Hartmann, Anthony Pagden, and Susan U. Phillips; for chapter 7, William Baxter, Garland D. Bills, Susan Blum, and Peter Landerman; and for chapter 10, Janise Hurtig, Conrad Phillip Kottak, and Joel Nevis. Finally, for chapter 8, I wish to thank Madeleine Newfield for her collaboration in the research on sound imagery and associative lexical influence and for her discussion of comparable English data, Robert Hoberman for discussion of Semitic, Jay Jasanoff for his discussion of comparable data from Indo-Iranian, and Eric Hamp for his criticism of the methodology of Mannheim and Newfield (1982).

An abbreviated version of chapter 2 appeared in *South American Indian Languages, Retrospect and Prospect* (1985) under the title "Contact and Quechua-External Genetic Relationships." An earlier version of chapter 3 appeared in *Language in Society* (1984) under the title "Una nación acorralada." A preliminary version of chapter 7 appeared in the *International Journal of American Linguistics* as "On the Sibilants of Colonial Southern Peruvian Quechua." I acknowledge the University of Texas Press, Cambridge University Press, and the University of Chicago Press for permission to use this material.

The research was supported in part by grants from the Organization of American States, the National Science Foundation, the Wenner-Gren Foundation for Anthropological Research, the Tinker Foundation through a grant to the Center for Latin American Studies of the University of Arizona, and the Horace Rackham School of Graduate Studies at the University of Michigan. In several stages this book was nurtured by the intellectual environment of the University of Michigan. The final manuscript was completed during a fellowship year at the Institute for the Humanities of the University of Michigan.

This book would not have been finished at all had friends, colleagues, and students in the Department of Anthropology at Michigan not been so understanding when I made myself unavailable for appointments, turned down dinner invitations, and retreated to the company of my computer. And during the last push to complete the manuscript in the dog days of 1988, David and Rolena Adorno, Norma Diamond, Beverly Rathcke, and David P. Watts provided moral support.

And, finally, praise be to the one to whom all praise is due.

A Note on Orthography and Citations

In this book, I follow the official Peruvian orthography for Quechua (with appropriate additions—see appendix 1): *Inka* rather than *Inca*, *khipu* rather than *quipu* 'knotted string,' *ziqi* rather than *ceque* 'straight line.' There are two main classes of exceptions: I use the traditional Spanish-based spelling for most Native Andean place names and personal names, as *Cuzco*, *Vilcashuamán*, *Roca* (but *Atawallpa*, *Thupa Amaru*); I use the spelling of the original source for quotations and citations—especially those from colonial-era sources—unless otherwise noted.

For many of the primary colonial-era sources, I follow the standard practice of citing the book in uppercase roman numerals, followed by the chapter in lowercase roman numerals, followed by the page number of the edition I used. The book and chapter citations allow the reader to consult other editions of the same work. Laws and decrees collected in the *Recopilación de leyes* and in Solorzano's *Política indiana* are cited by the date of the law, followed by the *libro* in uppercase roman, *título* in lowercase roman, and law in arabic numerals; these are followed by the volume and page number of the edition I used.

The Language of the Inka since the European Invasion

1 Introduction

In 1532, the Spanish empire came upon a multiethnic American empire, Tawantinsuyu, stretching across the Andes from what is today southern Colombia to northern Argentina, from the Pacific coast to small garrisons in the jungles of the eastern slopes. By 1533, Tawantinsuyu was in ruins, soon to be reduced to a small military enclave based in the lowlands northeast of Cuzco; to disorganized resistance among sectors of the population that had not collaborated with the invaders; and to a distant memory in national movements centuries later. The principal moment of the conquest was remembered by both sides to have taken place in the northern mountains of Cajamarca, in which the Inka Atawallpa rejected the (written) Word and was captured, ransomed, and killed. The disaster at Cajamarca was only the beginning of a campaign of military, economic, and cultural conquest that has achieved a peace that is at best uneasy and that threatens to dissolve in blood even as I write. The descendants of the Inkas, and the descendants of many of the people they had subjugated, have survived and to one extent or another have maintained many of their older practices and their languages; but they have survived as part of a new nation that was forged from their cultural and linguistic differences, a nation of peasants, a nation born in subjugation to the Spanish empire and the modern Andean republics.

This book is a study of the changes that have taken place in Southern Peruvian Quechua, the language of the former Inka state, since the European invasion in 1532. In writing it, I have three main purposes in mind: first, to describe the transformation of the social, cultural, and political settings of the language and the ways in which the use of Southern Peruvian Quechua was shaped by the circumstances of Spanish colonial domination (chapters 2 to 4); second, to understand the changes in the formal structure of the language, especially in its phonological system (chapters 5 to 9); and third, to use the history of Southern Peruvian Quechua as a case study in pattern explanations of linguistic change (chapters 9 and 10).

Part I, "The Historical and Social Setting," traces the changes in the cultural and social topography of the language, from the administrative tongue and lingua franca of a great multinational state to the stigmatized language of peasants, herders, and rural proletarians. I organize the discussion around the concept of the "social ecology of language," which consists of the ways in which linguistic differences are organized and located in a social landscape (whether also in a physical landscape or not), of the social evaluation of linguistic differences, and of the cultural and psychological resonances that these differences have for speakers. The notion of "social ecology" allows me to describe the sweep of changes in the social, cultural, and political contexts of language in a systematic way. Chapter 2, "The Ecology of Language Contact before the European Invasion," discusses the intimate, mosaic pattern of language contact in southern Peru and its implications for solving the problem of whether Southern Peruvian Quechua is related genetically to the neighboring Jaqi/Aru family, including Aymara. The southern Peruvian Andes were, in general, a cultural mosaic in which speakers of distinct and often unrelated languages lived cheek to jowl with one another; even though Southern Peruvian Quechua was the administrative language of an expansionist state, before the European invasion, it never became hegemonic, nor was it ever standardized, even in the territory immediately surrounding the Inka capital. After the fall of the Inkas, the linguistic landscape was subject to a process of homogenization, in a double sense. First, Spanish was implanted as the language of the dominant sectors of colonial society and eventually made its influence felt in every corner of Peru, either as the only language spoken or as the language through which the social domination was maintained institutionally. Second, during the colonial era, Southern Peruvian Quechua was promoted, by design and otherwise, at the expense of other Native Andean languages (chapter 3, "Language and Colonialism"). The modern-day spread of Quechua throughout the southern Peruvian highlands was achieved under European colonial rule, as the language of a conquered people. The preconquest pattern of interspersed multilingualism was replaced by a pattern in which two languages, Spanish and Southern Peruvian Quechua, coexisted in a relationship of domination—Spanish as the language of the dominant sector, Quechua as the language of the dominated. The relationship of domination has become so totalizing that today it is taken for granted by Quechua and Spanish speaker alike (chapter 4, "Linguistic Hegemony and the Two Dimensions of Language Variations").

The second part of the book, "Linguistic Change," is a reconstruction of linguistic innovations in the Quechua spoken in the former Inka capital, Cuzco. I use three kinds of evidence: evidence from comparative reconstruction of the Quechua language family; evidence from colonial-era and modern written texts, including grammars, dictionaries, collections of sermons, and literary works; and dialect evidence collected from modern-day speakers of the varieties of Southern Peruvian Quechua spoken in the Department of Cuzco. I rely most heavily on philological and dialectological evidence and bring in comparative materials only when they shed light on problems that are insufficiently clear from texts and modern recordings.

Part II establishes a chronology for the phonological changes that separate Southern Peruvian Quechua from the other members of the Quechua linguistic family and that distinguish the innovative Cuzco-Collao dialect from the more conservative Ayacucho-Chanka dialect. The formal chronology provides a general framework through which the rich colonial literature written in Southern Peruvian Quechua can be situated historically and socially (chapter 6). The reconstruction of older stages of Southern Peruvian Quechua clarifies the relationship between Southern Peruvian and the other Quechua languages. It also provides evidence for the nature of language contact in the pre-Columbian southern Andes (chapter 8). In general, historical phonology is the foundation for any other work in the historical sociology of language.

One of the most striking innovations setting the Cuzco-Collao dialect of Southern Peruvian Quechua off from other Quechua varieties is the presence of distinctive aspirated and ejective stops in Cuzco-Collao. These appear in loanwords from Jaqi/Aru languages and in onomatopoeic word stems. They have also diffused across families of semantically related word stems, to the point that some loans from Spanish also have ejective or aspirate stops even though these features do not appear in Spanish (chapter 8).

Cuzco-Collao Quechua has also undergone a series of mutually related consonant weakenings and mergers over the past 500 years. Stops weakened along an acoustic gradient, from those that concentrated acoustic energy in relatively higher portions of the auditory spectrum (*acute*) to those that concentrated acoustic energy in the lower portion (*grave*). The stops have generally merged into the fricatives *s* and *x̣*. The remaining consonants also weakened, merged, or reduced in frequency at the ends of syllables. These changes are clearly related to one another, despite the fact that the standard descriptive and theoretical frameworks of historical linguists would treat the changes as unrelated. Their spread is subject to several general conditions, some of which are phonological, some of which are not. The nonphonological conditions are the most interesting (and the most controversial) because they are unexpected by standard accounts of the nature of phonological change and yet make sense in terms of typological properties of Quechua morphosyntax. The progress of phonological changes through the word is a diagrammatic icon of the internal structure of the word (chapter 10). If my account of these changes is correct, we would expect sound change in typologically similar languages (strict subject-object-verb word order, agglutinative, suffixing morphology) to take place under the same conditions.

This book is addressed as much to anthropologists and historians interested in Andean language, culture, and history as it is to readers interested in the more theoretical issues of linguistic change broached in the later chapters. In order to make this work accessible to readers without linguistic training, I have tried to reduce the linguistic formalisms and technical vocabulary to the barest minimum required to describe the changes without losing precision. The main exception to this is chapter 10, in which I discuss the general principles of change and interpret them in terms of the morphosemantic structure of the Quechua word. A glossary of technical terms and a list of notational conventions appear in the appendices. I have also avoided casting the descriptive section of the book into a parochial theoretical framework; I hope that this will make it as useful to the agnostic scholar as to the theoretically committed.

There are at least two ways this book might be read. A nonlinguist who consults this book as a reference work on the history of the Cuzco-Collao dialect of Southern Peruvian Quechua will want to begin with the first part (chapters 2–4), turn to the descriptive second part (chapters 5–9), and avoid the more technical final chapter. A reader who is interested in the theoretical and methodological issues raised for historical linguistics will probably prefer to stay entirely within the second part and to concentrate on the final three chapters of the book.

The Language

Southern Peruvian Quechua is spoken in the contiguous highland departments of Apurímac, Arequipa, Ayacucho, Cuzco, Huancavelica, and Puno (see map 1). It is also spoken by urban migrants from these areas to the major cities. All told, there are approximately two million speakers of the language. Although there are fairly striking differences in phonology and lexicon, especially between the varieties spoken in Cuzco and Ayacucho, in broad terms the Quechua spoken in the southern highlands of Peru shares a fairly uniform morphology and

Map 1. The departments of Peru

syntax and should be considered a single unit for the purposes of regional language planning, as the Peruvian linguist Alfredo Torero has suggested (1974: 42–60). If it is appropriate to speak of the language of an area as a discrete entity even when the language has not been standardized, then *Southern Peruvian Quechua*, as it is referred to here, is such an entity.

At the time of the European invasion (1532), Southern Peruvian Quechua was the lingua franca and administrative language of the Inka state, Tawantinsuyu, and was called by the Spaniards the *lengua general del ynga.*[1] The word *Quechua* was already being used by the Spaniards as the name for the language by the mid-sixteenth century, as evidenced by its appearance in the *Lexicon* and *Grammatica* of Domingo de Santo Tomás (both 1560). The use of the word *Quechua* as the name for the language was possibly the result of the Spaniards' mistaking the word for 'valley', in the dialectal designation *qheswa simi* 'valley speech', for the name of the language. The term *Quechua* was also used in early sources to refer to unrelated languages such as Aymara and Mochica (Cerrón-Palomino 1987a: 32). Since the mid-sixteenth century, *Quechua* (from the sixteenth-century form **qhechwa*) has become a standard name for the language, so much so that the word has been borrowed back into Quechua as *kichwa, kichuwa, kechwa* and so forth.

Strictly speaking, the language had no "name" as such before the European invasion (cf. Cerrón-Palomino 1987a: 32). Quechua speakers referred to it as *runa simi* 'human speech', but in a generic sense rather than as the name of a language (Torero 1972 [1970]: 65). Today, in contrast, *runa simi* has come to be ambiguous, meaning both 'the speech of *Runa* (Quechuas)' and 'human speech' in a generic sense. Torero suggests that, after the European invasion, both *Runa* and its Aymara counterpart *Jaqi* narrowed semantically from 'human being' to 'Indian'. The main evidence comes from citations from the Jesuit lexicographers Gonçález Holguín and Bertonio, for Quechua and Aymara, respectively. I would argue, however, that as missionary lexicographers they were especially aware of the ethnic difference as a focus of their work and could only have taken *Runa* and *Jaqi* as the names of the non-Christian people to whom they preached. This is the relevant level of contrast elsewhere in the corpus of sixteenth- and early-seventeenth-century missionary material, especially in the trilingual catechism and sermonal of the Third Council of Lima. Thus, it would seem to me that *Runa* and *Jaqi* were generic terms for 'human' that were narrowed in, and for, certain contexts of use. In modern Cuzco, *Runa* maintains its ambiguity between 'human' at one level of contrast and 'indigenous person' at another. I agree with Torero, however, that in no sense did they function as the names of peoples or languages before the European invasion.

To give a proper name to a language requires a certain kind of consciousness of language, an assumption that languages can be standardized entities and that they can have names. There is no evidence that such a consciousness existed even during the period in which Southern Peruvian Quechua was the administrative language of the Inka state. The native expressions for the language in colonial sources designated speech varieties in one of three ways: by social contrast, by ecological contrast, or by place name. In order to get a sense of how this worked, let us consider the cultural semantics of the words used to talk about speech varieties.

First, labels for speech varieties could designate social contrasts. Historical sources frequently contain the expression *hawa simi*, which could be used for 'speech of the *puna*,' 'speech of outsiders to my group' with the speaker taken as the point of reference, or 'non-Cuzco speech' taking the elites of Tawantinsuyu as the reference point (Monzón 1586a: 220, 222; 1586b: 228; 1586c: 239; Garcilaso 1616: I, xxiii, 48; Torero 1972 [1970]: 72–74). This fits well with evidence from other social domains in which Southern Peruvian Quechua speakers evaluate social and ecological distinctions in terms of an opposition between *ukhu* 'inside' and *hawa* 'outside.' The opposition between *ukhu* and *hawa* was important in the political organization and marriage system of the Inkas (Zuidema 1971). The opposition between *ukhu* and *hawa* also represents a core feature of Quechua topography, especially for cultural geography (Quispe 1969: 12; Isbell 1978: 57–61, 187ff.) and the vocabulary of body parts (Stark 1969). The interpretation of the term *hawa* in its social sense, and so of *hawa simi* in its linguistic sense, depends upon the point of reference of *ukhu* 'inside.' The entire opposition could be understood from the point of view of either the speaker ('my speech' versus 'the speech of others') or of a socially determined center (Inka elites versus nonelites). It is therefore not possible to determine a precise referent for the colonial expression *hawa simi*.

Second, as an ecological contrast, linguistic varieties spoken in the warmer valleys, or **qhechwa* (modern *qheswa* or *qheshwa*), were opposed to those of the high plateau, *puna*, and were called **qhechwa simi* 'valley speech'. This is the likely source of the modern name of the language. For Quechua speakers, the *qheswa* zone is conceptually *ukhu* 'inside' as opposed to the *puna hawa* 'outside'; thus the spatial terms could also be applied to ecologically differentiated varieties of the language. The ecological distinction could be used on another level to oppose Quechua as the prototypically valley (*qheswa*) language to the prototypically high plateau (*puna*) language, Aymara, with which Quechua speakers have been in contact for perhaps more than a millennium. The authors of many of the early missionary grammars, dictionaries, and collections of sermons assumed that the valley speech of the Inka capital could be taken as a standard for the speech of the surrounding areas. They therefore based their works on the speech of *qheswa* people.

Third, any regional form of the language may be designated by the place name followed by the word *simi,* for example *Qosqo simi,* "the speech of Cuzco" (*la lengua del Cuzco,* in the early Spanish accounts). In Quechua culture, language is associated with territory. Southern Peruvian Quechua speakers identify themselves individually with their place of origin and trace that connection to a mythic emergence from the earth in a particular place. In Inka dynastic mythology, the culture hero who founded the royal dynasty was said to have ordered the groups that emerged from different places to speak differently. Modern Quechua speakers assert that their speech comes from the local water.

I have already suggested that the name *Quechua* was used by the Spaniards because they understood the expression 'valley speech' to be the name of the language. Since place names were used to talk about speech varieties, it is also possible that the name *Quechua* was taken from the name of the ethnic group, the *Quichuas* (Markham 1871a: 300). The Jesuit chronicler Bernabe Cobo (1653: XIV, i) wrote: " . . . speaking of the language of this kingdom, I speak only of Quichua as the lingua franca of all of the natives and inhabitants. The ones who had it for their own, and from whom the others got it, are the Quichuas, just as Castilian is called that because it is the mother tongue that we, the Castilians, speak."[2]

Thus Cerrón-Palomino (1987a: 33) suggests that the Spaniards adopted the name *Quechua* on analogy with their own use of *Castilian* to designate the language of Castile. Since Cobo's argument rested so much on analogy with Castilian Spanish, I am inclined to think that the association of *Quechua* as the name of the language with the ethnic Quichuas postdated *Quechua* coming into general use as the Spanish name for the language.

In this book, I use *Quechua* as the name of the language, for the sake of convenience. Southern Peruvian Quechua speakers normally refer to it as *Runa simi* 'human speech'. Keep in mind, though, that it is not only the name of the language that is an imposition from without, but even the idea that languages could be named at all. First-language speakers of Southern Peruvian Quechua nonetheless do prefer to call themselves *Runa* 'human' (or the Spanish *campesino* 'peasant', as an ethnic, not an economic term). I shall therefore refer to them as *Runa.*[3]

Quechua is the name of the language family, which includes genetically related languages spoken across western South America from southern Colombia to northern Argentina. The present work is about the history of one Quechua language, *Southern Peruvian Quechua*, the language of the Inkas, spoken today in the southeastern highlands of Peru; it is particularly about the varieties spoken around the former Inka capital, Cuzco.

The Place of Southern Peruvian Quechua in the Quechua Family

Until the 1960s, it was widely believed that the Quechua languages that were spread across the Andean highlands were all descended from the Inka lingua franca, influenced to a greater or lesser extent by pre-Inka substrate languages. The traditional view underestimated the diversity of the Quechua languages. Linguists were generally unaware of the existence of the Central Quechua languages. They also assumed, wrongly as it turns out, that the colonial expression *lengua general del ynga* referred to all of the modern Quechua languages.

Today, there is a consensus that there were several dispersions of the Quechua family, the earliest from a Quechua homeland usually placed in either central or coastal Peru. In this model, the Inka lingua franca was a thin overlay over a language family that was already spread widely and diversely across the central Andes. For a large, and relatively uniform, area including Southern Peruvian, Bolivian, and Argentine varieties of Quechua, a late dispersion is likely; for some areas, Quechua may have actually been introduced after the European invasion. The same may be true for the northernmost Quechua languages, including those spoken in modern Ecuador and Colombia, although the historical situation may be more complex. For all of these areas, Quechua languages are spreading at their geographic frontiers even today.

But the Quechua varieties spoken in the highland areas of the modern central Peruvian departments of Ancash, Huaylas, Huánuco, Jauja, and Junín have structural characteristics that set them off from the languages in the first group and from each other. There is considerably more diversity among the Central Peruvian languages than among the varieties most closely related to the Inka lingua franca. The relationships among the Central Quechua languages are themselves very complex, involving both genetic diversification and waves of changes that are shared by several geographically contiguous varieties. Most scholars today assume that the Central languages represent an earlier dispersion than do the languages related to the Inka lingua franca; most also locate the ancestral Quechua homeland either in this area or on the adjacent coast. The Italian linguist Benigno Ferrario (1956) is usually credited with proposing the multiple-dispersion hypothesis. The most important early classification of the Quechua family, including subgrouping and reconstruction, was carried out independently by Alfredo Torero (1964, 1968, 1970, 1974) and Gary Parker (1963, 1969b, 1969c, 1969f, 1971), who arrived at similar, largely compatible results, each proposing an initial division in the Quechua family between two main branches, which divide the Central Peruvian languages from those spoken to the north and the south. Although this classification has been challenged on morphological (Landerman 1978; Cerrón-Palomino 1979; Adelaar 1984) and phonological (chapter 7) grounds, it has not been replaced by a more comprehensive and detailed classification, and there is a working consensus around it (Hartmann 1972; Adelaar 1979; Cerrón-Palomino 1980, 1987a: 221–248; Torero 1983).

Central Quechua (Torero's Quechua I and Waywash, Parker's Quechua B) is represented by the modern varieties spoken in the central Peruvian highlands, particularly in the departments of Ancash, Junín, Huaylas, Huánuco, and Jauja. *Peripheral Quechua* (Parker's Quechua A and Torero's Quechua II and Wampuy) flanks Central Quechua both to the north and to the south. It is represented to the north by *Quichua* (spoken in Ecuador), *Inga* (spoken in Colombia), and the Peruvian varieties of Cajamarca, Lambayeque, and San Martín. To the south it is represented by the Bolivian varieties, Argentine Quichua, and Southern Peruvian Quechua.

The place of Southern Peruvian Quechua in the Quechua family is summarized in table 1.1, after Torero (1974). Varieties of Southern Peruvian Quechua are mutually intelligible. In general, intelligibility decreases drastically as one moves from branch to branch of the language family. Torero (1974: 36–51) has conducted intelligibility tests to demonstrate that Southern Peruvian Quechua and Central Quechua are *not* mutually intelligible, and my own experience with reactions to Central Quechua songs by speakers of Southern Peruvian Quechua from Cuzco supports his findings. This observation must be tempered by recalling that intelligibility is as much a social fact as a linguistic one, as Cerrón-Palomino's description of asymmetric intelligibility between Ayacucho-Chanka (Southern Peruvian Quechua) and Wanka (Central) demonstrates (1969: 3).

Southern Peruvian Quechua is spoken in the following places: the highland portions of the Department of Ayacucho; the Department of Huancavelica up to its northwestern border (excluding a small part of Tayacaja province), where it is contiguous with Huanca Quechua, spoken

Table 1.1. Place of Southern Peruvian Quechua within the Quechua Family

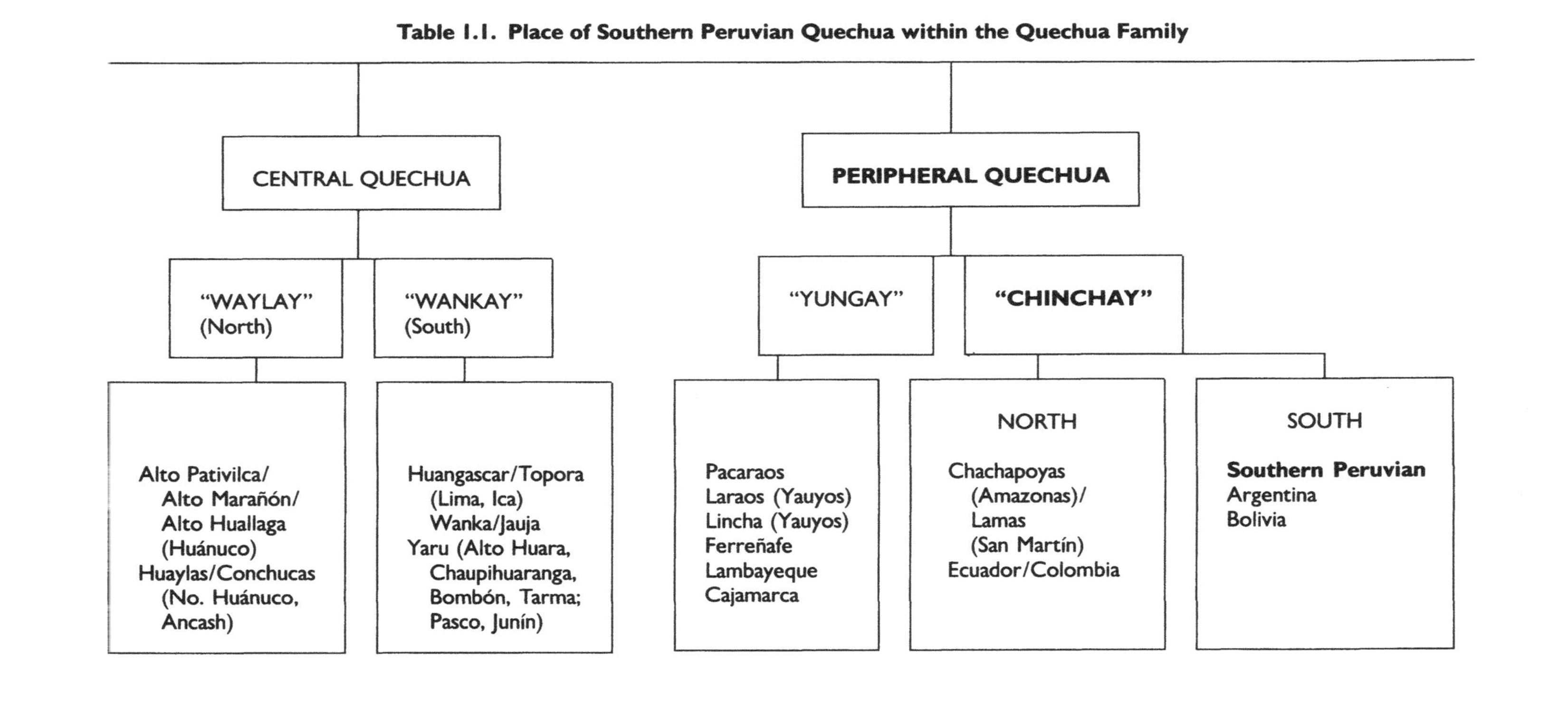

Table 1.2. Segmental Inventory of Ayacucho-Chanka Quechua

CONSONANTS

	labial	**alveolar**	**palatal**	**velar**	**uvular**	**laryngeal**
stop	p	t	ch	k		
fricative		s			q	
(retroflex) tap/fricative			r			
nasal	m	n	ñ			
lateral		l	ll			
glide	w		y			h

VOWELS

		front		**back**		
high		i		u		
low			a			

in Junín; the Department of Apurímac; the highland part of the Department of Cuzco and the jungle portion up to the Yavero River and the border with the Department of Madre de Dios; the highland portions of the Department of Arequipa (largely in the provinces of La Unión, Condesuyos, Castilla, and Cailloma) along with about 84,000 Quechua-speaking migrants mostly from Puno and Cuzco in the city of Arequipa itself; the northwest highland part of the Department of Puno, particularly the provinces of Carabaya, Melgar, Lampa, and western Sandia. Southern Peruvian Quechua is also spoken in the city of Puno itself, along with Aymara (Parker 1969a: 7; Torero 1974: 35; Adams 1976, 1979; Cerrón-Palomino 1976a: 30; Cusihuamán 1976a: 30f.).

Dialectology

The primary dialectal break within Southern Peruvian Quechua can be observed most clearly by contrasting the sound system of the Cuzco-Collao variety with that spoken in Ayacucho. The segmental inventory of Ayacucho-Chanka Quechua is seen in table 1.2.

Table 1.3. Segmental Inventory of Cuzco-Collao Quechua (The bracketed segments are distinctive in some subdialects, but not all)

CONSONANTS

	labial	alveolar	palatal	velar	uvular	laryngeal
plain stop	p	t	ch	k	q	
ejective	p'	t'	ch'	k'	q'	
aspirate	ph	th	chh	kh	qh	
fricative	< ϕ >	s	< sh >	< x >	< x̣ >	
(retroflex) tap/fricative			r			
nasal	m	n	ñ			
lateral		l	ll			
glide	w		y			h

VOWELS

		front		back		
high		i		u		
low			a			

Notice that Cuzco-Collao Quechua, in contrast, opposes three stop series, an ejective (or glottalized) and an aspirate series, in addition to a series of "plain" (neither ejective nor aspirate) voiceless stops, as in Ayacucho-Chanka. The segmental inventory of Cuzco-Collao Quechua is seen in table 1.3.

Glottalization (ejectivity) and aspiration are restricted to the initial stop in a word and may occur only in syllable-initial position. At the ends of syllables, the stops of Cuzco-Collao Quechua have been weakening and merging. These changes, which have taken place over the 450 years since the Spanish conquest, are the subject of later sections of this book. For the moment, let me illustrate the correspondences between the modern-day Cuzco-Collao and Ayacucho-Chanka dialects of Southern Peruvian Quechua with a few examples.

Ayacucho-Chanka plain stops correspond to Cuzco-Collao ejective or aspirated or plain stops in syllable-initial position, for example:

Ayacucho-Chanka		**Cuzco-Collao**	
**p**acha	'world, clothing'	_**p**acha_	'world'
		**p'**acha	'clothing'
**p**iñakuy	'to get angry'	_**ph**iñakuy_	
_ta**p**uy_	'to ask'	_ta**p**uy_	
**t**anta	'bread'	_**t'**anta_	
llan**t**u	'shade'	_llan**th**u_	
**ch**aki	'dry, leg'	_**ch**aki_	'leg'
		**ch'**aki	'dry'
min**ch**a	'the day after tomorrow'	_min**chh**a_	
**k**iki	'oneself'	_**k**iki_	
mis**k**i	'sweet'	_mis**k'**i_	
mull**k**uy	'to feel around for'	_mull**kh**uy_	
**q**asa	'frozen, freezing'	_**q**asa_	'frozen, frost'
	'notch, ravine'	_**q'**asa_	'ravine, something removed'
yar**q**a	'irrigation canal'	_yar**qh**a_	

and to Cuzco-Collao fricatives in syllable-final position, for example:

lli**p**ta	'ash lime chewed with coca'	_lli**ɸ**t'a_	
		~ _lli_^{w}_**x**t'a_	
		~ _lli**x̣**t'a_	
u**t**qay	'to hurry'	_u**s**qhay_	
_a**ch**ka_	'many, much'	_a**sh**ka_	
		~ _a**skh**a_	
cha**p**ra	'branch'	_ch'a**ɸ**ra_	'bush'
		~ _ch'a**wx**ra_	
		~ _ch'a**x̣**ra_	
_-**p**ti_	'subordinate clause, switch reference'	_-**x̣**ti_	
mi**t**kakuy	'to trip and fall'	_mi**s**k'akuy_	'to stub one's toe'
_u**ch**pa_	'ash'	_u**sh**pa_	
		~_u**s**pha_	
_-**ch**ka-_	'durative aspect'	_-**sh**ka-_	
		~ _-**s**ka-_	
		~ _-**sh**a-_	
		~ _-**s**a-_	
cha**k**ra	'field'	_cha**x**ra_	
lli**k**lla	'shawl'	_lli**x**lla_	

Moreover, Ayacucho-Chanka *q* became a fricative, [x̣], in all positions (Parker 1969a: 17, 19). Reflexes of final *q* are identical in the two varieties.

The nasals, laterals, and glides of Cuzco-Collao Quechua show a reduced inventory when compared to Ayacucho-Chanka Quechua. Of the nasals, *m* and *n* are opposed syllable-finally in Ayacucho-Chanka; they are merged in Cuzco-Collao, for example:

_ki**m**sa_	'three'	_ki**n**sa_
lla**m**kay	'to work'	_lla**n**k'ay_

-m	'assertion' (after vowels)	*-ŋ*
-wan	instrumental case	*-wan*

The opposition between the Ayacucho-Chanka laterals *ll* and *l* is neutralized before *t* where the *l* appears, and before *k* and *ch* where the *ll* appears. Cuzco-Collao laterals have the same distribution before all dental, palatal, and velar stops. Additionally, *ll* and *l* have merged to *l* before uvulars in Cuzco-Collao, for example:

allqo	'dog'	*alqo*
sallqa	'wild, savage'	*salqa*

Vowel-glide combinations in the Department of Cuzco are dialectally in the process of reduction: *ay* > *e:* > *i*; *uy* > *i*, under dialectally variable conditioning. The changes are favored after high consonants (e.g., *k* and *ch*) and disfavored after the grave consonants (e.g., *p* and especially *q*). Also, in Cuzco-Collao, syllable-final *w* has become *y* under dialectally and lexically variable conditioning, for example:

punchaw	'day'	*p'unchay*
wawqe	'male's brother'	*wayqe*

In summary, the Cuzco-Collao dialect of Southern Peruvian Quechua has a contrast among ejective, aspirate, and plain stops for the first stop in the word and has weakened, merged, or lost consonants at the ends of syllables. Ayacucho-Chanka Quechua has a single stop series (in place of Cuzco-Collao's three) but has maintained the consonants at the ends of syllables intact. Cuzco-Collao Quechua is spoken in the departments of Cuzco, Puno, and Arequipa. Ayacucho-Chanka is spoken in the departments of Ayacucho and Huancavelica. Both dialect types are attested in the Department of Apurímac, alongside transitional dialects. In the province of Aymaraes, for example, a lexically and grammatically Ayacucho-like dialect has distinctive ejectives and aspirates (though less prominently than Cuzco), but has not undergone the weakenings and mergers of syllable-finals. Apparently, this is the result of a relatively recent switch of cultural and linguistic allegiance from Ayacucho to Cuzco. Abancay Quechua, on the other hand, has aspirates but not ejectives, and in other respects resembles Cuzco-Collao Quechua, including in the weakenings of consonants at the ends of syllables.

In the Department of Cuzco itself, dialect variation results largely from: (1) lexical variation in ejectives and aspirates and in the ways in which words changed to conform to restrictions on these features; (2) variable rates of implementation of syllable-final lenitions and mergers; and (3) creation of new, low-yield phonemes (especially, *ϕ*, *x* and *sh*; bracketed in table 1.3) from one of the lenitions, along with local, lexically sporadic sound shifts and metatheses. A major department-wide variation pattern involves the sibilants *s* and *sh*. To the north of Cuzco and to the east of the Vilcanota River, the two sibilants (the latter the output of a *ch* > *sh* fricativization) tend to merge as *s*. To the south of Cuzco, they tend to converge on *sh* by means of phonologically conditioned, lexically diffused shifts of *s* to *sh*.

The Speakers

As the administrative language of the Inka state, Southern Peruvian Quechua was used as the lingua franca across an area that corresponds roughly to the spread of the Quechua family today. The Inka expansion occurred over a relatively brief period, perhaps less than a century. Although local elites were educated in the administrative language, the Inkas do not appear to have made an effort to implant a unified standardized language across the empire. On the contrary, even the area around the Inka capital itself was a linguistic mosaic. In the central highlands of Peru, Southern Peruvian Quechua represented an eggshell-thin overlay on the Quechua languages already spoken there. The relationship between the Inka lingua franca and the Peripheral Quechua varieties spoken in modern Ecuador and Colombia is more controversial (Rojas 1980: 33–35). The ethnohistorian Roswith Hartmann (1979) suggests that, although it is possible that there was Ecuadorian contact with Peripheral Quechua before the Inkas, the Ecuadorian and Colombian varieties were spread under Tawantinsuyu and during the colonial period. The modern-day diversity of Quechua in Ecuador and Colombia would then reflect aboriginal substrata.

At the time of the European invasion, the Inka state Tawantinsuyu occupied a territory from the southernmost portion of Colombia to northern Chile and Argentina (map 2).[4] Tawantinsuyu was a militarily expansive multiethnic empire. It incorporated neighboring ethnic polities into a redistributive economy controlled largely by indirect rule and a policy of resettlement of populations. Local communities were productively autonomous, but local households were required to donate labor to work the lands of the lords of local polities, the state, and the religion. The fruits of their labor supported the state bureaucracy and armies and were stored in a system of state-run storehouses against times of productive shortfalls. The relationships between levels of productive organization—households, larger aggregates of households, ethnic polities, and, finally, the state as a whole—were mediated by reciprocal obligations and rights that served to disguise the overall process by which the households' labor created wealth for the state. Exchange

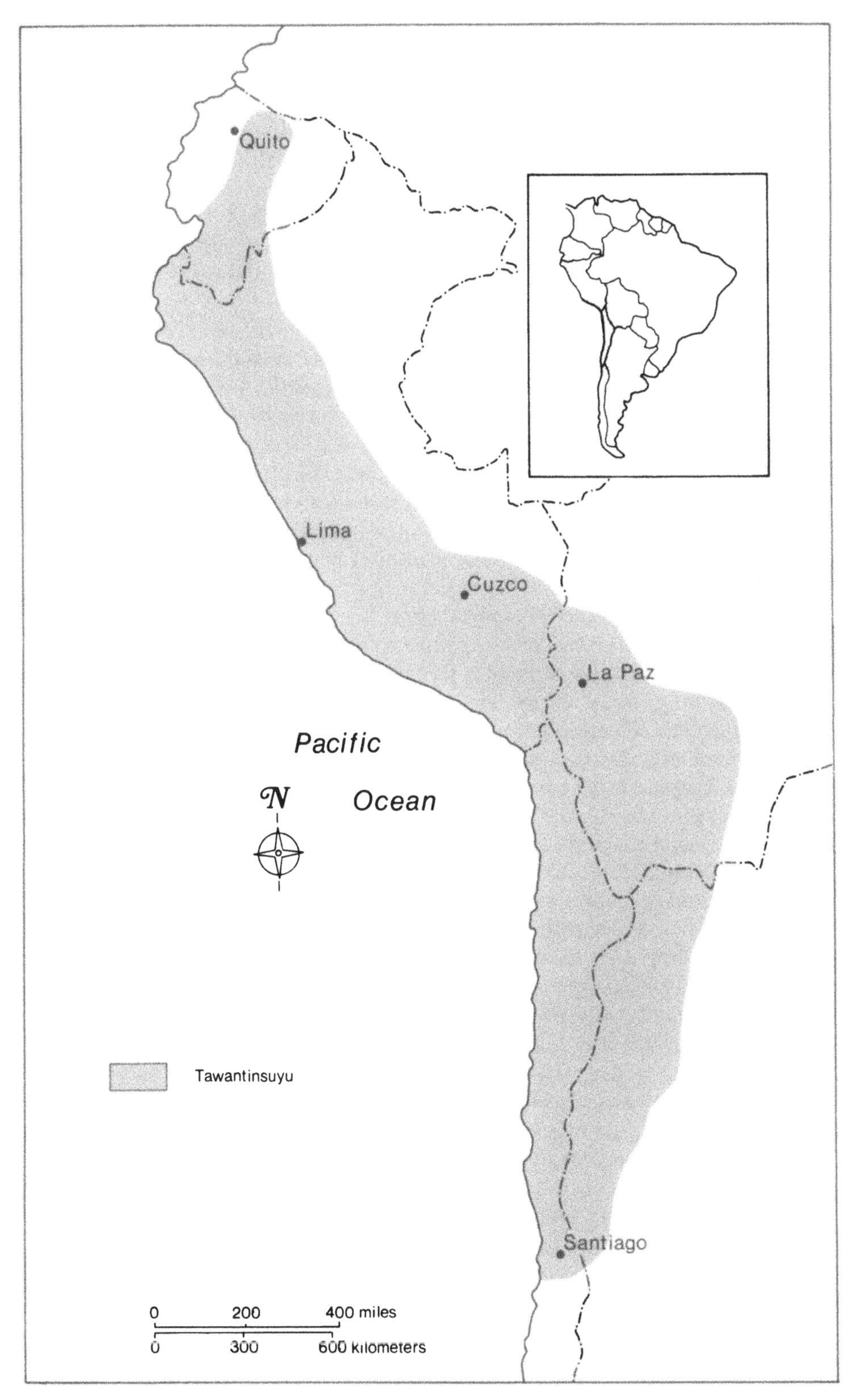

Map 2. The Inka state, Tawantinsuyu, at its greatest extent (adapted from John Hyslop, *Inka Settlement Planning*)

within the Inka heartland was mediated through the state-controlled redistributive economy rather than through markets, although market exchange and guild-controlled long-distance trade went on at the peripheries of the state. The Inka state is distinguished from other archaic multinational empires by the peculiar form in which surplus was extracted from local populations: in the form of labor and services rather than in the form of tribute.

The Inkas built their immense empire in less than a century, on the framework of older Andean polities. Inka statecraft followed the same principles of redistributive organization as the polities it was to incorporate, and so was able to annex their populations through a form of indirect rule, in which the relationships between local communities and the state were mediated by local ethnic lords. The state maintained, and perhaps even promoted, cultural and linguistic diversity among the conquered populations. Although local administrators were required to learn the Inka lingua franca, there is no evidence that the Inkas imposed their language and culture on the conquered peoples on a mass scale (see Cerrón-Palomino 1987c: 73–75).

The Inkas conceived of their state in terms of a fourfold division (*Tawantin suyu,* 'the parts that in their fourness make up a whole'), with the Inka capital, Cuzco, at its center. The Inkas did not distinguish among the ritual, administrative, military, and directly political aspects of statecraft. Cuzco was, at one and the same time, the sacred center of the Inka universe, the administrative center of the state, the ceremonial arena within which political alliances were cemented and political intrigues played out, and a template for the organization of the entire state. The Inkas maintained a system of 328 sacred places within a 60-kilometer radius of Cuzco, which embodied the articulation of the principle of fourfold division with two other basic axioms of Inka social structure, a moiety division into upper (*Hanan*) and lower (*Urin*) halves—each with its own ruler, and a threefold ranked hierarchy. The sacred places, including springs, rock outcroppings, shrines, and road bends, were situated on forty-one straight lines (*ziqi*), which radiated out from the sacred center of Cuzco, like spokes on a bicycle wheel. The *ziqi* lines were organized into ranked groups of three, which in turn were organized into larger ranked groups of three, which themselves represented each of the four major divisions of Cuzco (*suyu*). The four *suyu* radiated out conceptually to organize the entire civilized (Inka) world, each having distinct social and symbolic attributes associated with it: *Chinchaysuyu,* the civilized valley people toward the northwest, *Kuntisuyu,* the mountain and coastal people toward the southwest, *Antisuyu,* the lowlands on the eastern slopes of the Andes, and *Qullasuyu,* the high *puna* lands of herders, to the south.

The system of *ziqis* was used by the Inka state for several purposes: it served as the basis of an elaborate calendar system based on astronomical observation; it organized the distribution of irrigation water in the immediate vicinity of Cuzco; it associated each of the royal kin groups with certain ritual and calendric responsibilities and established a ranked hierarchy among them; and it likewise associated nonroyal kin groups in the immediate environs of Cuzco with the state organization of sacred space and social-political responsibilities. In short, it was a comprehensive organizing template through which the state organized many of its ceremonial, social, and political functions.

The descendants of the Inkas, Runa continue to live in the Inka heartland amid the ruins of settlements and of agricultural terraces. Like their ancestors, they are primarily agriculturalists and herders. And as among their Inka ancestors, social relations—at least among Runa—are tinged with an ideology of reciprocity and an axiology of loss. Reciprocity is the fundamental guiding principle of everyday life, of social interaction, etiquette, ritual relations with the earth and the lords of the mountains, relationships between humans and their herds, and even—in the longest run, after the millennium—between Runa and their non-Runa exploiters. But a pervasive sense of sorrow and loss is reflected in rite and song, perhaps as an implicit recognition that every reciprocal action is always one-half of a cycle, that reciprocity requires an initial surrender of the self to the gift of labor or object, and that the cycle of reciprocity is ever liable to rupture. "Why have you come from the mountains alone, why have you come single?" they will sing to an animal at an increase ritual. Andean economy and culture turn a famous anthropological principle on its head: all exchange is, at base, sacrifice (Gose 1986). Libations and payments to the earth, offerings to the mountain lords, and the accidental death of a member of a road construction crew are not different in kind from work prestations or *ayni*. All of these are performed with the hope that they will be repaid; an offering to the mountain lords might be repaid with fertility of the sacrificer's herds, work harvesting a field by other work harvesting, the road worker's death by successful completion of the project, but repayment is a moral, not a contractual obligation. Nonrepayment by humans of similar status can be penalized socially; nonrepayment by higher-status individuals, the mountain lords, or the earth cannot be.

To be Runa is to be a human being, to speak *Runa simi* 'Quechua', to be of a place, to live under the rule of reciprocity, *ayni*, and its attendant etiquette (but also 'to cry' over a sense of continual loss). To be otherwise is to be *q'ara*, 'naked', 'uncultured', 'uncivilized'. *Ayni* is understood by Runa, not as an abstract principle governing social interaction, but as the fundamental organizing basis of the material world. And so, throughout southern Peru, Quechua speakers treat the boundary between Quechua speakers who live by the law of reciprocity and Spanish speakers who do not as a distinction of primordial social importance. But however Runa may erect an ideological boundary to set off two quite distinct cultural and social logics, their lives have been tinged with the reality of global and regional mercantilism and capitalism since the first epidemics swept the Andes before the military invasion. The everyday lives of Runa reflect a myriad of personal, situational, and institutional compromises that suture the gulf between Runa and *q'ara* forms of life, as much as the functioning of the local economy requires it. This has been reality for Runa since the European invasion, no matter how physically remote their settlements may appear from the highland urban centers. And it has been a generating force behind the creation of a myriad of new cultural—religious, ideological, and aesthetic—forms that, however hybrid, are still Andean. Neither economy nor society, in the global sense, is dual. But there is a sense in which the Runa negotiate opposed sets of social principles and enter into productive relationships that function according to radically distinct logics (see Montoya 1987). As we shall see later on, this has important consequences for the ways in which Runa interpret dialect variation, and so for the nature of language change.

The striking cultural differences between Runa and the Spanish-speaking Peruvians with whom they live cheek to jowl is papered over by the official and widely accepted Spanish word for Runa: *campesinos* 'peasants'. This word reduces a cultural chasm to economics. But it also suggests static, monotonous uniformity, "a simple addition of homologous magnitudes, much as potatoes in a sack form a sackful of potatoes" (Marx 1957 [1852]: 109). The idea that Andean "peasants" are monotonously uniform does not hold up to scrutiny, although neither does the image of a sackful of potatoes. Andean tubers, after all, come in very many varieties; Weston LaBarre (1947) collected 209 named varieties of tubers in a single Andean community. Likewise, Arguedas (1983 [1972]: 252) wrote in a poem, *Pichqa pachak hukman papakunam waytachkan chay ñawikipa mana aypanan qori tuta, qollqi punchao allpapi. Chaymi ñutquy, chaymi sonqoy.* 'For five hundred and one (kinds of) potatoes blossom where your eyes can't reach in a land of golden night, silver day. They are my brains, they are my heart'.

The extent to which sets of cultural themes emerge and recombine in kaleidoscopic fashion over the expanse that once was Tawantinsuyu, the Inka state, is maddening to the anthropologist, in its variety of forms of social structure, ecology, economic organization, and authority structure, not to mention its variety of basic cultural patterns like gender relationships, cosmology, religious practices, and etiquette. However familiar a non-Runa visitor is with basic cultural practices, she is likely to be disturbed by those of another community but twenty or thirty kilometers away, as precious generalizations slip away. The most striking social and cultural differences are between the temperate valley (*qheswa*) communities that dedicate themselves primarily to agriculture and the high plateau (*puna*) herding communities. Here are two ethnographic vignettes, one of a *qheswa* agricultural community, one of a *puna* herding community, both from the Department of Cuzco.[5]

Qheswa: Lluthu (Province of Quispicanchi)

The two rivers that make up the territorial backbone of the city of Cuzco and of the department, the Huatanay and the Vilcanota, join at Huambutio, south of Cuzco (map 3). From this point south, the river (which flows north and east) is joined by a number of small tributary riverlets, each one of which forms a small river valley, along which there are a number of settlements, some former estates, and some working and abandoned textile mills. The landscape is heavily and abruptly broken up. For many settlements, lands ranging from 3,100 to about 4,300 meters above sea level are within a few hours' walk of the settlement. These communities engage in a mixed set of economic strategies, although agriculture—generally of grains—predominates here.

Lluthu, an agricultural community of about fifty households, along the Manqo River, is one such community (Hopkins 1983, 1985, 1988; Mannheim 1987). It was founded by the laborers of a small hacienda during the period of agrarian unrest that preceded the Agrarian Reform of 1969. They forceably evicted the administrator of the hacienda and razed the small manorial house. Their title to the hacienda was recognized by the government following the Agrarian Reform. The former laborers hold collective, communal title to the lands, which are worked as small household plots (*minifundios*) by reciprocal labor arrangements (*ayni*). Land is redistributed periodically among the households, at least in theory, according to need. The fertile, flatter land in the river valley is used primarily for maize production, the staple of the community. Hillier, higher-altitude lands are used for tubers—mainly potatoes—and broad beans. The highest-altitude lands are held communally as pasture, although herding—almost exclusively of sheep and bovine—is not the primary productive activity of the Lluthu Runa. The herds serve as a source of meat and wool, to be sure, but also as a readily convertible source of cash. Household wealth is conspicuously measured by herd size. There are also other, more marginal economic activities. Many households attempt to raise chickens from chicks that have been purchased at the provincial or department markets. Young men and women

Map 3. Six southeastern departments of Peru

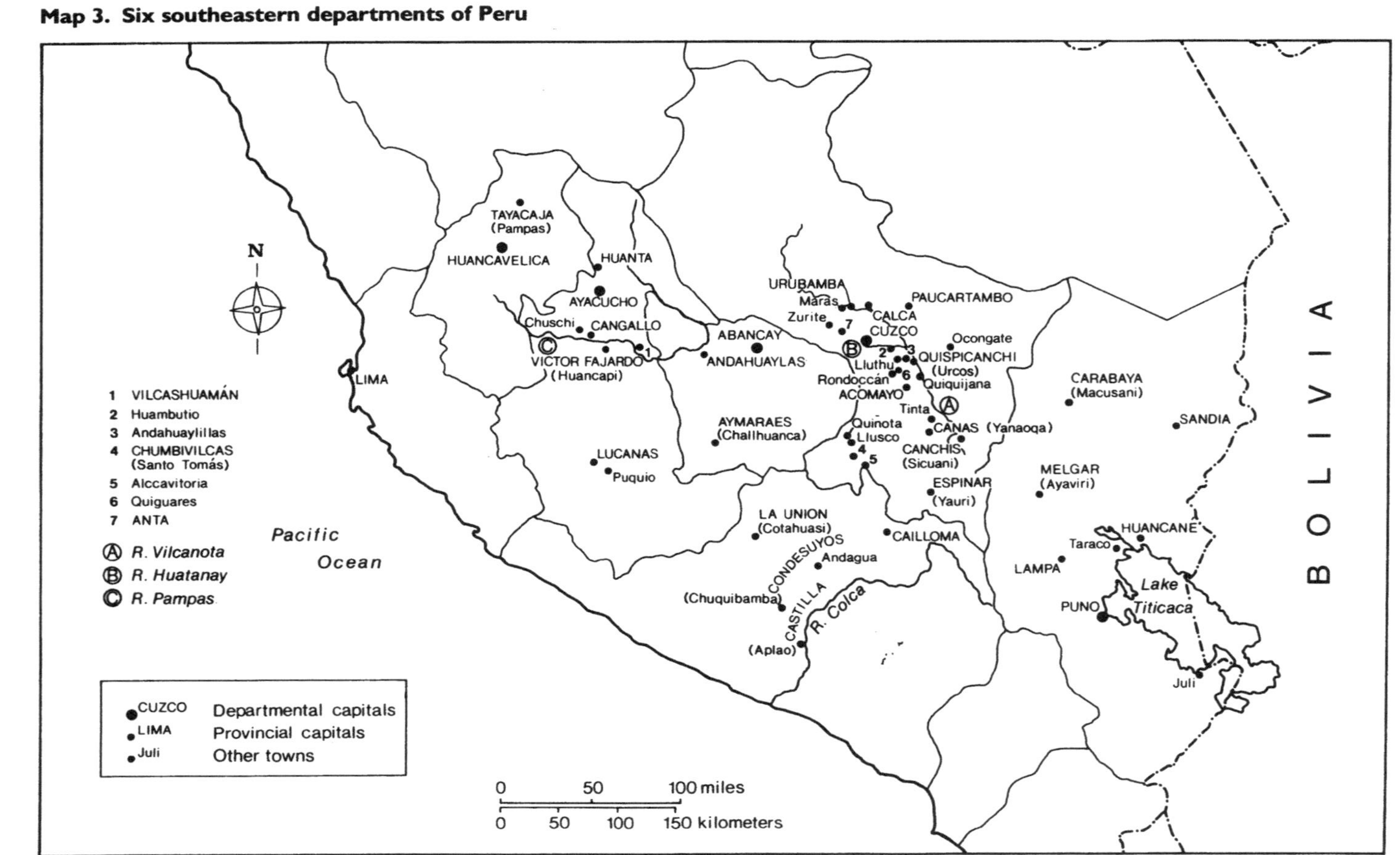

often sell their labor outside of the community—as agricultural, construction, menial, or domestic workers—for a period of time preceding marriage. And the community as a whole has invested in a grove of eucalyptus trees.

Labor is recruited by means of *ayni* relationships, ongoing and enduring relationships of reciprocal exchange, separately maintained by men and women among same-sex partners. Some residents of a nearby tuber-producing community are recruited for high-labor periods in exchange for a part of the maize harvest. Men are responsible for breaking the mother earth, to prepare a formerly fallow field, or to plow before planting—even the animals used for plowing must be male. Men often plant the seeds themselves (although elsewhere in the southern Andes this is a woman's job) and are always responsible for the labor of harvest. Women process the harvest and shuck and sort the maize. They are responsible for storing and maintaining sufficient seed for the following year. They are also responsible for managing the household's resources, in the broadest sense of the word. The sanction of whispers and loss of prestige that accompany a poorly managed household fall on the shoulders of the woman of the house. Exchange of goods is the ultimate responsibility of women. So is the care of the household animals. Women are responsible for food preparation. When large quantities of food are required (for example, to feed an agricultural work party), women call on their personal reciprocal networks for labor. Children are cared for by their mothers until they are weaned, when they are cared for by older siblings whenever possible.

When a couple begins to live together, they may live with, or adjacent to, either set of parents, depending on which is wealthier in land and animals. Wealth is inherited indistinctly among male and female children, except for animals, which are inherited matrilineally. The kinship terminology distinguishes parallel and cross cousins; parallel cousins receive the same terms as siblings. In the sibling terms, same-sex siblings are distinguished from cross-sex. Affinal terminology for parents' cross-sex siblings, which possibly reflected an earlier system of asymmetric marriage alliance, has been replaced by consanguineal loanwords, although the loan forms are rarely used for same-sex siblings of the parents, who receive parental terms. Age is critical for terms of address, particularly with siblings and parallel cousins. Discrepancies between generation and actual age (for example, a young girl addressing an older daughter-in-law) are resolved by using more distant and more respectful terms reflecting age, rather than generation.

Lluthu is a nucleated settlement, located just above the rich valley formed by the Manqo River. Lluthu Runa live in single-story adobe houses that are frequently partitioned into a cooking, eating, and social area and an area for storage and private sleeping. They may sleep on skins spread over a packed-earth floor, on a rolled straw mat, or on a sleeping platform or bed. There are a few small air holes; otherwise there is no ventilation, and the house is often clouded with the smoke from the dung fire in the earthen stove in the corner. Small crosses on the roof, centered above the main transom, hold the souls of the house.

The people of Lluthu are Roman Catholics. The Peruvian church, particularly the diocese of Cuzco, has recognized the peculiarly Andean form of Runa religiosity, and generally accepts—in practice, if not theology—many of the indigenous religious practices denounced by the parish priest over 350 years ago (Pérez Bocanegra 1631). Lluthu Runa attend mass either in the parish church in the municipal center or in a chapel in the community uphill from them, on special occasions and death. They practice the sacraments of baptism and marriage, in addition to the indigenous *rite de passage* of first haircutting, and form lasting bonds of kinship with the ritual sponsors of any of these occasions. Catholic ritual forms have been incorporated into payments to the earth, offerings to the mountain lords, and animal increase rites. The Catholic trinity and saints map onto the indigenous cosmos and sacred beings in multiple, mutually contradictory ways. Lluthu pays particular attention to the day of Santa Rosa of Lima, the only saint for which there is a rotated cargo. In theory the cargo is passed among single girls, although in practice their families are recognized as sponsors (Hopkins 1988). Saint John's day, the day of the sheep, is celebrated by household animal increase rituals, attended by the minimal matriline of the woman of the house. All Souls' and All Saints' days are celebrated with visits to the cemetery, ritual tables set up for the recently deceased, and a soccer game between the married and single men.

Puna: Alccavitoria (Province of Chumbivilcas)

Following the Vilcanota south, the landscape changes from the open alpine terrain to windswept high plateau (*puna*). Most of this land is above 4,200 meters, where agriculture is almost impossible. The agricultural settlements found downriver, to the north, are replaced by herding settlements; these are the *provincias altas*, or 'high provinces' of southwestern Cuzco, especially the provinces of Chumbivilcas and Espinar. The description of Alccavitoria is drawn from the ethnography of Glynn Custred (1974a, 1977a, 1977b, 1979, 1980).

Alccavitoria is a herding community of about 850 people, in the southernmost part of the Province of Chumbivilcas, bordering on the Department of Arequipa. The lands below 4,000 feet include a small alluvial fan and some of the slopes of the Velille River. These are suitable for agriculture, but make up a very small fraction of the total land base.

There are two types of pastureland: communal pasturelands on the mountain slopes and year-round pasturelands on the highest plateau. The lowest agricultural lands and the highest year-round pastures are owned by individual households. The people of Alccavitoria maintain residences in all three zones, practicing annual, cyclical transhumance between their primary residences and small huts located adjacent to their lower-altitude agricultural lands and their higher-altitude pasturelands. The primary residences are scattered into small household clusters throughout the territory of Alccavitoria. Eight households, including one mestizo family, live around the community center, near a school and chapel.

All of the members of the community are engaged in high-altitude agriculture of tubers, quinoa, cañihua, and barley, although, even in the best of years, no household could supply more than six months of food from agricultural labor. The main subsistence activity is herding of sheep, alpacas, llamas, and some cattle. Meat and wool from the sheep and camelids are consumed directly or used for sale and barter. Because the agricultural lands provide such a small part of the subsistence of the herders of Alccavitoria, they are forced to exchange for agricultural produce from lower ecological zones. Wool and dried meat are taken to neighboring *qheswa* communities to exchange for tubers, maize, and cereals. Wool and meat are also taken to regional markets, where they are sold; the proceeds of the sale are used to purchase trade items, which are taken on llama trains to *qheswa* communities, where they are exchanged for agricultural produce. The trading routes of herders like those of Alccavitoria can be quite extensive; for example, the community of Lluthu (described earlier) is visited regularly by traders from the *provincias altas*. For the herders, this form of trade represents subsistence, rather than entrepreneurial activity.

As in the other communities, labor is recruited by means of *ayni* partnerships. Labor in *ayni* is reciprocated with the same type of labor, if possible, or with money (*mink'a*), if not. The household, built around a nuclear family, is the basic unit of labor mobilization, production, consumption, and management of resources. *Ayni* is most frequently recruited among siblings and their spouses. Most productive tasks are shared by both sexes, including herding, weeding, digging tubers, spinning, and weaving. Men plow and carry on long-distance trading. Women cook and care for the house.

Inheritance of animals and land rights is bilateral. Children inherit at marriage; both partners bring their land and animals into the marriage, which becomes a new household, and a new land- and animal-holding unit. Residence is either virilocal or neolocal. The kinship terminology includes a set of core terms from Quechua, used for members of the nuclear family, and the families of the parents' siblings. These mark sex and generation, but not collaterality. A second set of terms in Spanish is used for lineal kin from two generations above and below ego, or for any kin outside of those for whom Quechua terms are used. These mark collaterality as well as sex and generation. Affinial terminology in Quechua is symmetrical and marked only for sex and affinity, not generation. Affinal terms marking generation are drawn from the Spanish set. The general rule seems to be that the Quechua terminological subset is used with the same kin with whom one cooperates most closely in economic activities. The Spanish terminological subset is used otherwise. Age is a critical parameter for terms of address.

Groups of brothers tend to reside close to one another. During periods in which year-round grazing lands are scarce, they are held by coresidential groups formed around up to three generations of agnates; the agnatic residence groups are the same units from which labor is recruited through *ayni* reciprocity.

The pattern described for Alccavitoria is a typically *puna* herding adaptation, much as the pattern described for Lluthu is typically *qheswa*. Within each of these types there is also considerable variation among communities, depending on such factors as the following.

—ecological circumstances: whether the community has direct access to multiple ecological micro-zones at different altitudes, such as the pattern described for Lluthu, or has a much more compact range of zones, such as the communities in the Pampa of Maras in Urubamba. In the latter case, the community will be much more oriented to market exchange than in the former.

—legal status of the community: whether a community is a "free community" descended from one of the colonial *reducciones* or an ex-hacienda. If it is an ex-hacienda, whether it was reorganized as a legal cooperative under state management, or whether it remained in the legal netherworld of a "peasant group" (as Lluthu did); if a cooperative, what the current relations are with neighboring communities; if a herding community, whether it has been incorporated into an Agrarian Service Cooperative; if a former ranch, whether it was incorporated into a government-run "cooperative" ranch after the Agrarian Reform of 1969.

—economic history of the community: if it is a free community, what its relations were to neighboring estates, and the nature of the labor owed to laboring estates; if adjacent to a mill or other larger-scale economic enterprise, what kinds of services were owed to the mill on a regular or seasonal basis, and what the relations were between the workers and the adjacent peasants.

—craft production: some communities specialize in craft production,

such as the manufacture of roof tiles, musical instruments, and ceramic wares, in addition to agriculture and herding. Each requires different kinds of labor arrangements.
—access to irrigation: availability and quantity of irrigation water, how distribution of water is regulated, how irrigation canals are maintained.
—political history: whether the community has been engaged in active legal or political battles to maintain its access to land in recent memory; whether there is active factional politics.

All of these circumstances can change the social configuration of a community in very drastic ways; many of these factors are responsible for the enormous variability among Runa communities in southern Peru today. In addition, there are specific historical factors, and imponderables such as political leadership, local pressures on community solidarity, Protestant missionaries, and so forth.

The Social Setting: A Preview

Southern Peruvian Quechua is spoken by about 90 percent of the population of the six south-central Andean departments of Peru; the main nonindigenous exceptions are urban areas. In the rural area, it is everywhere the language of everyday interaction. But at a national level, and in interaction with Spanish speakers, Southern Peruvian Quechua is an "oppressed language" in that its functional development has, since the European invasion, been the political, economic, and ideological prerogative of non-Quechua speakers. As the social world of Quechua speakers has come to embrace institutional, cultural, and interactional contexts that did not exist at the time of the conquest, the language has not kept pace. Although Quechua grammar and vocabulary have not atrophied, today, at the end of the twentieth century, monolingual Quechua speakers lead an atrophied existence, cut off from political, economic, social, and cultural arenas that affect their everyday lives. For this reason, many Southern Peruvian Quechua speakers have found knowledge of Spanish—even very limited knowledge—to be an indispensable resource. So Quechua speakers have a complex and often ambiguous set of responses to domination by Spanish Peru, including varying degrees of Quechua language maintenance and second-language skills in Spanish.

The survival of Southern Peruvian Quechua is not only a case of "language loyalty" in the limited sense of this expression, but reflects a comprehensive loyalty to a way of life with an exclusionary view of social interaction. Put another way, "language loyalty" in the contemporary agrarian communities of Southern Peru is bound up in a most profound way with loyalty to being Runa. To insist, along with Southern Peruvian Quechua speakers, that the language itself is properly called *Runa simi* 'Runa speech, human speech' is to agree to their identification of the language with both the natural and the social order.

I do not wish to imply that the stance of Southern Peruvian Quechua speakers toward Spanish is one of outright rejection, or even that there *is* a single stance. Since the institution of Spanish rule, access to Spanish language has been a necessary resource for Runa communities. A community's access to productive resources and its very survival may be called into question within the framework of administrative and legal systems in which all of the moves are made in Spanish. Bureaucratic control over the affairs of rural communities has grown considerably over the last decade, and with it the need for speakers who control Spanish at a sufficient level to negotiate the paperwork. The Spanish language is, moreover, a resource for individuals, particularly the unmarried youth who attempt to find temporary urban wage labor. Finally, there is to some extent an internalization of the national society's evaluation of the two languages: parents are often anxious that their children learn Spanish in the vague expectation that it will be useful to their household and ultimately to their children.

Runa, then, have the same ambivalence toward Spanish as they do toward *q'ara* institutions in general. In this context, language is emblematic of an intrusive social system whose values contradict the very order of the world. Recognition by Runa of the reality of national domination by Spanish-language institutions is tempered by an ethnocentrically tinted anger. On the model of *Runa simi* 'human speech', the Southern Peruvian Quechua name for their own language, Runa sometimes, with bitter humor, refer to Spanish as *alqo simi,* 'dog speech'.

It would be presumptuous to offer a prognosis for Southern Peruvian Quechua in view of the social and political complexity of the language situation. The present vigor of *Runa simi* in rural areas of the six southeastern departments of Peru suggests that reports of its imminent demise are premature, to say the least. But only an incurable romantic would deny the considerable institutional and political pressures applied to the language and its speakers in the context of a Spanish-speaking nation-state. As the institutional and cultural noose tightens around Southern Peruvian Quechua, its long-term prospects for survival are increasingly bound up with the creation of a self-consciously Quechua nation.

Part I The Historical and Social Setting

2 The Ecology of Language Contact before the European Invasion

Introduction

It is commonplace for historical linguists to assert that language change must be understood in its social setting. Frequently, this means that linguistic features, such as phonetic, lexical, stylistic, or language differences are correlated with social features such as socioeconomic status, age, and gender; or with social domains, such as ritual occasions, bureaucratic interviews, and rock concerts. Such analyses show fine-grained articulations between specific features of the linguistic landscape and specific features of the social landscape. They can most easily be carried out after the details of linguistic variability and social setting are well known. They are best suited to micro-analysis. But with some exceptions (largely in the fields of creolization, language death, and the political sociology of language) such analyses also assume that the social setting is relatively static and that the linguistic features are indices of inert social categories. In this part of the book I map out a social setting in which neither assumption is relevant. I shall be concerned with a macro-historical analysis of changes in the Southern Peruvian Quechua language, with a time scale of more than 500 years. I also sketch radical changes in the social setting over the same period. The changes in social setting are essential to understanding the nature of the changes that the language has undergone over that time and to understanding the nature of the evidence of those changes.

The central analytical concept I use is the "social ecology of language" (Voegelin, Voegelin, and Schultz 1967: 405; Haugen 1971). The social ecology of language consists of the ways in which linguistic differences are organized and set into a social landscape: of the ways in which language and dialect differences are institutionally channeled and used; of the degree to which diversity is encouraged or, conversely, restricted by language standardization; of the particular contexts of written attestations; of the social evaluation of linguistic differences;

and of the cultural and psychological resonances of linguistic differences for their speakers—in short, of the nature of speech communities as "organizations of diversity" (Hymes 1974: 433). Each of these features can vary considerably across cultures and across time. Since the mechanisms of linguistic change are determined by the social ecology, it is important to understand the cultural and political-economic underpinnings of the social ecology of language and to understand the ways in which it can vary. Case studies that focus on the social ecology of language are essential, in that they contribute to understanding how linguistic variation and change can be embedded in an extralinguistic context.

To get a sense of the ways in which the social ecology of language can vary, consider two contrastive examples, English in New York City (from Labov 1966a) and multilingualism in the northwest Amazon basin of South America (from Jackson 1974).[1] (Though these are specific speech communities at specific moments in time, I describe them in the "ethnographic present.")

English speakers on the Lower East Side of Manhattan (in the 1960s) comprise a single, fluidly stratified speech community. The speech of all members of the community varies along certain phonetic parameters, such as the extent to which *r* is dropped after vowels in words like *drawer* and *floor;* or the degree to which fricative *θ*(th) becomes affricate t^{θ} and then stop *t* in words like ***thing, thought,*** and ***through.*** All speakers use all of the values of these variables some of the time. The extent to which they do so indexes: (1) the socioeconomic status of speakers, and (2) the extent to which speakers are monitoring their own speech. Variables such as the different pronunciations of *th* are stable indices of socioeconomic status. The *θ*-variable maintains a consistent hierarchy reflecting the speaker's socioeconomic status regardless of the extent to which she is monitoring her own speech. The *r*-variable, on the other hand, is subject to conscious manipulation on the part of speakers. While in unguarded speech it reflects socioeconomic status in much the same way the *θ*-variable does, in more carefully monitored speech linguistically insecure speakers register a higher frequency of *r*s after vowels than even higher status speakers. Variables such as the *θ*-variable pattern below the speaker's threshold of awareness; variables such as the *r*-variable pattern above the speaker's threshold of awareness. The *r*-variable is in the process of change; the *θ*-variable is not. Two additional observations need to be made here: first, all of the members of the speech community share a set of evaluative norms according to which different speech styles have different prestige. Second, since the speech community is fluidly stratified, and the phonetic variables are indices of status, speakers can appropriate the style of a higher-status group in the same way as they appropriate other status markers to accrue prestige.

The Vaupés region of the northwest Amazon basin (in the 1970s) is a single, nonstratified, multilingual speech community, with three unrelated language families represented among twenty or so languages (Tukanoan, Carib, Arawakan). The people of the Vaupés have a generally homogeneous material culture and social organization. They are swidden horticulturalists who live in multifamily patrilocal longhouses, located from a few hours to a day from each other on foot. The longhouses are subunits of "language aggregates," who share a common father language. The language aggregates have no discrete territory, nor any other corporate existence. Speakers are required to marry someone who is not a member of their language aggregate. Any single longhouse, then, is multilingual, and a majority of interactions are between members of more than one language aggregate. Most speakers command at least three languages fluently, many four or five, and some understand as many as ten. Tukanoan is used as a lingua franca over the entire area. There has been a great deal of structural convergence between the languages spoken in the Vaupés region. Stratification is not a component of the language-aggregate system. The choice of a language in a particular interaction is very fluid. Though language differences are emblematic of social identity, in terms of the system of linguistic exogamy, speakers need not be continually reminded of it. There is no special prestige in speaking one language rather than another. Language identity plays a critical role in the marriage system and is therefore relatively stable.

I have contrasted two very different social ecologies in order to emphasize the range of variation. In New York City, fine-grained phonetic differences index the speaker's position in a fluidly stratified prestige hierarchy. In the northwest Amazon, approximately twenty languages are maintained in a single, nonstratified multilingual speech community, in which no single language has more prestige than another. The New York social ecology is marked linguistically by micro-differentiation of speech along a single prestige hierarchy. The northwest Amazon social ecology is marked linguistically by structural convergence, without any linguistically relevant prestige hierarchy.

The changes since the European invasion in the social ecology of Southern Peruvian Quechua are almost as dramatic as the difference between the New York and northwest Amazon cases. Immediately before the conquest, Southern Peruvian Quechua was the administrative language of the Inka state, Tawantinsuyu. Tawantinsuyu was a multiethnic empire, controlling territory running across the Andean region of South America, from what is today southern Colombia to northern Chile and Argentina. Southern Peruvian Quechua was the language of the people who were indigenous to the region of the Inka capital, Cuzco, the language of the ruling elite, and a lingua franca (or *lengua general*), a contact language for speakers of distinct languages within the state. But for much of the Inka state, including places close to the Inka capital itself, Southern Peruvian Quechua was but a thin overlay. The southern Peruvian Andes were, in general, a cultural mosaic in which speakers of distinct and often unrelated languages lived cheek to jowl with one another, much as is currently the case in other parts of South America, such as the northwest Amazon. Thus, even though Southern Peruvian

Quechua was the administrative language of an expansionist state, there is no evidence that it ever became hegemonic or was ever standardized, even in the nucleus of Tawantinsuyu around Cuzco. The archaeologist Craig Morris (1985: 478) has observed that "the brilliance of the Inka achievement seems to lie in its ability to accept, use, and perhaps even foster variability." This is as true of language as it is of Inka economy and society. The eighteenth-century European slogan "one nation, one people, one language" does not hold for the Andes, if it ever did for Europe.

Historical reconstruction of Southern Quechua and the nature of genetic relationships between Quechua languages and other language families must be understood in this light. Southern Peruvian Quechua, from among the Quechua languages, shares linguistic structures and patterns with neighboring languages. These might be explained by long-term, sustained, and close contact between the languages rather than by common inheritance. Southern Peruvian Quechua shows innovations of vocabulary that it partly shares with neighboring non-Quechua languages; these are also likely to have been borrowed into Southern Peruvian Quechua. Indeed, one of the earliest documents on the sociolinguistic setting of sixteenth-century Cuzco complains about the faddish tendency of the elites of Cuzco to borrow words from neighboring languages. And, if Southern Peruvian Quechua has undergone structural innovations that it does not share with other Quechua languages, then it would seem reasonable to look for the source of these innovations in the local setting of linguistic contact.

The European invasion and colonial rule drastically changed the linguistic ecology of southern Peru. The Europeans were struck by the diversity of languages, frequently complaining that "every valley had its own tongue." In order to make their new subjects easier to administer and proselytize, they set out to level the language differences. The European administrators set contradictory forces into motion as regarded Southern Peruvian Quechua. On the one hand, as one of the *lenguas generales*, one of the most widely understood languages of the region, Quechua was practical for religious and administrative purposes. The Spaniards consciously promoted Quechua—and the other *lenguas generales*, Aymara, Puquina, and Mochica (or Yunga), but Southern Peruvian Quechua above all—at the expense of local languages (*lenguas particulares*). European and Euro-American settlers had a stake in ensuring that native populations continued to speak a Native Andean language rather than Spanish, allowing the settlers to broker the involvement of native communities in the colonial economy and society. On the other hand, the Spaniards came armed with the conviction that languages were implanted by right of conquest, that religious indoctrination could only take hold through the medium of European languages, and that linguistic conversion would guarantee loyalty to the Spanish empire. The Spaniards conquered America fresh from their consolidation of power on the Iberian peninsula, where they had ruthlessly suppressed non-Christian religion and non-Romance languages. In theory, at least, the conquest of America was an extension of the conquest of Iberia. The ideology of linguistic conversion by right of conquest and a corresponding body of law and legal opinion were carried to America from the Spanish consolidation of power on the Iberian peninsula.

Southern Peruvian Quechua was thus caught in a double bind. At one and the same time, it was promoted at the expense of other indigenous languages and marked for extinction. And throughout the colonial era, and even since independence, some interest groups have argued for the total eradication of the language, just as other interest groups, for their own reasons, prevented Native Andeans from receiving schooling in Spanish, or promoted Quechua as a language of religious proselytization, or consciously cultivated it as a literary language. What is important to notice here is that the social and political geography of language shifted drastically after the European invasion. The fluid heterogeneity of languages that was present before the European invasion gave way to relative homogeneity and to relative hardening of a sociolinguistic hierarchy in colonial and modern Peru. Even though Southern Peruvian Quechua is still spoken by the vast majority of residents of the south central highlands, it is an oppressed language. Its use is stigmatized; its speakers are subject to the political-economic control of speakers of a foreign language. And if linguistic differences were indices of residential, ethnic, and political affiliation before the conquest (and these did have ramifications in political hierarchy), after the invasion, a single linguistic difference—Quechua versus Spanish—set off a small, empowered minority from the powerless majority.

The following chapters describe the changing social ecology of Southern Peruvian Quechua. Chapter 2 has two related objectives: to describe the pre-Columbian social ecology of language as a "base line" for understanding how the relationships among language, social identity, and territory were transformed by Spanish conquest and rule; and to set out a key debate in Andean historical linguistics and prehistory—namely, whether the Quechua languages are related to the neighboring Jaqi/Aru languages such as Aymara. I propose that the similarities between Aymara and Southern Quechua can best be understood as a consequence of intensive contact and structural convergence and discuss the social coordinates of contact between these languages. Chapters 3 and 4 discuss the politics of language in colonial and modern Peru, and its effect on the social ecology of language. Three effects are especially important:

(1) the movement from a mosaic geography in which language differences are evaluated in terms of locality to one in which a relatively homogeneous group is the object of domination by another, partly on the basis of language; (2) the ambivalence toward Quechua on the part of its speakers; and (3) the nonrecognition of local dialect variability within Quechua. In chapter 4, I also discuss native evaluations of language and dialect differences as an outcome of the process of homogenization of the linguistic geography of southern Peru.

Language Contact

From the first contact with Native South Americans, the European invaders were perplexed by their linguistic diversity (Cabello Valboa 1590: 218–219; Cobo 1653: XI, ix; c.f. Cerrón-Palomino 1987c). Bartolomé de las Casas expressed astonishment that "thousands of languages" were spoken in South America. For his part, José de Acosta (1577a: I, ii, 399, IV, viii, 517) guessed that there were more than 700 languages, "a true thicket [*selva*] of languages." Consider Cabello Valboa (1590: 104–105):

> . . . they speak so many languages, so different from each other . . . that I believe there aren't numbers high enough to count them, there are so many. This is so notable that in many provinces one doesn't go a league without coming across another language, as remote and distinct from the first as Castilian Spanish from Basque, or from English, or from African languages; in some lakes formed by the César branch of the great Magdalena River [of Colombia]. . . , there are some populated islands in plain view of each other, and on every island they speak a different language. In other parts of the Indies [Latin America], this reaches such an extreme that in one single village they speak two or three different languages, and in one house the woman and daughters happen to speak one language, and the husbands and sons another one very different from the first; and in some places it is considered immodest for women to speak in the language of men, and the men consider it contemptible to use the language and the words of women. . . .[2]

Cabello Valboa's remark that "there aren't numbers high enough to count" the languages spoken in South America may be hyperbolic, but the rest of the passage recalls modern descriptions of multilingualism in the eastern Colombian lowlands. Many Europeans took the linguistic diversity of native South America as a sign of the degree of barbarism of its inhabitants (Pagden 1982: 126–136, 180). According to sixteenth-century theories, civilization developed through economic and linguistic interaction (*communicationes*). Linguistic diversity was a sign that civil society had developed in only the most rudimentary ways. The central Andes were especially puzzling. The Inkas were recognizable as an empire, and the Europeans expected them to have unified their subjects linguistically. Instead, sixteenth-century eyewitnesses were astonished to find that "every village and every valley has its own language."

Andean multilingualism, then, created difficulties of both a practical and an intellectual order. For practical purposes, military, administrative, and religious, the Spaniards attempted to identify *lenguas generales*, languages that were spoken by broad segments of the aboriginal population, such as Southern Peruvian Quechua, Aymara, Puquina, and Yunga (or Moche). Often they found it convenient to require the use of a *lengua general*, or lingua franca, at the expense of local vernacular languages. Spanish administrators and missionaries thus became agents of the spread of the *lenguas generales* Quechua and Aymara.

For intellectual reasons, the Europeans sought to reduce the linguistic diversity they encountered, particularly in the Andean high civilizations. For instance, they assumed that the languages were dialects of one another or that they had sprung from a common root. Not only did the invaders reduce the languages in use by physical and cultural genocide; almost as if to add insult to injury, they sought to reduce the languages intellectually, by showing that the linguistic diversity of the Andes could be accounted for by showing that the languages came from a common source (Hymes 1973: 62–63). The impulse to find a single origin for the Andean languages has persisted through the centuries, as we shall see. In itself, there is nothing wrong with trying to trace historical origins; but, through the years, the search for origins has diverted intellectual energy from recovering the social, cultural, and historical dimensions of linguistic change: the processes by which Andean languages have diversified and changed and the social and cultural landscapes of linguistic diversity.

A case in point is the attempt made by many observers, colonial and modern alike, to show that the two most widely used of the *lenguas generales*, Southern Peruvian Quechua and Aymara, are related by descent from a common ancestor language. The point was argued over and over, often on the basis of spurious evidence or no evidence at all. And the debates did not lead to careful examination of the available evidence, much less to new research into Andean linguistic prehistory. These languages overlap in vocabulary and have typological similarities in phonology and syntax. As we shall see, the similarities can best be accounted for by contact and mutual borrowing rather than by common descent.

This chapter has two purposes. The first is to reconstruct the social ecology of language at the time of the Spanish conquest. The Southern

Peruvian Andes were "a thicket of languages," even in the vicinity of the Inka capital, Cuzco. The second is to show how contact between Aymara and Southern Peruvian Quechua fit the broader pattern of multilingualism in preconquest Peru. These purposes are inextricably woven together, in that the contact between Quechua and Aymara exemplifies the broader pattern and—at the same time—is inexplicable without setting it into the broader Andean patterns of appropriation of linguistic differences to cultural ends. Although I propose to reconstruct conquest-period patterns of multilingualism, my historical evidence is drawn entirely from postconquest written sources, especially from the first seventy years after the Spanish conquest.

Over the years, a number of claims have been made about the relationships between Quechua languages (most often Southern Peruvian Quechua) and other languages and language families, some geographically distant, some quite close. For example, Father Bernabe Cobo proposed in 1653 that Southern Peruvian Quechua was related to Aymara. Similarly, Sir William Jones, whose famous "Third Anniversary Discourse, on the Hindus" (1786) first identified the Indo-European languages, also claimed, in another (understandably less known) passage, that "the Hindus . . . had an immemorial affinity with . . . the Scythians or Goths, the Celts, the Chinese, Japanese, and *Peruvians*" (1967 [1786]: 20, emphasis mine). Even after the nineteenth century, when the notion of a "genetic relationship" took on a very specific meaning in historical linguistics, numerous writers claimed that Quechua was related genetically to other languages, supporting their claims with little or no evidence.

The criteria for a genetic relationship are strict. A genetic relationship requires systematic comparison of morphology and vocabulary and postulation of systematic sound correspondences. In order to be explicit and testable, a proof of a genetic relationship must include a reconstruction of a parent language and a set of testable hypotheses about the evolution of each of the daughter languages, including the postulation of sound laws, morphological and restructuring processes (Kuryłowicz 1973), and lexical and grammatical etymologies (Goddard 1975).[3] The ultimate goal of a genetic reconstruction is not simply to show that two given languages are related through common descent, but to reconstruct the linguistic history of each in what Saussure (1971 [1915]: 291ff.) called a "prospective reconstruction," that is, a reconstruction forward from the parent language. Raw similarities between word-stems do not tell us anything in and of themselves.

Unfortunately, the less that is known about the internal diversity of the Quechua family, the more the speculations about outside genetic relationships. Only recently have linguists working on Quechua understood how diverse the language family really is. As some of the less-studied varieties of Quechua receive more attention (in works such as Torero 1968 and Taylor 1982 for Ferreñafe and Taylor 1984 for Yauyos), and, as details of the linguistic history became better known (for example, Landerman 1978 on the person system; Cerrón-Palomino 1979, 1987b; Adelaar 1984), it has become clear that even more work remains to be done.

It is only within the last twenty-five years that linguists have begun to focus on diversity within the Quechua linguistic family. This orientation is probably the most important achievement of Quechua linguistics in this period. Only a small portion of its potential has yet been realized. For example, Quechua is rich morphologically, and much of the diversity in the modern languages is due to morphological change; Quechua has a lot to teach us about the nature of morphological change. Similarly, once more is known about the processes of phonological and morphosyntactic change, it will be possible to reconstruct changes in the vocabulary, and this will have important implications for Andean prehistory. A more realistic view of the internal evolution of the Quechua languages will also make it possible to gauge distant genetic relationships more realistically. Until now, all of the attempts to relate Quechua to other genetic groupings of languages (e.g., Harrington 1943; Swadesh 1969) have been based on thin evidence: sometimes the Quechua evidence has come from only one language in the family (usually Southern Peruvian Quechua); sometimes from only one branch (Peripheral); sometimes indiscriminately from among the Quechua languages; and sometimes indiscriminately from Quechua and a neighboring language family, Jaqi/Aru.[4]

The most persistent suggestions for outside genetic relationships have been with Aymara, a language that borders on Southern Peruvian Quechua. Aymara has now been shown to be a member of another language family, Jaqi/Aru, along with the two Peruvian languages Jaqaru and Kawki (Hardman-de-Bautista 1966b, 1976, 1978, 1985; Torero 1972 [1970]: 64–76; Briggs 1976). From the Quechua side, the suggestions of a genetic relationship with Aymara have almost always used evidence from the Southern Peruvian and Bolivian languages. But these are precisely the Quechua languages that have been in closest contact with Jaqi/Aru languages. The issue at stake here is the following: how do we account for the phonological and lexical similarities between Southern Quechua and Aymara? Are they the result of language contact or of common inheritance? This is the point at which the notion of "ecology of language" is especially important. If there is good evidence that the languages were geographically intermeshed, then the similarities might be the result of language contact. And if there is little evidence that the similarities can be accounted for by common inheritance, then the language contact hypothesis would be the stronger of the two. I argue that the similarities between Southern Quechua and Aymara are the result of language contact and convergence rather than common inheritance. The ethnohistorical evidence suggests that the linguistic landscape of pre-Colombian Southern Peru was extraordinarily complex and conducive to areal diffusion of linguistic forms and structures through language contact.

Quechua and Aymara

Bernabe Cobo wrote in 1653 that "the two languages, Quechua and Aymara . . . belonging to two neighboring and coterminous peoples, have such a similarity in vocabulary and construction, that even someone who knows as little of them as I do could hardly deny that both have originated from a single forerunner, in the same fashion that Spanish and Italian were born from Latin" (1956 [1653]: XI, ix, 29).[5]

Cobo's assertion was later endorsed by renowned Andean scholars such as J. J. von Tschudi (1853), Clements Markham (1871a), Heymann Steinthal (1890), and Jacinto Jijón y Caamaño (1941–1947). For the most part, the claims that Quechua and Aymara were related by common descent were based on two observations: the phonological inventories of Aymara and Cuzco-Collao Quechua are similarly patterned; approximately 20 percent of the vocabulary is identical or similar in the two languages. But neither observation says anything one way or another about a genetic relationship. In the nineteenth and early twentieth centuries, Peruvian historians debated whether to attribute the archaeological remains in southern Peru and Bolivia to "Quechuas" or "Aymaras." In the context of this debate, a number of baseless statements were made that one language could be "derived" from the other (e.g., Markham 1871a; Villar 1890; von Buchwald 1919; Valcárcel 1936–1941; and Lira 1944).

Modern advocates of a genetic relationship include J. M. B. Farfán, Carolyn Orr, Robert Longacre, and Yolanda Lastra de Suárez. Farfán (1954) simply assumes that there is a genetic relationship between the two language families and attempts to "date" it using lexicostatistics. Orr and Longacre's proposed "Proto-Quẹchuamaran" (1968) uses the comparative method to reconstruct a prototype parent language for the two families. The Orr and Longacre proposal includes a systematic comparison of vocabulary from the two language families, but is fraught with methodological problems.

Orr and Longacre select nine dialect witnesses from the Quechua family to reconstruct a prototype parent language for Quechua. The nine witnesses are not representative of the linguistic family. Only one witness represents the entire Central Quechua branch; three, including Southern Peruvian Quechua, border on Aymara-speaking areas; and four of the witnesses are Ecuadorian varieties that are probably descended from the Inka lingua franca, Southern Peruvian Quechua (Hartmann 1979). Orr and Longacre unwittingly bias their dialect sample toward varieties of Quechua that have been in contact with Aymara (cf. Cerrón-Palomino 1982: 238). Since these are the Quechua dialects that share the most vocabulary with Aymara and most resemble it structurally, Orr and Longacre's sample is biased in favor of their hypothesis.

In addition, Orr and Longacre consider only vocabulary that is present in all nine of the Quechua witnesses. This favors the thin overlay of vocabulary associated with the Inka expansion and the Aymara-influenced Inka lingua franca (Parker 1969c: 72). Even with these limitations, the Orr and Longacre reconstruction of proto-Quechua is problem-ridden, since the correspondences between the manners of articulation are irregular (Parker 1969f: 158ff). They are less regular still in a more representative sample of dialect witnesses, especially for ejectives and aspirates (Stark 1975: 214).[6]

There are similar sampling problems in the Aymara part of the reconstruction. Although descriptive material on the other Jaqi/Aru languages was in print at the time of the Orr and Longacre study (Matos 1956; Hardman-de-Bautista 1966a), they used only Aymara in the comparative reconstruction. Of the Jaqi/Aru languages (Hardman-de-Bautista 1966a, 1978), Aymara has had the closest contact with Southern Quechua and is structurally the most similar to the Quechua languages used by Orr and Longacre. The other two Jaqi/Aru languages, Jaqaru and Kawki, are structurally more different and more difficult to account for under the "Proto-Quechuamaran" hypothesis.

Yolanda Lastra (1970) also suggests that Quechua and Aymara are related genetically. She compares the positional classes and grammatical categories of Aymara and Ayacucho-Chanka Quechua and observes that, even though the suffixes have different morphological shapes, they have similar meanings and occur in the same relative order (cf. Hymes 1955). Lastra concludes that the match between position classes is evidence of a genetic relationship and might allow positional categories to be reconstructed for a proto-language. Yet a match-up of morphological position classes is neither sufficient nor necessary to demonstrate that two languages are related genetically. On the contrary; languages in contact frequently converge to the point that the relative order of grammatical elements matches (Gumperz 1967; Gumperz and Wilson 1971). Einar

Haugen (1971: 335) writes, "In stable bilingual communities there is . . . accommodation between symbiotic languages, such that they cease to reflect distinct cultural worlds: their sentences approach word-for-word translatability, which is rare among really autonomous languages." Thus the position class match-up, far from being an indication of a deep genetic relationship, is a predictable consequence of stable multilingualism.

Moreover, both languages are typologically similar. Both are internally consistent verb-final languages; they are exclusively suffixing and agglutinative. Quechua agglutination is transparent, while it is obscured by complex morphological adjustments in Aymara and the other Jaqi/Aru languages. In Quechua, the relative order of suffixes is semantically iconic in a way that accords with the other typological facts (see chapter 10). Briefly, the linear order of the suffixes reflects a semantic hierarchy obtaining among them. The suffixes are divided into three major classes: (1) derivational, (2) inflectional, and (3) discourse-level suffixes, which follow the word-stem in that order. Within each major suffix class, the sequential order of suffixes reflects their relative subjectivity, semantically more subjective suffixes following semantically less subjective. Since the order of affixes is iconic, it is of as little use in attesting to a genetic relationship as onomatopoeia. Finally, the labels for grammatical categories that are used in Lastra's study are so vague that it is not clear to what extent there really is a match-up in the meanings and to what extent it reflects the words used to label the suffixes. Joseph Davidson (1977, 1979: 11) has tested Lastra's proposal in greater detail and finds no evidence that the languages are related genetically.

One of the critical issues in the debate over whether the Quechua and Jaqi/Aru languages are genetically related has been the source of the ejective (or glottalized) and aspirate stops in Southern Quechua, including the Cuzco-Collao dialect of Southern Peruvian Quechua and the Bolivian dialects. Advocates of a genetic relationship suppose that the ejectives and aspirates were inherited from a common Quechua-Jaqi/Aru ancestor. Opponents of a genetic relationship assert that the ejectives and aspirates were borrowed into Southern Quechua from the Jaqi/Aru family (Ferrario 1956; Parker 1963; Hardman-de-Bautista 1964; Torero 1964; Cerrón-Palomino 1984: 106–107). They observe that: (1) there are no known reflexes of either feature in the Central Quechua languages; and (2) ejectives and aspirates appear only in those Quechua varieties that have been in contact with Jaqi/Aru languages. The only exceptions to the second observation are Ecuadorian varieties descended from or influenced by the lingua franca (Cerrón-Palomino 1987a: 183–188). According to the critics of the "Proto-Quechuamaran" hypothesis, the ejectives and aspirates are areal and cannot be reconstructed for proto-Quechua. Indeed, there is even some doubt about their status in earlier stages of Southern Peruvian Quechua (chapters 5 and 8).

Critics of the hypothesis that Quechua and Aymara are related genetically—such as Max Uhle, Benigno Ferrario, Martha J. Hardman-de-Bautista, Gary Parker, and Alfredo Torero—contend the resemblances between Southern Quechua and Aymara are the result of long-term contact. Their position has two components: first, to show that past attempts to reconstruct a common ancestor language are flawed methodologically or empirically; and, second, to show that the similarities between the languages can better be accounted for by language contact. The first component, that a genetic relationship has *not* been demonstrated successfully, is important for methodological reasons. The notion of "common ancestry" rests entirely on positive evidence; it cannot be demonstrated that two given languages are *not* related genetically (Bright 1970). Once past genetic explanations of the similarities between Southern Quechua and Aymara have been discarded, it remains to construct a positive explanation for the similarities: language contact. The language contact hypothesis becomes compelling if: (1) there is independent evidence for widespread language contact; and (2) it clarifies linguistic phenomena that would otherwise be incomprehensible. In the following sections I present ethnohistorical evidence that the ecology of language in southern Peru and Bolivia was far more complex than it is today, with widespread multilingualism between territorially interspersed languages. The colonial sources on Andean multilingualism are consistent enough to reconstruct a general pattern and to evaluate it in social and cultural terms. I then turn to the variability in Southern Peruvian Quechua ejectives and aspirates and show how the variability can be accounted for more fruitfully under the contact than the genetic hypothesis.

Historical Evidence for Language Contact

There is good evidence that several other languages were spoken alongside Quechua in pre-Columbian and sixteenth-century southern Peru. The evidence is especially strong for Aymara and Puquina, two of the most widely spoken languages in the first decades after the Spanish conquest (Toledo 1575b; Torero 1965: 26–29; 1972 [1970]: 52; Bouysse-Cassagne 1988: 48–62). Aymara was spoken in much of the area in which Cuzco-Collao type varieties of Southern Peruvian Quechua are spoken today, including the *provincias altas* of the departments of Cuzco (Canas, Canchis, Chumbivilcas, and Espinar) and Arequipa (Tercer Concilio Limense 1584: f. 78r; Ramírez 1597: f.

15v; Anonymous 1600: II, 402; Bertonio 1603: 10, 1612: f. A3). The nature of contact-era and colonial multilingualism has been the subject of pointed debate, much of which has been conjectural. Let me review the evidence here.[7]

The best sources on the linguistic situation in colonial highland Peru are local reports from priests and colonial administrators. By the 1570s, the older Andean pattern of discontinuous settlements had been disrupted by the Spanish reorganization of the colony, especially by the consolidation of settlements. Nevertheless, many of the most useful sources come from the period immediately after the reorganization. These sources include the surveys and tax assessments that accompanied the reorganization of the colony under Viceroy Toledo (Bouysse-Cassagne 1976, 1977; Cook 1977) and the systematic survey of the empire conducted under King Philip II (*Relaciones geográficas de Indias*). Other sources were less useful, although they provided occasional data. The classic sources on the Inkas, the colonial chronicles, tend to discuss language in normative terms and are neither specific nor reliable enough. On the other hand, local documents, especially trial records, usually refer to the local language with a generic expression, such as *lengua índica.*

In the 1586 survey, the provincial administrator (*corregidor*) of Chumbivilcas, Francisco de Acuña, reported that in Llusco and Quiñota "some . . . speak the Aymara language and others the *lengua general* of the Inka [Quechua]."[8] He also reported the existence of a local language, "Chumbivilcano," which was spoken alongside the Inka lingua franca, Quechua, in the provinces of Chumbivilcas, Espinar, and Grau (Acuña 1586: 313, Alccavitoria; 1586: 318, Capamarca; 1586: 320, Santo Tomás and Colquemarca; 1586: 322, Velille; 1586: 324, Livitaca). Paul Rivet (1924: 652) suggested that "Chumbivilcano" was an Aymara-related (Jaqi/Aru) language, but this was pure conjecture on his part. There is no written evidence for "Chumbivilcano," nor is it spoken today. The speakers of Chumbivilcano were lower-status herders and dispersed across the *punas*; the speakers of Quechua were villagers with ties to the Inka state. The Aymara speakers in the region were likewise of higher status than the Chumbivilcanos (Poole 1987: 260).

The same 1586 survey described a system of ethnic symbiosis in the province of Collaguas. There were two ethnic groups, each with its own distinctive dress and distinctive form of cranial deformation; each group also had its own origin myth establishing a distinctive relationship to the local territory. One group, the Collaguas, spoke Aymara, and the other, the Cavanas, spoke Quechua (*la lengua general del Cuzco corruta y muy avillanada*) (Ulloa 1586: 328–329; cf. Pease 1977: 140; Manrique 1985: 30–34; Gelles 1988: 9–10). The Cavanas were relative newcomers; the Collaguas occupied herding lands in the frigid plateaus and the poorest agricultural lands in the valleys.[9] In 1620 the bishop of Arequipa warned of the necessity of teaching Spanish as a prerequisite to Catholic indoctrination because of the linguistic diversity of the parishioners: "Cuzco . . . has villages of Quechua, Aymara, and Puquina Indians; the same diversity is also found in the Bishopric of Arequipa" (Millones 1971: 303; Almonte 1813: 307).[10] In eighteenth-century Andagua (Condesuyos, Arequipa), Quechua was the most widespread secular language, but Aymara was used as a liturgical language by pagan priests (Salomon 1984: 25; 1987: 160). Even as recently as the beginning of the nineteenth century, a priest in the province of Condesuyos reported that even though Quechua was the most widely understood language, Aymara, Coli, Isapi, and Chinchaysuyo (Northern Quechua?) were spoken there as well (Almonte 1813: 307).

Closer to Cuzco, the 1586 report on Zurite and Anta (Department of Cuzco) mentions that "the majority have distinct languages, but speak the lingua franca [*la general*]" (Fornee 1586: 17);[11] the rest of the report on the Province of Abancay routinely reports only that the people speak the Inka lingua franca, Quechua. Finally, a *Censo de Indios* (1633–1641) lists a number of communities in the present-day departments of Cuzco and Apurímac, often including Aymara ethnic names or the designation "Aymara" next to community names.[12]

The reports for the Ayacucho region in the 1586 survey are more difficult to interpret. According to historical sources and oral tradition, the Inkas evacuated the region, especially around Vilcashuamán, and resettled it with colonists (*mitmaq*) from the other regions of Tawantinsuyu. The *mitmaq* colonists maintained their own ethnic identities, marriage ties to their homelands, and languages. Moreover, rather than settle the *mitmaq* in geographically contiguous regions according to ethnic polity of origin, the Inkas interspersed *mitmaq* of distinct ethnic origin and language (Zuidema 1966: 69–71, 1968: 504, 1970: 154–155; Purizaga 1972: 54–62; Earls and Silverblatt 1977; B. J. Isbell 1978: 63–65; Salas 1979: 17–30).

In Ayacucho, the Inka lingua franca served as a means of communication among ethnically distinct *mitmaq* settlers, and between different ethnic polities and the state. Rodrigo de Cantos (1965 [1586]: 307) wrote that there were so many local languages that all local authorities (*caciques*) were required to learn "the *lengua general* that they call Quechua" for the purposes of contact with the Inka state (compare Acosta 1577a: IV: viii, 517). In the immediate vicinity of the modern city of Ayacucho, according to Ribera y Chaves (1965 [1586]: 187–188), "They have different languages because each community speaks its distinct language although all speak the lingua franca of Cuzco, as the

Inkas ordered them to speak. And out of necessity they have continued their use of the Quechua *lengua general,* using their own native language."[13] Likewise, in Vilcashuamán, Carabajal (1965 [1586]: 206) observed that, although Quechua was used as a lingua franca, the *mitmaq* continued to speak the tongues of their places of origin. Carabajal reported that Aymara was spoken alongside Quechua in the modern-day provinces of Cangallo and Víctor Fajardo (Ayacucho). As late as the middle of the seventeenth century, "Indios aymaraes" are mentioned in litigation records from Chuschi (Cangallo, Ayacucho; B. J. Isbell 1978: 65; also Earls and Silverblatt 1977: 162–163). There is also evidence of Wanka (Central Quechua) settlements in the same region (Víctor Fajardo, Ayacucho; Earls and Silverblatt 1977). Luis de Monzón wrote of the Atunsoras (Huamanga, Ayacucho): "now they speak the *lengua general* Quichua of the Inka. They have another language that is native to them, the Aymara language, and they have other languages that they speak and understand, that are called *hahuasimi,* which is to say 'language outside of the *lengua general*' ['outside speech']" (1586a: 220).[14]

Monzón again, writing of two other populations in Ayacucho—Atunruncana and Rucanas: "in this *repartimiento* there are many different languages because each ethnic lord (*cacique*) has his language, although all speak and understand the language of the Inka. And the languages that they speak and understand other than the language of the Inka are called *hahua simi,* which is to say, 'language outside of the general language', which is the language of the Inka, and in which they interact and speak with the Spaniards, and they are understood by the Indians" (1586b: 228).[15] "In this *repartimiento* there are many different languages. Those of Antamarca have their own ancient language, those of Apcaraes another, the Omapachas another, and the Huchucayllos another. And these languages don't have their own name; rather they all call their own language *hahuasimi,* which is to say 'language outside of that of the Inka', which is used in common . . . and which all understand and speak" (1586c: 239).[16]

The reports that in many places Aymara was spoken alongside Quechua in southern Peru are frequently understood to mean that Aymara once covered a contiguous territory beginning in the modern Aymara-speaking area around Lake Titiqaqa through Cuzco, Ayacucho, and Huancavelica. It is undoubtedly true that Quechua has expanded across southern Peru at the expense of Aymara, as it is doing today. But in light of the descriptions of the social ecology of Ayacucho and Huancavelica, we cannot discard the possibility that the Aymara presence there might be the result of Inka *mitmaq*-resettlement policies rather than the remnant of a pre-Inka Aymara-speaking population stratum (Diez de San Miguel 1964 [1567]: 81). The pattern of *mitmaq* resettlement of the region appears to have been determined in part by the cultural associations of Quechua and Aymara. Speakers of Quechua, the stereotypic valley (*qheswa*) language, were settled in the valleys; speakers of Aymara, the stereotypic high plateau (*puna*) language, in the plateaus (Kubler 1946: 332–333). And we need to reexamine the question of the genesis of Ayacucho-Chanka Quechua and its relationship to Cuzco-Collao Quechua varieties in the light of the social ecology of language in sixteenth-century Ayacucho and Huancavelica. It is unclear to what extent Ayacucho-Chanka Quechua is a late offshoot of the Inka lingua franca and to what extent it reflects an earlier, pre-Inka variety of Quechua.

The Puquina Language

Along with Southern Peruvian Quechua and Aymara, a third language, Puquina, was widely spoken in the south of Peru until the seventeenth century (Anonymous 1600: II, 61; Créqui-Montfort and Rivet 1925; Torero 1965: 17–29, 1987: 343–351). The Cuzco synod of 1591 required the use of Puquina along with Quechua and Aymara in the Diocese of Cuzco, and the Arequipa synod of 1638 likewise ordered indoctrination in all three languages in the Diocese of Arequipa (Créqui-Montfort and Rivet 1925: 222–223; Torero 1965: 18–19, 1972 [1970]: 57–58; Galdos 1987: 244–245). In addition, the bishop of Arequipa, Pedro de Villagomez, assigned a Puquina translation of the Catechism of the Tercer Concilio to two priests, Alvara Mogrovejo of Carumas and Miguel de Azana of Ilabaya and Locumba (Vargas 1953: 50; Torero 1987: 344). Taraco (Huancané, Puno), today a Quechua-speaking district bordering on Aymara, is reported to have Puquina spoken as late as the middle of the seventeenth century (Torero 1987: 346; also Ghersi and Arquinio 1966).

The evidence for Puquina is less reliable than for Aymara and must be interpreted cautiously. As a case in point, consider the seventeenth-century village of Andahuaylillas, located about thirty kilometers southeast of Cuzco, in which a seemingly straightforward piece of evidence appeared conclusively to indicate Quechua-Aymara-Puquina trilingualism. The portal of the baptistry has the baptismal formula "I baptize you in the name of the Father, of the Son, and of the Holy Spirit. Amen" inscribed around the portal in five languages: in Latin, on a medallion held by three angels; in Spanish across the painted frieze around the doorway; in Quechua (*Ñocam baptizayqui Yayap Churip Espiritu Sanctop Sutinpi Amen*) over the doorway arch; and in Aymara and Puquina on the doorway pillars (Keleman 1967 [1951]: I, 175, II, 113; also Mesa and Gisbert 1962: 40–41; Macera 1975: 70, 84; see Torero 1987: 346–

347, 358, for a discussion of the Puquina inscription). Torero (1972 [1970]: 63, 1987: 347, 399) took the inscriptions as evidence that Aymara and Puquina were spoken alongside Quechua in the seventeenth-century village. Yet a careful search for documentation of colonial Andahuaylillas (Hopkins 1983) did not turn up evidence of Puquina speakers.

The parish priest in the early seventeenth century was Pérez Bocanegra, famous for a Quechua doctrinal manual based on his experiences in Andahuaylillas. (For a discussion of the text, see chapter 6.) In the early seventeenth century, the Jesuits pressed a claim for Andahuaylillas as a mission parish. The Jesuits maintained that Andahuaylillas would be an ideal language-training parish for Quechua missionary work like the Aymara training parish they had established in Juli (Cisneros 1601: 285; Vázquez 1637; Vargas Ugarte 1960: 368–369; Hopkins 1983: 186–190). Their detractors argued that they really wanted it as a base from which to oversee their nearby haciendas.

The Jesuits actually gained control of the parish from 1628 to 1636. Much of the artwork in the church dates from that period. The inscriptions on the baptistry have not been dated (Macera 1975: 50), but, judging from its morphology, the Quechua inscription cannot be more recent than the seventeenth century. Apart from the inscriptions, there is no evidence that either Aymara or Puquina was spoken in Andahuaylillas.[17] The parish of Andahuaylillas is unusually well documented linguistically, and all evidence points to Quechua as the parish language. During the 1620s and 1630s, when the church was completed, Andahuaylillas was a center for mission-oriented linguistic work, so it is reasonable to conclude that the multilingual inscriptions were painted on the baptistry to stand for its avocation. One cannot be certain whether the inscription was done under the curacy of Pérez Bocanegra or of the Jesuits; but, in the latter case, it could represent a reaffirmation of the Jesuit dedication to the work with Quechua, Aymara, and Puquina begun by the Jesuit scholars Barzana and Acosta in the late sixteenth century. In sum, there is considerable evidence that Puquina was spoken in the southern Peruvian Andes, especially in the first century after the conquest, but there is almost none on the circumstances of its use, geographical or social; this will require careful coordination of local ethnohistoric and linguistic sources.

The Social Ecology of Noncontiguous Territory

The description of sixteenth-century Ayacucho and Huancavelica and the case of Puquina point up how important it is to contextualize the colonial distribution of languages in an overall "ecology of language," conceived of in terms of Andean patterns of language use. To do so is to lay the basis for a "diachronically slanted sociolinguistics" (Malkiel 1968a: 28; Romaine 1982) oriented toward understanding the social and cultural meaning of dialect and language in the Andes. There are four themes to keep in mind: (1) noncontiguous territorial organization; (2) the association of speech and locality; (3) the use of ethnic differences to situate groups in a social hierarchy without a necessary correspondence between language and ethnic identity; and (4) the organization of social differences on a stable, rather than contingent (or aleatory) basis.

Noncontiguous territorial organization. Geographic contiguity was not a criterion for the territorial distribution of languages in the south-central Andes until it was imposed as conscious policy by the Spanish colonial administration. As we have already seen, southern Peru was extremely complex linguistically in the period immediately following the European invasion. The linguistic complexity was socially significant. For instance, in Vilcashuamán language differences were used as one of the bases for determining the pattern of resettlement of *mitmaq* colonists, with Quechua speakers assigned to the temperate valleys (*qheswa*) and Aymara speakers assigned to contiguous high *punas*. In Collaguas and Cavanas (Arequipa), the Quechua-speaking Cavanas maintained a stable symbiotic relationship with the Aymara-speaking Collaguas.

Before the European invasion, one strategy for maximizing access to complementary productive resources was for a social unit to organize itself in "archipelago" fashion. The social unit maintained noncontiguous islands located in areas with access to other productive resources than its core settlement (Murra 1967: 384ff., and 1972; Salomon 1985; Galdos 1987; Glave 1987). Regional polities were also organized in a discontinuous spatial pattern. Sixteenth-century land records show discontinuous settlements in the Vilcanota and Huatanay valleys right in the heart of the former Inka state (Rostworowski 1970a; Espinoza 1974). Even states were organized on the basis of a noncontiguous geography. The Aymara-speaking Lupaqa state, for example, had a core settlement on the shores of Lake Titiqaqa. But its 20,000 domestic units controlled zones up to fifteen days' walk from the center, east into the montaña and west to the coast (Murra 1968). Recent archaeological work on the Inka state suggests that it is best conceived of as a web of "overlapping tiers of [discontinuous] units" (Morris 1985: 484). A second form of noncontiguous geography that built on the archipelago model was the *mitmaq* resettlement policy of the Inka state, which moved entire populations into new locations, sometimes to provide specialized services to the state, sometimes to secure state control over a region. *Mitmaq* settlements continued to identify with their places of origin socially, ritually, and linguistically.

Speech and locality. In Andean cultures, speech varieties are intimately tied to the places in which they are spoken. Each local group was associated with a way of speaking, as well as a mythological place of origin, a style of dressing and braiding the hair, and a pattern of cranial deformation. According to the indigenous chronicler Santa Cruz Pachacuti Yamqui (c. 1613), the legendary founder of the Inka dynasty, Manqo Qhapaq, ordered that the clothing and speech of each people be different, so that its place of origin would be easily identifiable. Manqo Qhapaq brought order to the world, in part by joining together language, cultural identity, and territory. Even today, to be Runa involves an identification of one's person with a place, and an ethnocentric commitment to one's own local ways of speaking, insofar as they are accessible to the speaker's awareness. A person is imbued with the very essence of a place; language is part of that identity.

Noncorrespondence between ethnic identity and language. While territory and language were associated in essentialist ways, language and ethnicity were not. Pre-Columbian polities used ethnic differences to situate groups in a social hierarchy without a necessary correspondence between language and ethnic identity (Zuidema 1973; Torero 1987: 336–337; Wachtel 1987: 393). In the sixteenth-century Audiencia of Charcas (southernmost Peru and Bolivia), for example, the term *Uru* was used in tax records and other descriptions to describe lower-status, autochthonous peoples, who lived alongside higher-status Quechuas and Aymaras. *Uru* designated an organizational and functional position in the economy, rather than a language (Bouysse-Cassagne 1976: 99; Torero 1987: 335). During the early colonial period, ethnic and linguistic identity were both changing, but followed different paths. Ethnic identity was used to differentiate indigenous people along class lines. On the other hand, linguistic differences were being flattened out by the expansion of the colonial *lenguas generales* at the expense of the Puquina, Uruquilla, and other local languages (Klein 1973; Bouysse-Cassagne 1976, 1977).

Throughout Charcas, however, the local language was spoken by a lower-status group and lost at the expense of an intrusive, higher-status indigenous language. The linguistic situation described by Acuña for sixteenth-century Chumbivilcas and by Ulloa for the Collaguas is similar, in that the intrusive languages are of higher status than the local ones. The parallel between Chumbivilcas and Charcas reopens the question of whether *Chumbivilcano* was the name of a language or the name of (a possibly multilingual) "ethnicity" that had been organized along class lines.

The organization of social differences on a stable rather than contingent basis. In pre-Columbian polities, linguistically significant social differences were constituted within a larger organization, rather than in terms of temporary, contingent exchange relationships. The pattern of intrusive ethnic groups having a higher status than local groups (Duviols 1973) was set into a durable hierarchy that was reinforced by language, dress, ritual practices, and different mythological relationships to territory. Members of one group could not, as individuals, appropriate the ritual practices or language of the other. In central Peru, stable linguistic and cultural boundaries have been shown to have persisted since the European invasion and have been traced backward archaeologically to about 1,000 years before the conquest (Bird 1984). The groups involved are ecologically complementary and have maintained *stable* exchange relationships across the boundary. Similarly, the larger-scale Andean polities used ethnic and language differences as the basis of stable, ascriptive hierarchies.

This feature of the social ecology has two consequences for linguistic change. First, the type of sociolinguistic pattern found in societies in which prestige status can be changed by the way that individuals appropriate language, with conscious imitation of higher-prestige forms, cannot have been the basis of either language spread or linguistic change, since individuals cannot manipulate linguistic markers to achieve social mobility.[18] Second, it is unlikely that the Andean languages spread by means of trade networks, since trade was a relatively peripheral activity in the Andean states, tended to occur in the context of linguistic and cultural differences, and tended to be conducted silently (Rojas 1980). The Andean states, including the Inkas, had redistributive economies, at least in their core territories. Each producer's place in the redistributive system was rigidly determined; there was little room for trade within the polity. In such a system, trade takes place at the margin, and special-status groups of traders are described for the northernmost frontier of the Inka state and for the Pacific coast (Rostworowski 1970b; Salomon 1978: 97–99). In his description of "the most widespread customs that all Indians observe," Bernabe Cobo (1956 [1653]: XI, viii) emphasized that trade was conducted silently (cf. Mayer 1974: 28; Rojas 1980: 65). Modern ethnographic evidence supports him on this.

These four themes—noncontiguous territorial organization; association of speech and locality; noncorrespondence between language and ethnicity; and stability of social and linguistic distinctions—have resonances in colonial and modern times (chapters 3 and 4). The connection between speech and locality is maintained today, especially in the connection between the local native languages and ritual access to place deities. The power of local languages is in their ritual use to address the local deities, who control the everyday fortunes of Runa households: agricultural production, fertility and health of domestic animals, and human fertility and well-being. The relationship between a high-status intrusive language set off in a stable bilingual setting from a low-status local language seems to be repeated in the modern relationship between Spanish and Southern Peruvian Quechua. Two aspects of the relationship between Spanish and Quechua can be understood in that light: (1) the differentiation of sources of power that are associated with the languages—the ritual power of the locality as opposed to the power of the national political economy and the formal structure of the state (Harvey 1987); and (2) the homogenization of Quechua as the autochthonous language as opposed to Spanish as the intrusive language.

There are critical differences between pre-Columbian and modern bilingualism. Before the conquest, the boundaries between intrusive and autochthonous languages were maintained rigidly; today, from the standpoint of the national society, Quechua and Spanish are part of a prestige system that allows individual mobility and appropriation of the higher-status language. Partly as a consequence, Spanish is implanting itself as the hegemonic language, its social dominance diffusely penetrating all aspects of everyday life (see chapter 4). The pre-Columbian system, in contrast to the modern, depended on continued differentiation and on neither language becoming hegemonic.[19]

The geography of language in pre-Columbian and early colonial southern Peru was a quilt of socially stable linguistic differentiation. Moreover, language and ethnicity did not necessarily correspond. Thus, it is not possible to interpret the territorial domain of linguistic communities in uniform and geographically contiguous terms; nor is it necessary to postulate migrations of populations in order to explain territorial discontinuities (e.g. Lathrap 1970: 68, 80; W. H. Isbell 1974; Stark 1985). The social conditioning of discontinuity is more subtle than that. Consider two postconquest cases in which languages changed their territorial spread: since the Spanish conquest, Southern Peruvian Quechua has been expanding southward against Aymara; similarly, southern Peru has become more homogeneous linguistically. In both of these cases, languages have moved across populations, instead of populations moving with their languages. To say that languages move across populations is the more productive way to look at the problems of territorial discontinuity and language spread, since it requires specification of the historical and social conditions for such movement. Theories of migrations of populations, on the other hand, tend to be circular: the only evidence is the linguistic distribution that was to be explained in the first place.

Language Contact and Linguistic Convergence

Let me turn now from ethnohistorical to linguistic evidence bearing on the Quechua-Aymara problem. The issue of whether ejective and aspirate stops are genetic (in Quechua) or areal has been considered crucial to claims as to whether Quechua and Aymara (Jaqi/Aru) are genetically related. All partisans of a genetic relationship between Quechua and Aymara have assumed that the ejectives and aspirates are genetic. Orr and Longacre (1968) have reconstructed them at the levels of both proto-Quechua and the proposed Quechua-Aymara ancestor. It is not surprising, then, that the status of the ejectives and aspirates has become a major focus of contention. As we have seen, ejectives and aspirates are present only in the Quechua varieties that have been in contact with Jaqi/Aru languages, or in dialects that have been influenced by these varieties; there are no reflexes of ejectives and aspirates in the Central Quechua branch. Opponents of the genetic hypothesis have offered four additional arguments against reconstructing ejectives and aspirates in proto-Quechua (Hardman-de-Bautista 1964; Stark 1975): (1) that words with ejectives and aspirates are disproportionally represented in the vocabulary shared by Aymara and Southern Quechua; (2) that the ejectives and aspirates are too variable to reconstruct systematically in Southern Quechua, much less in proto-Quechua; (3) that there is evidence that many of the Quechua words with ejectives and aspirates recently acquired those features; and (4) that, if it is assumed that ejectives and aspirates were borrowed into Southern Quechua relatively recently, other changes in the language become more comprehensible. I consider each of these points in turn.

First, Southern Peruvian Quechua lexical stems containing ejective or aspirated steps show a disproportionate number of lexical stems that are similar in both form and meaning in Aymara: 67 percent as opposed to 20 percent without either (Stark 1975: 212–213). Were the features genetic, one would expect a more equal distribution of supposed cognates, since the presence of particular phonological features can influence lexical borrowing, but not lexical retention. In many cases, it can be ascertained that word-stems have moved from Aymara to Quechua, sincc glottalization and aspiration have different distributions in the two languages. In Quechua, they are restricted to the first oral stop in a word. (For a formal statement of the restrictions, see chapter 8.) In the Jaqi/Aru languages, it is possible for a word to contain more than one of these stops. Any word with more than one of the ejective and aspirate stops in Aymara for which there is a similar stem in Quechua with an ejective or aspirate would have to have been borrowed from Aymara to Quechua. This is so because there is an independently motivated explanation for the loss of the feature in that direction; were an ejective or aspirate acquired on a later stop in Aymara, the process would be entirely arbitrary.

Second, comparison of cognate lexical stems from Southern Peruvian Quechua (Cuzco-Collao) and Bolivian Quechua (Cochabamba and Sucre) shows that the ejectives and aspirates are highly variable, so much so that reconstruction of the two features is problematic even at the level of Southern Quechua: Southern Peruvian, Bolivian, and Argentine Quechua (Stark 1975: 214ff.) A word with an ejective stop in one Southern Quechua dialect might have a nonejective stop in another. There are also doublets of related words within the same dialect, in which one has an ejective or aspirate where the other does not. Even within Cuzco-Collao Quechua, glottalization and aspiration are variable, though to a lesser extent. Presence of glottalization and aspiration on particular lexical items (e.g., *irqi* ~ *hirq'i* 'child'; *allpa* ~ *hallp'a* 'ground'; *haqay* ~ *haqhay* and *chaqay* ~ *chhaqay* 'that, there [deictic of situation]') is one of the few phonological variables that is consciously perceived by speakers (cf. Stark 1975: 217–218 on the Quechua of Cochabamba, Bolivia).

Third, there is evidence that, apart from the loanword core discussed above, glottalization and aspiration further diffused through the lexicon by means of associative lexical influence, in which the shape of one word influences the shape of a semantically related word. The features spread across lexical domains. This process is discussed in some detail in chapter 8, but for the moment, note the agreement of glottalization and aspiration in the following lexical sets: 'to become flat': *p'aqpakuy, p'arpakuy, last'ayukuy, p'alayukuy, t'aslayakuy*; 'foam': *phusuqu, phuqpu, phullpu*; 'curved, bend': *q'iwiy, p'akiy*; 'curved, crooked': *q'iwi, wist'u, t'iksu*; 'worn out': *thanta, mullpha*; 'limp': *wist'uy, hank'ay, wiqruy* (glottalization blocked on the last); 'narrow space': *k'iski, t'iqi, q'iqi*; 'narrow object': *k'ikllu, p'iti*; 'dusk': *arkhiyay, laqhayay, rasphiyay* (Parker et al. 1964: 35, 45, 54, 56, 81, 90, 93). Associative lexical influence was still alive after the conquest, as Spanish loanwords that likewise acquired the features attest: *khuchi* 'pig' < Sp. *cochina*; *phustullu* 'blister' < Sp. *pústulla* (modern *pústula*); *mut'uy* 'mutilate' < Sp. *mutilar* (cf. Stark 1975: 212).

Sound symbolism, "an inmost . . . similarity association between sound and meaning" (Jakobson and Waugh 1979: 178), also motivated the spread of ejectives through the lexicon. Again, Spanish loanwords are valuable witnesses: *hach'a* 'ax' < Sp. *hacha*; *hasut'i* 'whip' < Sp. *azote*; *hich'ay* 'throw out' < Sp. *echar* (Stark 1975: 212).[20] The words for 'narrow' mentioned above are examples of both associative lexical influence and sound symbolism; they are sound symbolic in that the ejective feature reflects 'narrowness', as does the preponderance of high, front (narrow) vowels in the set.

There are other sources for the modern Southern Quechua ejectives as well. Many (though not all) of the words that had apical affricates and sibilants in proto-Quechua have ejectives in Southern Peruvian Quechua, though not necessarily in the same place in the word. Apart from the ejectives that reflect proto-Quechua apicals, the stems containing glottalization and aspiration divide into a large common core in which the features are consistent throughout the varieties of Quechua that use them, plus a periphery through which the features diffused somewhat less systematically by means of associative lexical influence and sound symbolism.

A fourth and final argument that glottalization and aspiration were borrowed into Southern Peruvian Quechua, rather than having a genetic status, is provided by the subsequent direction of change in the varieties that have acquired these features. To my mind, this argument is more speculative than the others. One of the main dialect differences within Southern Peruvian Quechua is between varieties with ejectives and aspirates and varieties without. The varieties with ejectives and aspirates are spoken more to the south, including the Department of Cuzco; those without, more to the northwest, including the Department of Ayacucho. The Cuzco-type dialect (Cuzco-Collao Quechua) has a three-way opposition at the beginning of syllables, among ejective, aspirate, and plain stops. At the ends of syllables, most of the consonants have weakened; most of the distinctions between (even plain) consonants that appear at the beginnings of syllables are lacking at the ends. Conversely, the Ayacucho-type dialect (Ayacucho-Chanka Quechua) has neither ejective nor aspirate stops; the consonants at the ends of syllables reflect the full range of ancestral distinctions. The conservatism of the Ayacucho-Chanka type of consonant system at the ends of syllables is supported by three kinds of evidence: cognate forms in other Quechua varieties, internal reconstruction of Cuzco-Collao Quechua, and four centuries of written records.

Are these facts related? Is it an accident that Cuzco-Collao Quechua, with a three-way opposition in syllable-initial position, has systematically merged its finals? Consider the following: with the three-way opposition among ejective, aspirate, and plain stops, the combination of a consonant and a vowel has a mean frequency of .0133 in Cuzco-Collao Quechua. In Ayacucho-Chanka Quechua, in contrast, the same combination of a consonant with a vowel following it has a mean frequency of .0256. The information carried by a sound or combination of sounds is the inverse of its frequency. That is to say, the more predictable it is, the less information it carries. The greater the range of choices, the more information that is carried in each one. Almost twice as much information is carried in the selection of a consonant-vowel combination in Cuzco-Collao Quechua as in Ayacucho-Chanka. Now consider the frequencies of canonical syllables in Cuzco-Collao and Ayacucho-Chanka. The canonical consonant-vowel-(consonant) (obligatory initial consonant, optional final one) combination in Ayacucho-Chanka Quechua has a mean frequency of .00216; the same combination in modern Cuzco-Collao Quechua, .00222. In other words, in a Cuzco-Collao Quechua dialect that has undergone the weakenings and mergers of consonants at the ends of syllables, the information carried by a canonical syllable is of the same scale as a canonical syllable of Ayacucho-Chanka Quechua *without the ejectives and aspirates, and without the consonant weakenings and mergers.*

Both dialects of Southern Peruvian Quechua have very similar morphosyntactic systems; the morphosyntactic system can thus be held constant. If we consider the information carried in the phonological systems, it looks as though the weakenings and mergers of consonants at the ends of syllables in Cuzco-Collao Quechua represent a kind of compensation for the addition of ejectives and aspirates. The ejectives and aspirates increase the informational load of the perceptually stronger syllable onset; consequently, the informational load of the perceptually weaker syllable finals has been eliminated, gradually though systematically. In short, the changes that the Cuzco-Collao-type varieties have undergone over several centuries become intelligible if ejectives and aspirates were acquired, rather than inherited features.

This argument must remain entirely speculative, since there is no general framework within which formal phonological structures and changes can be described in terms of the information they carry. Linguists normally assume that phonology is autonomous from the rest of the speaker's cognized grammar and rarely consider the informational implications of formal phonological structures.[21]

The linguistic arguments that Southern Peruvian Quechua glottalization and aspiration were borrowed in the course of language contact, then, are as follows. (1) Ejectives and aspirates are disproportionately represented among lexical stems that are similar in the two language families, so much so that they appear to have been borrowed preferentially. Although phonological factors such as the presence of ejectives and aspirates influence borrowing, they do not normally influence genetic retention. Were the features genetic, one would expect them to have been retained in the same proportion as any other feature. (2) Ejectives and aspirates are so variable in the Southern Quechua languages that it is problematical to reconstruct them even for Southern Quechua, not to mention proto-Quechua. They do not have reflexes outside of the Quechua languages that either were in direct contact with Jaqi/Aru languages or reflect older varieties that were in direct contact. (3) There is evidence that, aside from a core lexicon of loanwords, glottalization and aspiration have spread through the Quechua lexicon by means of primary sound symbolism and associative lexical influence (secondary sound symbolism). The affected lexicon includes some loanwords from Spanish, so that these processes are still very much alive. (4) The dialects of Southern Peruvian Quechua with distinctive glottalization and aspiration have undergone a series of weakenings and mergers over the last 500 years that speculatively might be interpreted as compensatory changes.

Let me turn now to an argument that ejectives and aspirates were *not* borrowed from Aymara, proposed by the linguist Lyle Campbell (1976: 83).

As a rule of thumb, borrowed segments (or features) tend to lose restrictions on their distributions in the course of borrowing. But notice that there are *more* restrictions on the distribution of ejectives and aspirates in Southern Quechua than in the Jaqi/Aru languages even though by the contact hypothesis the direction of borrowing was from the Jaqi/Aru languages to Southern Quechua (Campbell 1976: 191–192).[22] The rule of thumb suggests that Southern Quechua should show *fewer* restrictions on the distribution of ejectives and aspirates. Campbell concludes that "if the hypothesis that diffused segments lack distributional restrictions of the donor language should survive investigation, then the question of whether Quechua owes the origin of its glottalization and aspiration to Aymara would receive a negative answer, and the question of Quechua-Aymara affinity would need to be investigated from a new perspective."

It may be that the hypothesis is a useful rule of thumb but not valid in a hard and fast way. As we have seen, there is evidence to suggest that stems with ejectives and aspirates *were* borrowed preferentially and that the features subsequently diffused through the Southern Peruvian Quechua lexicon. Or it may be that the hypothesis is correct in its essentials but vague in the way it has been applied to this case. What exactly is it that is generalized: the sequential distribution of the ejectives and aspirates, the rule(s) governing their sequential distribution, or the way in which they function in the Southern Peruvian Quechua phonological system? In this case, it appears to be the last of these, in two senses.

First, the ejectives (and possibly also the aspirates) are *culminative* (Jakobson and Halle 1956: 20) in addition to having the ordinary phonological function of distinguishing words and utterances (see chapter 8). They are culminative in that they mark the word as a phonological unit, in that every word can have at most one ejective. They also mark the hierarchy of morphological elements that make up the word, by making lexical stems as against suffixes; only stems can even carry ejectives and aspirates. It is common in the world's languages for ejectives to have a culminative function, that is, marking the word as a unit (Greenberg 1970a: 16–17). Notice, though, that insofar as the ejectives are restricted to occurring once per word, they are less integrated in the phonological system than are ordinary, nonculminative features.

Second, the "once per word" restriction on both features is a *generalization* of the sense-discriminative function of the features to its simplest form: words are distinguished by the presence or absence of a feature (glottalization, aspiration) whose position in the word is nearly predictable and whose domain is the entire word. In short, even if we grant the hypothesis that restrictions on distribution are generalized or lost in the process of borrowing, it is not clear how it is to be applied to the problem of whether the Southern Quechua ejectives and aspirates are borrowed. Although the *formal* distribution of ejectives and aspirates is indeed more restricted in Southern Quechua than in Aymara, from a functional point of view, the Quechua distribution is more general. The question of whether the ejectives and aspirates are borrowed is not addressed by Campbell's proposal in a clear-cut way.

Finally, even if a Jaqi/Aru areal source for ejectives and aspirates is precluded by the general principle, are we to assume that they are genetic to the Quechua family and reflect a common Quechua-Jaqi/Aru inheritance? The answer, quite plainly, is that we cannot do so without the evidence of careful, systematic comparative reconstruction within each of the families. Even if the hypothesis that distributional restrictions are generalized or lost in the process of borrowing proved to be applicable, it could only take its place alongside the standard criteria of proof of a genetic relationship. It could never supplant them.

Genetic Relationships and Social Ecology

Three conclusions can now be drawn about the issue of whether Quechua and Jaqi/Aru are genetically related. (1) There is no substantive evidence that they are, once the Orr-Longacre reconstruction has been set aside for methodological reasons (Cerrón-Palomino 1982: 238). (2) There are substantive linguistic reasons for concluding that the similarities between Southern Quechua and Aymara are either typological, and thus not evidence for a genetic relationship, or the product of long-term, intensive contact. (3) The social ecology of language in southern Peru provided the appropriate conditions for the languages to converge structurally. These included stable interdigitated multilingualism and the propensity of the Inka elites to borrow words from neighboring languages and to introduce them into wider use in Southern Peruvian Quechua.

If debate about the genetic relationship between Quechua and Jaqi/Aru seems elusive to nonspecialists, it is perhaps due to the notion of "genetic relationship" itself. It cannot be demonstrated that two given languages are *not* related; rather, the notion of "common ancestry" rests entirely on positive evidence. On the other hand, it is perfectly sensible to say that two languages are not related within a specific period; within a limited time span, it is perfectly appropriate to require the proof positive of phonological correspondences and well-argued etymologies, as the only criterion for a genetic relationship (cf. Goddard 1975: 255). It is especially important to avoid unsubstantiated pronouncements in cases like this.

The Indo-Europeanist Paul Thieme argues that a proof of common ancestry between languages—or, as is the case here, between language families—requires first a detailed, accurate, and reasonably thorough command of the relevant data, and, second, in Thieme's (1964: 585) words, that it be "demonstrably evident that there is no other hypothesis that would serve the purpose better or as well." As we have already observed, the attempts to demonstrate that Quechua and Aymara are genetically related have not provided appropriate evidence. In fact, the way in which the problem itself has often been posed, assuming a direct correspondence between the Quechua language most influenced by Jaqi/Aru (Southern Peruvian Quechua) and the Jaqi/Aru language most influenced by Quechua (Aymara), actually precludes meeting the standards of evidence. The first of Thieme's requirements has not been met; that is to say, no genetic relationship has been demonstrated. Turning to the second requirement—that "no other hypothesis . . . would serve the purpose better or as well"—I have built up a case that the resemblances between the languages can be explained more parsimoniously as resulting from contact and massive borrowing than from common inheritance (cf. Torero 1970; Stark 1975; Cerrón-Palomino 1982; Hardman-de-Bautista 1985). As Cerrón-Palomino has put it, "the attempts to establish a genetic relationship between the [Quechua and Jaqi/Aru] linguistic families do not resist a serious confrontation with empirical data and appear to be vitiated from the beginning because of their unilateral selection of testimony languages within the families. . . . In view of the fact that the hypothesis of common origin has proven unproductive, convergence remains the more probable theory, at least until deeper synchronic and diachronic study of both language families permits proof to the contrary" (1982: 238, my translation).

The success with which this position can be developed depends on progress in dialectology and detailed reconstruction of the processes of language change in the two families. Moreover, ethnographic study of the linguistic, social, and cultural aspects of modern contact between Quechua and Aymara would shed light on the ecology of language contact in the past: on the processes of structural convergence between these languages in contact, on the motivation for change on the part of the speakers, and on the speakers' own evaluation of the situation. The key to understanding the way in which the languages have changed as formal systems is to view them within the changing social ecology of language.

Although the attempts to demonstrate a genetic relationship between Quechua and Aymara produced negative results (conclusively, as such matters go), the debate has been productive in that it brought into focus several important problems of language structure and language use. How did Quechua accommodate structurally to the Jaqi/Aru languages with which it was in contact? Though we are far from detailing the morphological, syntactic, and semantic dimensions of linguistic convergence, the details of phonological accommodation are increasingly clear, as we shall see in later chapters (chapter 8, on the ejectives and aspirates; chapter 7, on the sibilants). What were the social conditions of language contact in the southern Peruvian Andes? In order to answer this question, we need to coordinate linguistic and historical evidence. At the time of the conquest, the region was a mosaic of territorially interspersed languages, less a linguistic melting pot than a cauldron of differentiation. In the decades that followed, the linguistic heterogeneity of southern Peru was leveled out as native Andeans were fused into a culturally cohesive "oppressed nation," as we shall see in the following chapters.

3 Language and Colonialism

The most important feature of the social setting of Southern Peruvian Quechua since the European invasion in 1532 may be summed up by the slogan "Spanish is the language of the dominant sector, and Quechua the language of the subjugated sector" (Escobar, Matos, and Alberti 1975: 53). In terms of institutional structure, politics, economy, and culture, Southern Peruvian Quechua has been an "oppressed language," to use a phrase suggested by the Bolivian linguist Xavier Albó (1973, 1974: 223–225).[1] The repertoire of contexts in which it can be used is restricted; its two million speakers are stigmatized. Only individuals can overcome the stigma attached to their Quechua identity, and only then by abandoning the language and the cultural universe that accompanies it. The rhetoric of economic development, which is as pervasive in Peru as elsewhere in the Third World, actually encourages the stigmatization of Southern Peruvian Quechua language and culture by labeling their abandonment "integration into national society." In effect, this only projects a strategy for individual social mobility on the larger community of Quechua speakers.

For developmentalists, Quechua speakers will advance economically only when they cease to be Quechua. But what developmentalist language planners miss is that, even though cultural domination makes language abandonment a necessary condition for advancement in economic status, it is not a sufficient condition (cf. Varèse 1972: 765–766; Mayer 1982: 276ff.). In order to see this, we need only place Quechua-speaking people from the southern highlands alongside their impoverished Spanish-speaking counterparts from the mountains above Lima. That coastal peasants speak Spanish does not ease their economic, political, or social marginality. Moreover, since resolution of the language problem is almost always focused on the individual speaker, it covertly legitimizes the stigma associated with Quechua. In brief, Southern Peruvian Quechua is an oppressed language because, since the European invasion, policy decisions that vitally affect its social existence have been made, just as they are today, by institutions and individuals who are foreign to its speech community.

In this chapter, I trace the history of Southern Peruvian Quechua's status as an oppressed language from the mid-sixteenth century until the end of Spanish political rule in Peru. There are two sides to this story. First, Quechua came to displace other Native Andean languages in southern Peru, through a combination of conscious Spanish policy and the unforeseen consequences of other political decisions. The modern linguistic homogeneity of southern Peru was achieved under Spanish colonial rule. Second, the relationship between Spanish and Quechua came to reflect and reproduce the relationships of domination between their respective communities of speakers. This was also achieved under colonial rule by a combination of conscious policy and unforeseen consequences of other actions.

In the course of this discussion, I also hope to redress a curious historical myopia that has afflicted many students of Andean bilingualism. That myopia is rooted in the uncritical (and often unacknowledged) use of analytic models that have not been sufficiently honed to the concrete social reality of the region.

By a recent, conservative count, approximately 90 percent of the inhabitants of the south-central highlands have a Native Andean language as their mother tongue, despite the pervasive presence of the dominant linguistic, cultural, and economic systems in even the most remote localities for the last four centuries (Mannheim 1985: 483–488). In approaching this phenomenon, one analytic model, the "dual society" model, assumes that language policy consists of intervention in an otherwise nearly automatic shift of allegiance by individuals from one cultural group to another. According to this model, the mere existence of a large and geographically concentrated population of indigenous speakers indicates recent contact between the two groups; otherwise, a much lower percentage of indigenous language speakers would be expected.

Another model, the "internal colonialism" model, assumes that maintenance of an indigenous language over a long period is a matter of convenience for purposes of economic exploitation and political control. There is a large grain of truth in this observation. Many legal and political measures were designed to minimize Quechua access to viceregal and republican political, economic, and legal structures. However, internal colonialism models have not acknowledged that Quechua speakers have played an active role in maintaining their language and culture. Moreover, these models have been used, perversely, in a context in which the legitimacy of national domination is taken for granted.

Not surprisingly, then, under this analysis the appropriate political response to the problem of language domination is the end of the dominated nationality as such, not the end of the structures of domination (cf. Mosonyi 1982).

The internal colonialism model assumes that maintenance of Quechua and other Native Andean languages served the interests of the dominant groups in colonial and modern Peru. But if it is in the interests of the dominant groups to maintain ethnic boundaries by maintaining language difference, how can we explain the efforts made by Hispanic and Peruvian authorities over four centuries to erase them? Proponents of the internal colonialism model ignore these efforts, just as proponents of the dual society model ignore four centuries of contact. Thus, users of both models have reinvented the social history of Southern Peruvian Quechua and its speakers to conform to their presuppositions.[2]

These attitudes toward history become particularly striking when we observe the strong continuity between colonial and present-day language policy and the continuing relevance of the colonial language debate to contemporary planning. The policy options, arguments used to justify them, and methodology of implementation have in their essentials persisted for over four centuries (see Heath and LaPrade 1982: 143, for a similar assessment). Only the words change: where the unity of the Spanish empire was once at stake, today it is the unity of the Peruvian nation-state. Where it once was suggested that Quechua lacked the vocabulary to express European religious ideas, today it is said that it lacks the vocabulary of advanced technology. And where the Jesuits promoted religious and cultural indoctrination in Quechua to ease ideological access to the conquered, now liberal educators promote bilingual education programs designed to ease the transition of Quechua speakers into a Spanish-speaking world (Paulston 1973: 98–99; López 1987: 358 and note 8; Solís 1987: 650–651). The teaching *cartillas* have replaced the catechism with distillations of European children's stories. In short, where once the continued existence of Southern Peruvian Quechua culture was debated in the rhetoric of "language and religion," now it is debated in the rhetoric of "language and development." But the discontinuities in the jargon used to talk about the politics of language obscure a more fundamental continuity in language policy and politics. Not only does every generation reinvent the wheel, but it is the very same wheel.

Language, Religion, and Empire

"Language was always the companion of empire" wrote Nebrija in the preface to the first Castilian grammar (1492: f.1r), published in the same year that Columbus arrived in the New World.[3] The statement is apt for several periods of Southern Peruvian Quechua. First, prior to the European invasion, Quechua served as the administrative language of Tawantinsuyu, the Inka state, and was the medium of communication among the diverse peoples who were incorporated into the state.[4] (As we saw in chapter 2, Quechua did not achieve linguistic hegemony during Tawantinsuyu's brief existence, even in the immediate vicinity of the Inka capital, Cuzco.) After the European invasion, the Spaniards recognized Quechua's potential as a *lengua general* (lingua franca) for administrative purposes and especially for proselytization, and consciously promoted it as a vehicle of linguistic homogenization (Toledo 1572: 407, 1573: 50, 1575a: 359; Blas Valera, cited by Garcilaso 1609: VII, iii, 249; Romero 1964: x; Torero 1974: 181–198). Under these conditions, the former Inka lingua franca continued its expansion even after the conquest.

Finally, Nebrija's slogan sums up the overriding circumstance under which Southern Peruvian Quechua was to develop: as the language of a vanquished people, its development was restricted according to a language policy dictated to fit the political, economic, and ideological needs of the Spanish empire and its local heir, the Peruvian republic. Importantly, such policy was implemented through the institutional apparatus of the Spanish empire inherited by Spanish-speaking Criollo elites after independence.[5]

Language policy in the Spanish empire was molded by competing interest groups, each of which staked its claim before the Council of the Indies (Heath 1976: 50; Rivarola 1985: 26–27).[6] As a result, the council frequently shifted back and forth between radically different approaches, depending upon which pressure group was able to gain its attention. The extent to which the council's policies were actually implemented was similarly determined by competing interests, this time at a local level.

The ideological mission of the Iberian expansion in the New World was religious conversion. Even before the Inka defeat at Cajamarca (1532), the laws of Burgos charged *encomenderos* (grantees of the population of Indian settlements as laborers and spiritual wards) with instruction in Catholicism and Castilian (Heath 1976: 67). The counter-reformist Council of Trent (1545–1563) promoted the use of vernacular languages in religious instruction, allowing tighter integration between secular and religious language policy. During the first years, the council approved provisions on popular education and ordered publication of catechisms in vernacular languages (*vulgarem linguam*) whose fidelity to Latin catechism was overseen by local bishops (Condero 1979: 10). But at the same time that the new emphasis on the vernacular boosted the status of Castilian by permitting a unified language policy in the religious and political spheres, it served as a charter for proselytization in the principal indigenous languages. Within a few years of the Trentian order, the missionary priests who were charged with this task were informally translating catechism and improvising teaching *cartillas* in the major vernacular languages of Peru. Many, however, worked through mestizo translators.

The ecclesiastical authorities could not guarantee that the translations were theologically sound and reacted to improvised translations with characteristic severity (Toledo 1571, 1572: 407, 1579a: 187, 1582: 125; *Recopilación de leyes* 1681: I, xv, 5, reprint 1: 132;[7] Garcilaso 1616: I, xxiii, 50).[8] For example, Archbishop Loayza outlawed vernacular teaching *cartillas*. Religious and secular authorities were afraid not only that Christian doctrine would be distorted, but that they would lose political control over the growing population of bilingual mestizos.[9] Bilingual interpreters used their positions in many aspects of native life, from the confessional to the courtroom, to their own advantage. Not only did they abuse their monolingual Quechua countrymen, but they were seen as a threat to the emerging colonial order (Archbishop of Cuzco Fernando de Vera, letters to the king of 24-iii-1635 and 1-iii-1638, in Santisteban 1963: 28). The subsequent measures taken against bilingual mestizo interpreters were not limited to their positions as religious translators: mestizos who aspired to the clergy faced restrictions, and mestizos were barred altogether from becoming notaries.[10]

At the same time, the colonial government encouraged native hereditary elites to learn Spanish (*Recopilación de leyes* 1681: V, viii, 40, reprint 2: 153). The religious orders opened schools known as *colegios de caciques* for the children of hereditary headmen (Galdo 1970; Cardenas 1977; Wood 1986: 79–84). But by the seventeenth century, the *colegios de caciques* aroused the same anxieties as did earlier religious and secular interpreters. According to their detractors, the *colegios de caciques* educated their charges too well, for any native lord who could speak Spanish was a potential threat to the regime (Archbishop de Vera, in Santisteban 1963: 28; Jesuit Provincial Antonio Vázquez, letter of 22-iii-1637, reprinted in Eguiguren 1940: 876).

Influenced by the Council of Trent, the First Provincial Council of Lima (1551–1552) took steps to promote use of Native Andean languages in religious contexts. It ordered priests to learn the vernacular and to use it in their work in indigenous parishes (*doctrinas*) (Condero 1979: 10). It also reversed Archbishop Loayza's ban on vernacular teaching *cartillas* (Vargas 1942: 13f.; Castillo 1966: 48). A course of study in Quechua, founded a year earlier in the Cathedral of Lima, was formally inaugurated (Castro 1963). The first attempts to standardize a Quechua catechism are reported for the same period. The Second Council of Lima (1567–1568) went still further in legitimizing Quechua as a language of religious discourse, ordering teaching activity in the vernacular and use of the standard catechism, and prohibiting use of interpreters (*sayapayaq*) (Vargas 1942: 110, 410, 1951–1954; Castillo 1966: 49). Yet the Jesuit superior, José de Acosta (1577a: IV, iii, 507–508), complained about the general lack of knowledge of the vernacular by priests of indigenous parishes and lamented the still too common situation of priest and parishioners who could not understand each other, even with the Quechua catechism.

By the time of the Third Council (1581–1583), numerous Quechua *cartillas* and catechisms were in use (Tercer Concilio Limense 1584: prologue; Castillo 1966: 50). The Third Council charged a committee headed by Acosta with the task of writing a single, unified catechism, a confessional, and a sermonal (Acosta 1583; Tercer Concilio Limense 1583, 1584, 1585; Anonymous 1600: II, 17; Vargas 1951–1954: vol. 1, acción II, cap. 3; Rivet and Créqui-Montfort 1951–1956: I, 4–16; Bartra 1967; see chapter 6 for a description). The council also took the extraordinary step of contracting a printer, Antonio Ricardo, to come to Lima from Mexico and to set up the first printing press in the Peruvian colony in order to supervise the printing of the catechism and ensure its speedy publication (Vargas 1942: 271f.; Condero 1979: 17–25).

The Third Council was especially concerned about the ways in which critical points of faith could be lost in translation. The most salient problems of translation were collected in the "Annotations" of the *Doctrina christiana.* For instance, the council recommended using the verb *ruray* instead of *kamay* to refer to the creation of the universe. The verb *kamay* would have suggested a god who is the soul (or hidden principle) of the world, rather than its creator (Tercer Concilio Limense, 1584: f. 77v). The annotations also discussed grammatical problems of translation, such as the distinction between "inclusive" and "exclusive" plural in the first person (Mannheim 1982). The annotations observe that throughout the region, " . . . inclusion and exclusion are used in the first person plural in both pronouns and verbs. Inclusion is when we include the person or persons with whom we speak in the matter, as (for example) if we were speaking to pagans we might say, 'We people are created for heaven' as *ñocanchic runacuna hanacpachapac camascam cãchic.* Exclusion is when we exclude the person or persons with whom we speak from the matter, as (for example) if we were speaking to pagans we might say, 'We Christians worship one god' as *ñocaycu christianocuna huc çapay Diosllactam muchaycu.*"[11]

Standardization of religious materials in Quechua was also an incipient form of standardization of the language, since the same materials would be used among Quechua speakers throughout the viceroyalty (see Cerrón-Palomino 1987c: 86–88). As we have already seen, it was policy by the late sixteenth century to encourage linguistic homogeneity among Native Peruvians by propagating the Inka lingua franca at the expense of other Native Andean languages, Quechua as well as non-Quechua. The Third Council followed the same strategy, deciding to use the Quechua of Cuzco itself, but in a simplified form, hoping that simplification would make the work accessible to Quechua speakers from outside Cuzco, "all those who are called Chinchaysuyos" (Tercer Concilio Limense 1584: f. 74r).[12] It did so in part by omitting glottalization and aspiration from the orthography and reproved the Cuzqueños who "use such exquisite and obscure words and ways of speaking that they cross the borders of the language" (Tercer Concilio Limense 1584: f.74r).[13]

The publication of the Third Council's works stimulated others to prepare grammars, collections of sermons, and related religious materials in Quechua. In addition, several courses in Quechua were established in Lima. Besides the aforementioned course in the Cathedral of Lima, the Jesuit Colegio de San Pablo began a course in 1569 under the supervision of Blas Valera (*Recopilación de leyes* 1681 [1580]: I, xii, 51, reprint 1: 205; Martin 1968: 49). A third chair of Quechua was founded at the University of San Marcos by Viceroy Toledo in 1579 in recognition of the importance of vernacular language skills to religious conversion and indoctrination. The university chair was charged with certifying the linguistic skills of all priests in the indigenous parishes, and no additional priests were to be assigned without examination by the chair (Toledo 1579a: 185, 1579b: 593ff., 1582: 126). The chair was given broad powers in certification of priests; a requirement that priests learn the vernacular was given the force of civil law by several royal decrees;[14] and an examination in Quechua became part of the process of certification of priests (*Recopilación de leyes* 1681 [1580]: I, xv, 6, reprint 1: 132–133; royal decree, 19-ix-1580, in Eguiguren 1951: vol. 2, 602–605; Gibbs 1979: 91, 96). Even so, complaints continued throughout the colonial period that priests were unable to communicate with their parishioners (Viceroy Enríquez, letter of 12-ii-1583, in Eguiguren 1951: vol. 2, 618; Concolorcorvo 1773: 368f.; Colin 1966: 143). The requirement that rural priests be certified in the Native Andean languages was honored most in the breach. Whether Native Andean languages were actually used in a parish was determined by local conditions and the inclinations of individual priests.

Antivernacular Reaction

The liberal positions taken at Trent and increasingly adopted during the sixteenth century by the viceregal government and church were opposed from many quarters, secular and religious alike. In order to understand the vehemence with which many of the colonists opposed liberal policies toward Quechua, we need to consider how they conceived of the relationships among language, culture, and society. These were threefold: that speaking the same language forges bonds among the speakers; that a language can be imposed on a defeated population by right of conquest; and that language preserves cultural identity. Not only did the Spanish empire have a right to impose its language on possessions in the New World, but it had the obligation to do so, at the risk of allowing subjects to maintain distinct cultural and political identities—that is, at the risk of losing them. This cluster of ideas is as much a source of passion in modern Peru as it was in the early viceroyalty.

This view of language has its roots on the Spanish peninsula. The Spaniards colonized the New World fresh from their consolidation as a nation-state. With the defeat of Granada in 1492, the Kingdom of Castile conquered the last remnants of Moslem rule on the Spanish peninsula. The Castilians conceived of their consolidation of power as a divinely appointed mission to spread Christianity and required their non-Christian populations to convert or face expulsion. Such nonreligious practices as language, style of dress, and table manners were understood to be external signs of religious identity and religious deviance. Although the church prohibited specifically religious practices—such as observing Ramadan, Friday prayer, circumcision, and Islamic prayer—other customary practices were also banned, such as songs and dances and Arabic personal names. The state supplemented these restrictions by banning Arabic language and literature, veiling, public baths, Moorish clothing, and couscous (Kamen 1985; Root 1988: 125–126). All of these—private bodily practices as much as public—were carefully policed by local denunciations to the inquisition and the state. What is especially salient is that language, religion, and other cultural practices were identified with each other, and all three with the newly emergent Spanish state.

The rhetoric of conquest developed in Europe was extended to the new American colonies. The Spaniards justified their conquest of the New World as a Christianizing mission similar to the Christian conquest of Spain and pursued similar cultural policies. For instance, the seventeenth-century jurist Solorzano Pereira (1647: II, xxxvi, 36, 1930 edition 1: 402) argued that the indigenous languages of the New World could be treated in the same way as Arabic was on the peninsula and suppressed by decree.[15] Similarly, the Spaniards prohibited newly converted Indians from eating seated on the ground, a practice that had been identified with Moslems on the Spanish peninsula.

The politics of cultural conformism was expressed in other ways as well. The colonists brought the idea that speakers of the same language were drawn together by natural bonds. Blas Valera's expression of the notion that "similarity and conformity of words almost always leads to reconciliation and brings true union and friendship to people" (quoted by Garcilaso 1609: VII, iii, 248; cf. Zúñiga 1579: 95) was cited approvingly by Solorzano (1647: II, xxxvi, especially paragraph 30),[16] as part of an argument that the imposition of Castilian in the New World was justified by natural law.[17] Likewise, in the late eighteenth century, Concolorcorvo (1773: 369) argued that linguistic differences were at the root of the hatred that Native Andeans felt for Spanish speakers.

Opponents of liberal language policies also observed that language played an important role in maintaining Native Andean cultural integrity. Language was the source and pillar of cultural memory in a political context that called for forgetting. This contributed to the vehemence of ecclesiastical opposition to church use of the vernacular, opposition that was spearheaded by the Franciscans. The sixteenth-century priest Antonio de Zúñiga epitomizes clerical opposition to the use of Quechua by churchmen. In a letter to King Philip II, Fray Antonio complained that the Native Andean languages helped to maintain pagan religious practices. They did so, he argued, by codifying native religious concepts and by not possessing vocabulary appropriate to Christian ideas. Wrote Zúñiga (1579: 92), "among them there is no language sufficient to explain the mysteries of our holy Catholic faith, because all lack the vocabulary."[18] Zúñiga listed language third among impediments to religious conversion, after coca (whose importance to native religious life he acknowledged) and witchcraft (1579: 90ff.). The complaints were legion: Native American languages were obscure; they had no terms for abstract concepts like time, being, or virtue; there were no terms for important religious concepts such as God, faith, angel, virginity, or matrimony; and there was no way to express the concept of Holy Spirit (Acosta 1577a: IV, ix, 518, 1590: V, iii, 142; Barnadas 1973: 445–446; Pagden 1982: 181–182).[19] Conversely, for Garcilaso de la Vega (1616: I, xxiii, 49) it was not the lack of Christian vocabulary, but rather the presence of pagan vocabulary that was at fault. Garcilaso argued that elimination of native religious vocabulary would wipe out the memory of pagan cultural practices.

Nor were the complaints limited to vocabulary. José de Acosta (1577a: IV, ix, 518) conceded that Native Andean languages were generally weak on philosophy and theology. It was impossible to explain the paradox of the Trinity when there was no way to talk about paradox. And there was no way to discuss belief with people who are not accustomed to talking about language and cannot even understand what "belief" is (Pagden 1982: 157, 180). Although the churchmen invented a Quechua neologism for the concept, the discourse contexts and cultural resonances were so different that it is impossible to imagine any overlap between the two (see chapter 6).

Even the relatively liberal Third Council of Lima asked in a sermon, "How can we, as Runa, talk to God?" (1585: sermon xxviii, 405). Zúñiga (1579: 94) recommended that the king give indigenous speakers a year or two to learn the Spanish language under sanction of rigorous punishment, "for it is for such a holy end as putting in them the Catholic faith of our lord Jesus Christ."[20] The Council of the Indies (Consejo 1596) submitted a proposal similar to Zúñiga's for outlawing Native American languages, but it was rejected by King Philip II.

The Spaniards perceived a closer relationship between linguistic and cultural integrity than even their emphasis on religious vocabulary would indicate. For the Spaniards, religious conversion was not restricted to doctrinal and liturgical matters, but was culturally comprehensive, including economic and social practices (Konetzke 1965: 201; Duviols 1971: 237; Baciero 1986: 139–148; Borges 1986; Wood 1986). Evangelization included teaching "good manners and civilized life," and "to have a good life and good customs and to hate and forget their vices, rites, and pagan customs" (Toledo 1579b: 593).[21] Thus, the First Council of Lima (1551) prohibited such idolatrous practices as sleeping on the ground, not eating from a table, and chewing coca. Furthermore, the council stipulated concentration of settlements and observance of religious festivals in part to stimulate economic exchange and commerce (Vargas 1942: 110).

By the mid-seventeenth century, Philip III had concluded that the relatively liberal language policies pursued by his predecessor had failed and that Hispanization was fundamental to successful Spanish control of the Andes (*Recopilación de leyes* 1681: I, xiii, 5, reprint 1: 96; Heath 1976: 70). A hard-line policy against indigenous languages, promulgated in a royal decree in 1634 (Royal *cédula* of 2-iii-1634, cited by Santisteban 1963), was wholeheartedly endorsed by the bishop of Cuzco, Fernando de Vera (1635), who compared imposition of Castilian by the Spanish to Inka, Greek, and Latin linguistic imperialism. Yet Vera's successor, Manuel de Mollinedo y Angulo (1699), was to complain that, although he was complying with a royal order decreeing the teaching of Castilian, the students were "pigs in pronouncing it and giving the right meaning to words,"[22] so he was forced to continue religious use of Quechua. Over the next century, the Spanish authorities repeatedly issued decrees promoting Castilianization, including a late-seventeenth-century decree mandating education until age ten and forbidding it to anyone older.[23]

Although these decrees were enforced unevenly (Heath 1976: 71f.), the change in royal policy brought about a decline in official religious literature in indigenous languages. From the middle of the seventeenth century on, publication of original linguistic work in the aboriginal languages virtually halted. The need for religious works in the native languages was met by reprinting the *Artes* and catechisms of the late sixteenth and early seventeenth centuries. This coincides with a general decline of interest in the culture and history of the conquered on the part of the colonial bureaucracy.

The Quechua Renaissance

At the same time that religious and secular officials lost interest in developing a literature in Quechua, Quechua language and literature were cultivated in a self-consciously nationalistic way by the provincial elites of Cuzco. The appropriation of Quechua as a literary vehicle by the provincial landed class reveals the ambivalence of language as a national symbol.

By the late seventeenth century, a Criollo (native-born, Spanish-speaking) landed class had developed in Cuzco. Although the landowners held Spanish titles and had accumulated their wealth through colonial commerce, systematic encroachment on indigenous land, and exploitation of Quechua labor, the landowners considered themselves thoroughly Andean and attempted to establish their political legitimacy by laying claim to the Inka past (Kubler 1946: 350; Colin 1966: 138ff.). The eighteenth-century marquises of Valle Umbroso, for instance, disputed the authority of colonial administrators (in one case to the point of rising against the *corregidor* or provincial authority), claimed to be descendants of the Inkas, were addressed with the Quechua title *apu* 'lord', wore "Inka" clothing, and spoke Quechua (Colin 1966: 143ff.; Denegri 1980: xlix; Tamayo 1980: 88–93; Lavallé 1987: 143–146). When wealthy Criollos identified themselves with the Inka past, they did so to legitimize their possession of estates and wealth; to claim political autonomy from the Spanish administrative apparatus; and to deny any connection between coeval Quechua peasants and the achievements of the Inkas. To a great extent, the modern images of the ancient American empires are a product of the eighteenth-century imagination (Pagden 1987a, 1990).

Functionalist reason tells us, to be sure, that the use and promotion of "indigenous" cultural forms and language by those who were among the worst exploiters of Native Andean labor permitted them to maintain tighter control of the terms of articulation between Native Andean agriculturalists, herders, and weavers and the larger colonial economy. At the same time, such use and promotion of Quechua language and arts served to legitimize despotic political and economic control in the hinterland. Certainly these were factors in the emergence of *indigenismo* among rural Andean landlords during the first half of the present century (cf. Favre 1967: 130; for a comparable Mesoamerican example, see Diebold 1961: 501). But at the same time the very existence of the Criollo landed class was threatened by the bureaucratically top-heavy, metropolis-centered politics of the time. The appropriation of the native symbolism of power, including the language, supplied legal and political legitimacy to the landed Criollo class, at least in the broader context of the viceroyalty. In that light, when Criollo landowners acted as patrons of the arts in imitation of peninsular forms of prestige, it was to sponsor Andean visual art and literature.

The visual art of the late seventeenth and early eighteenth centuries was a stylistic anachronism, adapting Rococo forms to Andean contexts well beyond the decline of Rococo in Europe (Macera 1975: 68). Similarly, the formal literature of this period derived from the Baroque *culteranismo* movement—a literary movement given to flowery excess—but was changed to meet local circumstances, especially to fit the pretensions of local elites. The European *culteranistas* idealized the European classical civilizations and used them as cultural models; the Andean *culteranistas* substituted the Inkas. A major local author of the period, Juan Espinoza Medrano (1632– 1688), wrote a defense of the *culteranista* Luis de Góngora well after Góngora had fallen out of favor in peninsular literary circles (Espinoza 1662; Jammes 1966).[24] Espinoza, rector of the Cathedral of Cuzco, himself wrote sermons and verse in Quechua, Spanish, and Latin, including several *autos sacramentales*, religious versified dramas, in prosodically measured verse in which the text, save for stage directions, was written entirely in Quechua (Cosio 1941; Yepez 1946: 26–27; Rivet and Créqui-Montfort 1951–1956: I, 128–129). Even though he composed the dramas in Quechua, Espinoza Medrano followed the versification principles of Golden Age Spain.

A number of such versified dramas dating from the late seventeenth century to the late eighteenth circulated in manuscript among Cuzco elites. This period, often referred to as the "literary dark age" of Quechua (Rowe 1950: 145), turns out rather to have been a golden age. The well-known anonymous works *Usca Paucar* and *Ollanta* (in at least two manuscript traditions) and Gabriel Centeno's *El pobre más rico* can be assigned to this period on the basis of phonological innovations in the manuscripts of these works.[25] The format of Espinoza Medrano's *autos sacramentales*, including an untranslated Quechua text written according to Spanish literary norms and occasional Spanish stage directions, appears in the later versified dramas, as much in the secular *Ollanta* as in the religious *El pobre más rico.*

The idealization of the Inkas in the visual and literary art of the seventeenth and eighteenth centuries was an important part of the resurgence (Rowe 1954). The new landed elites appropriated the memory of the Inkas as a source of legitimacy, at the same time recreating the Inkas in their own likeness. They established continuity with the Inkas, but displaced them into the past, *their* past, not the past of Runa agriculturalists and laborers. Nonetheless, the newly invented "memory" of the Inkas played a critical role in the social upheavals of the eighteenth century, as it galvanized local elites to resist the authority of the Spanish viceroyalty.

The Quechua literary renaissance took shape against a background of social convulsion. From 1730 until 1780, there were no fewer than thirty-seven local uprisings in the modern-day Southern Peruvian Quechua–speaking departments (Colin 1966: 171–183; O'Phelan 1976, 1985), culminating in the massive rebellion of 1780. The British opening of Buenos Aires to cheap English cloth had led to the collapse of primitive cloth factories (*obrajes*) in nuclear Cuzco (the Vilcanota valley south of the city, up to the *provincias altas*), which could not successfully compete for markets with European cloth (Moscoso 1965). The ensuing economic collapse set large numbers of landless laborers adrift and added fuel to the rebellion, the last large-scale colonial revolt in Southern Peru to have a decidedly Quechua nationalist tone. The revolt was coordinated through a network of local-level indigenous lords led by Tomasa Titu Condemayta and Micaela Bastides and her husband José Gabriel Thupa Amaru, who was titular head of the movement. His name 'resplendent *amaru*' was emblematic of the occasion: the *amaru* is a mythic reptile associated with *pacha kuti* 'the world returning to itself', the nexus between the death and rebirth of world order. Although the story is probably apocryphal, Antonio Valdéz, the priest of Tinta, is said to have staged the Quechua drama *Ollanta* before the leaders of the rebellion. Valdéz is in fact closely associated with two of the codices of *Ollanta*, the Justiniani and Sahuaraura, though I have not been able to trace either the source or the veracity of the account; traditional histories of the uprising, such as Lewin (1943), usually refer to secondary sources. The two most likely sources are the *Museo Erudito* account of the existence of *Ollanta* (revealed by Valdéz's nephew Narciso Cuentas: Palacios 1837), and Clements Markham's descriptions of his discovery of the Justiniani manuscript in which he attests to Pablo

Justiniani having seen the play performed in Tinta (Markham 1856: 172) and that it had been performed before Thupa Amaru (Markham 1912: 90). Although Valdéz was not among the priests tried for supporting the uprising (he died in 1816 of natural causes), he did sympathize with the rebel cause, and acted as a courier between the bishop of Cuzco and Thupa Amaru's cousin, Diego Cristóbal Thupa Amaru (Villanueva 1983: 301–323, esp. 315).[26]

What is beyond dispute is that the colonial government associated the cultivation of Quechua drama and other literature with political nationalism and the revolutionary movement. After the rebellion failed in 1781, Quechua theater and other literary expressions were explicitly banned (Areche 1781; Rowe 1954: 30–31; Hopkins 1982: 7–9).

Eradication and Resistance

The defeat of the rebellion brought a firmer resolve on the part of the Bourbon colonial administration to eliminate Quechua language and culture. The sentence of death against Thupa Amaru carried the instruction that "in order that these Indians remove the hatred of Spaniards which they had conceived . . . they are to dress in our Spanish clothing and speak the Castilian language. The use of schools will be introduced with more vigor than up to now under the most rigorous penalties for those who do not attend" (Areche 1781: 772).[27] *Visitador* Areche gave Quechua speakers all of four years in which to learn Spanish and abolished the chair of Quechua at the University of San Marcos. Areche prohibited the literary artifacts that American-born elites used to construct a vision of the Inka past, including Garcilaso's *Comentarios reales* and plays such as *Ollanta.* The genealogical proofs of royal descent that were used to claim indigenous lordships were restricted. Ultimately the hereditary lordships (*cacicazgos*) were suppressed altogether (Areche 1781: 773; Lewin 1943: 382; Valcárcel 1947: 191; Rowe 1954: 39).

The bishop of Cuzco, Juan Manuel Moscoso (1781), expressed the Spanish rage eloquently:

> If we consider that the language stayed with the Indians without any change—in some places so integrally that not a word has been lost from the dialect that those rural people use—it is yet another matter worthy of shame for the Spanish nation. I understand well that the presses are wearing out from printing ordinances and laws to take the Indians' language away from them, and that in keeping with the royal edicts about this matter, earnest prelates order it with grave asperity during inspections of their diocese, prescribing that the young be taught Spanish. But what good does this do, when the Indians continue to

speak their own languages, and so tenaciously, that they speak three languages as completely different as Quechua, Aymara, and Puquina? We have had more than 200 years of conquest and even though conquerors bring their language to the conquered, our Spaniards haven't thought about anything else than letting them hang onto their language, and have even accommodated to it, since we see that they [the Spaniards] use it more often than their own language [Spanish]. The inconveniences that this causes are obvious to the blindest person, and God, the king, and public interest suffer greatly from this reprehensible practice.[28]

One of the immediate goals of the newly organized Bourbon administrative apparatus, the intendant system, was "the extirpation of the Indian language" (Alvarez y Jiménez 1792: 57),[29] a slogan that recalls the late-sixteenth- and early-seventeenth-century campaigns against indigenous religious and cultural practices. The intendant of Arequipa, Alvarez y Jiménez (1792: 75), claimed to have established schools in several provinces (*partidos*) but went on to lament that "total elimination [of indigenous languages] isn't easy."[30] But the Bourbon policy of forced Castilianization by means of compulsory education was ultimately frustrated by the ever-present play of conflicting interests. Spanish and Criollo elites understood well that their knowledge of how the system worked was an important mechanism of social control. It was in their interest to use the language barrier to maintain an ethnically reinforced social hierarchy. Seeing education and Castilianization as a threat to that hierarchy, they actively undermined the state educational policy (Macera 1967: 218f.). Likewise, the rural priest could not be counted on to use his parish to sponsor a school because that would jeopardize his own use of the position to commercial ends, which was facilitated by his position of mediation between community and state (Hopkins 1983: 111–142). The state could not be called upon to bear the financial burden of a rural educational system without disturbing the profit from colonial taxation. The state was, moreover, already in a position of borrowing from the taxes on communities. The state therefore proposed to have each community set aside lands that were to be worked to support a local school (Macera 1967: 223). The 1782 royal order to establish schools filtered through a state and religious bureaucracy that for a variety of reasons and because of a variety of interests was unwilling to carry it out (Konetzke 1965: 203). As late as 1820, the colonial government sent orders to establish a school in each parish.[31]

For the new Bourbon administration, the language barrier was an impediment to national unification. But for local landowners and officials in an empire founded on bureaucratic paperwork (a scribe, after all, accompanied the *conquistadores*), the language barrier meant that they were playing a poker game in which they not only set the rules, but held all the cards. Beside the ravages of disease, forced resettlement, forced labor, and burdensome taxation that the indigenous population had to endure, the very means of subsistence, the land base, was subject to disintegration through legal means in a language they could not even understand, not to mention a byzantine legal system. The literature on the growth of Spanish and Criollo landed property, haciendas, is filled with cases of land sales in which announcements of sales were made in Spanish so that indigenous people could not protest in time to prevent the sale of land out from under them.[32] Complaints were also kept to a minimum by announcing the visit of political, judicial, and religious authorities in Spanish only (cf. Ramírez 1986: 89). Moreover, at such times as native communities did enter the judicial arena, they were dependent on the honesty, good faith, and capability of legal interpreters.[33]

One way in which Runa communities could defend themselves was to have a bilingual *cacique*, a community head. Matienzo's (1567: 21) plan for the reorganization of colonial society strongly urged that *caciques* learn Spanish, and the Jesuits established schools specifically for that purpose (Galdo 1970; Cardenas 1977). Guaman Poma (1615: 738) considered literacy in Spanish an essential attribute of the ideal *cacique*, the better to defend his subjects in court. He took the task quite personally and dedicated his life to writing his thousand-plus-page protest against colonial abuses, in which he proposed suggestions for their remedy to the king (Guaman Poma 1615). The ability of a Spanish-speaking *cacique* to seek legal redress on behalf of his subjects was explicitly condemned in complaints against the Colegios de Caciques. Both laity and clergy criticized the Jesuits for teaching the children of *caciques* "too well," so that their alumni were able to turn around and make formal complaints about abuses by clergy and layperson alike (above and Duviols 1971: 328).[34] To this day, the practice continues of making sure that some members of a Quechua community learn Spanish in order to speak for the community in legal situations.

Language and Domination

As Spanish dominion in the Andes came to a close, the die had already been cast—in all its detail—for the political setting of the language conflict. Although until recently the Spanish-speaking population of Peru has been a numerical minority, it has had effective and continuous control of political and legal institutions since the mid-sixteenth century. This is the unquestioned foundation of the political sociology of language in the Andes and has been since the solidification of the Spanish and Criollo institutional structure; it is at the root of the complexity of the language issue, because, at one and the same time, the language barrier is both a hindrance to and a tool for ideological and social control of the large Quechua-speaking population. For Quechua speakers themselves, learning Spanish is also a double-edged sword: rudimentary knowledge of Spanish is necessary for physical and cultural survival, but in the long run, it is a threat to Quechua culture (Cerrón-Palomino 1983: 115).

This unquestioned foundation also establishes limits to the range of available options in the Peruvian language debate. Since the late sixteenth century, two clear positions have developed with respect to use of Native Andean languages. The two positions have been remarkably consistent for more than four centuries: the modern versions can be easily inferred from the colonial arguments by substituting the words *development* and *nation* for *religion* and *empire.*

One position, which we might wish to refer to as "liberal" or "soft assimilationism," was promoted by the Jesuits and was in ascendancy during the late sixteenth and early seventeenth centuries, which was also a period in which Quechua was used as a literary language. The other, which we might call "Hispanist" or "hard assimilationism," was proposed on the model of peninsular linguistic unification and persisted throughout the colonial period as an ultimate goal. It achieved dominance under the Bourbons but was implemented only piecemeal during the period in which Spain lost its grip on America. It was the latter position that the republic inherited: postindependent Lima was intellectually modernist, and the literary revival of Quechua taking place in Cuzco was ultimately lost in the provincial backwater of a centralist state. The new Peruvian republic was to become a Spanish-speaking country.

With a few remarkable exceptions, including the brief officialization of Quechua under the nationalist Velasco government (Gobierno Revolucionario 1975), the "Hispanist" position has dominated national language policy and education since independence from Spain (1821). Only in 1979 did adults who were not literate in Spanish receive the right to vote. Despite the dominance of the "Hispanist" position, the "soft assimilationist" position has been consistently promoted by educators and social scientists, Peruvian and foreign. On several different occasions, the "soft assimilationist" position became the law of the land, but it never received the massive support necessary to implement it (compare Rojas 1983; López 1987: 356).

From the European invasion until today, the politics of language has been a politics of social subordination. Overtly, colonial language policy was schizophrenic in its shifts between maintaining the Native Andean languages as a step toward assimilation and suppressing them altogether. Covertly, the entire political spectrum was suffused with social domination; any political choice tended to reinforce the relationship summed up by the slogan "Spanish is the language of the dominant sector, and Quechua the language of the subjugated sector." It is significant that the actors in the language debate represented the dominant sector; the debate was conducted in Spanish. The absence of Native Andean voices—except through stubborn refusal to bend to one or another policy—casts a utopian pall over the entire debate.

There is only the hint of these voices in colonial sources. Modern Andean people are notoriously ethnocentric about linguistic differences, be they differences of dialect or of language; they are proud of their own way of speaking. The same attitude was reported throughout the colonial period. For instance, Blas Valera observed that Qollas (Aymara speakers) and Puquinas were perfectly happy with their own languages and in fact looked down on the Inka lingua franca (Garcilaso 1609: VII, iii, 248). Valera himself took a Cuzco-centric view of the matter: " . . . the Puquina, Collas, Urus, Yuncas, and other nations of Indians are crude and stupid and even speak their own languages badly because of their stupidity. When they get to learn the language of Cuzco, it appears that they throw off the crudeness and stupidity that they had and aspire to political and courtly things, and the smarter ones try to raise themselves to even higher things" (Garcilaso 1609: VII, iii, 251).[35]

Writing in the late eighteenth century, Concolorcorvo pointed out the same linguistic ethnocentrism in Native Andean attitudes toward Spanish speakers: "They try to hide from any Spaniard or mestizo who doesn't speak to them in their own language, and they consider them [Spanish speakers] as we consider them [Quechua speakers], barbarians" (1773: 368).[36] Understandably, Runa had little interest in learning Castilian (cf. Toledo 1582: 135; Garcilaso 1616: I, xxiii, 49). Even today I have heard Quechua speakers refer to Spanish as *alqo simi* 'dog speech' on analogy with their expression for their own language, *Runa simi* 'human speech'.

When Native Andeans express their views of linguistic domination directly, as they do when they call Spanish dog speech, or through the myths discussed in the next chapter, they are amazingly perceptive about how it works; yet they express themselves through bitter irony—irony that takes their subjugation for granted. The courses of action posed in the language debate are posed from the perspective of power, posed for a monolingual, not a bilingual Peru.

Beyond that, the politics of social subordination reshaped the linguistic landscape: before the European invasion, the Andes were a linguistic mosaic of interspersed languages and peoples. The heterogeneity encountered by the first European soldiers, travelers, and settlers has been replaced by a situation in which language difference maps directly onto political domination.

4 Linguistic Hegemony and the Two Dimensions of Language Variation

Linguistic Hegemony

The changes in the social ecology of language from the European invasion onward were double. First, Spanish was established as the language of the dominant social sectors. Second, the native *lenguas generales* were promoted by the colonial government and clergy at the expense of local languages. The linguistic diversity encountered by the first Europeans was homogenized through a combination of population losses, reorganization of Native American settlement patterns, and conscious language policy. These changes lent a degree of linguistic unity to the indigenous sector that it did not enjoy before the European invasion (see Matos 1974 [1970]: 106–107; Moya 1981: 144). Quechua, then, is an "oppressed language" in a sense additional to those that I discussed in the last chapter. *It was constituted under colonial rule; it has always been a captive nation.* The modern-day unity of Southern Peruvian Quechua was achieved under European colonial rule. (To a greater or lesser extent, this is true for the other Quechua languages as well: to a greater extent for Ecuadorian or Argentine Quichua, to a lesser extent for the varieties spoken in Yauyos.) But this in no way diminishes the modern-day relevance or "authenticity" of Southern Peruvian Quechua. Quechua communities continue to reproduce themselves as part of what the ethnographer-novelist José María Arguedas called *una nación acorralada*, an enclosed nation.

Although language differences were linked to hierarchy and social domination before the European invasion, after the invasion the nature of domination changed dramatically. In modern Peru, Spanish is *hegemonic* in a way that no other language, even the Inka *lengua general*, ever was. The concept of hegemony is often used to account for the ways in which social domination is maintained through time without direct physical or institutional coercion, often with the consent of those who are dominated (Gramsci 1971 [1929– 1935]: 12–13, 55–57, 180–

183, 245–246, 1985 [1929–1935]; Anderson 1976; Scott 1977: 273–277; Williams 1977: 108–114; Mouffe 1979; Adamson 1980: 171–179; Woolard 1985; Orent 1988: ch. 1).[1] In this sense, hegemony is believed to contrast with more direct forms of physical coercion and violence. But from a historical perspective, physical and institutional coercion are often stages in the consolidation of hegemonic domination and are often called upon to support a faltering hegemony, as we saw in the last chapter. The hegemony of Spanish in modern Peru is a historical achievement that was built up over centuries of domination. It cannot be laid at the feet of any single political decision, law, or institutional mechanism. Rather, as we saw, the relationships of power were such that any individual political move, however enlightened or well-intentioned, tended to reinforce Spanish dominance.

When I say that Spanish is hegemonic, I mean that social dominance is reproduced in every act of speaking, diffusely, but inescapably. Social domination is a lived reality every day in the lives of every single Quechua speaker. It is reproduced in different ways in every act of speaking, be it in Spanish or Quechua; in the choices that bilinguals make to speak one or another language in a particular setting even when the choice is to speak Quechua; in the gnawing closure that it places on the lives of Quechua monolinguals; in the silence of Quechua-speaking children in a Spanish-speaking classroom; in the pride with which a Quechua peasant *writes* his name; in the shame of a military draftee who cannot understand the Spanish spoken around him; in crude bilingual puns used in the marketplace; in the insults shouted at a monolingual Spanish speaker who cannot understand them, since that is the only way that she can be insulted with impunity; and in countless other situations.

Social domination is reproduced in the duality of powers that affect the everyday lives of Quechua peasants.[2] The earth mother and the mountain lords affect the day-to-day survival of the households; they allow the crops to grow, the animals to give birth, and women to have children. They are spoken to in Quechua. The landlords, the police, the judge, the priest, the schoolteacher, the "agronomy engineer," the civil servant, and the clerk at the Ministry of Agriculture have other kinds of power, power to mete out arbitrary punishment and violence, or power to despoil lands, require fines, receive bribes, and withhold the loan needed for this year's seed. They expect to be spoken to in Spanish, even if they speak Quechua back; at the very least, they speak Spanish among themselves. It is as if the words themselves give Spanish speakers their power. Quechua speakers live at the intersection of these two domains. But the two domains are not mutually exclusive. If you are a victim of witchcraft, in Quechua, it will cause your crops to fail, and animals and family members to die. Witchcraft must be counteracted by "curing" the household by making offerings to the earth and the mountain lords, in Quechua. The cautious victim will also go to the police post, a Spanish-language domain, and denounce the person who is responsible.

After the European invasion, Quechua speakers added new stories to their mythology to account for the arbitrary power of Spanish words (Arguedas 1967; Ortíz 1973). Pizarro's capture of the last Inka, Atawallpa, is told as a contest, in which Atawallpa is asked to read. He examines the book (a bible), sees the squiggles dancing across the leaves, and throws it on the ground in frustration. He is decapitated as punishment. In Chayanta, Bolivia, Quechua speakers annually reenact the capture and death of Atawallpa in a play. They nullify the power of the Spaniards by removing the words from their mouths. The instructions for the part played by Pizarro read: *Simillanta kuyuchin* 'He makes only his lips go around' (Lara 1957: 92ff.; cf. Wachtel 1971: 35ff.). As another example, consider the following story about some peasants whose lands were threatened with judicial action by a local landowner. The peasants of the story are from Huanta (Ayacucho), a province that is known for its violent and abusive landlords and for periodic peasant uprisings. The narrator is from elsewhere in the Department of Ayacucho; the narrative was recorded in Lima, the Peruvian capital.[3]

The landowner is able to grab the lands because he speaks Spanish and is therefore capable of mobilizing judicial power on his behalf. The peasants, who do not speak Spanish, have no means with which to defend themselves. They recognize their disadvantage and select some members of their community to go to Lima to *buy* some Spanish talk (*castellano rimay*). But Spanish proves to be costly. Let me quote the story at length (from Ortíz 1973: 176–83).[4]

In the town of Huanta, one time a few years back, an *hacendado* wanted to grab a community's lands.
So the Runa of the community said,
"By speaking Spanish, he'll defeat us in this court case," they said.
"So what'll we do?" they said.
"It's best we go to Lima," they said.
So one Sunday, they had an idea [*yuyarisqaku*].
They selected three Runa with good memories [*allin yuyaysapa*] to come to this town of Lima to buy Spanish. Each one could only manage to buy one Spanish expression, because they cost so much.
So they said,
"Which should we buy?"
"*Ñuqayku*" ['we' or 'us', excluding the addressee].
"And another to go with it?"
"*Munaspayku*" ['because we want to . . .'].
"And after that?"

"*Chaytam munaniyku*" ['that's what we want'].
So the three Runa came toward the town of Lima on foot, until they got to La Mejorada. From La Mejorada they came to the city of Lima in a train. When they arrived in Lima, they went to the home of a fellow Huanteño to rest.
So, while they were in Lima, the Huanteño asked them,
"How come you came?"
So the people who came from Huanta said,
"We came to buy Spanish, dear brother."
"What do you want to buy Spanish for?"
So the Runa who came from Huanta said,
"Dear brother, this landlord is trying to throw us off of our community's land by speaking Spanish, so we also came to buy Spanish in order to defend ourselves."
So the Huanteño who was here [in Lima] said,
"What expressions would you like?"
"We want just three."
So the Lima Huanteño said,
"*I* can sell them to you."
So one of the Huanteños spoke again,
"How much will you charge us for each expression?"
So the Lima Huanteño said,
"I'll sell them to you for fifty each expression."
So the Huanteños said,
"Give us a discount, dear brother, it's for our hometown."
"*Entonces sesenta soles* [sixty *soles*], I'll charge you for each one."
"All right, dear brother."
"Which of you will buy first?"
So one of them said,
"Me first."
"And what expression do you want?"
"*Ñuqayku*" ['us'].
So the Lima Huanteño said,
"*Nosotros.* That's how that expression is said," he said.
Then another said,
"Now to me."
So the Lima Huanteño said,
"And you, what would you like?"
So the Huanteño said,
"*Munaspayku*" ['because we want to . . .'].
So the Lima Huanteño sold him this expression,
"*Porque queremos.*"
And then the Lima Huanteño said to the other,
"You, what would you like?"
So the last Huanteño said,
"For me, *Chaytam munaspaykum*" ['that's what we want'].
So the three Huanteños learned by buying.
So, after they learned [the words], they traveled back toward their village by train until they got to La Mejorada, and from there went on foot.
So, as they were going on a mountain, they came upon a dead person, still fresh, dripping with blood.
When they came upon him, the Huanteños said,

"What kind of heart to have killed him like this!"[5]
While they were saying that, three Civil Guards came, seated on horseback.
"*¿Quién mató a este hombre? ¡Hablen! ¡Hablen!*" [who killed this man? speak up! Speak up!].
So the Huanteños ran off in fear. Then they said,
"They are making us squander ourselves [causing us to spill out] by speaking Spanish," they said.
"But we were buying Spanish in order to defend ourselves," they said.
And the Civil Guard spoke to them only in Spanish. That being so,
"You! You bought the first. You answer!"
So the first Huanteño to buy Spanish came back at the Civil Guard,
"¿Quién mató a este hombre?" [who killed this man?] he was asked.
"*Nosotros*" [us], he said.
So the Civil Guard asked,
"*¿Porqué lo mataron?*" [why did you kill him?].
And the Huanteños said,
"Now you!"
So the second purchaser of Spanish came back at the Civil Guard,
"*¿Porqué mataron?*" [why did you kill him?].
"*¡Porque queremos!*" [because we wanted to].
So the Civil Guard said,
"*Pues ahora van presos*" [then you are under arrest].
So the last one said,
"*¡Eso queremos!*" [that's what we want!].
So as the Civil Guards led them off they said,
"They'll give us a prize for sure; that's why they are leading us off. Justice is great!" they said.
So now they arrived before the judge, who questioned them in Spanish.
The Huanteños looked at each other.
"We bought Spanish in order to defend [ourselves]," they said.
So the judge asked,
"*¿Quién de ustedes mató a este individuo?*" [which of you killed this individual?].
So the first Huanteño who bought Spanish began when the judge asked,
"*¿Quién lo mató?*" [who killed him?].
"*Nosotros.*" [us].
"*¿Porqué lo mataron?*" [and why did you kill him?], he continued.
"*¡Porque queremos!*" [because we wanted to!].
"*Entonces los condeno a veintecinco años de cárcel*" [in that case, I sentence you to twenty-five years in prison].
"*¡Eso queremos!*" [that's what we want].
So, up to now, the Huanteños have been sitting in jail. Now that you know about their lives, bring them a little something, even if it is only coca.[6]

On a superficial reading, this story is about three country rubes who go to the big city, are cheated by their countryman, and get in over their heads because they pretend to be something that they are not, Spanish speakers. But there is more going on than that, as much in what the story assumes about the world as in what it states explicitly. Spanish is associated with state and judicial power, a power that is experienced as arbitrary by the Runa. The landowner is able to pursue his ambition of seizing the lands of the community *by speaking Spanish* and is thereby able to mobilize judicial power on his behalf. The Huanteño in Lima is able to raise the price of Spanish arbitrarily and to cheat his Runa countrymen by switching from Quechua to Spanish. The Civil Guards speak to the Runa in Spanish and the Runa lose themselves: "By speaking Spanish, they are causing us to spill out" (*usuchiwachkanchikmi castellano rimaspan*), they say. They try to respond in Spanish, but are taken off by the Civil Guards anyway. The judge speaks to them in Spanish and sentences them to twenty-five years in prison, during a court procedure that they cannot understand. The Runa regard their own possession of a word and two phrases of Spanish as equally magical talismans that they can use to defend themselves from the arbitrary power of Spanish words and from Latin Peru. They assume that the power is invested in the words themselves.

For Runa, Quechua is a natural, generic language, *Runa simi*, 'human speech'. For its speakers, Quechua is intimately connected to the everyday world. The verb *yachay* 'to know' designates everyday, practical (rather than abstract) knowledge; it is used frequently, without further modification, to mean 'to know Quechua'. Spanish, on the other hand, is pure artifice. It is associated with state power, especially with the urban areas in which state power is concentrated. Spanish can be bought and sold there; so in order to win their court case, the Huanta peasants go to the Peruvian capital Lima, not to appeal to the national political authorities, but to buy Spanish. They even imply that the landowner acquired his Spanish by buying it.

However much Quechua is linked to the everyday lives of Quechua peasants, that life is subject to the encompassing control of Spanish-language institutional structures. The encompassing institutions and economy threaten the physical existence of the Quechua peasants. As individuals, they are subject to the coercive power of the state, which appears in the form of three Civil Guards on horseback and a Spanish-speaking judge. As a community, they are subject to the loss of their land base through the courts, a loss that threatens the community's survival. The peasants in the story are unable to challenge the power or legitimacy of the encompassing political and economic systems. Rather, they are restricted to operating within the parameters set by the encompassing systems. Even so, their challenges are futile.

The encompassing institutions establish Spanish hegemony even when the choice of language is subject to negotiation. Consider the following exchange in the office of a justice of the peace in a bilingual community in southern Peru, Ocongate (Quispicanchi, Cuzco), from the ethnography of Penelope Harvey (1987: 115):[7]

> . . . a man struck his wife and insulted her while he was drunk. The woman entered the room first, speaking Quechua, and told the judge what happened. Later her husband entered and began to explain in Spanish that he could neither confirm nor deny his wife's story because he had forgotten everything. The judge didn't let him speak in Spanish and interrupted him saying, "*Manachu Runasimita yachanki? ¿Eres misti o qué cosa?*" in Quechua, "Don't you know Quechua?" now in Spanish, "Are you a *misti* [mestizo] or what?" They continued in Quechua. The woman spoke in Quechua for a long time, telling the judge what had happened, and of the way in which the man mistreated her and their children.
>
> The judge listened to the two and later sentenced him. He began speaking in Quechua, and said that drunkenness was no excuse for the man's behavior. Above all, he was concerned about the children and tried to explain to the man that children have a different psychology. At this point, he began to switch from Quechua to Spanish, since in Quechua it was difficult to express some of the ideas he wanted to communicate. When he spoke in Spanish, he had a much softer attitude toward the accused.

The man was sentenced to twenty-four hours' detention. Harvey (1987: 116) observes that the justice felt positively toward the man and displayed his positive feelings by speaking to him in Spanish.

In this case, the justice manifests his power not by requiring that the couple speak Spanish in his dispatch, but by determining which language the defendant could speak when. He begins by demanding that the defendant speak Quechua, but he does so by first asking in Quechua, "Don't you know Quechua?" then continuing in Spanish "Are you a *misti* or what?" (in my opinion, sarcastically). His move here is to deny the defendant access to the language of power and then to undermine the defendant's self-identification as a Spanish speaker by suggesting that he is trying to pass himself off as someone who is both more powerful and despised. *Misti* is a derogatory term used by Quechua speakers to refer to local elites such as shopkeepers, landowners, and hacienda overseers.

But once the judge establishes his authority by requiring the defendant to speak Quechua, he maintains it by acting as a linguistic gatekeeper. The justice himself switches to Spanish as his feelings toward the defendant soften, and Spanish becomes a vehicle of solidarity between the two men. In the judge's dispatch, as in the story about the peasants from Huanta, an implicit evaluation of the two languages is behind the judge's choice of languages and the defendant's attempt to address the judge in Spanish. Spanish is the language of the state power invested in the justice of the peace, and it is up to the justice to maintain his association with state power by regulating its use. But, just as in the story of the three peasants from Huanta, the association of Spanish with acts of domination and with the dominant sectors of Peruvian society lurks in the background, unspoken, but taken for granted by all.

Anecdotes such as these could be repeated endlessly. The point is not that Spanish domination is established in one or another instance; it is rather that Spanish domination is reproduced in the background of any social interaction in which both languages come into play. It is the tacit acceptance of Spanish domination as one of the background assumptions of social interaction that reflects and builds linguistic hegemony.

Up to now, I have sketched only one aspect of what the relationship between Spanish and Quechua means to the modern Quechua speaker. Spanish is unquestionably the language of power. But as the judge's comment to the defendant implied ("Are you a *misti* or what?"), there are also distinct social personas and moral orders associated with Spanish and Quechua. For Runa, the moral order associated with Quechua is counterposed to the hierarchy of power. Although the Quechua moral order does not directly oppose the hegemony of Spanish domination, there is an inherent tension between the two. In the judge's question there was an invocation both of the power dimension associated with Spanish and of the moral order associated with Quechua. The invocation of power might be paraphrased as "Are you pretending to be something you are not?"; the alternative Quechua moral evaluation is implied by the use of the word *misti,* from the Spanish word *mestizo.* It is not used in any racial sense, but rather to lump together the rural elites at whose mercy Quechua peasants often find themselves: the landlord, the Civil Guard, the schoolteacher, the shopkeeper, and the political authorities. *Misti*s are regarded as avaricious outsiders whose only purpose in life is to abuse and otherwise exploit Runa. For a Quechua peasant to use *misti* to describe another Quechua peasant is to put the second one beyond the moral pale. For the judge to do so is as effective as it is disingenuous, since he is manipulating the moral order associated with Quechua on behalf of the hegemony of Spanish. Let us examine the way in which the linguistic and cultural oppositions are constructed from a Quechua perspective.

Runa and *Q'ara*

Throughout southern Peru, Quechua speakers make a distinction in their social universe between *Runa* and *q'ara* (Ayacucho-Chanka Quechua *qala*). In its broadest sense, *Runa* means 'human being' or 'person', as opposed to animals, for example. As a social term, *Runa* refers to 'human being' only in the fully socialized sense of the word, as Quechua speakers who are engaged in ongoing relationships with the place they were born in, with its sacred mountains and place-shrines, with other *Runa,* and with their animals. Runa take part in a ritual complex that regulates their relationships with local territory, with their animals, and with other human beings. They reenact the relationships of reciprocal interaction in everyday etiquette: in greetings, eating, drinking, chewing coca, and working together. The principles of reciprocal action are also built into the categorial structure of the language. In each of these instances, from ritual at its most condensed to grammar at its most distilled, Runa are continually reproducing the general principles of reciprocity. Here I discuss the categorial structure of these principles, but keep in mind that the principles of reciprocity are as implicit in everyday social interaction as the relationships of power discussed earlier.

Q'ara is opposed to *Runa* in the narrower sense in which the latter is used to refer to a 'fully socialized person'. To be *q'ara*, 'naked', 'uncultured', or 'uncivilized', is to live outside of the Runa moral order. *Q'ara* are outsiders to the place and as such maintain no ritual relationship with it. They also exempt themselves from the obligations of reciprocity, be it with other people or with the place.

Q'ara include lowland Indians (*q'ara ch'unchu*) and the city dwellers whom Runa encounter when they go to the city to market goods or attend to bureaucratic paperwork. The focal *q'ara* are the *misti*s who live in or near rural communities: priests, shopkeepers, itinerant salespeople, schoolteachers, landowners, and political leaders (Cotler 1968; Earls 1969; Flores 1974). *Q'ara* are perceived to be greedy and wealthy with ill-gotten profit. As Runa live from food, especially from the maize they produce, so *q'ara* are said to "live from money." This is an early and enduring perception that Runa have of outsiders. In Guaman Poma's (1615: 369) letter to the king there is a drawing of a Runa handing a Spaniard some gold, asking, "Do you eat this gold?" The interest of outsiders in rural Peru and rural Peruvians is suspect, as well it might be. The early chronicler Cristóbal de Molina "el Cuzqueño" (1574: 79) described a rumor that "they had sent from Spain . . . for Indian body fat, to cure a certain disease, for which no medicine could be found except for body fat. Because of that, in those days the Indians went around very circumspectly, and they avoided the Spaniards to such an extent that they didn't want to carry firewood, herbs, and other things to the house of a Spaniard, so they wouldn't be killed for their fat once they were inside."[8]

Rural *misti*s, especially priests, are the targets of similar stories today. They are said to have the power to extract the fat from Runa entrails and process it into church candles, Nivea cream, or North American machinery (Morote 1952; Solá and Cusihuamán 1967a: ch. 8; Vallée and Palomino 1973; Liffman 1977; Taussig 1987: 238–241). The victim dies a terrible, lingering death. In the mining areas of Huancavelica, the harvest of human body fat is even described as an organized extractive industry (Favre 1987). Occasionally, similar suspicions are directed against nonlocal people, including non-Peruvians, but the targets are most often *misti*s from the southern highlands.

The Resonances of Reciprocity

Runa live and work, eat and marry, drink and pray, and think and fight in a universe governed by reciprocity. The defining characteristic of fully social beings is that they maintain relations of reciprocity with other Runa; with the earth, the mountains, and the place; and with their animals. Human beings regulate relationships of reciprocity with mother earth and the mountain lords through seasonal and everyday ritual practices. People care for their domestic animals as their domestic animals care for them.[9] The two-sided, reciprocal relationship between humans and their animals is reflected in the word used for domestic animals, *uywa*. *Uywa* is a "zero"-nominalized form of a verb stem.[10] Although nominalized verbs in Quechua are usually marked as to whether the derived noun is the agent or the recipient of the related action, *uywa* is not. In a sense, *uywa* 'domestic animals' are both *uywasqa* 'cared for' and *uywaq* 'carers'. Reciprocity permeates all aspects of domestic life. Although dogs are generally not well treated, on the way to the hereafter a deceased person must pass through a world of dogs where the dogs are able to repay the person's treatment of dogs in this life (Núñez del Prado 1970: 110). Children at play are said to "carry out reciprocity (*ayni-*) with god." As they get older, they reciprocate each other's labor by taking the household's animals to pasture.

The most rudimentary form of reciprocity is *ayni*, a service that is performed with the expectation that it will be reciprocated in kind. Most of the day-to-day tasks involving more than one person—agricultural labor, herding, food preparation, and house building—are organized by *ayni* primarily, though often not exclusively. Individuals maintain networks of others with whom there are long-standing relationships built on the exchange of services. In any given household, individuals maintain separate networks of *ayni* partners. These networks are gender-segregated. Thus, the men recruited by the male head of household to perform a labor-intensive agricultural activity might have food prepared for them by women recruited by the female head of household who are not married to any of the men. (In theory, the *ayni* networks are entirely separate; in practice, it is unlikely that they are entirely so, communities being as small as they are.) At the same time, one of the children might be out pasturing animals with her own separate *ayni* network.

Idyllic as this may sound, it needs to be qualified in several ways. First, *ayni* work is done in the *expectation* of similar work being returned. Although Runa calculate the *ayni* they owe and that is owed them very carefully, there is room for imbalances to develop, particularly as a household develops other resources (for example, cash or rights to use part of the household's lands) for recruiting labor. *Ayni* is balanced only in theory. Second, although the English word *reciprocity* conjures up pleasant images of people sharing life's responsibilities equally, in Southern Peruvian Quechua culture, *ayni* is morally neutral. The early lexicographers Domingo de Santo Tomás (1560b: f. 107v) and Diego Gonçález Holguín (1608: 40) translate *ayni* as 'recompense' and 'revenge' (cf. Murra 1970: 21). *Ayni* can involve repayment of work in kind, but it can also be invoked in a blood feud.

Ayni, then, is a comprehensive principle governing the conduct of social life. More than that, it is an ontological premise, an assumption about how the world is organized. Everything—every action—in the world evokes *ayni*. All Quechua rituals, from the most mundane etiquette to animal increase rituals, in one way or another maintain *ayni* as a basic ontological axiom. Though *ayni* itself is morally neutral, it is a basic ontological axiom, and a prescription for how to live and what to expect from others. Here a moral evaluation does come into play, since there are those who do not live by its premises, who live from pure will, desire, and greed. Such individuals, if they live in a Quechua community and do not have other sources of power, might face social ostracism and ultimately face expulsion from their community and lands. There are strong social pressures that maintain and regulate *ayni* as a social norm. One such way is to regard those who pretend to live beyond its scope, *misti*s and other *q'ara*, as barbarians and to suffer them only reluctantly.

Reciprocity saturates the organization of the Quechua lexicon and grammar. The categorial organization of grammar and lexicon has a special status in maintaining reciprocity as a basic ontological premise of Southern Peruvian Quechua culture. Like the hegemonic relationships of power examined earlier in this chapter, the categorial organization of the lexicon and grammar remains in the background of every act of speaking, implicit and outside of the speaker's awareness, yet compulsory. Whenever a speaker invokes part of the network of lexical meanings surrounding reciprocity and other forms of cyclicity, she is unconsciously reaffirming the ontological status of the larger network of meanings. Whenever a speaker draws upon the obligatory grammatical richness of the language, he is unconsciously but compulsively subscribing to its axioms. As with the earlier discussion of linguistic hegemony, the axioms of reciprocity do not exist in an abstract netherworld; rather, they are latent in every act of speaking (Sapir 1949 [1924]: 153, 1949 [1929]: 162; Gramsci 1971[1929–1935]: 323; Boas 1938: 132f.; Jakobson 1959; Hymes 1983 [1970]: 160ff.). Thus, to explore the network of lexical and grammatical meanings in which reciprocity is embedded is to explore the cultural resonances and force that it has for the speaker.

Reciprocity and, more abstractly, cyclicity are coded in several forms in the Cuzco-Collao Quechua lexicon and grammar (Dumézil 1955; Urbain 1980). The base forms of many of these lexical stems are verbs; they denote actions rather than institutions. (They frequently need to be translated as nouns in English, however.) Since Runa communities vary considerably in the ways in which they organize work institutionally, the specific uses of these terms also vary from community to community. The following are typical: *ayni-* is used as a verb and as a zero-nominalized noun, *ayni,* to denote direct reciprocity, which as we have seen, is carried out in the expectation of return *ayni* (Dumézil 1955: 4–7). In theory, it is symmetrical. *Mink'a-,* also both as a verb and as a zero-nominalized noun, denotes reciprocity that is asymmetric, hierarchically organized, and redistributive (Dumézil 1955: 7–16). Work that is organized in *mink'a* can involve *ayni* relationships between individual workers and the person organizing the *mink'a.* Thus, although the overall organization of work in *mink'a* is hierarchical, individual participants can be recruited into it in *ayni,* among other ways. *Maña-,* as a verb and as a derived noun (*mañay,* which takes the nominalizer of process, *-y*), denotes a prestation that receives a delayed counter-prestation in kind. For example, ritual offerings to the lords of the mountains are often accompanied with a *mañay* request for a counter-prestation of fertile lands and herds. *Mañay* prestations are made as part of an ongoing relationship of mutual rights and obligations in terms of a system in which such relationships have the character of "total social phenomena" (Mauss 1925: 32). In this respect, *mañay* contrasts with *manuy,* a loan that is made as a contingent economic transaction and incurs a specific debt.

All of these terms are part of an elaborate lexical network denoting circularity, circular motion, curvature, twisting, and reversal. (Much of the larger network has been marked with glottalization by means of associative lexical influence; see chapter 8.) One of the pre-Columbian epithets for the deity Wiraqucha is *tiqsi muyu,* 'beginning (or root) circle'. Circular motion with the hands is even a common and typically Quechua gesture.

Two of the terms in the lexical network for 'circular motion' are especially relevant to the present discussion: *mit'a* and *kuti*. *Mit'a* is labor taken in turns. It is asymmetric and, in theory at least, "loaned." *Mit'a* is probably related to the Common Southern Quechua verb **mitmay* (also in both zero and agentive, *-q* nominalized forms). In the Inka state, **mitma* was used for outlier settlements in discontinuous archipelago systems and for resettled populations. In the early colonial period, *mitma* had a strong connotation of 'outsider'. The word *mit'a* itself was adapted during Spanish colonial rule to denote forced native labor, usually in mining and care of Spanish rest stations (*tambos*). In theory, *mit'a* laborers were drawn in turns for a period of several years from the native tribute-paying population; many did not return from the horrors of the colonial mining *mit'a*.

Kutiy, which as a verb denotes 'return', is also used in a zero-nominalized form to mean 'turn' or 'times', as in *iskay kuti* 'two times'. Some speakers in Cuzco have analogically constructed a verb *qutiy* 'to return a prestation' on the basis of *kutiy* and *quy* 'to give'. In the 'return' sense of *kutiy*, it differs from *ripuy* 'to return to one's place' in that *kutiy* specifically implies that the action is part of a cycle, whereas *ripuy* only specifies the existence of a goal for the action. The expression *pacha kuti*, in which *kuti* appears in a zero-nominalized form, indicates a turn in the basic ontological assumptions constituting an evidential model or "world." Southern Peruvian Quechua speakers regard history as a sequence of worlds (*pacha*), each governed by a set of assumptions about the order of the world. Each of the worlds is separated from the next by *pacha kuti*, in which some basic ontological postulates are inverted. Both past and future are cast in this mode. The Inka state was reorganized by a culture hero, Pachakuti Inka; the European invasion was a *pacha kuti*; and many Runa speak of a future *pacha kuti* after which money will be worthless, city dwellers will have only their money to eat, and the *mistis* will have to serve Runa rather than the reverse.

Among the grammatical morphemes, four verbal suffixes are especially important for the vocabulary of reciprocity: *-paku-*, *-naku-*, *-nachi-*, and *-ysi-*.[11] The sequence *-paku-* may be added to a verb stem with the sense of 'to perform an action reciprocally to an end'. Thus from *llank'ay* 'to work' we get *llank'apakuy* 'to work together on each other's behalf'; from *ayniy*, *aynipakuy* 'to reciprocate (one another) to a particular end'. The suffix *-pa-*, which frames the endpoint of a predication, appears with the ambivalent stem *yana*, abstractly 'complement', as *yanapay* 'to help', literally, 'to act as a complement to an end'. The sequence *-naku-* attached to a verb stem is roughly the equivalent of 'each other'. Thus, *ayni-nakuy* 'to reciprocate-one another', *maqa-*

nakuy 'to hit-one another, to fight', and so forth. In contrast, the sequence *-nachi-* requires an external agent to initiate the reciprocal action, as *ayni-nachiy* 'to make others reciprocate-one another', and *maqa-nachiy* 'to cause others to fight'. The suffix *-ysi-* (colonial *-wsi-*) attached to a verb stem means 'to assist (someone) to perform the action denoted by the stem'; thus *papata hasp'iy* 'to dig out potatoes' becomes *papata hasp'iysiy* 'to help (someone) dig out potatoes'.

The center of gravity of this lexical and grammatical network is *ayni*, symmetric reciprocity. The idiom of *ayni* may be used to express reciprocal relations regardless of their political-economic context. *Ayni* itself may thus be converted into a device for masking inherently asymmetric, hierarchical relationships. But *ayni*, and the rhetoric of reciprocity in general, is more than an abstract conceptual tool for thinking and speaking about an already constituted social world. Reciprocity is constituted in everyday practices, in the seemingly trivial details of etiquette, and in the tacit underside of Quechua lexicon and grammar.

Thus, in addition to building *ayni* and other forms of reciprocity into their lexicon and grammar, Runa follow a careful etiquette in exchanging, serving, and consuming food, hard liquor, maize beer, coca, and cigarettes. The etiquette for each of these actions is not simply a social lubricant to make the actions flow smoothly; rather, the forms of etiquette powerfully condense the principles and forms of reciprocity. These include such everyday practices as the ways in which a small cup of cane alcohol is offered to a co-worker, the order in which plates of food are served when people sit down to eat, and the way in which a companion is invited to chew coca. For example, when two Runa exchange and chew coca leaves, they establish or confirm a certain affective density to their relationship by the formula they chose to invite each other, by the formula with which they acknowledge the invitation (by thanking the other person or by naming the relationship), and by the exchange of coca itself. They also confirm relationships to the mountain lords, the earth mother, and the local place in a whispered invocation in which the sacred principles receive the essence of the coca. Finally, the chewed coca is carefully returned to the earth. Coca chewing is an especially resonant expression of reciprocity and "Runa-ness" (Allen 1978: 166ff., and 1981). It has been such a pivot of Runa cultural cohesion that it has often ranked high on the list of cultural characteristics targeted by advocates of cultural assimilation. For example, the letter to Philip II by Antonio de Zúñiga (1579), which advocated eradicating the Quechua language, placed speaking Quechua only third on a list of undesirable cultural practices, after coca chewing and witchcraft. The modern debate over the role of coca in Quechua life (Allen 1976, 1988; Cáceres 1978; Mayer 1978; Ugarte 1978) is muddled by the production of cocaine for the international drug trade, but it is argued along similar lines as the debate over persistence of the native languages, and with much the same vehemence.

The Dimensions of Language Variation

Runa must thus contend with two conflicting political-economic orders. Their own moral order, based on a comprehensive framework of reciprocity, is encompassed by the national Peruvian economy and society. The texture of social relationships experienced along these two dimensions is fundamentally different. Within the framework of reciprocity, be it amiable or hostile, the exchange of services, goods, or enmity takes place within an ongoing relationship, often a relationship of kinship or *compadrazgo* (ritual kinship). The values exchanged express and reshape the relationship within a framework of mutual rights and obligations. In contrast, along the second dimension, social relationships are contingent and subject to continuing change; they are mediated through strict economic interest and through the money economy (even if they involve direct exchange of goods); and, because they are contingent, relationships of power and domination must continually be reasserted.

Each of the two social dimensions is associated with a separate social ecology of language, that is, a separate framework for evaluating language variation. Variation that has its roots within Southern Peruvian Quechua, for which I will use the phrase *endogenous variation,* is evaluated within a Runa moral economy. Variation resulting from language contact between Southern Peruvian Quechua and Spanish is evaluated in a twofold way: (1) against the background of relationships of power by means of which Quechua culture and society are encompassed by the national Peruvian economy and society; and (2) as a reflection of the extent to which speakers are orienting their behavior toward an urban, Spanish-language prestige system.

The two social ecologies, one that structures endogenous variation, the second that structures contact variation, are unequal. The sociology of Quechua-Spanish contact partly determines the social evaluation of endogenous language variation, but not vice versa. One aspect of the social hegemony of Spanish is that Southern Peruvian Quechua is treated as a single, undifferentiated, stigmatized language. This is internalized by Quechua speakers in evaluating Quechua dialects as equivalent socially and undifferentiated. Another aspect of Spanish hegemony is that Spanish has a metalanguage for talking about the linguistic markers of bilingualism; the metalanguage focuses attention on certain linguistic features of the speech of bilinguals and consciously stereotypes (and stigmatizes) some of the features. In contrast, there is no popular meta-language, either in Quechua or in Spanish, for talking about linguistic variation within Quechua. In the following sections, I discuss the social ecology of endogenous variation and contrast it to contact variation. Because of differences in the social ecology and in the texture of social relations implicated in each kind of linguistic variation, the nature of language change is different in the two instances.

The social ecology of endogenous variation is by and large comparable to the social ecology of pre-Columbian language variation (chapter 2), especially in the association between speech and locality. There are four basic, interrelated themes: (1) most variation, especially subphonemic variation, is linguistically and socially *covert*; (2) different ways of speaking are treated as socially *equivalent*—there are no varieties that have greater or lesser prestige than others; (3) however, for features that occur above the threshold of awareness, Quechua speakers are *ethnocentric* and expect others to conform to their own variety; and (4) language differences are *locally structured,* without an overall system of social evaluation.

Covert

Linguistic variables differ in the extent to which speakers can become aware of them. Lexical differences are relatively accessible to the awareness of speakers, particularly if their attention is called to the differences. Differences in grammatical morphology are obvious to speakers, although they do not understand grammatical morphemes that are not also present in their own variety. Subsegmental phonological variation is linguistically covert, that is, below the threshold of social and linguistic awareness. As a rule, Quechua speakers do not recognize subsegmental differences even when their attention is called to them. I tested this by arranging conversations between speakers of phonologically distinct varieties from different parts of the Department of Cuzco. I advised them that the purpose of the conversation was to allow me to "extract speech differences." I would frantically take notes on phonological differences, but would invariably be asked why I had bothered to arrange the conversation, since their speech was the same. On the other hand, speakers were able to solicit lexical differences, particularly once a few had been pointed out to them.

It is significant that endogenous phonological variation is linguistically and socially covert, since this is not true in other sociolinguistic settings. For contrast, consider the conscious sensitivity shown to subsegmental phonological variation by speakers of English, particularly in such linguistically complex settings as New York City. Subsegmental variation resulting from contact between Quechua and Spanish, as we shall see, is more like variation within English than variation within Quechua, in that the variation is subject to conscious evaluation on the part of bilingual speakers.

Equivalence

As we have seen, four centuries of Spanish linguistic domination lent a degree of linguistic unity to Native Peruvians that did not exist before the European invasion. During the colonial period, there was a conscious effort made to homogenize the linguistic variability that existed before the European invasion. The distinction between Quechua and Spanish has assumed an importance that looms larger than any local linguistic differences. In addition, Runa have internalized the tendency of non-Quechuas to treat Native Peruvians as an undifferentiated mass. Thus, they generalize from their own local experiences and assume that their local experiences represent the epitome of what it is to be Runa. When they travel in southern Peru, Runa may notice differences in lexicon or cultural practices. But within a major dialect of Southern Peruvian Quechua, such as Cuzco-Collao Quechua or Ayacucho-Chanka, phonological differences go unnoticed and remain unnoticed even when the speaker's attention is called to them.

In addition, Runa refuse to accept that a Quechua language that differs extensively from their own is Quechua at all. When they hear songs on the radio sung in Central Peruvian varieties of Quechua, Southern Peruvian Quechua speakers assume that they are sung in a different language; I was told several times that Central Peruvian Quechua songs were "Aymara." Likewise, Torero played recordings of speech in several Central Peruvian varieties of Quechua to speakers of Southern Peruvian Quechua and vice versa. He was told that the recordings were incomprehensible or that they must be a foreign language like "Japanese" or "Russian" (Torero 1974: 40–42).

Ethnocentrism

Quechua speakers are locally ethnocentric about speech differences above the threshold of awareness. Outsiders who join a community are expected to conform to local ways of speaking and are corrected when they do not, most effectively in a joking way. Apart from local preference for their own way of speaking, linguistic differences are not evaluated hierarchically. There are no better or worse dialects, no varieties accorded prestige or stigma. Local ethnocentrism has both pre-Columbian and colonial roots. As we saw in chapter 3, linguistic ethnocentrism was a feature of the social ecology of language before the European invasion. But it is maintained in part because of the assumption that local varieties of Quechua are equivalent to one another, so that outsiders *should* speak and behave like members of the speaker's own community.

Unsystematic

Southern Peruvian Quechua speakers do not interpret linguistic variation as anything more than local difference, regardless of whether the variation is tacit or overt. There is no systematic interpretive matrix through which speakers assign social meaning to dialect differences, except that the speakers are from different communities. Localized, (socially) unsystematic dialect patterning is a common pattern in rural Native American peasant communities. Paul Friedrich (1971: 169) has coined the phrase "pueblo dialectology" for this and related features of linguistic variation in Tarascan and other Native Mexican languages; Wick Miller (personal communication, 1987) has observed localized dialect patterning among Tarahumara speakers in northernmost Mexico.

The localized, socially nonsystematic patterning of endogenous phonological variation contrasts with the patterning of linguistic variation induced by Spanish-Quechua bilingualism and with the dialect patterning in other speech communities in which linguistic variables index social stratification. Consider once more Labov's study of variation in the English spoken on the Lower East Side of Manhattan. According to Labov (1966a: 651; 1972 [1970]: 248–249), even though speech is systematically variable, the speech community shares a uniform set of social attitudes toward language. Labov (1972 [1970]: 249) observes that "the correlate of regular stratification of a sociolinguistic variable in behavior is uniform agreement in subjective reactions towards that variable." In order for linguistic variation to index nonlocalized social characteristics, the speech community must constitute a single "community of reference" (Cancian 1979: 34ff.), in which speakers from different social strata share a common set of evaluative norms against which they interpret dialect differences. Whenever social stratification is invoked to explain linguistic changes in progress or stable sociolinguistic variation, it assumes that speakers share a systematic matrix that indexes the variable to social characteristics and provides an evaluation of the variable in terms of the speaker's social values.

Contact Variation

We have already seen that the domination of the Spanish language encompasses and penetrates all aspects of Runa life and livelihood. For bilinguals, the choice between Quechua and Spanish is a function of power relationships as they are expressed in specific institutional and interactional settings. It is also an index of the extent to which bilingual speakers are orienting their behavior to the urban, Spanish-oriented prestige system. Bilingual speakers accommodate to Spanish linguistic norms to different degrees, affecting their speech in Quechua as well as their Spanish. Variation of this kind is a matter of individual accommodation, rather than wholesale change in the grammar of Southern Peruvian Quechua. The reason is that the individuals who have accommodated most to Spanish tend to interact least with other Southern Peruvian Quechua speakers, especially when, for one reason or another, they lose contact with their home communities. Bilinguals do not, therefore, serve as a source of spread of enduring linguistic changes in Quechua. Surprisingly, the areas of substantive change in Southern Peruvian Quechua are few.

The main long-term impact of Spanish on Southern Peruvian Quechua is in the Quechua lexicon. Many word-stems have been borrowed into the Southern Peruvian Quechua lexicon (cf. Hoggarth 1973). These include stems for objects (*awiyun* < *avion* 'plane'), institutions (*inlisa* < *iglesia* 'church'), social relations (*tiya* < *tía* 'aunt', with the semantic range it has in modern Spanish), time concepts (*lasuna* < *la una*, 'one o'clock'), and other concepts (*kriyiy* < *creer* 'to believe') that did not exist before the European invasion or that were not culturally salient (e.g. *riru* < *dedo* 'finger'; Spanish number words for counting money). A few grammatical morphemes have also been borrowed (*asta* < *hasta* 'until', but always with the Quechua counterpart *-kama* suffixed to the until phrase; *-s* 'plural', mainly in the speech of bilinguals; *si* 'if' in conditional constructions, but often with Quechua affixes attached). The syntactic impact is less clear-cut, but is strongest in the most bilingual speakers. Virtually no phonological changes can be attributed to the impact of Spanish. In addition, there are no "interlanguages" found in southern Peru such as the *chawpi lengua* 'middle language' spoken in Ecuador, where Spanish word-stems are combined with Quechua grammatical morphology and syntax (Muysken 1979, 1981). Apparently, the sociolinguistic setting and history of the Ecuadorian dialects are different from Southern Peruvian Quechua.[12] All told, the norms implicit in the Quechua grammatical system are quite distinct from those implicit in Spanish, at least for speakers of Southern Peruvian Quechua who either are monolingual or use Quechua as their main language.

Accommodation to Spanish-language norms, then, is an individual, rather than a speech-community-wide affair. There are important personal and political reasons for learning Spanish (Montoya 1987: 43). We have already seen that Spanish is required by communities for their legal defense. It is common for young men and women to leave their communities just before marriageable age to work at manual labor, domestic service, and petty commerce. The cash they bring in pays for items of personal consumption (shoes, a nice set of store-bought clothes, a radio, soccer cleats), as well as items that their household cannot acquire other than with cash (salt, sugar, noodles, veterinary services, liquor, farming implements such as plow blades). Young men are subject to the military draft at the same age. In both cases, reasonable working knowledge of Spanish is absolutely necessary.

Communities, particularly the new communities carved out of former estates, such as Agrarian Production Cooperatives and Peasant Groups, are subject to governmental regulation, especially through the Ministry of Agriculture, and are required to maintain frequent contact with the appropriate bureaucrats. They must also keep proceedings of community assemblies and account books. For these purposes, Spanish literacy is required of the community secretary and treasurer. The practical requirement that community leaders be literate in Spanish creates political anomalies, such as when a literate college student is chosen as a community authority over older eligible people. Traditionally, age confers respect and authority. In addition, older people have gone through a series of political-ritual offices that make them eligible for leadership in the community. But more and more frequently, the traditional criteria for office are ignored in favor of literacy.

Finally, there is the age-old problem of legal proceedings. The sheer quantity of regulations and frequent shifts in the legal regimen of the agrarian sector leave considerable space for conflicts of interpretation and lawsuits. Communities must protect their basic productive resource, their land, from neighboring communities, from the families of former landowners, and from ingenious schemes by bureaucrats. In order to pursue legal claims in the courts and in order to defend themselves from the legal maneuvers of outsiders, responsible members of the community, preferably the legally recognized officials, must have working knowledge of Spanish.

As we saw earlier, Runa do not question these external constraints requiring them to use another language as a condition for their survival; their world has been like that for four and a half centuries now. Rather, they recognize the practical value of linguistic skills in Spanish and send their children to school with that specific goal in mind. Programs to teach in Quechua along with Spanish have sometimes met with opposition from the community, for very straightforward and practical reasons. Community members argue that the schoolchildren were already speaking Quechua at home; since there is no written literature available in Quechua, Quechua literacy is a luxury (Zúñiga, Lozada, and Cano 1977; Zúñiga 1979: 34; Hornberger 1987: 218–222). On the other hand, there is considerable interest in rural Cuzco in Quechua literacy and literature (Boothroyd 1979); the local opposition generated by bilingual education programs reflects the marginal status of Quechua in the national society and especially in the state bureaucracy. The problems faced by bilingual education programs in Quechua are not different in kind from those faced by bilingual education programs in oppressed languages and language varieties in the United States (cf. Paulston 1973; Labov 1982).

We often imagine bilingualism in Spanish to involve assimilation to Spanish cultural and linguistic norms, and we imagine that process to be unidirectional. For Runa in rural Cuzco, the language contact situation is far more complex than that. My ethnographic work turned up individuals who learned Spanish at one stage in their lives but shifted back to Quechua, to the point that they were virtually monolingual. Such people, often returned migrants from urban areas, usually had good passive control of Spanish but refused to speak it or spoke it badly, as if to shed an uncomfortable set of clothes. I noticed deterioration in the Spanish of several people I knew over the course of my field research; perhaps they simply tired of their second language. This came as a surprise for me. Like many, I had come to Peru with an image of Quechua as a vestige, rather than the choice that it is.

But for the people who abandon rural life, it is absolutely appropriate to speak of one-directional language shift. These include voluntary outmigrants who seek upward mobility in the urban money economy and people who have been expelled from their home communities, because they consistently reneged on reciprocity obligations. Expulsion, including loss of land rights and animals, and shunning is the ultimate social sanction for maintaining a rural reciprocity-based moral order. For speakers who abandon their peasant homes, language is a badge of upward social mobility. Upward mobility depends in part on taking on an appropriate status image, including accumulating commodities (often ostentatiously) and controlling the regional variety of Spanish.

Individuals acquire Spanish by progressive approximation of Spanish grammatical and phonological targets. Some of the characteristics of incomplete acquisition of Spanish have become stereotyped as *sociolinguistic markers*, that is, consciously evaluated emblems of an individual's place in the status system (Labov 1972 [1965]: 178–179). Markers can be manipulated, above the threshold of awareness. It is common for speakers who are acquiring regional Spanish to overshoot grammatical and phonological targets, in other words, to be *hypercorrect.* Insofar as markers can be consciously manipulated, hypercorrection from above the threshold of awareness comes into play as a factor in linguistic change. The most remarked-upon examples involve the mismatch between the vowel systems of Quechua and Spanish and the efforts of Quechua speakers to overcome the mismatch in their Spanish. It is the target of ridicule in editorial cartoons in the Lima newspapers, in television comedies, and in crude ethnic jokes. The following eighteenth-century anecdote is typical: "A certain Spanish lady, pretty and well dressed, was on the balcony of her house with a rose in her hand, and as 'a speaker of elegant words' came by, he wanted to flatter her with the following Spanish adage: 'The rose knows well in whose hand it rests'; to which she responded with great satisfaction: '*Qui [que] rosa, qui [que] no rosa, qui [que] no te costó to [tu] plata*' [What do you know from roses, it didn't cost *you* any money]" (Concolorcorvo 1773: 372).[13]

The young woman in the story has replaced her *e*s with *i*s and her *u*s with *o*s. Concolorcorvo suggests that this phenomenon, known popularly as *motosidad* (from Vulgar Latin *muttum* 'growl'; Cerrón-Palomino 1975: 128), reached the highest strata of eighteenth-century Cuzco society. There are two aspects of *motosidad:* (1) perception and articulation of Spanish vowels in a Quechua pattern by first-language Quechua speakers, or *interference,* and (2) overcompensation for the differences in the vowel systems of both languages by first-language Quechua speakers, or *hypercorrection.* Let us consider each in turn.

Modern Southern Peruvian Quechua speakers have a conceptual (or phonemic) three-vowel system, diagrammed below. (The vowels correspond to *i, u,* and *a* in the official Quechua orthography).

These vowels are phonetically lower in some circumstances (next to a uvular [q, *qh, q*], with some intervening consonants permitted), as:

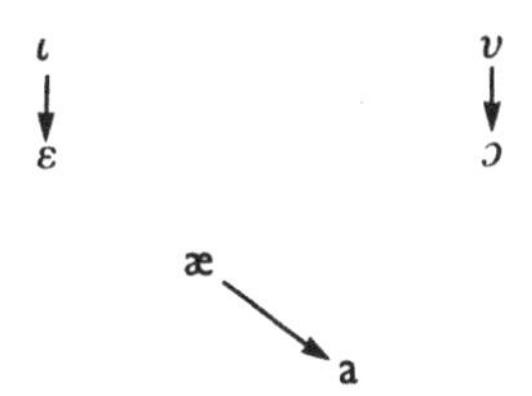

They are raised phonetically before a high, front glide.

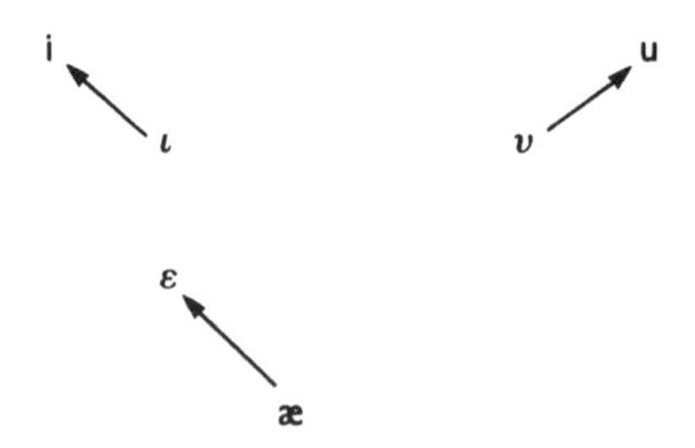

Compare these patterns to the five canonical vowels of Spanish:

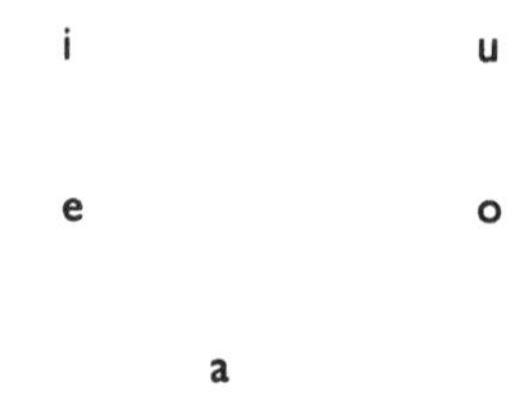

The basic form of the Quechua vowels (described in the first Quechua pattern) are more lax and centralized than their Spanish counterparts. It is not that Quechua has only part of the Spanish five-vowel system; the three vowels it has are phonetically different from any of the five vowels of Spanish (Albó 1970: 236–238; Cerrón-Palomino 1975: 134). Some educators have assumed incorrectly that the Quechua vowels could be identified phonetically with Spanish *i*, *u*, and *a*, and have proposed a five-vowel orthography for Quechua for use in bilingual education programs. But studies made by the Experimental Bilingual Education Project of Puno have shown that, by beginning with a five-vowel orthography, a Quechua schoolchild is misled into identifying the Quechua pattern with the Spanish and later encounters difficulty with Spanish (cf. Jung and López 1987; Zúñiga 1987).

A first-language Quechua speaker who is speaking Spanish will normally use the first Quechua pattern to pronounce the Spanish vowels. For such a speaker, the Spanish mid vowels, *e* and *o*, will be merged with the respective high vowels *i* and *u*, since the closest corresponding relationships between high and mid vowels are automatic (allophonic) alternations caused by the adjacent sounds. It is part of a Southern Peruvian Quechua speaker's tacit knowledge of her language that any variation in vowel height is caused by adjacent sounds. But when a Quechua speaker uses the three-vowel Quechua pattern to produce Spanish words, *all* of the sounds corresponding to Spanish high and mid vowels are heard as "wrong" by a first-language Spanish speaker. If the Quechua vowels ι and υ (corresponding roughly to the vowels in Standard American English *pin* and *book*) are used where the Spanish mid vowels should be, such as *mιsa* for *mesa* 'table', then the Spanish speaker interprets them as high vowels and hears *misa*. If the same Quechua vowels are used where the Spanish high vowels should be, such as *mιsa* for *misa* 'mass', then the Spanish speaker interprets them as mid vowels and hears *mesa*. *Motosidad* is a problem of both interference in the Quechua speaker's pronunciation of Spanish and the Spanish speaker's misperception of it.

Motosidad is also the object of conscious social censure. Of all the features connected with linguistic interference from Quechua in the speech of bilinguals, it is the vowels that attract the most attention and are the subject of social stereotype. The interference of the Quechua vowel system is as socially salient as the loss of post-vocalic *r*s in New York English. First-language Quechua speakers who are trying to accommodate to a Spanish-speaking world are well aware of the problem and of the social stigma connected with it (Cerrón-Palomino 1975). As a result, many of them overcompensate for it in both their Spanish and Quechua and use etymologically inappropriate vowels; linguistically insecure speakers hypercorrect by substituting the low vowel *a* for the *e*, even in Quechua (Albó 1970: 240).

It is not surprising that linguistic stereotypes such as *motosidad* should cause so much anxiety for the bilingual speaker. In highland cities such as Cuzco, as well as in some of the smaller provincial capitals, the choice of language and the markers of bilingualism are the subject of almost continual negotiation of status in face-to-face interaction. The constant monitoring and evaluation of interpersonal status contribute much to the tension of everyday life.

I have described some of the effects of language shift for individuals who are exposed to Spanish relatively late in life. For many young urban bilinguals, however, exposure to Spanish began so early and has been so strong that they have restructured their Quechua along Spanish lines. For such speakers, hypercorrection involves the inappropriate spread of Spanish features into Quechua, often beyond their presence in Spanish. Some common features are fricativization of [h] (pronounced like English *h* in *house*) to [x] (*jota*; pronounced like German *ch* in *ach*) at the beginnings of words, acquisition of a Spanish-like vowel system, with the vowels tensed and lexically reassigned in Quechua, and morphological and syntactic reshaping of Quechua on a Spanish model. A bilingual who is dominant in Spanish cites Quechua infinite verb forms with the Spanish infinitive ending *-r* (borrowing both morphology and the metalinguistic speech register), and prefers subject-verb-object word order instead of Quechua subject-object-verb order. Since both Quechua and Spanish have relatively flexible word order, word order remodeling is most noticeable in Quechua when it violates constraints that are followed in monolingual speech. For example, a Spanish-dominant bilingual might put a copula between the possessor and the thing possessed in a possessive phrase, *X-pa kashan Y-n* 'the *Y* is *X*'s'; this construction violates a syntactic constraint in the speech of monolinguals that a possessive phrase cannot be interrupted by another word.

Linguistic Change and Awareness: Hypercorrection

I turn now to the problem of hypercorrection in the speech of bilinguals, in order to point out some striking differences between the social ecology of linguistic variation within Quechua and the social ecology of contact variation. As we saw, subsegmental phonological variation within Quechua is linguistically covert. Larger-scale linguistic differences are treated as socially equivalent, except the Quechua speakers are locally ethnocentric about them. Finally, linguistic variation is not interpreted as anything more than local difference, regardless of whether the variation is tacit or overt. There is no systematic interpretive matrix through which speakers assign social meaning to dialect differences, except that the speakers are from different communities. What is critical here is that there are no social mechanisms that would by themselves encourage speakers to imitate one another, except in the very localized setting of face-to-face interaction.

For contact variation, on the other hand, the first-language Quechua speaker is consciously appropriating a second language. The markers of non-native production of Spanish are well known and subject to manipulation above the threshold of awareness. Speech differences are interpreted in terms of a larger social pattern that assigns prestige values to them; the prestige structure identifies speech differences with other markers of social stratification, including dress, occupation, and acquisition of commodities. Speech differences are conspicuously consumed in the same manner as other commodities.

What implications do these differences have for the nature of linguistic change in the two contexts? Labov (1972 [1965]: 178–179) contends that linguistic change occurring above the speaker's threshold of awareness follows a different trajectory from change below the threshold of awareness. Arguing from complexly stratified social settings in the northeastern United States (Martha's Vineyard, the Lower East Side of Manhattan), Labov proposes that change begins with the generalization of a linguistic variable to members of a social group. At this point, the linguistic variable is a simple index of group membership. From here, the change is expanded by succeeding generations of speakers within the group. Labov refers to the expansion of a change as "hypercorrection from below the threshold of awareness." (I refer to it here simply as "expansion" of the change.)

In contrast to "hypercorrection from below," "hypercorrection from above" supposes a complex social setting in which variables are stylistic and social markers of prestige. Markers indexing the highest-status group in the system are prestigious; others are stigmatized. Some speakers of stigmatized forms shift their most careful speech toward the prestige target and beyond it (Labov 1966b, 1972 [1970]: 244–245, 1980). This may take the form of overcompensating for their own deviance from the prestige norm as when Quechua speakers use low [a] when they are trying to produce mid [e]. Or it may take the form of a linguistic innovation that reverses an earlier innovation, but goes beyond it, as when English speakers from San Francisco who drop *r* after vowels innovate by introducing *r*s in contexts that did not have them in the first place (DeCamp 1972). It is changes such as these that were traditionally known as "hypercorrection" (or 'hyperurbanism'; Bloomfield 1933b); I use it in the following sections as a shorthand for Labov's "hypercorrection from above the threshold of awareness."

Hypercorrection is more than just a late stage in the evolution of sound change. It reflects certain features of the social landscape. In order to get hypercorrection (from above the threshold of awareness): (1) the linguistic variable must be stratified, both stylistically and socially; (2) it must be open to conscious evaluation as a marker of social stratification by members of the speech community; and (3) the stylistic and social stratification of the variable must form a system that is shared by members of the speech community.

Most importantly, it must be possible within the social system to manipulate linguistic variables and other status markers to accumulate prestige or to acquire a certain social status. This means that hypercorrection from above the threshold of awareness is limited to social settings in which status is negotiated in terms of a commonly accepted prestige hierarchy. Within the prestige hierarchy, language is only one of several status indices. Because the hierarchy both is commonly accepted and is used to evaluate other social phenomena such as education, profession, dress, and acquisition of material goods, prestige accrued in one of these domains can be transposed into prestige in another (Bourdieu 1982). Another way of putting this is that all of the status markers, including contact variation, form a single social field within which status is negotiated.

Thus, the pattern of linguistic innovation found in hypercorrection (from above the threshold of awareness) reflects a broader pattern of social innovation, also seen in such nonlinguistic domains as agricultural technology (Cancian 1979: 84ff.) in which innovation reflects the social anxiety of an insecure position in a prestige hierarchy, one that is neither prestigious nor stigmatized. The broader pattern, in turn, requires a certain kind of social consciousness, in which social relationships are understood and constructed in terms of the relationships between commodities and other indices in the prestige hierarchy. The crux of the matter, according to Lukács (1971 [1922]: 83), is that "a relation between people takes on the character of a thing and thus acquires a 'phantom objectivity', an autonomy that seems so rational and all-embracing as to conceal every trace of its fundamental nature: the relationship between people."

Within the social ecology of contact between Quechua and Spanish, social relationships are negotiated in terms of prestige attributes. The prestige hierarchy is experienced by bilinguals as having an objective structure of its own to which they must orient their own use of language. In order to move up in the prestige hierarchy, they must aim at acquiring the attributes of higher statuses, including higher-status ways of speaking. Bilinguals are thus trapped on a treadmill of linguistic insecurity, ever attempting to refine their Spanish, ever overcompensating for the linguistic interference of their native language. Notice that the struggle of bilinguals to master Spanish has the same repercussions as the negotiation of language choice discussed at the beginning of this chapter: it reinforces the linguistic hegemony of Spanish. As Quechua speakers attempt to master Spanish, Latin Peru comes to master them, again!

Variation within Southern Peruvian Quechua is linguistically covert and understood as a mere expression of local differences; for all intents and purposes, local dialects are socially equivalent. Contact variation is evaluated in terms of a shared hierarchy of prestige in which linguistic differences are associated with other status markers and with other forms of social domination. Speakers consciously try to manipulate speech differences to social ends. These two dialectological patterns are each associated with a different moral order and political economy. In the rural setting of endogenous variation, production is oriented primarily (though not entirely) toward immediate subsistence. As we have seen, production is organized according to deep-rooted axioms of reciprocity, which are practiced in the context of enduring social relations of ongoing rights and obligations. Being Runa involves commitment to the language, to local territory, and to an ontology of reciprocity. In Runa communities, prestige is accrued by a number of different means, including ritual-political offices, reputation as a worker, and accumulation of movable wealth in domestic animals (*uywa*).

In the predominantly urban setting of contact variation, on the other hand, production is organized by wage labor and oriented primarily toward market exchange. Prestige in the urban setting is also determined by a complex set of criteria, but by far the primary determinant of urban prestige is the conspicuous accumulation of commodities. The rural Quechua political economy is encompassed by the broader regional and national economies, to be certain, but it is experienced in a fundamentally different way from the latter two. For Quechua speakers, social relations in the two domains are organized by different principles and have different textures.

The differences between the social ecology of endogenous variation and the social ecology of contact variation correspond to the differences in productive relationships and prestige structures. In the urban setting of commodity production organized by wage labor, language becomes just one more commoditized emblem of class. Language differences are evaluated within a shared set of normative standards that assign prestige to some forms and stigmatize others; the basis for the prestige scale is the extent to which the linguistic forms approximate the regional norms for Spanish. The pattern of conscious hypercorrection observed in contact dialectology is a direct consequence. In contrast, language variation within Southern Peruvian Quechua is evaluated merely as local difference, without the overarching assignment of social values to linguistic differences, or the anxiety of trying to speak in someone else's voice, or conscious hypercorrection of linguistic differences. That is why in Xavier Albó's (1970: 224) study of linguistic variation in Cochabamba, Bolivia, it appeared to him that "most of the variation with social significance can be traced back to bilingualism."

There are two very general consequences for the nature of phonological change in Southern Peruvian Quechua since the European invasion. First, as we shall see in the second part of this book, the changes take place in an orderly sequence and in an orderly pattern. The major phonological changes in the Department of Cuzco have internal linguistic motivations. The process by which they spread is regular and predictable (chapters 9 and 10). The normal structural consequences of hypercorrection do not occur in the postinvasion linguistic history of Cuzco-Collao Quechua. The structural indications of hypercorrection include unmotivated phonological restructuring of lexical representations and the addition of phonological rules undoing the effect of earlier innovations (but in a broader set of linguistic contexts; DeCamp 1972; Zonneveld 1980). There is no evidence of either in my data. Although this is an "argument from silence" (or at least, an observation of silence), it is a significant one, since some historical linguists assume that hypercorrection and imitation of prestige forms are the normal, if not the only, way for languages to change (Hock 1986: ch. 20). I would maintain that this cannot be true.

Second, the two dialectological patterns are relatively autonomous. Variation induced by contact with Spanish is a matter of individual accommodation, rather than wholesale change in the grammar of Southern Peruvian Quechua; as I have already pointed out, individuals who have accommodated most to Spanish tend to interact least with other Southern Peruvian Quechua speakers. Surprisingly, only one of the phonological changes in Cuzco-Collao Quechua since the European invasion might be traced to the influence of Spanish. The tap ɾ becomes a fricative ɹ adjacent to a word boundary (i.e., at the beginnings and ends of words). All other fricativization processes in Southern Peruvian Quechua take place at the ends of words or at the ends of syllables (see chapter 9), so that the fricativization of *r* is an anomaly. But local varieties of Spanish also have a fricativized *r* adjacent to a word boundary, and structurally similar processes (usually turning *r* into a trill *r̃*) take place throughout the Spanish-speaking world. It seems reasonable to conclude that the spread of Quechua fricativization to word boundaries was influenced by the model of Spanish.

Summary

The European invasion reshaped the social distribution of language across the Southern Peruvian landscape. Before the European invasion, Southern Peruvian Quechua was in intimate contact with other Andean languages, with which it was interspersed in a noncontiguous pattern. Although Southern Peruvian Quechua was the administrative language of the Inka state, there is no evidence that it ever became hegemonic or was ever standardized. Speech differences were associated with local places; these were understood to be stable. In pre-Columbian Peru, linguistically significant social differences were constituted within a larger organization, rather than in terms of temporary exchange relationships.

European colonial rule drastically changed the linguistic ecology of Southern Peru. The Europeans promoted Southern Peruvian Quechua for the purposes of religious proselytization and local rule, at the expense of local languages. The new settlers had a stake in ensuring that native populations continue to speak a Native Andean language rather than Spanish, in order to broker the place of native communities in the colonial economy and society. Thus, Southern Peruvian Quechua came to be spoken over a large contiguous territory, but as the language of a subjugated people.

The fates of the Southern Peruvian Quechua language and culture were subjects for debate under Spanish colonial rule. No matter how well-intentioned, each of the political choices made tended to reinforce Spanish domination over Quechua. By the time of independence, the social ecology of language in southern Peru had been altered irremediably. The linguistic mosaic encountered by the first European invaders was replaced by relative homogeneity, which was keyed into sociopolitical domination: Spanish as the language of the dominant social sector, Southern Peruvian Quechua as the language of the oppressed.

The social ecology of modern Southern Peruvian Quechua is shaped in part by the circumstances of linguistic oppression. Speech differences are evaluated in terms of two relatively autonomous social matrices. Variation within the major dialects of Southern Peruvian Quechua has a social ecology that is by and large comparable to the social ecology of pre-Columbian language variation, especially in the association between speech and locality. Most variation within Southern Peruvian Quechua is linguistically and socially covert. Different ways of speaking are treated as socially equivalent. However, for features that occur above the threshold of awareness, Quechua speakers are ethnocentric and expect others to conform to their own variety. Finally, language differences are locally structured, without an overall system of social evaluation.

Linguistic variation resulting from contact between Spanish and Quechua, on the other hand, is interpreted in terms of a larger social pattern that assigns prestige values to them; the prestige structure identifies speech differences with other markers of social stratification, including dress, occupation, and acquisition of commodities. The markers of non-native production of Spanish are well known and subject to manipulation above the threshold of awareness. As a result, speech differences resulting from language contact are subject to hypercorrection (from above the threshold of awareness). Endogenous speech differences appear not to be.

In part II, I turn to a formal description of the linguistic changes in the dialect of Southern Peruvian Quechua spoken in and around the former Inka capital, Cuzco, from the time of the European invasion until the present. I use three kinds of evidence: (1) comparative and internal reconstruction of the ancestor of the language, as it was spoken before the European invasion; (2) written sources, beginning less than thirty years after the European invasion, but concentrating most on the late sixteenth, seventeenth, and eighteenth centuries; and (3) study of the modern dialects of Southern Peruvian Quechua spoken in the Department of Cuzco, Peru.

Part II Linguistic Change

5 Common Southern Peruvian Quechua

Southern Peruvian Quechua (marked with asterisks on the simplified family tree in fig. 5.1) is the Quechua language spoken in the six southeastern departments of Peru: Apurímac, Arequipa, Ayacucho, Cuzco, Huancavelica, and Puno. It shares a common morphological and syntactic history with the other Southern Quechua languages spoken in Argentina, Bolivia, and Chile and is mutually intelligible with the latter two. Southern Peruvian Quechua was the lingua franca of the Inka state. The most closely related Quechua languages outside of the Southern group are those spoken in Ecuador and southern Colombia; these were either descended from or heavily influenced by the Inka lingua franca.[1]

Today Southern Peruvian Quechua is divided into two major dialects, Cuzco-Collao and Ayacucho-Chanka (also marked with asterisks). In order to elucidate the history and diversification of Southern Peruvian Quechua, I assume that these two dialects are descended from a single common ancestor language, which I refer to as *Common Southern Peruvian Quechua.* Common Southern Peruvian Quechua is a hypothetical reconstructed (or proto-) language, of a relatively shallow order; it should not be confused with proto-Quechua, the hypothetical, reconstructed ancestor of the Quechua linguistic family.

The two dialects of Southern Peruvian Quechua are virtually identical morphosyntactically, but differ significantly in phonology and lexicon. There are two main phonological differences. (1) The Cuzco-Collao dialect has distinctive ejectives (glottalized stops), aspirates, and plain voiceless stops, whereas the Ayacucho-Chanka dialect has only plain voiceless stops. The ejectives and aspirates are relatively recent features of Cuzco-Collao, but they are now solidly installed in the sound system. Cuzco-Collao shares these features with the neighboring Bolivian varieties of Quechua, and with neighboring non-Quechua languages, includ-

Figure 5.1

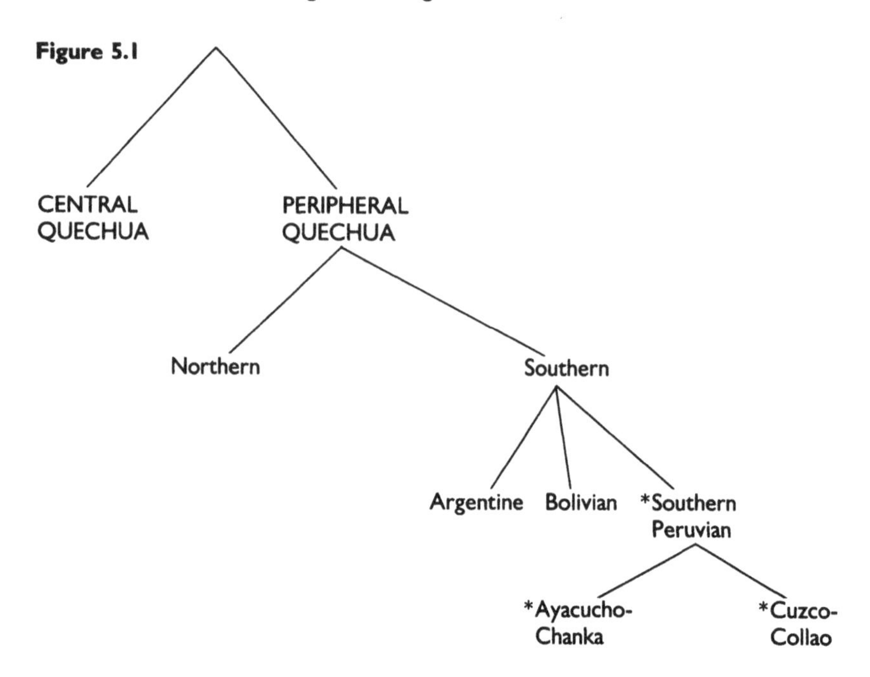

ing Aymara (Hardman-de-Bautista, Vásquez, and Yapita 1974) and the Quechuanized Puquina of the Callawayas of Bolivia (Oblitas 1968; Stark 1972; Torero 1987). (2) The Ayacucho-Chanka dialect has distinctive stops and fricatives at the ends of syllables, while Cuzco-Collao has only fricatives in the corresponding position. The Cuzco-Collao stops have weakened and merged with the fricatives. In addition, other classes of sounds, including fricatives, nasals, laterals, and glides, have weakened and/or merged with other members of the same phonological class. There is some lexical homophony in Ayacucho-Chanka, in words that are distinguished by glottalization or aspiration in Cuzco-Collao. There is very little homophony in Cuzco-Collao as a result of the mergers of consonantal endings. There are major lexical-semantic differences between the dialects as well, although these are less patterned and more variable locally.

There are several reasons for concentrating so narrowly on the history of Southern Peruvian Quechua. First, there are advantages to be gained from taking a finer rather than broader perspective on linguistic reconstruction and change. A finer perspective allows for more precise control over the relevant evidence and allows a more detailed picture of the historical processes by which the language changed to emerge. In a broader perspective, a reconstruction of the linguistic history would have to be stated in terms of correspondences rather than specific innovations, if only because of the limits of current comparative Quechua studies. Correspondences are algorithms for stating the differences between related dialects or languages. But, in a finer perspective, it is possible to focus on linguistic innovations, that is, on actual historical events, and to embed them much more specifically in the historical and social circumstances in which they took place. In addition (and, I might add, paradoxically), because a narrower-gauge perspective focuses on innovations rather than algorithmic correspondences, it is possible to raise issues of general theoretical and methodological import that would be missed entirely were linguistic history to be treated entirely in terms of algorithmic correspondences, as is often the case in Native South America. For example, the lenitions and mergers of consonant endings in Cuzco-Collao followed a course through the word that mirrored its grammatical-semantic organization (chapter 10). This was entirely unexpected and sheds new light on the cognitive and semiotic organization of sound change. It also makes it possible to construct a testable model of the relationships between different local dialects and historical states of the language and to set up an accurate chronology for the changes.

Second, Southern Peruvian Quechua is of special interest because it was the language of one of the Native American high civilizations, the Inkas. As such, the social and historical processes by which it developed reflect on Inka history and society and afford us another form of access to Inka culture in general. Although the classic writings of colonial grammarians, lexicographers, dramatists, poets, and chroniclers have been subject to intense scrutiny by scholars since the fall of the Inka state (especially during the nineteenth century), such work was carried out without a general framework within which ancient texts could be situated socially and historically, and without a sense of how these texts were related to each other, chronologically, socially, or linguistically. One aim of the present work is to provide such a framework, by means of a detailed reconstruction of the phonological history of Cuzco-Collao Quechua. Historical phonology is the essential foundation of any other linguistic or literary history and of any future historiography of Quechua-language sources. In spite of masterful work by nineteenth century historian-philologists such as Tschudi (1853, 1876), Markham (1864, 1871a, 1871b), Pacheco (1878), and Middendorf (1890a, b, c, 1891), modern literary philologists such as Galante, Lara, and Meneses (1950, 1976), and anthropological philologists such as Trimborn and Hartmann, this basic groundwork had yet to be done.

Third, Southern Peruvian Quechua, especially the Cuzco-Collao dialect, is the best-attested Quechua language from a literary point of view. There is a rich literature in Southern Peruvian Quechua beginning as early as a few decades after the European invasion, an almost inexhaustible but largely untapped vein of religious works, mythology, poetry, and drama (cf. Lara 1969), which has continued to be enriched in modern times, by the formal poetry of Arguedas (1972), Alencastre (n.d.), and Lara (1975), and by the folk poetry of countless composer-performers of highland *huayno* music (Roel 1959; Escobar and Escobar 1981; Montoya, Montoya, and Montoya 1987). The chronological framework established here will allow us to place much of this material in its proper historical and social setting. For example, it was common to refer to the period from the late seventeenth to the early eighteenth century as the "dark age of literary Quechua," but we now know that it was rather the "golden age of literary Quechua," a period of intense cultivation of the language by a small, self-consciously nationalistic elite that patronized Quechua literature and art in order to legitimize its economic and political power in the south-central highlands (chapters 3 and 6).

Until the middle of the twentieth century, literary and scholarly cultivation of Southern Peruvian Quechua, whether by Peruvians or foreigners, was closely associated with the estate-owning elites of Cuzco and Arequipa. The landowning class maintained an interest in Quechua language and literature through local journals and publications (in the work of Pacheco, for example), by private preservation of manuscripts as antiquities (in the independence-era papers of Justo Apu Sahuaraura), and by supporting and orienting foreign scholarship on Quechua language and literature (the work of Markham, Middendorf, and Tschudi; cf. Tamayo 1980: 144–152). The antiquarian interest of provincial urban elites continues to be an important strand in Quechua studies, particularly in provincial "Academies of the Quechua Language" and in provincial university courses. A professionalized, technical linguistics did not take root in Peru until the 1960s, with the sociopolitical rise of urban commercial and professional classes.

The antiquarian study of Quechua language and literature reflected its class character, not least of all by asserting the superiority of the Quechua spoken by the provincial elites of Cuzco and Arequipa. Elite *indigenistas* promoted the dogma that Quechua spread only with the Inka expansion, that Cuzco was the Quechua homeland, and that other varieties were "mere corruptions" of the classical language of the Inka. They also identified pre-Columbian Quechua with their own speech, "pure Quechua of the Inkas," and therefore discarded the two most important sources of linguistic data: written sources from the colonial period and Quechua as it is spoken today in the rural hinterlands as an everyday, living language. The scholarly folklore built up around Quechua linguistic history diverted attention from basic, detailed historical work. The debates of the late nineteenth and early twentieth century about whether Quechua could be "derived" from Aymara or vice versa (see chapter 2) are a good example of the work produced from this perspective.

In addition, linguistic reconstruction was hindered by a lack of basic descriptive work of sufficient quality and detail to be usable in a comparative reconstruction. The best-documented Quechua language, Cuzco-Collao, was described with sensitivity by Gonçález Holguín at the beginning of the seventeenth century, but few other grammarians even approached his sophistication until Middendorf (1890a). Even into the 1970s, linguistically informed descriptive work on Southern Peruvian Quechua was scarce: a journal article on Cuzco-Collao morphology (Yokoyama 1951), a mimeographed reference grammar of Cuzco-Collao (Solá and Cusihuamán 1967b), and a morphological grammar of Ayacucho-Chanka (Parker 1969a) were its full extent. No book-length, linguistically informed reference grammar of Cuzco-Collao was published until 1976 (Cusihuamán 1976a). Quechua scholars had focused their attention on pedagogical materials that by their nature must be limited in detail. Considering the scarcity of primary descriptive studies, the achievements of historical linguists and philologists such as Teodoro Meneses, John Howland Rowe, Alfred Torero, and Gary Parker have been nothing short of remarkable.

Sound Patterns in Three Inka Dialects

The earliest detailed study of Southern Peruvian Quechua linguistic history was John Howland Rowe's "Sound Patterns in Three Inca Dialects" (1950). Rowe was the first to observe the systematic correspondences between the modern Cuzco-Collao and Ayacucho-Chanka dialects, which he compared with early-seventeenth-century Cuzco Quechua as described by Gonçález Holguín (1607, 1608). Rowe noticed that the ejectives and aspirates present in modern Cuzco-Collao Quechua and attested in Gonçález Holguín's *Vocabulario* were absent from the Ayacucho-Chanka dialect. Conversely, modern Cuzco-Collao showed a narrower range of segments in syllable-final position than either Ayacucho-Chanka or colonial Cuzco. The syllable-final stops of colonial Cuzco-Collao and modern Ayacucho-Chanka have merged with the corresponding fricatives.

Rowe used this evidence to reconstruct an earlier stage of Southern Peruvian Quechua that was close to the dialect described by Gonçález Holguín. The reconstructed proto-language, which he named "Classic Inca," had the syllable-final stops of Ayacucho-Chanka dialect and the ejectives and aspirates of modern Cuzco-Collao dialect. Rowe identified his reconstructed language with the Inka lingua franca. But since he considered it the parent language of modern Cuzco-Collao and Ayacucho-Chanka Quechua, it corresponds to the stage I would call Common Southern Peruvian.

Rowe followed a time-honored procedure in reconstructing "Classic Inca." Wherever two segments in one of the dialects corresponded to one segment in the other, he reconstructed the prototype system with two segments and reconstructed a diachronic merger for the second dialect. For example, Cuzco-Collao plain, ejective, and aspirate stops all correspond to Ayacucho-Chanka plain stops. There is no phonological algorithm to explain how a plain series could have split into three, whereas none is needed for a merger. Rowe therefore reconstructed three stop series—plain, ejective, and aspirate—for "Classic Inca," which merged into one in Ayacucho-Chanka. Similarly, Ayacucho-Chanka has both stops and fricatives at the ends of syllables, while Cuzco-Collao has only fricatives. Rowe's "Classic Inca" has the stops and fricatives of Ayacucho-Chanka, which merged in modern Cuzco-Collao.

It is heuristically useful to reconstruct all correspondences as separate proto-segments, although it leads to unrealistically complex proto-systems and unrealistically simple linguistic histories. Fortunately, Rowe also had the written evidence supplied by Gonçález Holguín and the other colonial grammarians, as well as unusually perceptive insights into the structure of modern Southern Quechua phonology. The phonological system reconstructed for "Classic Inca" was corroborated by Gonçález Holguín. His reconstruction of the syllable-final consonants is also corroborated by patterns of dialect variation in the modern language. Most phonological variation in modern Cuzco-Collao can be traced to the weakenings and mergers of the syllable-finals (chapter 9). There are also traces of the mergers in the synchronic phonology of Cuzco-Collao Quechua, in the form of several phonological rules that fricativize syllable-final stops or merge other syllable-final consonants. Finally, the reconstructed syllable-finals also correspond exactly to cognate forms in the other, non-Southern Quechua languages (Parker 1969c, 1969f, and 1971), although Rowe could not have known that at the time.

Rowe's reconstruction of ejectives and aspirates in Common Southern Peruvian Quechua is less strong. From a comparative viewpoint, neither can be reconstructed outside Southern Quechua (Southern Peruvian, Bolivian, and Argentine varieties), although there are possible witnesses in Ecuador that may ultimately be of Southern Peruvian origin as well. Reconstruction of ejectives and aspirates is highly problematic even at the level of Southern Quechua, for there is considerable lexical variation in the presence of glottalization and aspiration throughout the

Figure 5.2

	A Cuzco-Collao	B Ayacucho-Chanka	C Ancash
'to sneeze'	hach'iy	hachiy	akchiwsaay
'roasted grain'	hank'a	hamka ~ qamka	ankay
'toad'	hamp'atu	hampatu	ampatuy
'to catch'	hap'iy	hapiy	
'how much'	hayk'a	hayka	ayka
'to urinate'	hisp'ay	hispay ~ ispay	ishpay

Southern Quechua languages. The distribution of ejectives and aspirates in modern Cuzco-Collao into patterned, but variable associative sets suggests that the variability of these features resulted from a long-term process of lexical diffusion and split (chapter 8). There is a small amount of evidence that Ayacucho-Chanka Quechua once also had these features, in the form of an *h* that precedes words that etymologically should begin with a vowel.

Words beginning with a vowel were preceded by a predictable glottal catch. But in the Southern Quechua languages that have ejectives and aspirates, there is a word-structure constraint that restricts glottalization to once per word. Words preceded by a glottal catch that also contain an ejective (glottalized) stop are incompatible with the constraint. The initial glottal catch was therefore replaced by an epenthetic *h* in such words. Some examples from contemporary Cuzco-Collao Quechua are listed in column A of figure 5.2.

Column B lists the Ayacucho-Chanka cognates (from Parker 1969a and Soto 1976b) to the Cuzco-Collao examples and column C lists cognates from a Central Quechua language, Ancash (from Parker and Chávez 1976).[2] (The Ancash cognates are from a dialect that has preserved etymological initial *h*. In most of the rest of Ancash-Huailas Quechua, $h > \emptyset$.) Each of the Ayacucho-Chanka words has an initial *h* whose presence is not accounted for by its usual etymological source, as the Ancash cognates attest. In one set, there is a dialect variant with the expected form (*hispay* ~ *ispay*); in another the initial *h* is in the process of being reinterpreted as a variant of the uvular fricative *q* (*hamka* ~ *qamka*). Each of them also corresponds to a stem in Cuzco-Collao Quechua that has an initial *h* that was conditioned by the ejective. These Ayacucho-Chanka stems (and others like them) either were borrowed from a variety that had ejectives or represent the residue of an epenthetic *h* that formerly was conditioned by the presence of glottalization in Ayacucho-Chanka Quechua. In the latter case, it would be plausible, though far from certain, that Rowe was correct in assuming that Common Southern Peruvian Quechua had ejectives.[3]

Rowe (1950: 146ff.) also reconstructed two sibilants on the basis of the orthographies of Domingo de Santo Tomás (1560a, 1560b) and Gonçález Holguín (1607, 1608). Comparative and philological evidence supports his conclusion that Common Southern Peruvian Quechua had two sibilants even though all modern Southern Peruvian Quechua varieties show only one as a reflex of both (chapter 7). Some modern dialects of Cuzco-Collao Quechua distinguish two sibilants, / s / and / ʃ /, but the distinction is a more recent innovation. / ʃ / has two sources: fricativization of palatal stops at the ends of syllable and palatalization of *s* after a front vowel.

At the time Rowe wrote his article, very little was known of the Quechua family apart from Southern Quechua. His statement that "the known modern dialects, including those of Cuzco and Ayacucho, derive from the form of the language spoken in Cuzco in the 16th century rather than preserving older local differences" (1950: 137) has turned out to be inadequate in the light of more intensive work in the Central Quechua languages. Rowe was one of the first scholars working in Native American languages to recognize the value of written evidence for diachronic work. But he underestimated the diversity of the Quechua languages. As a result of the relatively shallow genetic perspective in which he was working, he overestimated the relative importance of written sources as opposed to comparative reconstruction. His emphasis on written sources is fine within the confines of Southern Peruvian Quechua, but is misplaced in the broader context of the Quechua family. There are few colonial texts of secure provenience from outside of Cuzco, and the depth of differentiation of the Quechua family is far greater than the four and a half centuries that can be documented with texts. He appears to have considered his reconstruction as deep and as wide in scope as the evidence permitted. Although it was not a family-wide reconstruction, it is of enduring value as a historical account of Southern Peruvian Quechua.

Rowe's article served as the basis of the Southern Peruvian portions of two later, family-wide historical studies, which I shall review more briefly. The first full-scale comparative work in Quechua was carried out independently by Gary Parker (1963) and Alfredo Torero (1964), who arrived at similar, largely compatible results. Each proposed to group the Quechua languages into two main branches, which divide the Central Peruvian languages from those spoken to the north and the south.

Both men recognized the importance of the Central Quechua varieties for reconstructing proto-Quechua. Their reconstruction of proto-Quechua show it to resemble the Central Quechua languages more closely than the Peripheral. Parker and Torero assume that Southern Peruvian Quechua is innovative in several respects, including morphologically, in the acquisition of distinctive ejectives and aspirates, in the loss of an archaic distinction between two sibilants (reconstructed as *s and *ʃ), in the loss of an earlier distinction between two affricates (*č and *ç̌), and in the erosion of consonantal endings.

Torero and Parker disagree on the chronology and genetic depth of the innovations.[4] Parker (1963, 1969b) proposes that ejectives and aspirates were borrowed into a stage of Peripheral Quechua that is the ancestor of the modern Ecuadorian and Southern Quechua varieties ("Ecuadorian-South"), but does not include the Peripheral Quechua varieties spoken in Cajamarca or Amazonas. According to Parker, they subsequently merged in Ayacucho-Chanka and Argentine, and partly merged in Ecuadorian. Parker (1969b: 271) also attributes the loss of the distinction between the two palatal affricates to "Ecuadorian-South." The loss of the sibilant distinction, which (as we see in chapter 7) was still recorded during the sixteenth and seventeenth centuries, is described as an independent innovation in each of the Southern Quechua languages. The erosions of consonantal endings are also treated as independent innovations in Bolivian and Cuzco-Collao Quechua. Torero (1964), on the other hand, treats the ejectives and aspirates as an areal feature introduced into some parts of Southern Quechua and reflected in Ecuadorian by an overlay of influence from the Inka lingua franca. The merger of proto-Quechua *ç̌ > *č is attributed to the same stage as in Parker's reconstruction, although Torero (1964: 463) also suggests that the affricate merger is areal. The loss of the sibilant distinction is also described in areal terms by Torero. The erosions of consonantal endings are treated as innovations in Cuzco-Collao (1964: 464).

Parker presents his material within a rigorously conceived "tree" model, in which the Peripheral Quechua languages are subgrouped by means of shared innovations. A careful reading of Parker's text, however, produces several contradictory subgroupings of the Southern languages. I have deliberately avoided presenting Parker's and Torero's accounts of Southern Quechua in terms of subgrouping by shared innovation. Let me justify that decision with two examples of contradictions that would be produced by the strict use of shared innovations to subgroup Southern Quechua.

Both Parker and Torero attribute the unconditional merger of the proto-Quechua affricates to a stage of Ecuadorian-Southern unity. For Parker, this was the same stage at which glottalization and aspiration were acquired. For Torero, only a subset of the dialects that lost the affricate distinction acquired glottalization and aspiration. If shared innovation is rigorously followed as a criterion for subgrouping, then the varieties with ejectives and aspirates would form a subgroup of the varieties with the loss of the affricate distinction. But Torero (1964: 464) provides evidence that the older affricate distinction is partly reflected in the modern distribution of ejectives (see chapter 7). In order for this to be the case, the affricate distinction would have had to be lost *after* ejectives and aspirates came into Southern Quechua, that is, at a later stage than a strict subgrouping by means of shared innovations would suggest. Torero himself avoids this paradox by treating both innovations as chronologically unordered areal phenomena. Another problem is offered by the merger of the sibilants. The sibilant merger is attested in all of the Southern Quechua varieties. If subgrouping by shared innovation were followed consistently, the merger of sibilants would identify Southern Quechua as a genetic subgroup. But the sibilant distinction is attested historically until the end of the seventeenth century (chapter 7), long after the loss of Southern Quechua unity. Neither Parker nor Torero proposes a subgrouping on this basis even though it would be called for methodologically.

The Sound Pattern of Common Southern Peruvian Quechua

The paradigmatic segmental inventory in figure 5.3 may be reconstructed for Common Southern Peruvian Quechua. (I have placed the ejectives and aspirates between brackets to indicate their problem status.) The distributions of Common Southern Peruvian Quechua segments are reconstructed on the basis of a "minimum common denominator" principle. When a feature or process is attested for both modern varieties and not specifically ruled out by written evidence, I assume that it was present in the common language. The canonical syllable structure was CV(C) with the initial consonant slot filled by a glottal catch for phonemically vowel-initial words. Contextual variation of vowels was roughly the same as in modern Cuzco-Collao except that: (1) the modern processes that raise vowels adjacent to *y* were absent, and (2) the rule that lowers high vowels adjacent to a uvular was narrower in application. (In addition, certain morphologically governed vowel alternations and morpheme fusions either have expanded in application or were introduced since Common Southern Peruvian Quechua.) Glides were derived from underlying vowels as in both of the modern varieties.

Figure 5.3

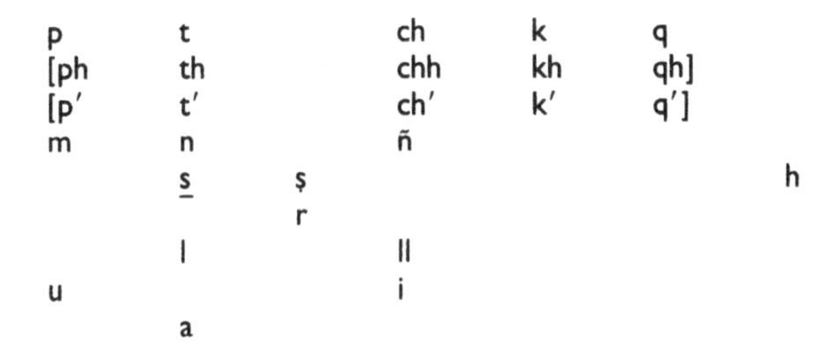

The syllable-final consonants were reconstructed as they appear in modern Ayacucho-Chanka Quechua. All of the nonejective and non-aspirated stops occurred at the ends of syllables as stops with the single possible exception of the uvular. It is impossible to tell from colonial texts whether it had become a fricative.[5] Nasals other than *n* occurred at the ends of syllables; *ñ* was restricted to prepalatal position;[6] *n* was realized as [ŋ] before glides, nasals, and laterals; *r* was realized as [ɹ] word-finally; *ll* depalatalized before the alveolar series; *l* was infrequent.

Three areas are especially significant for understanding the history of Southern Peruvian Quechua.

Sibilants As Rowe first observed, until the end of the seventeenth century, Southern Peruvian Quechua had two sibilants, which have merged unconditionally in the modern dialects. The phonetic nature of the sibilants and the course followed by their merger is discussed in chapter 7.

Ejectives and aspirates I have already discussed the ejectives and aspirates in the context of contact between Southern Quechua and the Jaqi/Aru languages (chapter 2). Ejectives and aspirates appear only in the Southern Quechua languages, including Southern Peruvian Quechua, although there are reflexes of aspirates in some Northern Quechua languages; there are none in Central Quechua. Reconstruction of the ejectives and aspirates is problematic no matter how shallow the time frame. Of the two major dialects of Southern Peruvian Quechua, only Cuzco-Collao Quechua has ejective and aspirate stops; Ayacucho-Chanka Quechua lacks them. As we have seen, the evidence that Ayacucho-Chanka Quechua ever had these features is slim. The ejectives and aspirates are irregular even *within* Cuzco-Collao Quechua. The ejectives and aspirates are discussed in chapter 8.

Erosion of consonantal endings As we have already seen, the phonological system of Cuzco-Collao Quechua has been transformed by a series of weakenings and mergers of consonants at the ends of syllables. The weakenings and mergers of syllable-final consonants, discussed in chapters 9 and 10, account for much of the dialectal diversity in modern Cuzco-Collao.

In the following chapter I turn to some of the problems involved in using written sources as evidence of the history of the language.

6 Reading Colonial Texts

Southern Peruvian Quechua has a written literature of a depth and scope that is rivaled only by Mexicano (Nahuatl) and Quiché among Native American languages. This literature includes systematic linguistic observations, in the form of grammars and dictionaries, from as early as 1560; collections of sermons, catechisms, and other religious materials, some of them stylistically quite elegant, beginning in the 1580s; Christian hymns, beginning around 1600; indigenous ritual texts and songs, recorded beginning less than twenty years after the European invasion; versified secular and religious dramas, beginning in the seventeenth century; and lexical notes on the language almost from the time of the conquest. In addition, there is a single corpus of Andean myth, written entirely in Southern Peruvian Quechua, from the early seventeenth century. The four-volume *Bibliographie des langues aymará et kičua,* by Paul Rivet and Georges de Créqui-Montfort, lists almost 5,000 items from 1560 until 1955, the overwhelming majority of which are in or concern Southern Peruvian Quechua.[1]

These materials document the changes in the language from the time of the European invasion until today. To a lesser extent, they also document changes in Quechua rhetoric and verbal art and provide the source material for a socially sensitive literary history of a people who are themselves without writing. For example, the songs included by Felipe Guaman Poma de Ayala in his *Primer nueva corónica i buẽ gobierno* (1615) are different in formal structure from modern Quechua folksong (Mannheim 1986). Both are semantically regulated rather than prosodically regulated, but the songs included in the *Nueva corónica* have a more complex and open texture than their modern counterparts. Similarly, the works of the eighteenth-century Quechua literary renaissance reveal the fantasies and social anxieties of the landowning elites of the provincial highlands, played out in their attempts to find a source of social and political legitimacy in the Andes, rather than in distant Lima or even more distant Spain.

The written sources in Quechua are not quite a "vision of the vanquished." Rather, they were shaped by the colonial social and political circumstances in which they were written. Most were written for European purposes: grammars and dictionaries as guides to the language of the conquered; collections of sermons for priests whose Quechua was not sufficient to compose the sermons themselves; an official catechism to avoid inadvertently introducing heretical doctrines because of poor translation; hymns to the European god; reports on the customs and practices of the conquered. And after independence: official decrees announcing independence from Spain; schoolbooks with European-style animal stories; expensive modern editions of colonial-era texts. Most were also written by Spanish speakers, or by bilingual mestizos whose primary language was Spanish. No texts were ever written by monolingual Quechua speakers, and very few by speakers who did not acquire Quechua as a second or later language.

Throughout the colonial period, first-language Quechua speakers were legally barred from the two professions in which a Spanish-derived indigenous scribal practice might be established, priest and notary (*escribano*). Thus, there was no indigenous scribal tradition, not even one derived from Spanish orthography, as there was in colonial Mexico. Moreover, although many of the sixteenth- and seventeenth-century Quechua writers were familiar with each other's work, there was no effort to standardize the writing system. Colonial writers largely fended for themselves.

For the purposes of using writings in Quechua as evidence of the spoken language, this situation offers both advantages and disadvantages. The absence of standardization and of a native scribal tradition means that, for the most part, written texts in Quechua are good witnesses of the ways in which it was spoken at the time the texts were written. Quechua writers were generally not bound to a tradition of writing, nor to a written literature in Quechua. Instead, they adapted the Spanish alphabet and orthographic conventions to writing Quechua, often in their own ways. They did not force the written language to conform to written prescriptions, especially to spelling conventions; rather, they wrote Quechua as it sounded to them. The absence of an indigenous scribal tradition means that we can observe the progress of sound changes without the hindrance of archaisms in spelling.

Many of the colonial sources are also useful for studying morphology and syntax for much the same reason. Since grammarians had no models for many Quechua grammatical processes and categories in classical grammar, they were forced to construct realistic descriptions of the ways in which the language was actually used, as best they could. The descriptions of the Quechua distinction between the inclusive and exclusive person in the grammar by Domingo de Santo Tomás (1560a) and in the annotations to the *Doctrina christiana* of the Third Council of Lima (1584) are the very model of clarity and provide genuine insight into the ways in which these categories were used by Quechua speakers. Similarly, Gonçález Holguín's description of verbal derivation in his *Arte* (1607) was far more sensitive to the complexities of meaning of these categories than most modern descriptions. It is true, though, that most verbal and nominal inflectional categories, especially tense, aspect, and case, were generally described by colonial grammarians in rigid Latinesque terms. The collections of sermons are eloquent testimony to formal Quechua rhetoric, which their writers did their best to imitate. These must also be used with caution, since, to different degrees, the writers model Quechua syntax and style on Spanish. The influences of Spanish aesthetics and style are even more pronounced in formal verbal art, such as the seventeenth-century hymns and the eighteenth-century versified dramas.

The fact that Quechua was written in terms of Spanish orthographic conventions, mostly by people who did not speak Quechua as a first language, also had a clear disadvantage: written Quechua was warped by the fact that it was filtered through a differently constructed linguistic system. Written Quechua does not reflect what the writers heard, but rather what they *thought* they heard, in terms of the Spanish system to which their perceptions were attuned. At certain critical points, we are thwarted in our efforts to understand even the distortion itself because the exact nature of the Spanish system is in doubt. For many years, the distinction between the colonial Quechua sibilants withstood analysis because the Spanish sibilants in colonial America were also phonetically puzzling (see chapter 7).

In this chapter, I explore some general problems in using colonial texts as evidence. I mean "colonial texts" in a double sense: texts from the colonial period, to be sure, but also texts that were produced in a colonial situation, texts that were written in a colonized language by the colonizers. Since my main purpose is to use these texts as evidence of phonological change, I concentrate on problems of interpretation that arise from the mismatch between the sound patterns of Spanish and Southern Peruvian Quechua. I then give a brief description, in chronological order, of each of the sources I used as witnesses to the historical transformation of Southern Peruvian Quechua. The descriptions include biographical information on the authors, if known, and certain linguistic characteristics: evidence bearing on the sibilant problem, their treatment of aspirate and ejective stops, the extent to which they show weakening of consonants at the end of syllables, and other morphological and lexical characteristics that situate the sources with respect to one another. The written sources are treated as *witnesses* of a historical dialect of Southern Peruvian Quechua. When several sources reflect a single historical dialect, they are treated as a single witness. Conversely, when a scribe records more than one historical dialect in different texts, each text is treated as a separate witness. The written sources are cited by a witness number corresponding to the description of sources later in this chapter. For example, Juan de Aguilar's 1690 grammar is cited as "witness 9."

Exuberances and Deficiencies

In an important essay on the nature of cross-linguistic and cross-cultural interpretation, Alton L. Becker (1982) argues that all such interpretation is at once exuberant and deficient. Exuberances and deficiencies arise whenever there are differences between patterns in the interpreter's language and the language being interpreted. An interpretation is exuberant whenever the categories of the interpreter's language require something to be added to the original in order to be intelligible to the interpreter. An interpretation is deficient whenever the categories of the interpreter's language fail to account for significant patterning in the original. According to Becker, exuberances and defiencies are not a matter of interpretation badly done. Rather, they are the condition of all cross-linguistic interpretation, at any points at which the categories of one language do not correspond to the categories of another.

Consider the following sentence in Cuzco-Collao Quechua, from the autobiography of Gregorio Condori Mamani (1977: 25), with its closest English equivalent:

(i)

Chaypaqsi *extranjero* Mama Killata rin.
For that, the foreigners went to the moon.

There are several points at which the Quechua sentence and its English "equivalent" do not correspond. In Southern Peruvian Quechua, a speaker must distinguish between events that he is personally willing to vouch for and hearsay. The first word in the Quechua sentence has the reportive suffix *-si,* to mark the narrated event as hearsay. There is no corresponding grammatical distinction in English, even though we can translate it with a phrase like *it is said that* or *they say.* But the suffixes that mark these categories are ubiquitous. If they were translated consistently, most declarative sentences would begin with either *it is said that* or *I vouch that.* The result would resemble a translation from Japanese in which all honorifics were translated with the word *honorable,* or a translation from Italian in which all gender was translated with the words *male* and *female.* Example (i) was hearsay; the translation was deficient in that the category *hearsay* could not be expressed with the same subtlety in English as in Quechua.

Another deficiency of the translation is that Condori calls the moon *Mama Killa* 'Mother Moon', in a habitual, ordinary sense. But to translate it as 'Mother Moon' would give the English a poetic or at least a euphemistic sense that does not reflect the ordinariness of the original.

The translation is exuberant as well. The Quechua distinction between singular and plural is not obligatory; its English counterpart is. In the Quechua *extranjero* (from Spanish) is not marked as plural, but it is understood to be plural from the linguistic context. The translation is exuberant in requiring a plural where the original has none, because, otherwise, *foreigner* could only be understood as singular. Quechua makes no distinction between definite and indefinite, whereas English requires all countable nouns to have an article (at least in certain syntactic contexts) and requires a choice between a definite and an indefinite article. There are no articles in the Quechua, and they must be added to the English translation. Finally, the Quechua sentence is unmarked for tense. It is understood from the context that the event took place in the past. But in English *For that, the foreigners go to the moon* would have a different meaning from the Quechua. It would suggest that the foreigners habitually go the moon or could be the weary response of someone who was being told a tall tale about foreigners who go to the moon and find nothing: *For that, foreigners go to the moon!* But in Quechua it was a definite, past action. The English translation requires a past tense.

Undoubtedly, I could find a way to make up for the deficiencies of the translation by using long technical paraphrases. It is more difficult to work around the exuberances of English. The point, though, is that exuberances and deficiencies of one kind or another are inherent in any cross-linguistic interpretation. I spoke of the exuberances and deficiencies of the English translation rather than of the Quechua, because I was trying to express a Quechua sentence in English. The shoe could as easily have been on the other foot.

In working with colonial Quechua texts, there are at least two levels of exuberances and deficiencies that must be accounted for. First, there are those brought into the text by the Spanish-speaking scribe, who interprets Quechua patterns in terms of Spanish, even when he writes in Quechua. Second, there are the exuberances and deficiencies of an English speaker (or a modern Spanish speaker) interpreting a text written four hundred years ago for one set of purposes, today, with an entirely different set of purposes in mind. In the following section, I examine some of the problems interpreting several short Quechua texts from the sixteenth and seventeenth centuries. I am especially interested in the differences between the sound pattern of Quechua and the sound pattern and writing conventions of Spanish.

Consider the following passage from a seventeenth-century manual for priests in Quechua parishes, Juan Pérez Bocanegra's *Ritual formulario e institución de curas* (1631; witness 8). Pérez was one of the great colonial stylists of the language and had an intimate familiarity with everyday life in rural Cuzco. The passage, on dream interpretation, is in a question-and-answer format designed for use in a confession (1631: 143).[2] In the *Ritual formulario* it is preceded by a Spanish paraphrase.

(ii)

Moçcoscaiquicta Iñecchu canqui? allintam moçconi manallictam moçconi, moçcoscaimã tupu chayapuan ñispa ñecchu canqui? Pimampas villacchu canqui, vnanchapuay moçcoscaita ñispa Puñuspa moçcoiñijquipi chacacta purispa, raquipacmi moçconi ñispa ñecchu canqui?

Pérez Bocanegra represented his questions as continuous running text, in two columns, following printer's conventions for Spanish. But his Quechua is highly stylized. The printing conventions obscure the Quechua rhetorical conventions that Pérez Bocanegra followed, including extensive grammatical parallelism and quotation. Here is the same passage, rewritten in lines to reflect the rhetorical structure implicit in Pérez Bocanegra's Quechua. A line-by-line English translation follows.

(ii′)

1 Moçcoscaiquicta Iñecchu canqui?
allintam moçconi
manallictam moçconi,
moçcoscaimã tupu chayapuan ñispa
5 ñecchu canqui?
Pimampas villacchu canqui,
vnanchapuay moçcoscaita ñispa
Puñuspa moçcoiñijquipi
chacacta purispa,
10 raquipacmi moçconi ñispa
ñecchu canqui?

1 Do you accept your dreams?
"I dream well,
I don't dream well,
What I have dreamt has arrived to me in measure"
5 Do you say it?
Do you tell someone,
"interpret me my dream"?
While asleep, in your dream
crossing a bridge
10 "it's for separation I dreamed?"
Do you say it?

The word *Iñecchu* (line 1) is a semantic exuberance, a neologism intended to translate Spanish *creer* 'to believe'. *Iñiy*, however, is made up of an interjection I (which Pérez marked by capitalizing it) followed by the verb *ñiy* 'to say' (Tercer Concilio Limense 1584: 77v; Cerrón-Palomino 1987a: 199–200), literally, 'to say *I*; to say "yes"; or to accept'.[3] In Pérez Bocanegra's Spanish and in our English, belief is an inner state that can be held by an individual (*Iñiy* is also used to translate the *Credo*); *Iñiy*, however, is a social transaction.[4] *Iñiy* never took root as a verb outside of a religious context. It is used in the *Credo* even today. José Gregorio Castro (1961 [1906]: 7), for example, wrote it as *I-ñinim*, using the hyphen to indicate that it is not a single verb.

Pérez Bocanegra's orthography is exuberant in distinguishing *e* from *i* and *o* from *u*, even though the distinction is predictable from context: *ñispa* but *ñecchu*. Pérez filtered the Quechua vowels through the five-vowel Spanish system. This is useful, because most midvowels occur adjacent to uvular stops (e.g., *ñecchu*, the second *o* in *moçconi*), and he did not distinguish the uvulars from the velars. The deficiencies of his writing system are as follows.

Ejectives and aspirates The three-way distinction among ejective, aspirate, and plain voiceless stops is not represented at all in Pérez Bocanegra. This might suggest that Pérez was writing in a dialect that lacked ejectives and aspirates, but internal evidence indicates that the text was written in Cuzco-Collao Quechua, which did distinguish the consonant types.

Velars and Uvulars Southern Peruvian Quechua distinguishes velar consonants from uvular. Pérez Bocanegra underdifferentiates this distinction as well, writing both with the Spanish symbols *c* and *qu*, as in *canqui* (kanki), *chacacta* (chakakta) but *villacchu* (willaqchu) and *moçconi* (muzquni). (Normalizations are between parentheses.) The Quechua vowels are lowered and backed adjacent to a uvular (chapter 4; Rowe 1950: 139; Cusihuamán 1976a: 48–51; Esquivel 1979). Thus, Pérez Bocanegra's overdifferentiation of the vowels allows some (but not all) of the uvulars to be identified in his orthography.

Finally, let me make two more observations about the writing system in the *Ritual formulario.* Pérez Bocanegra distinguishes two sibilants, *ç* (written as *c* before *i* and *e,* and sometimes as *z,* syllable initially) and *s* (written *ss* between vowels). The letter *v* is an orthographic variant of *u,* at the beginning of a word, as in *villacchu* (willaqchu) and *vnanchapuay* (unanchapuway).

As a second example, consider the following passage from a song included in Felipe Guaman Poma de Ayala's *Primer nueva corónica i buẽ gobierno.* Guaman Poma was an early-seventeenth-century local-level indigenous headman, who composed a letter of protest to the king of Spain, Philip III, running well over a thousand pages of text and drawings (Ossio 1977, 1978; Adorno 1978, 1980, 1986; Husson 1985; López-Baralt 1988). Guaman Poma argued for restoration of native lands and traditional native rule within the Spanish empire, and for strict physical separation between the colonists and native peoples. The *Nueva corónica* includes a long narrative history of the New World, describing pre-invasion Peru within the framework of a Christian universal history, an equally lengthy and detailed denunciation of social conditions after the European invasion, and the author's prescriptions for a just social order.

Guaman Poma was a first-language speaker of Quechua who was literate in Spanish and was familiar with the major religious and historical publications on the New World. He followed the conventions for a printed book in assembling his manuscript. He wrote on both sides of the page and included the first word of the next page at the end of a page to signal the continuity. He even justified his handwritten prose on the right margin. His text is written in a Spanish that follows Quechua patterns of rhetorical organization, leaving much of his writing opaque to modern Spanish-speaking readers. There are long Quechua passages inserted within his Spanish text, for several reasons: to quote songs associated with festivals, to say something politically charged, to make fun of the sermons of colonial priests, or to describe the interactions between Native Peruvians and their conquerors. Guaman Poma was from Lucanas, a province of the modern Department of Ayacucho in which Ayacucho-Chanka Quechua is spoken today. He describes himself as descended from the Yarovillca Allauca Huánuco, which perhaps associates him with another region of the Andean highlands as well, but by and large he seems to have spoken a seventeenth-century Ayacucho-Chanka Quechua (Urioste 1980: xxii–xxiii). He was enormously sensitive to dialect and style differences in Quechua, a sensitivity that is reflected in some of the Quechua passages of his chronicle (Urioste

1980: xxvi–xxvii). The full range of variability in his Quechua still needs to be sorted out. The following passage is taken from a song included in one of his festival narratives.[5]

(iii)

unoy uiquellam apariuan yacuy parallam pusariuã / chay llicllayquita rycuycuspa chay acsoyquita cauaycus / pa • mananam pachapas chiciancho • tuta riccharipti / pas • mananatacmi pacha pacarincho • camca coya cam / pas•[ca] mananachi yuyariuanquicho • cay sancaypi poma / [a]toc micouaptin • cay pinaspi • uichicasca quicasca tiapti • palla /

Guaman Poma's Spanish narrative (not reproduced here) is as highly stylized as Pérez Bocanegra's Quechua. His Spanish follows oral Quechua rhetorical conventions.[6] The Quechua is semantically regulated verse, which I have rewritten in lines to reflect the poetic structure of the passage, along with a line-by-line English translation.

(iii')

unoy uiquellam apariuan	My water, just tears, is brought to me,
yacuy parallam pusariuã	My water, just rain, is led to me,
chay llicllayquita rycuycuspa	Looking at that shawl of yours
chay acsoyquita cauaycus / pa •	Gazing at that skirt of yours
mananam pachapas chiciancho •	Though the world no longer enters evening
tuta riccharipti / pas •	As by night I awaken
mananatacmi pacha pacarincho •	The world even no longer dawns
camca coya cam / pas•[ca]	You, you still are *qoya*
mananachi yuyariuanquicho •[7]	Perhaps you no longer remember me
cay sancaypi	In this prison of mine
poma / [a]toc micouaptin •	Where the puma-fox eat me
cay pinaspi •	In this captivity
uichicasca	Separated,
quicasca	Out of reach,
tiapti •	As I remain
palla	Gather[ed?]

I arrived at the line divisions on the basis of two kinds of semantic parallelism: grammatical parallelism, such as *mananam pachapas chiciancho* •// *mananatacmi pacha pacarincho* •// *mananachi yuyariuanquicho* • 'Though the world no longer enters evening // The world even no longer dawns // Perhaps you no longer remember me', in alternating lines; and semantic couplets, such as *unoy uiquellam apariuan / yacuy parallam pusariuã* 'My water, just tears, is brought to me, / My water, just rain, is led to me'. "Semantic couplets" are a peculiarly Quechua poetic device in which two lines that are otherwise identical morphologically and syntactically are bound together by the alternation of two semantically related word-stems. The stems are a semantic *minimal pair;* they differ by a single semantic property, and there is no word-stem with a value for that property midway between them. It is especially striking that metrical structure is not a defining characteristic of the poetic line.

Guaman Poma used a raised dot ("•") to indicate line divisions. The raised dots appear less frequently than the line divisions that were determined on the basis of internal poetic criteria, but the raised dots never appear anyplace that it is not also a line break by the internal criteria. Guaman Poma's raised dots and other orthographic devices such as brackets, dashes, and commas partly compensated for the deficiencies of the Spanish printing conventions he chose to follow in his manuscript. I would argue that Guaman Poma's use of these devices to indicate line divisions—ones that are otherwise lost in the Spanish printing conventions that he followed—more than justifies restoring the line structure in a modern transcription.

The fact that Guaman Poma was a first-language speaker of Quechua does not spare him from the exuberances and deficiencies required by the conventions of Spanish writing. Guaman Poma's orthography is exuberant and deficient in many of the same ways as Pérez Bocanegra's. Guaman Poma writes with the five Spanish vowels, although it is evident from his Spanish that he was unable to distinguish them systematically. He frequently interchanges the Spanish mid vowels *e* and *o* with their high counterparts, *i* and *u* (Urioste 1980: xxix). Like Pérez, Guaman Poma uses *e* and *o* adjacent to a uvular, although not consistently, as in *uiquellam* (wiqillam) and *coya* (quya), and *acsoyquita* (aqsuykita). He does not distinguish the uvulars from velars orthographically, although they were present in his speech, but uses *c* and *qu* for them nondistinctively, as in *llicllayquita* (llikllaykita) and *camca* (qamqa). He does not distinguish palatal from alveolar nasals, as in *mananam* (manañam); nasal consonants are written with a tilde at the end of a line, as in *pusariuã* (pusariwan). Guaman Poma does not distinguish the sibilants consistently either in his Spanish or in his Quechua, except in a parody of the priest Cristóbal de Molina (see witness 2).

The preceding short texts from Pérez Bocanegra's *Ritual formulario* and Guaman Poma's *Nueva corónica* are especially useful to illuminate some of the technical difficulties in interpreting colonial Quechua texts, in that these two men were exemplary in their knowledge of the language and of rural life and undoubtedly showed the greatest care and sensitivity in constructing their texts. Guaman Poma, as we saw, was a first-language speaker of Quechua; Pérez Bocanegra was one of the most skilled interpreters of his time and had deep, firsthand experience in the rural Quechua-speaking countryside outside of Cuzco. The exuberances and deficiencies of their texts, written representations, and translations attest to the inherent difficulties of translation, especially across languages as structurally different from each other as Southern Peruvian Quechua and Spanish. The difficulties of translation are most striking at the points at which the structural patterns of the two languages correspond least, for example, when Pérez Bocanegra is forced to construct a Quechua neologism to translate the Spanish verb *creer* 'to believe', or when Guaman Poma cannot fit the Quechua vowels to the Spanish orthographic system, or indeed, fit the Spanish vowels to his native Quechua system in a consistent manner. In the following section, I summarize the main stumbling blocks to using colonial texts as phonological evidence.

Deficiencies: The Ejectives and Aspirates, Uvulars and Velars

Quechua orthographies based on the Spanish writing system were inadequate to the task of representing Quechua phonologically. This problem was explicitly addressed by some colonial writers who either deliberately ignored these distinctions (Tercer Concilio Limense) or addressed them by inventing special characters ad hoc. Two well-known sites of ambiguity or orthographic underdifferentiation—the uvular/velar opposition and the distinction among ejectives, aspirates, and plain voiceless stops in Southern Peruvian Quechua—were pointed out by Garcilaso de la Vega (1609: II, iv), who complained that the orthographic confusion led Europeans to construct fantastic etymologies and, in turn, to misinterpret Andean culture: " . . . *huaca* . . . with the last syllable pronounced at the top of the palate means 'idol' . . . and is a noun that does not permit verbal derivation in order to say 'commit idolatry'."[8]

Garcilaso (1609: II, v) continued with the observation that "the same expression *huaca,* with the last syllable pronounced deep inside the throat, becomes a verb which means 'to cry'. Thus Spanish historians who didn't realize the differences said, 'the Indians enter their temples to sacrifice crying and showing grief; that's what *huaca* means.' . . . The truth is that the different signification results only from the different pronunciation without changing a letter or an accent."[9]

Garcilaso also recounted having met a Dominican in Córdova who had held a chair of Quechua in Peru for four years but was unaware of the Southern Quechua distinction among ejective, aspirate, and plain voiceless stops. The Dominican pointed out that the same word, *pacha* (Cuzco-Collao [pacha]), that denoted 'world', 'universe', and 'sky' was also used for clothing (Cuz. [p'acha]). Wrote Garcilaso, "I showed him the pronunciation of this noun and others *viva voce;* it can't be taught any other way" (1609: II, v).[10]

The Southern Quechua ejectives and aspirates were the orthographic Waterloo of colonial grammarians. Of the texts that explicitly were written in or about colonial Cuzco-Collao Quechua, none adequately and consistently represented the distinctions among ejective, aspirate, and plain stops until the nineteenth century. The earliest works that can be securely identified as Cuzco-Collao Quechua, the *Cathecismo* and *Sermones* of the Tercer Concilio Limense, intentionally omitted indication of glottalization and aspiration in an effort to strip the sermons of "exquisite and obscure ways of speaking" peculiar to Cuzco (Tercer Concilio Limense 1584: 74r).[11] Moreover, the authors of the *Doctrina christiana y cathecismo* were not up to the task of "looking for new characters to differentiate them" (Tercer Concilio Limense 1584: 75r). The Quechua annotations to the *Doctrina* indicate that by the 1580s such orthographic devices as doubling stops, adding *h* to them, and the letter *k* were used to write the sounds that Spanish lacked. But the authors lamented the fact that the special symbols had not been standardized. As we saw, Pérez Bocanegra also chose to ignore the ejectives and aspirates, with a few rare exceptions. Aguilar's late-seventeenth-century grammar used a special symbol, *cc,* for the uvular, but made no indication of glottalization and aspiration.

Gonçález Holguín, on the other hand, used a variety of special characters including doubling the character to indicate both glottalization and aspiration, *h* to indicate aspiration, *cc* for the plain uvular stop, and *k* for uvular aspirates and fricatives. Unfortunately, Gonçález Holguín was inconsistent in his use of special characters, frequently writing the same stem two or three different ways. When he used double *cc* or *qqu,* he seemed to be indicating only that the stop was not a plain velar stop, but not whether it was ejective or aspirated, or any of the three uvulars. The *k* indicated that a uvular was not a plain voiceless stop, but not whether it was an ejective, aspirate, or uvular fricative. Nor does the lack of a doubled letter necessarily indicate a plain voiceless stop. The same special symbols, though more inconsistently, appear in a number of manuscripts more or less contemporary to Gonçález Holguín's grammar and dictionary. All of these manuscripts seem to use the special characters even more inconsistently than Gonçález Holguín did.

In some cases, it can be determined whether a word has glottalization from an epenthetic *h* that appears at the beginning of the word. In Southern Quechua a word structure constraint restricts glottalization and aspiration to the initial oral stop in the word (chapter 8). Words beginning with a vowel were preceded by a predictable glottal catch. But words preceded by the glottal catch that also contained an ejective violated the constraint; the glottal catch was replaced by an epenthetic *h* in such instances. Epenthetic *h*, then, can be used as evidence for the glottalization feature in those orthographic systems in which *h* is used consistently. This can often be determined independently. For example, Gonçález Holguín was very consistent in using nonepenthetic *h*. Thus, when epenthetic *h* does not appear on vowel-initial stems in which glottalization is attested, for example, *açuttacuni* 'to whip oneself (first person)' (< Sp *açotar; tt* is evidence of glottalization), it should mean that the word did not have an epenthetic *h*. In contrast, the anonymous versified drama *Usca Paucar* was inconsistent about initial *h;* in *Usca Paucar* the presence or absence of an initial *h* would be meaningless as evidence for glottalization.

Exuberances: The Vowels

Colonial writers overdifferentiated the vowels, assigning the three Quechua vowels to five Spanish vowel symbols. As we saw with Guaman Poma, they were sometimes inconsistent in their use of the symbols for the Spanish high (*i, u*) and mid vowels (*e, o*). Phonetically, the Quechua vowels do not correspond directly to any of the Spanish vowels (see chapter 4), although there are two phonetic processes by which the Quechua high vowels [ι] and [υ] are lowered to the approximate area of the Spanish mid vowels. All three Quechua vowels are lowered and backed adjacent to a uvular. (A uvularized nasal or an *r* may come after the lowered vowel, but before the uvular.) The vowels are also lowered by a prosodic tendency to lax and centralize vowels late in a word. In either situation, the Quechua vowels occurring in the mid region were usually written with a Spanish mid vowel symbol. As I have already pointed out, this provides a partial corrective for uvular/velar underdifferentiation since high vowel symbols adjacent to a *c* or *qu* indicate that it is nonuvular.

In order to reconstruct the sound patterns described in colonial-era written sources, then, one must take into account not only the document itself, but also the author's phonological pattern and orthographic conventions. The pattern incongruities between the language that is being described—Southern Quechua—and the language in which it is written—Spanish—impose exuberances and deficiencies on the description. There is no way in which the Quechua sound pattern can be restored mechanically; interpretation of colonial written sources requires knowledge of the author's linguistic background, the audience for the material, and the circumstances under which it is written.

Written Sources

The written sources span the period from the late sixteenth century until the late nineteenth century. These include priests' manuals, collections of sermons, and other religious literature, Quechua texts cited in early chronicles written by speakers of the language, grammars and dictionaries, and literary works, especially versified dramas. In each case, I sampled several running passages from the text (in the case of dictionaries and grammars, running sequences of entries) and charted out the changes witnessed by the texts. The sample included a number of republican-era texts, but my efforts were concentrated on the colonial-era materials, for which the evidence was sketchier and more difficult to interpret. The colonial-era materials included the following: Santo Tomás 1560a and 1560b, Molina "el Cuzqueño" 1574; Tercer Concilio Limense 1584 and 1585; the anonymous *Vocabulario* of 1586; the anonymous manuscript that begins *Runo yn° niscap machoncuna* . . . (Anonymous, Huarochirí, early seventeenth century); an anonymous fragment of notarial records from 1605–1608; Gonçález Holguín 1607 and 1608; Santa Cruz Pachacuti Yamqui 1615; Pérez Bocanegra 1631; Aguilar 1690; Centeno n.d.; and the anonymous versified dramas *Usca Paucar* (Sahuaraura codex), and *Ollanta* (Sahuaraura and Justiniani codices). I also sampled approximately twenty other colonial-era sources and an equal number of texts from the nineteenth and the first half of the twentieth centuries.

The seventy years or so following the Third Council of Lima (Tercer Concilio Limense) (1583) represent a high point for Quechua literary production. This period coincides with a relatively liberal language policy, influenced by the Council of Trent and its calls for proselytization in the vernacular. The linguistic work of this era centered around making the former Inka lingua franca accessible to priests in native parishes (*doctrinas*). Along with dictionaries and grammars, vernacular priests' manuals were prepared for parish priests, who often lacked the linguistic skills to hear confession or preach in the indigenous languages. Such manuals include short analytic catechisms (*cartillas*), synthetic *catecismos,* and collections of sermons. The sermons are especially rich sources of information on rhetorical form. The Tercer Concilio's sermons, for example, were punctuated in such a way that phrasing and intonation in formal rhetorical style could be read from the printed page, so that even a Quechua neophyte could sound like a skilled orator. The Tercer Concilio's *Sermones,* the collections of sermons by Avendaño (1649) and Avilá (1648a, b), Pérez Bocanegra's *Ritual formulario,* and other similar texts (Oré 1598, 1607; Jurado 1649; Molina 1649) also supply information on the process by which Roman Catholic doctrine and religious symbolism were incorporated into indigenous ritual practices.

Quechua texts and lexical material appear in colonial secular reports as well, although the linguistic quality of these materials is uneven.[12] Those reports that were written by mestizos and others who were in close contact with Quechua speakers are especially interesting. The manuscripts by Cristóbal de Molina "el Cuzqueño" and Santa Cruz Pachacuti Yamqui contain short religious orations. Felipe Guaman Poma de Ayala's thousand-page letter to the king complaining about colonial social conditions includes a number of songs, satirical pastiches of Quechua religious sermons by missionary priests, occasional narrative shifts into Quechua, and lexical information. The anonymous manuscript of Huarochirí is a lengthy compilation of local mythology, written entirely in Quechua.

Although I am concerned most of all with the Quechua spoken in the former Inka capital, Cuzco, I have also used several sources of mixed or uncertain dialect provenience. Two proved especially useful, with appropriate limitations: Santo Tomás (1560a, 1560b) and the anonymous manuscript of Huarochirí. Santo Tomás worked with informants from both major branches of the Quechua family. The anonymous manuscript of Huarochirí is of uncertain dialect provenience. On the other hand, I have made only limited use of the *Nueva corónica* by Guaman Poma, who was a speaker of an Ayacucho-Chanka variety of Southern Peruvian Quechua.

I used sixteen colonial-era texts more intensively than the rest, as witnesses of historically and geographically situated dialects. Occasionally, I considered more than one text by a single author or committee of authors, such as the grammar and dictionary of Gonçález Holguín, or the catechism and sermons of the Third Council. I treated multiple texts by the same author as a single witness. On the other hand, I treated some works that are available in several versions as multiple witnesses, as in the case of the two codices of the versified drama *Ollanta*. The different codices of the dramas, regardless of whether they were different versions of the "same" work or different codices by a single scribe (Sahuaraura), represented different states of the language and so were treated as distinct sources. I refer to this set of sources collectively as the "textual sample." Three formal features of the texts are especially important: (1) ejectives and aspirates (discussed in chapter 8), (2) the status of syllable-final consonants (discussed in chapters 9 and 10), and (3) the treatment of the sibilants (discussed in chapter 7). Evidence of ejectives and aspirates is also sufficient (but not necessary) to show that the variety attested is a Southern Quechua language other than Ayacucho-Chanka Quechua. Cuzco-Collao Quechua underwent a series of weakenings and mergers of syllable-final consonants, which began before the last attestation of the sibilant distinction; these changes establish the dialect provenience and the relative chronology of the texts.

I especially relied on the following materials.

1. Domingo de Santo Tomás, o.p., *Grammatica o arte* and *Lexicon*, both from 1560

Santo Tomás (b. Seville, d. 1568) arrived in Peru in 1540 and spent most of his first five years in America on the coast and in the central highlands, though he was later to travel to Cuzco as well (Roze 1878: 157–168; Mendiburu 1934: 10, 76–79; Vargas 1947; Cisneros 1951; Porras 1951, 1986 [1962]: 32; Rivet and Créqui-Montfort 1951–1956: I, 3). Like his colleague in Chiapas, Bartolomé de las Casas, Fray Domingo was an important spokesman for Native American rights (Santo Tómas n.d.; Roze 1878: 162; Vargas Ugarte 1938: 154; Barnadas 1973: 251–255, 281, 327; Murra 1980: xviii). The *Grammatica* was written by 1550. Santo Tomás spent the five-year period from 1556 to 1561 in Italy and Spain, where he arranged for publication of the *Grammatica* and *Lexicon*. He was named bishop of Charcas (modern Bolivia, northern Argentina and northern Chile) in 1562.

Santo Tomás was aware of the dialect differences in the Quechua language family (1951 [1560a] 15–19; Cerrón-Palomino 1984: 94); he worked with informants from both the Central and Peripheral branches of the Quechua language family (Santo Tomás 1951 [1560b]: 15).[13] The *Grammatica* shows Southern inflectional morphology, and both the Central and Peripheral words for 'four', *chuzco* and *tagua*, respectively (Santo Tomás 1560b: 35v). Entries in the *Lexicon* with sibilants often appear in two forms, an [ʃ]-form, representing Central Quechua pronunciation, and an [s]-form, representing Southern pronunciation. Likewise, Santo Tomás cites both variants of the Peripheral/Central *hamuy* ~ *xamuy* ([ʃamuy]) lexical shibboleth. Another possible dialectal shibboleth is that Fray Domingo reported a single palatal stop, although it is not clear whether this reflects Spanish orthography or the merger of $\check{ç}$ > $\check{c}$ in most Peripheral languages. Palatal stops fricativize syllable-finally. Dentals appear to have fricativized sporadically in the same environment. There is no evidence of the ejectives and aspirates that are characteristic of Southern Quechua, excluding Ayacucho-Chanka Quechua. Santo Tomás systematically distinguished dorsal and apical sibilants, { ç } (= [*s*]) and { s̲ } (= [ṣ]).

Santo Tomás's *Lexicon* is essentially a listing of stems, with verbs cited in first and second person. According to Santo Tomás himself (1951 [1560a]: 14), the *Grammatica* is an approximation oriented to the practical use of Spanish speakers who required rudimentary knowledge of the language for evangelical purposes. There is evidence that Santo Tomás overregularized the inflectional paradigm (Mannheim 1982: 148ff.).

2. Cristóbal de Molina "el Cuzqueño," *Relación de las fábulas y ritos de los Yngas* (1574)

Molina (b. Baeza, Andalucía, 1529–1585), a parish priest in Cuzco and *provincial visitador eclesiástico*, was famed for his abilities in Quechua and florid rhetoric (Guaman Poma 1615: 611; Romero 1916; Porras 1943, 1986 [1962]: 349–355; Rivera 1949; Rowe 1953; Meneses 1962, 1965; Urbano 1989).[14] The *Relación* includes eleven Quechua ritual texts. These texts are important both as historical witnesses to the language and as rare examples of Inka ritual poetry. Unfortunately, the surviving manuscript found among Avila's papers is a sixteenth-century copy made by someone who did not speak Quechua (cf. Porras 1943: 97; Rowe 1953). Although the manuscript is inconsistent with respect to the sibilant distinction, the sibilants are distinguished often enough to suggest that the distinction was a feature of Molina's speech. There is independent evidence of this. The sibilant distinction in Guaman Poma's (1615: 611–612) short satire of Molina's preaching style is consistent with the sibilant entries in Gonçález Holguín (1608).

3. Tercer Concilio Limense, *Doctrina christiana y cathecismo* (1584) and *Tercero cathecismo . . . por sermones* (1585)

The linguistic materials designed by the Tercer Concilio Limense were written by committee. The council was concerned with standardization of the catechism and other religious instruction in the vernacular languages, and so charged a committee headed by José de Acosta (b. Medina, c. 1539–1600) with writing an official catechism, *cartilla,* and sermon collection that were translated into Quechua and Aymara (Acosta 1577a: V, xv, 568, 1583; Tercer Concilio Limense 1583; Anonymous 1600, I, 275, I, 285, I, 311–312, II, 17; Torres 1882: 9–10; Medina 1904: 3–36; Vargas Ugarte 1941: 141–142, 1947: 91, 1951–1954: I, 266, I, 317, III, 94ff.; Rivet and Créqui-Montfort 1951–1956: I, 10f.; Bartra 1967: 359–372; Durán 1982; García 1986). Acosta himself played a major role in writing the Spanish text (Durán 1982: 239–255; García 1986: 206–208). The Quechua translation was carried out by Juan de Balboa (d. 1591), chair of Quechua at the Cathedral of Lima, and three residents of the southern highlands. Blas Valera (b. Chachapoyas, 1551–1597) was among the ecclesiastical censors (see Mateos 1944: 48–62). It is widely believed that a manuscript catechism by the doyen of colonial Jesuit linguists, Alonso Barzana (b. Córdoba, 1527–1595), served as the basis for the Third Council's catechism. The

Doctrina consists of a twenty-page *doctrina,* a simple catechism, an extended catechism, and *plática,* all in Quechua, Aymara, and Spanish. A set of annotations explaining points of orthography and culturally sensitive translation problems is appended to the *Doctrina.* The Quechua annotations include a brief discussion of dialect variation and an explanation of the distinction between inclusive and exclusive forms in the person system.[15] A short lexicon of religious figures and untranslatable vocabulary follows. The *Cathecismo . . . por sermones* (1585) consists of thirty-one trilingual sermons. The Quechua sermons are set and punctuated so as to make it possible to "read" the rhetorical structure of the sermons.

The *Doctrina* and *Cathecismo . . . por sermones* are of a piece linguistically. Three of the four translators, Alonso de Martínez and Francisco Carrasco, both from Cuzco, and Bartolomé de Santiago (c. 1548–1589), from Arequipa, were speakers of a Cuzco-Collao-type variety of Southern Peruvian Quechua. But the committee complained about the ostentatiousness of Cuzco Quechua and settled on a simplified version that it hoped would allow the work to be of wider use. Ejectives and aspirates are therefore not marked as such in the orthography even though the translators state that they are writing in the Quechua of Cuzco. The consonant distinctions of Common Southern Peruvian Quechua are intact at the ends of syllables; none of the weakenings or mergers are attested. The Third Council distinguished the two sibilants, although they are at slight variance for the [s̲]; the *Cathecismo* uses { c } before *i* and *e* and { z } elsewhere; the *Doctrina* employs { ç } as well, syllable-initially.

4. Anonymous, Huarochirí, *Runa yn[di]o niscap machoncuna ñaupa pacha . . .* (early seventeenth century)

The Huarochirí manuscript is a book-length collection of mythology written entirely in Quechua without translation (Duviols 1966; Urioste 1973, 1982; Hartmann 1975, 1981; Taylor 1980, 1985, 1987; Salomon 1982; Acosta 1987). It was located among the papers of Francisco de Avila (b. Cuzco, d. 1647), who used it as the basis of an uncompleted report on rite and myth in the province of Huarochirí (Lima) (Avila 1608). There are several modern editions of varying quality and a morphological grammar based on it. The manuscript has been translated into Spanish, French, Latin, Polish, Dutch, and German. (An English translation by Frank Salomon and George Urioste is forthcoming.) Formal study of the text has not been carried out in sufficient detail to bring internal evidence to bear on a number of vexing problems surrounding the manuscript, including its authorship, the relationship

Figure 6.1

Huarochirí	Gonçález Holguín 1608
quimça (101r)	quimça (684) 'three'
socta (97v)	çocta (86) 'six'
canchis (81r)	canchiz (1607: 218) 'seven'
escon (64v)	yzccon (270) 'nine'
llocsi (64v)	llocsi- (215) 'to leave'
ricsi (64v)	ricci- (655) 'to recognize'
cosa (67v)	coça (361) 'husband'
sacha (106v)	çacha~hacha (74) 'brush'
çuma~sumac (64v)	çumac (89) 'beautiful'
causa- (64v)	cauça- (415) 'to live'

of the text to the language spoken in Huarochirí, and the extent to which the texts suffered stylistic deformation in the process of being put to paper. It frequently has been assumed that the language of the text is seventeenth-century Cuzco-Collao Quechua, but there is no orthographic evidence for ejectives and aspirates, and the Central word for 'four' *chusco* (f. 96r) appears alongside its Southern counterpart, *taua* (f. 64v; cf. Arguedas 1966: 14).[16] Both sibilant orthographic types { ç/z } and { s/ss } were used, but inconsistently. The sibilants are also inconsistent with other texts from the same period. Thus *sasa* appears alongside *saça* 'difficult' (f. 64v; compare Gonçález Holguín [1608: 74], *çaça*), and *sapa* is corrected on the manuscript to *çapa* 'each' (f. 64r; compare Gonçález Holguín [1608: 327, 441], *çapa*). The forms in figure 6.1 show correspondences between the Huarochirí manuscript and Gonçález Holguín. Notice that the correspondences are inconsistent.

Why are there discrepancies between the anonymous manuscript of Huarochirí and Gonçález Holguín? It appears that the Huarochirí manuscript was written by a scribe who had a single sibilant ({ ç }) Spanish system but was attempting to account for a two-sibilant native system. The discrepancy is orthographic rather than a reflection of phonological change in progress, for the merger involved a shift of { s } > { ç }, and the errors are all { ç } > { s }. It is also possible that the scribe had a single-sibilant Quechua system and was attempting to restore a lost distinction in his own speech.

5. Anonymous notary, *Cay q[ui]quin llactapi cabildo tantanacucuna . . .* (1605–1608)

The manuscript is one of two fragments of Quechua language notary records that have been discovered thus far.[17] Long runs of Nahuatl notary records have been located in Mexican archives, but other than these documents the Mexican notary materials have no counterparts in Peru. This may have been the result of strict enforcement on the part of Viceroy Toledo of a royal decree (1576) forbidding mestizos to occupy the office of notary (see chapter 3). The document consists of fragments of a longer notarial register, including wills and land demarcation as well as bestowal of staves of authority (*cazpi*, now *vara*) on indigenous community leaders. The text is set up in two parallel columns, Spanish on the left and Quechua on the right. The notary took care to assure that lines matched their respective translations. The Spanish text shows that the notary had only limited acquaintance with Spanish legal formulas. There is syntactic and rhetorical borrowing in both directions. There is a short vocabulary list in the register in which the notary attempted to construct Quechua equivalents for Spanish legal terms. Place names indicate that the document is from the present-day Calca-Urubamba area (Department of Cuzco). Syllable-finals are unchanged from Common Southern Peruvian Quechua. Ejectives and aspirates are unattested. The sibilant distinction appears, but the notary is even more inconsistent with the sibilants than the writer of the Huarochirí manuscript.

6. Diego de Gonçález Holguín, s.i., *Gramática y arte nueva* (1607) and *Vocabulario de la lengua general* (1608)

Gonçález Holguín (b. Cáceres 1552–1618) was the best colonial grammarian of Quechua. A Jesuit, he was sent to Cuzco shortly after his arrival in Peru in 1581, where he was ordained and where he began his study of Quechua (Piñas 1585: 620; Anonymous 1600: I, 292–293, II, 125–126; Torres 1882: 68–70; Mendiburu 1933: VI, 268–273; Porras 1952: xx–xxiii; Millé 1968: 76).[18] Gonçález Holguín's linguistic training included serving as superior at the Jesuit Aymara language training parish in Juli. He also spent time as the vice-rector of the Jesuit *colegio* in Quito (Ecuador), where his requests for leave time to work on his grammar were rejected by the Jesuit provincial. The *Gramática*, written in the late 1590s, includes a Latinate treatment of the inflectional system and a detailed, semantically sensitive analysis of the complex verbal derivational system. It ranks with the best linguistic descriptions of a Quechua language for any period. Gonçález Holguín paid considerable attention to discourse-level suffixes marking scope of affirmation, negation, hearsay, emphasis, and so forth, as well as to sentence connectives and interjections. Such topics were otherwise rarely or inadequately covered in colonial grammars. The *Vocabulario* has entries for fully inflected and derived Quechua words and phrases along with the usual stem listings and so is especially rich as a cultural source (cf. Golte 1973). Gonçález showed a clear concern for the nuanced differences between Quechua and Spanish lexical and cultural worlds. But even though Gonçález Holguín was an exceptionally careful observer, he based his entries on unsystematic elicitations in both languages, essentially a "card file." The entries sometimes make sense in terms of a Quechua cultural logic and sometimes make sense in Spanish. Gonçález Holguín's *Vocabulario* frequently includes a derived and inflected word or phrase in Quechua defined by a phrase in Spanish. The phrase entries are frequently loan translations, in both directions, from Spanish to Quechua and from Quechua to Spanish. Therefore, the phrase entries must be used with caution.

Gonçález Holguín stated that he was describing the court language of Cuzco. Glottalization and aspiration are both attested in his orthography, but they are not always distinguished. He is also inconsistent in the way he represents the distinction between velar and uvular consonants. The sibilants are clearly and consistently distinguished, though he spelled some words with both sibilants and said that some were variable. The *Vocabulario* represents the [s̱] with *c* (occasionally replaced by *ç*) before *i* and *e*, *ç* syllable-initially elsewhere and *z* syllable-finally. The grammar uses *z* in all contexts for the same segment. In both the grammar and the *Vocabulario*, [ṣ] is written as *s* in all environments, except between vowels where it alternates with *ss*. The care with which Gonçález Holguín observed lexical variation in the use of sibilants makes his work the standard for understanding the colonial sibilants.

7. Santa Cruz Pachacuti Yamqui, *Relación de antigüedades deste reyno del Pirú* (c. 1615)

The *Relación* is one of the most important colonial sources for indigenous myth and cosmology (see Harrison 1982; Salomon 1982). The author, an indigenous headman from the southernmost part of the Department of Cuzco, includes ritual texts with a content and structure similar to those of Molina "el Cuzqueño." The ritual texts are woven into a mythic history in which they are associated with each of the Inkas. Santa Cruz Pachacuti Yamqui also includes a condensed visual representation of the Inka cosmos alongside Quechua religious utterances. The narrative itself is peppered with Quechua lexical stems. The Quechua is badly garbled in all of the modern editions.

Santa Cruz Pachacuti Yamqui made ad hoc and inconsistent orthographic distinctions between velars and uvulars, and among ejective, aspirate, and plain stops. Although both { ç } and { s } are represented in his orthography, there does not seem to be a clear or consistent pattern to their use. Many stems are written with both. The *Relación* was found in the same volume of papers belonging to Francisco de Avila as the Huarochirí manuscript and the text by Molina "el Cuzqueño."

8. Juan Pérez Bocanegra, *Ritual formulario e institución de curas* (1631)

Pérez Bocanegra (d. 1645) taught Latin grammar at the University of San Marcos (Lima), and served as a singer in the Cathedral of Cuzco, choir book corrector, and parish priest in Belén in the city of Cuzco, before assuming the positions of *examinador general* of Quechua and Aymara for the diocese of Cuzco, and *párroco* of Andahuaylillas (Province of Quispicanchi), a village south of Cuzco (Mendoza 1665: 551; Esquivel y Navia 1753: 31, 58; Eguiguren 1951: 1, 54, 358; Vargas Ugarte 1960: 368f.; Stevenson 1968: 280ff.; Zuidema 1982b; Hopkins 1983: ch. 3; Mannheim 1987; chapters 1 and 2 of this book). The *Ritual formulario,* completed in 1622, is rich in information on indigenous, non-Christian ritual practices. It includes citations of indigenous ritual utterances, a discussion of dream interpretation and other forms of divination, and a Quechua-language hymn to the Virgin, which identifies her with the Pleiades. The hymn was the first piece of vocal polyphony to be published in the Americas (Stevenson 1968: 280).

Internal evidence (including reference to the moieties of Andahuaylillas, p. 619) indicates that the text was written in Cuzco-Collao Quechua, although there is no direct orthographic reflex of glottalization and aspiration. The sibilant distinction is represented consistently. Laminal [s̲] is represented by *ç,* in variation with *c* before *i* and *e,* and in variation with *z* syllable-initially; apical [ṣ] as *s,* with *ss* used between vowels. The Quechua text of the *Ritual formulario* is well written and, apart from frequent use of *chay* as an article in nondemonstrative contexts, remarkably free of Spanish syntactic influence.

9. Juan de Aguilar, *Arte de la lengua quichua* (1690)

Aguilar was assistant *cura* of the Cathedral of Lima at the time the *Arte* was composed. Aguilar's *Arte* is the last source in which the sibilants were more or less consistently distinguished. It is striking that they are not distinguished in his Spanish. The *Arte* shows leveling of the postvocalic form of the accusative, *-cta* > *-ta.* Fricativization of syllable-final palatals appears as a change in progress; compare *-chuch* (98) and *-chus* (28). The *-sha-* form of the durative is first attested in variation with *-chka-* (69, 75). A form of the inclusive plural that survives today in Arequipa, *-chicc* (likely to reflect [chiq]), is attested (25).[19] The grammar underlying the forms of Aguilar's *Arte* thus lacks the diachronic word-final palatalization, *k* > *č* / *i*__# which today covers the Department of Cuzco. It has the beginnings of syllable-final uvularization of velars and fricativization of uvulars. Figure 6.2

Figure 6.2

	Aguilar	Others
	-chik	-chik
palatalization	—	-chich
lenition of palatals	—	-chish
merger of final sibilants	—	-chis
uvularization	-chiq	—
attested	-chicc	-chis

summarizes the differences between the Aguilar grammar and later colonial sources.

None of the final four sources I considered shows any trace of the sibilant distinction. All four are from the Cuzco region; though none is dated, a fairly good case can be made that they are from the eighteenth century. Each of these texts shows innovations that are not attested in the first nine witnesses, including weakenings and/or mergers of syllable-final consonants. All four are versified dramas, written in lines of eight or nine syllables. All were written in Quechua, except for Spanish-language stage directions.

10. Gabriel Centeno, *El pobre más rico* (n.d.)

Nothing is known about the author or circumstances of the play *El pobre más rico,* which is set in the city of Cuzco. Ejective and aspirate stops are both indicated by double letters. Epenthetic [h], which is a reflex of ejectives in etymologically vowel-initial stems, appears in the text, as in *herque* [herq'ẹ] 'child' (line 182), and *hampatu* [hamp'atu] 'toad' (line 287). Lenition of syllable-final palatals, which was variable in Aguilar's (1690) *Arte,* has gone to completion except for a single paradigm regularization in which the dubitative *-cha,* which drops the vowel when it follows a vowel, remains as *-ch#*. In all cases of the lenition of palatals, the reflex is [s̱]. (There is a possible occurrence of durative *-chka-* > [ʃa] reflected in { cha }; *caparcachanco* [line 421].) The inclusive plural is *-chic* word-internally and *-chis* word-finally. The remaining syllable-final stops are unchanged.[20]

Laterals depalatalize before uvulars. Neutralization of syllable-final nasals is variable. In Centeno's synchronic grammar *n* assimilates to *m* before labial stops (*n* → *m*/__*p*) variably, although orthographic use of { n } for synchronically underlying *m,* as in *cutinpuchun* (line 139), indicates that the assimilation of *n* to *m* before labial stops is widespread enough for the scribe to infer that all *m*s before *p* are derived from *n;* in addition, *m* becomes *n* before another *m* (*m* → *n*/ __*m*). The postvocalic variant of the witness affirmation suffix continues to appear as *-m*. The post-vocalic form of the accusative is level with the postconsonantal form, *-ta,* for example, *michipacunata* (379); *camachiscayquita* (117).

11. Anonymous, *Usca Paucar* (n.d., Sahuaraura)

Usca Paucar is represented by several codices. The only one that is publicly accessible today is a copy made in 1838 by the nationalist priest from Cuzco, Justo Apu Sahuaraura. Sahuaraura's copy, collected with the famous play *Ollanta,* selections from Garcilaso's *Royal Commentaries,* and Sahuaraura's own royal lineage, is held by the National Library of Peru (Meneses 1950: 1–21, Rivet and Créqui-Montfort 1951–1956: I, 315ff., Lara 1969: 150f.).[21]

Both ejectives and aspirates are represented by doubling the stop. Alternatively, aspirates are represented by an *h* following the stop. Lenition of syllable-final palatals has gone to completion with a regular *s* reflex, except where aspiration is permitted on a following stop, in which case the reflex is s[STOP]^h, as in *ascca ascca* (< *achka*) (line 122) 'many', where the double *cc* indicates [k^h],[22] and *huspha* (< uchpa) (line 64) 'ash'. The dubitative is regularized to *-cha* with the loss of the *-ch* variant. The inclusive plural is leveled to *-chis* both within and at the ends of words: *huyaichis* (line 46), *noccanchispan* (line 1578). The subordinate clause marker for switch reference appears both as *-pti-* (lines 142, 162, and 536) and *-cti-* (line 465), the latter reflecting $p \rightarrow \dot{x}/\_\$$. No other lenitions of syllable-final stops are in evidence.[23] Lateral depalatalization before uvulars is variable, as in *El pobre más rico.* The rule assimilating nasals to a following labial stop ($n \rightarrow m/\_p$) is so regular that occurrences of *m* are usually written as { n } before *p* even where the segment is lexically *m,* as *panpapin* (line 113), *ranpa* (line 252), *hanpunqui* (line 179, when *n* reflects the morpheme *-mu-*). Nasals are neutralized word-finally, where *n* is written, and likely reflects { ŋ } as it does today. The postvocalic variant of the witness suffix is thus *n.* Initial { h } sporadically appears without apparent motivation.

12. Anonymous, *Ollanta* (n.d.b., Sahuaraura)

Ollanta, the most famous literary piece in Quechua, has a shadowy past. It has been the subject of acrimonious debate over its origin, authorship, and cultural provenience (cf. Markham 1856: 169–200, 1912: 89–94; Rojas 1939; Cosio 1941; Rivet and Créqui-Montfort 1951–1956: I, xxv–xxxii; Lara 1969: 62–90; Landerman 1982).[24] At least nine distinct manuscript versions of *Ollanta* have at one time or another come to light, and most have served as the bases for published editions. There are appreciable textual differences between the manuscripts. Despite the attention that has been paid to *Ollanta*, no systematic comparison of the codices and editions of the play has yet been attempted. The Sahuaraura codex is part of the same collection as *Usca Paucar* and so also dates to 1838. Sahuaraura himself attributed authorship of *Ollanta* to Antonio Valdéz, the priest of Tinta during the late eighteenth century. It is striking that Sahuaraura's *Ollanta* and *Usca Paucar* codices represent different stages in the history of the language. Each is internally consistent in that respect. *Usca Paucar* is clearly the more archaic of the two. Sahuaraura evidently copied the texts, rather than editing them. In spite of the late date associated with the Sahuaraura codices, they are faithful copies of older manuscripts. Moreover, Sahuaraura's manuscript of *Ollanta* is in turn more archaic than the Justiniani codex, which dates (on all accounts) to the 1770s or 1780s.[25] By phonological criteria, all four of the versified dramas represent more recent states of the language than Aguilar's *Arte* (1690). Assuming that Aguilar's *Arte* indeed represented the speech of the end of the seventeenth century, and that it was written by him and not plagiarized from an earlier grammar,[26] we can assign the four dramas to the ninety-year period from 1690 to 1780, the so-called literary dark age. The relative chronology of the texts can be established by means of the internal logic of weakenings of syllable-final consonants.

This result is startling, for it forces us to revise entirely the usual view of eighteenth-century provincial letters as a backwater in a decaying colonial system. The anachronistic Baroque *culteranismo* of Espinoza Medrano (1632–1688), who composed in both Quechua and Spanish, was part of a movement to establish a Quechua literature that lasted to the end of the eighteenth century and was not a mere flash in the pan (see chapter 3).

The Sahuaraura manuscript of *Ollanta* follows different orthographic norms from the Sahuaraura version of *Usca Paucar*. There can be no doubt that they were copied from earlier manuscripts written by different scribes. The sporadic initial [h] that appears in *Usca Paucar* does not appear in *Ollanta*, where all occurrences can be accounted for etymologically. As in *Usca Paucar*, lenition of syllable-final palatals is complete, resulting in *s* plus aspiration on the following stop when this is phonotactically permitted, such as *uspha* 'ash' (p. 115), and *s* in suffixes and in stems in which aspiration is not permitted, such as *quisca-man* (p. 116) <**kichka* 'to the thorn', *huesccarccoscca* (p. 118) <**wichq'ay* 'to close'. Syllable-final *t*, which never was attested in suffixes, regularly remains in stems, as in *utccaitan* (p. 114) 'quickly'; *mitcascaita* (pp. 114, 116) 'stumbling'; *chutquicca* (p. 114); *utcu* (p. 119) 'cotton'. The only occurrence of syllable-final *k* in suffixes is definitively lost through the leveling of the accusative **-kta* > *-ta*. There is no evidence of any change in the status of syllable-final *k* in stems. Lenition and uvularization of syllable-final *p* is advanced over *Usca Paucar,* but still variable.[27] The postvocalic variant of the genitive is regularly uvularized, but both *-pti* and *-cti* variants of the switch reference subordinate clause marker are in evidence, although the *-pti* form is infrequent, as in *ppiñacuptinpas* (p. 114). Syllable-final *p* is intact in stems: *upyanchis* (p. 114) 'we drink'; *rapra* (p. 117) 'wing'; *chapchactin* (p. 116) 'eating like a bird, grain by grain'. (Notice though, *-pti* > *-cti.*) There is no evidence of change in the status of uvulars.

The nasals have merged at the ends of syllables, as evidenced by *quinsa* (< *kimsa*) (p. 126) 'three'. By this time, they had the same distribution as in modern Cuzco-Collao Quechua: at the ends of syllables, nasals assimilate to the place of articulation of the following stop or fricative and are realized as [ŋ] in other syllable-final contexts, including at the ends of words. Depalatalization of laterals prior to uvulars continues to be irregular. The nominalizer **-nqa* has now definitively lost its uvular stop. There is no evidence yet of loss of uvulars from r[CONSONANT][VOWEL] suffixes or of velars from *-yku* ~ *-yka.* The shift of syllable-final *w* to *y* has taken place in suffixes, as in *pureisihuai* (p. 114) 'help me to travel', but is lexically specific (as it is today) and variable in stems: *punchau* ~ *ppunchau* (pp. 113, 116, 117, 126) ~ *ppunchai* (pp. 114, 126, both word-internal) 'day, daylight', as against invariable (and stem-internal) *ñaupac* (p. 114) 'earlier' and *chaupinpin* (p. 116) 'in its center'.

13. Anonymous *Ollanta* (n.d.a., Justiniani)

The Justiniani codex of *Ollanta* has been dated to the 1770s–1780s. It is similar in character to the Sahuaraura manuscript, although there are numerous textual differences, ranging from lexical substitutions to differences in entire verses. Lenition and uvularization of syllable-final *p* is completed in suffixes. Syllable-final uvulars are represented as { cc } rather than the { c } (at least normally) of the Sahuaraura codex. It is not clear whether there is a phonetic motivation for representing the uvular this way or whether it is one more idiosyncrasy in an especially problematic area of Quechua orthography. The Justiniani codex also has persistent but irregular use of hyphens following syllable-final stops, for example, *thup-rascaña* (p. 7), *quechip-rancuna* (p. 10), *rap-ra* (p. 8), but *chapchacctañi* (p. 5) and *tapya* (p. 5); *ric-rãchis* (p. 8), but *ticranapacc* (p. 7); *ac-llanajq.chu* (p. 9). It is not clear whether the hyphens indicate syllable divisions or fricativizations of the preceding stops. There are two reasons to suppose that they indicate fricativizations: (1) no syllable-finals other than stops are followed by a hyphen; (2) fricativization and uvularization of labials had already gone to com-

Table 6.1. Seventeenth- and Eighteenth-Century Changes

	Aguilar	Centeno	Anon, *Usca Paucar* (Sahuaraura)	Anon, *Ollanta* (Sahuaraura)	Anon, *Ollanta* (Justiniani)
č > s/__$	%	+	+	+	+
-chicc > -chis (lev)	—	%	+	+	+
-cha ~ -ch (lev)	—	—	+	+	+
p > x̣/__$ (suf)	—	—	%[a]	%[b]	+
—kta > -ta (lev)	—	—	—	+	+
w > y/__$ (suf)	—	—	—	+	+
w > y/__# (stem)	—	—	—	%	+

[a] Sporadic.
[b] More frequent than in *Usca Paucar.*

(suf) = in suffixes.
(stem) = in stems.
(lev) = morphological alternation leveled.
\+ = regularly attested.
% = variably attested.
— = not attested.

pletion in the suffixes; fricativization could have been expected to filter into the stems. The Justiniani manuscript has regular word-final *w* > *y* whereas in the Sahuaraura codex it was still variable.

Several lexical observations are worth making. The two manuscripts of *Ollanta* are on opposite sides of a lexical isogloss, already attested as a variable by Gonçález Holguín. Where Sahuaraura has *saqi-* for 'abandon' (< **zaqi-*), Justiniani has *haqi-* (Sahuaraura p. 119; Justiniani, pp. 10 and 11; cf. Justiniani, p. 7, line 116, p. 21). The form *saqi-* is now generalized. The archaic form of 'to enter', *yayku-*, which persists in the modern language in the *provincias altas* (the southern high plateau) still appears (p. 21). The present-day lexical variable *hurqu-* ~ *urqu-* 'extract' is attested as *horccohuai* (p. 4).

The chronological order of the Sahuaraura and Justiniani texts is established by the completion of the lenition and uvularization of syllable-final *p* in suffixes and the completion of the spread of *w* > *y*/__$ from suffixes to stem-final position in the Justiniani manuscript.

I have summarized the phonological and morphological changes that are diagnostic of the relative chronology of Aguilar's (1690) *Arte* and the four versified dramas in table 6.1. A plus (+) sign indicates a change that has gone to completion; a minus (–), a change that is unattested; a percentage sign (%), a change that is attested variably. The changes include three phonological changes: (1) lenition of syllable-final *č* and merger with *s*, (2) lenition and uvularization of syllable-final *p*, and (3) shift of syllable-final *w* to *y*; and three instances of paradigm regularization: the inclusive plural *-chicc*, word-internally as the residue of two regular sound changes, was leveled to *-chis*; the postvocalic form of the accusative *-cta* was leveled to *-ta*; the dubitative was regularized to *-cha* with the loss of the postvocalic *-ch* variant.

7 The Sibilants

For some of the phonological contrasts in colonial-era written sources, we have a clear idea of the nature of the linguistic system being described and the corresponding contrasts in the scribe's language; these are relatively straightforward. The underdifferentiation of ejectives, aspirates, and velars versus uvulars and the overdifferentiation of the vowels, discussed in the last chapter, are good cases in point. For the sibilants, on the other hand, we have neither the direct evidence of the native language nor a clear idea of the nature of the corresponding contrast in the scribe's language. At the very moment at which Southern Peruvian Quechua was first documented, the scribal language, Spanish, was itself in the midst of significant changes in its fricative system, including its sibilants. The medieval antecedents of the colonial Spanish sibilants and the modern outcome of the changes are well known. But the phonetic nature of the sixteenth-century sibilants and the course the changes followed have been the source of acrimonious debate. The Spanish sibilant changes affected scribal practice in Native American languages, but we are in the dark when it comes to the phonetic course of the changes and the sociolinguistic allegiance of the scribes.

Thus, the sibilants have been one of the most intractable areas in the reconstruction of colonial Southern Peruvian Quechua phonology. Although a contrast between two sibilants is attested in written sources, and cognate distinctions are made in other Quechua languages, there is no evidence internal to Southern Peruvian Quechua as to their phonetic nature. The colonial sibilants have merged to modern Southern Peruvian [s], with the exception of dialectally restricted palatalizations (s > ʃ) adjacent to high front vowels and glides, several word-initial correspondences with modern [h], and at least one syllable-final correspondence with modern [x]. The phonetic values of the orthographic symbols for sibilants in colonial texts { s, ss, ç, z, x } cannot therefore be recovered by analogy with modern forms. Nor are the phonetic values recoverable by applying the comparative method to dialects of Southern Peruvian Quechua: all modern Southern Peruvian Quechua varieties have either a single underlying sibilant or a distinction of recent origin that is irrelevant to reconstructing the colonial distinction.

The problem of the sibilants was first pointed out in Rowe's (1950) reconstruction of Common Southern Peruvian Quechua. Rowe observed that, although there was evidence for two colonial Quechua sibilants, it was not possible to interpret Spanish scribal practices as to their nature. Peter Landerman (1979, 1983) has since formulated a solution that is at once elegant and convincing. Landerman's solution is based on evidence from language contact and from colonial-era written sources. The former draws on loans among Quechua, Aymara, and Spanish; the latter involves Quechua and Aymara texts written by Spanish speakers. He concluded that Southern Peruvian Quechua had a distinction between a dorsal [s̲], represented as {ç, c (before front vowels), and z} and an apical [ṣ], represented as {s, ss}. Spanish had the dorsal/apical distinction as well as a palatal [ʃ], represented as {x}. Aymara had a single sibilant, ṣ, orthographic {s}. It is clear from sixteenth- and seventeenth-century Southern Peruvian Quechua texts that there were at least two phonemically distinctive sibilants. I believe that Landerman's analysis of the phonetics of the distinction is correct. In the passage that follows, I summarize the relevant portions of his argument before examining the philological details that bear upon the issue. (The passages that summarize Landerman [1979, 1983] are indented.)[1]

> At the time of the conquest, the Spanish of Toledo distinguished the six sibilants represented by the orthography in figure 7.1.[2] [{c} was usually written without a cedilla before *i* and *e*. Word-initial {s} alternated with {ss} elsewhere to represent the voiceless segment. Word-internal {s} represented the voiced segment. {g} was usually used in place of {j} before *i* and *e*.]

Figure 7.1

voiceless	{ç / c}	{#s / ss}	{x}
voiced	{z}	{s}	{j / g}

> The regional dialect of Old Castile merged the voiced and voiceless sibilants as in figure 7.2. By the mid–sixteenth century, sibilant devoicing, which had been a regional characteristic of Old Castile, spread to Toledo and Madrid. Even the most learned individuals of

these cities accepted unvoiced forms of the former voiced sibilants as the norm by the 1570s. It is a point of controversy whether the {ç}:{z} distinction persisted as an opposition between affricate and fricative a half-century beyond the loss of voicing.[3]

Figure 7.2

$\begin{Bmatrix} \text{ç} \\ \text{c} \end{Bmatrix} \quad \begin{Bmatrix} \#\text{s} \\ \text{ss} \end{Bmatrix} \quad \{\text{x}\}$

The regional dialect of Andalusia commonly merged $\begin{Bmatrix} \#\text{s} \\ \text{ss} \end{Bmatrix} > \begin{Bmatrix} \text{ç} \\ \text{c} \end{Bmatrix}$ and {s} > {z} through the mid–sixteenth century. By the end of the sixteenth century, the loss of the voicing distinction led to a system in which a single segment reflected earlier $\begin{Bmatrix} \text{ç} \\ \text{c} \end{Bmatrix}$, {z}, $\begin{Bmatrix} \#\text{s} \\ \text{ss} \end{Bmatrix}$, and {s}, as in figure 7.3 (for a summary, see Catalán 1957: 317ff.). It is normally assumed that Andalusian was the prototype for Latin American Spanish.

Figure 7.3

{ç} {x}

Finally, in both dialects {x} shifted to a phonetic velar. The modern counterparts of figures 7.2 and 7.3 are indicated by their respective primes.[4]

Figure 7.2′

$\begin{Bmatrix} \text{z} \\ \text{ç} \end{Bmatrix} = [\theta] \quad \{\text{s}\} = [\text{ṣ}] \quad \{\text{j}\} = [\text{x}]$

Figure 7.3′

$\begin{Bmatrix} \text{z} \\ \text{ç} \\ \text{s} \end{Bmatrix} = [\underline{\text{s}}] \qquad \{\text{j}\} = [\text{x}]$

Landerman (1979: 6f., 1983: 208–209, following Canfield), has used Nahuatl orthography to set the initial parameters of orthographic system in figure 7.2. A first approximation of the phonetic content of figure 7.2 can be obtained by observing the scribal practice of a speaker of the system in figure 7.2 describing a sibilant that is independently attested. Consider Alonso de Molina's sixteenth-century dictionary of Nahuatl. Figure 7.4 shows correspondences between the Nahuatl phonological system and Molina's orthography (Karttunen 1981: 109).

Figure 7.4

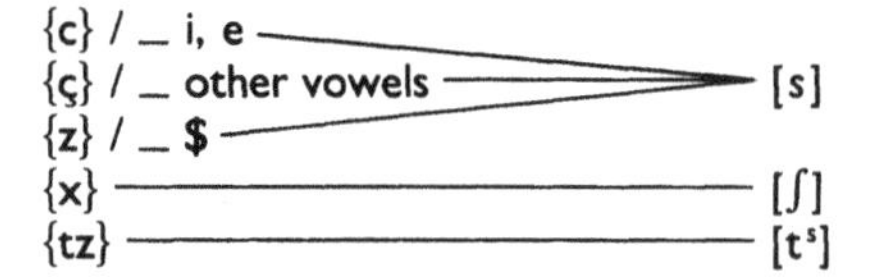

There was no Nahuatl segment that corresponded to {s}; it was borrowed into Nahuatl as [ʃ]. Thus, *señora* appears in early documents as *xinola* (Karttunen and Lockhart 1976; Lockhart 1981: 109). In a figure 7.2 type of orthography, such as Molina's, {ç} and {z} represented a single segment, which was a fricative [s̲] and not an affricate [t^s]. Further, {s} was perceived as more like [ʃ] than like either [s̲] or [t^s].

Returning now to Cuzco-Collao Quechua, Gonçález Holguín (1608) followed a similar orthographic practice in his dictionary some forty years after Molina with respect to { ç } and { z }. Orthographic *c* was used before *i* and *e*, *ç* elsewhere syllable-initially, and *z* syllable-finally.[5] The { ç } segment contrasted with { s }, written *ss* between vowels and *s* elsewhere (Gonçález Holguín occasionally substituted *s* for *ss* between vowels, as *cusi* ~ *cussi* 'happy': 1952 [1608]: 56).

Gonçález Holguín stated explicitly that there was no { x } in the language.

Writing in the mid-sixteenth century, Domingo de Santo Tomás (1560a, b) also distinguished { ç } and { s } in Quechua. The former was consistently written as *ç* syllable-initially and *z* syllable-finally, the latter *ss* between vowels, and *s* elsewhere. Santo Tomás identified substantially the same instances of { ç } and { s } as Gonçález Holguín.

Santo Tomás, who worked with speakers of several Quechua varieties, observed that there was a word-initial { s } : { x } dialect shibboleth (1560a: iv, 73v, 1951 [1560b]: 14), and cross-listed a number of stems in his *Lexicon* between { x } and { s } initials. Though many witnesses observed that the language spoken in Cuzco lacked { x },[6] it appeared as { ʃ } in most of the Central and Northern languages, as it does today. Diego de Molina (1649), a Franciscan who preached in Huánuco, described { x } as an emblem of local identity in contrast to the lingua franca. Apart from using { x } in appropriate Central Quechua forms, Santo Tomás used it syllable-finally in place of an etymological palatal stop,[7] as in *pixca* 'five' (< *pichqa*) and *vixcani* 'I close' (< *wichqay*) (1560b: 38v, 38r; cf. Landerman 1983: 209).[8] The correspondence North and Central { x } : Southern { s } and the syllable-final reflex of the palatal stop both demonstrate that, just as in the Nahuatl case, we are still dealing with { x } = { ʃ } until at least the middle seventeenth century.

For both Santo Tomás and Gonçález Holguín, { ç } and { z } represented a single segment in Quechua, which was distinct from { s } and from phonetic { ʃ }. If we assume (along with the standard interpretation [Alonso 1955]) that { ç/z } represents [t^s], then we are faced with several problems. (1) This contradicts the orthographic situation in Nahuatl, where { ç/z } represents a dorsal sibilant. (2) It also causes a serious problem for comparative reconstruction within the Quechua family. The modern reflex of Southern { ç/z } is { s̲ }. The cognates of { ç/z } in the Central and Northern languages are also { s̲ } or reflexes of an earlier { s̲ }. This suggests that the proto-Quechua ancestor of { ç/z } was a dorsal sibilant. If we interpret { ç/z } as { t^s } for Colonial Southern Peruvian Quechua, we are forced to reconstruct a stage of the language between changes of *s > *t^s and *t^s > s̲ without any independent evidence or motivation. The interpretation of { ç } as { t^s } must therefore be rejected in favor of { s̲ }.

The { s } was a sibilant, and by process of elimination was neither [ʃ] nor [s̲]. Moreover the phonetic value of { s } in the Spanish system in figure 7.3 is generally assumed to have been [ṣ] like its modern Castilian reflex. Landerman concludes that Southern Quechua { s }, cognate to / ṣ / in Wanka and / ʃ / in other Central and Northern Quechua varieties, also represented the apical sibilant [ṣ].

The orthographic representations diagramed in figure 7.5*a* are reconstructed for sixteenth- and seventeenth-century Southern Peruvian Quechua. In addition, the correspondence in figure 7.5*b* appears in sixteenth- and seventeenth-century texts, though [ʃ] was not distinctive in colonial Southern Peruvian Quechua. The segments within brackets are the phonetic values of the orthographic representations. The starred segments are the corresponding reconstructed phonemes of Common Southern Peruvian Quechua. (I follow Rowe [1950] in using the symbol *z* for the Common Southern Peruvian Quechua dorsal. I do so to bring the reconstructed symbols into line with the orthographies of Santo Tomás, Gonçález Holguín, and the works of the Tercer Concilio, all of which are cited frequently by Andean historians and anthropologists. The choice of symbols is phonetically awkward, but more accessible to nonlinguists.)

Minimal pairs for the / z / : / s / opposition attested by colonial grammarians include *açua* 'chicha': *assua* 'more' (Santo Tomás 1560b: 106r and 86r, respectively); *uça* 'flea': *usa-* 'to accomplish' (Gonçález Holguín 1608: 632 and 333) and *maça* 'work pair': *masa* 'reciprocal term for male member of affine group' (Gonçález Holguín 1608: 221).[9]

Consider now some otherwise perplexing early loan correspondences. Southern Peruvian Quechua had the system in figure 7.5*a*, with a distinction between [s̲] and [ṣ]; Spanish speakers varied between the sys-

Figure 7.5

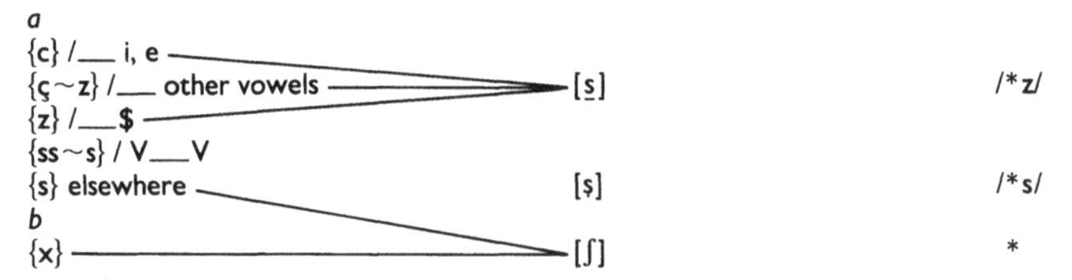

tem in figure 7.2, which distinguished three sibilants [s̠], [ṣ], and [ʃ], and the system in figure 7.3, which distinguished two sibilants, [s̠] and [ʃ]. Each involves a correspondence between modern Quechua [s̠] and modern Peruvian Spanish [x]. *Oveja* 'sheep', which formerly had [ʃ], now has two Quechua reflexes, *uwisa* and *uwixa*. Recall that there was no [ʃ] in early colonial Southern Peruvian Quechua. Spanish [ʃ] was thus borrowed as its closest Quechua counterpart, [ṣ] hence, *uwiṣa. The Southern Quechua *ṣ* > *s̠* merger resulted in the form *uwisa*. In Spanish, [ʃ] velarized to [x] as in its modern form.[10] The word was borrowed a second time as *uwixa*. At present, the older form is restricted to song.[11] Several loanwords from Quechua to Spanish evidence an Andalusian-type fricative system (fig. 7.3) for Spanish speakers who adopted the loans. The word for indigenous sandals attested in colonial sources as [uṣuta] (> modern [husut'a]), entered Spanish with a [ʃ].[12] The present form, *ojota*, arises from velarization (apart from the normal high ~ mid vowel reassignment). *Jalca* 'high plateau' likewise has its source in [ṣallqa] 'savage puna'. *Jora*, the Peruvian Spanish term for the sprouted maize used for corn-mash, was attested in seventeenth-century Quechua as [ṣora], again with initial [ṣ] (Garcilaso 1609: VIII, ix; Gonçález Holguín 1608: 18). *Sora* appears as a Peruvianism in modern Spanish dictionaries with initial { s }. The initial { s } could reflect either borrowing through a three-sibilant (fig. 7.2) system (rather than the two-sibilant Andalusian system), or its orthographic presence, as *sora*, in Garcilaso's *Comentarios*. The place name in Cuzco *Quiquijana* has a modern Quechua reflex [kikis̠ana], presumably from *[kikiṣana]; the sibilant followed the usual path in the Spanish counterpart, [ṣ] > (by loan) [ʃ] > [x]. It was borrowed back with [x].

The Achilles heel of phonetic reconstructions of the sixteenth-century sibilants is that they ultimately refer to what Spanish speakers wrote and what they thought they heard. But in this sense the historiographic problem is no different from any parallel problem of cultural interpretation. Whenever we interpret a cultural document from the colonial period, we are reconstructing not only the indigenous cultural system but the colonial one as well. Moreover, to assume that the orthographic sibilants are arbitrary variants of one another, as most scholars of colonial Quechua have done, is to assume the null hypothesis. By assuming that the distribution of the orthographic sibilants is neither random nor an imposition of Spanish orthographic norms, we are able to investigate the nature of the sixteenth- and seventeenth-century Southern Peruvian Quechua sibilants.

The Sibilants Reconsidered

In order to explore the nature of the colonial sibilants, I follow a double strategy. First, I use comparative evidence from the Wanka language (Central Quechua) to show that the sibilant distinction in colonial sources is a consistent cognate of a phonological distinction made elsewhere in the Quechua family. This establishes that the distinction we are tracking is proper to the Quechua family and establishes some phonetic parameters for the genetic reconstruction of the sibilants in colonial Southern Peruvian Quechua. Second, I amass written evidence to establish that the distinction was recorded reliably by independent observers. The inconsistencies in the written record shed light on the social backgrounds of the scribes and allow us to frame the problem of the historical disappearance of the sibilant contrast.[13]

The last source to distinguish the sibilants is Aguilar's *Arte* of 1690 (witness 9). It presents strong support for the persistence of the distinction up to the end of the seventeenth century because: (1) the sound changes (particularly the palatal lenitions) preclude the possibility that Aguilar copied it from an early-seventeenth-century source; and (2) Aguilar was not orthographically consistent in his Spanish. This accounts for the numerous substitutions { s } for { ç }, when the direction of the sound change was the opposite, { ş } > [s̱]. At this point, the Andalusian type of sibilant system had become universal in Peruvian Spanish.

But there is still a problem with the pre-Aguilar texts. On the one hand, there is a high tradition of materials written by well-educated individuals in which the sibilant distinction is more or less consistently maintained, including Santo Tomás's *Grammatica* and *Lexicon* (witness 1), the Third Council's sermons and *Doctrina* (witness 3), Gonçález Holguín's *Arte* and *Vocabulario* (witness 6), Pérez Bocanegra's *Ritual formulario* (witness 8), and, last, Aguilar. (Anonymous [1586], Garcilaso [1609] and [1616], Avendaño [1649], Jurado Palomino [1649], and D. de Molina [1649] may be added to this list. Landerman [1979, 1983] has observed that Oré [1598], Huerta [1616], and Torres Rubio [1619] also made the sibilant distinction.) On the other hand, there are works in which two orthographic sibilants types are used, but not consistently distinguished. These include the texts by Molina (witness 2), Santa Cruz Pachacuti Yamqui (witness 7), and the Huarochirí manuscript (witness 4), and a single early-seventeenth-century text with no distinction between the two, that of the anonymous notary (witness 5). Molina, Santa Cruz Pachacuti Yamqui, and the Huarochirí manuscript were all among Francisco de Avila's papers, and in the latter two cases it is possible that we are dealing with scribes who were trained by the same individual, a speaker who did not consistently distinguish the segments in his Spanish. Molina's *Fábulas y ritos* is a second-generation copy made by a late-sixteenth- or early-seventeenth-century scribe who was apparently not very familiar with Quechua and doubtless had an Andalusian-type system in his Spanish. The anonymous notary used { s } for both reconstructed segments, but errors in the Spanish text indicate that the { ç/z } : { s } distinction was a received orthographic convention. We are dealing here with a complex sociolinguistic setting in which the Andalusian type of system with a single sibilant was to take over from the learned two-sibilant system. It should therefore not be surprising that the variation between sibilant systems is reflected in occasional underdifferentiation of the Southern Peruvian Quechua sibilants in texts as well as in the trajectories of loanwords.

I have qualified the consistency of the sibilant distinction among texts of the high tradition with the words "more or less." Landerman's analysis of the sibilants—which I have adopted here—is strengthened if it can be shown: (1) that the distinction in colonial Southern Peruvian Quechua is cognate to the sibilant distinction in the Quechua languages that maintain it today, and (2) that the texts that distinguish the sibilants are consistent with each other in this respect despite other orthographic differences. In order to demonstrate these points, I chose a sample of 120 stems with sibilants; occasionally the stems had sibilants in one of the cognates, but *h* or "zero" (Ø) in another. The stems were selected to maximize the number of cognates between texts. For comparative evidence, I used the non-Southern Wanka language, which has a relatively conservative sibilant system. Junín-Wanka Quechua has a two-way sibilant contrast, between a dorsal s̲ (written *s*) and an apical ș that palatalizes to [ʃ] adjacent to *i* and *y* (written *sh*).

Comparative Evidence

I used the *Arte* and *Vocabulario* of Gonçález Holguín for the comparison with Wanka because: (1) I could find examples of almost the entire 120-word set in that corpus; and (2) there is a problem in establishing the provenience of the only other source for which a relatively complete sample could be found, the *Lexicon* and *Grammatica* of Santo Tomás. The Wanka material is from Rodolfo Cerrón-Palomino (1976a). A lexically irregular word-initial *s* > *h* shift distinguishes the Waylla and Waycha varieties of Wanka from those spoken in Jauja. I shall here refer to the former two varieties as Wanka and the latter as Jauja (cf. Cerrón-Palomino 1976a) and include evidence from both sides of the isogloss.

Table 7.1 lists Wanka cognates for stems with orthographic { ç/z }, Common Southern Peruvian Quechua */ z / (dorsal [s̱]).

With overwhelming frequency orthographic { ç/z } in the colonial Cuzco-Collao Quechua *Vocabulario* of Gonçález Holguín (=[s̱]) corresponds to the dorsal sibilant ([s̱]) in Wanka. Regular correspondences are shown in table 7.1 (*a, b,* and *c*). The initial *h* for non-Jauja varieties of Wanka in (*b*) and (*c*) reflects a change internal to Junín-Wanka Quechua (Cerrón-Palomino 1977: 13ff.). The correspondence of initial *s* ~ *h* variation in early-seventeenth-century Cuzco to this change (*c*) is intriguing. It suggests both that initial *s* ~ *h* variation might be older than one would guess from either the present-day or colonial distribution of the stems and that the divergence between Junín-Wanka and Southern Peruvian Quechua may be younger. The stems cited in (*d*) are exceptions, but in each case there is disagreement among colonial lexicographers as to whether the form has { ç/z } or { s }. The irregularity of (*e*) in the Jauja form may be a Wanka-internal development.

Table 7.2 lists Wanka cognates for stems with orthographic { s } in Gonçález Holguín's work, Common Southern Peruvian Quechua */ s / (apical [ṣ]). Recall that Wanka { sh } is phonetically [ṣ] except adjacent to a front vowel or glide.

Regular correspondence of orthographic { s } (= [ṣ]) in colonial Cuzco-Collao Quechua to Wanka / sh / (= [ṣ] ~ [ʃ]) is shown in (*a*). The stem *hamu-* 'to come' (*b*) has undergone an *ṣ* > *h* change in Southern Peruvian and Bolivian Quechua. The regular reflex appears in poetic texts reported by Garcilaso and Guaman Poma. The stem *samu-* was reanalyzed as radical *sa-* and suffix *-mu-*, which in the context of a motion verb indicates movement toward the speaker, and analogical reassignment of the radical to *ha-* on the model of *haku* 'let's go'. *Haku* in turn was interpreted to consist of radical *ha-* and middle voice *-ku.* Much the same process is taking place in the change *yaykuy* ~ *haykuy* 'to enter', currently restricted to nuclear Cuzco.[14] The verb *yaykuy* is reanalyzed as radical *ya-* and suffix *-yku,* which contextually denotes motion inward (cf. Gonçález Holguín, 1842 [1607]: 246). The radical is again reassigned to the incipient verb stem *ha-*.[15] In (*c*), Waylla and Waycha Wanka show the regular reflex / sh /, while Jauja shows / s /. The change in (*c*) again appears to be Wanka-internal. The only irregularities, then,

Table 7.1. Wanka Cognates for */z/

Gonçález Holguín		Jauja	Wanka	
(*a*) Gonçález Holguín {ç/z} : Wanka /s/				
quimça (684)			kimsa	'three'
çocta (86)			suqta	'six'
puçac (292)			pusaq	'eight'
yzccon (270)			isqun	'nine'
upiyay maci (455)	'drinking partner'		masi	'partner'
çenca (598)			sinqa	'nose'
huaci (324)			wasi	'house'
riccicapuni (655)	'recognize from afar'		lisqiy	'to recognize'
coça (361)			qusa	'husband'
çumak (89)			sumaq	'beautiful'
çaça (74)			sasa	'difficult'
cauçani (51)			kawsay	'to live'
çacça (74)	'gluttony'		saksay	'to swell up'
uça (632)			usa	'flea'
ciqui (84)			siki	'buttocks'
ciça (82)	'flower'		sisay	'to flower'
muzpachini (253)	'to cause to lose judgment'		muspay	'delirium'
ccaci (59)	'useless'		qasilla	'behave yourself'[a]
çua (559)	'thief'		suway	'to steal'
ccaça (497)			qasa	'frost'
huapci (181)	'vapor'		wapsiy	'to evaporate'
çupay (89)			supay	'devil'
çuchuni (87)	'andar asentadillas'		sutru	'feeble person'
pazcani (279)			paskay	'to untie'
acini (14)			asiy	'to laugh'
maça (221)	'work pair'		masa	'pair'
chazquini (98)			traskiy	'receive'
(*b*) Gonçález Holguín {ç/z} : Jauja /s/ : Wanka /h/				
çapa (441)	'each'	sapalla	hapalla	'alone'
çara (79)		sala	hala	'maize'
çaruni (79)		satruy	hatruy	'to step on'
çamani (75)		samay	hamay	'to breathe, to rest'
cirani (463)		silay	hilay	'to sew'
cecanni (81)		siqay	hiqay	'to climb'

Table 7.1. *(continued)*

Gonçález Holguín		Jauja	Wanka	
(*c*) Gonçález Holguín {ç/z} ~ *h* : Jauja /s/ : Wanka /h/				
huc (687) ~ çuc(lla) (87)		suk	huk	'one'
hacha ~ çacha (74)		satra	hatra	'bush'
(*d*) Gonçález Holguín {ç/z} : Wanka /sh/ [ʃ]				
ticci[b] (687)	'origin'		tiqshiy	'to create'
ccazpi[c] (64)	'staff'		kashpi	'thin stick'
azpini[d] (42)	'to scrape'		ashpiy	'to scrape the earth'
canchiz[e] (1607: 218)			qantrish	'seven'
aznani[f] (42)			ashnay ~ asyay	'to stink'
(*e*) Gonçález Holguín {ç/z} : Jauja /sh/ : Wanka /s/				
vçuni	(350) 'to be lost'	ushuy	usuy	'to spill'
(*f*) Gonçález Holguín {ç/z} : Jauja /sh/				
ñauça		ñawsha		'blind'

All Gonçález Holguín citations are from the *Vocabulario* unless otherwise noted. Verbs are cited by Gonçález Holguín in the first person. The sequence {cc} after a vowel and before a front vowel represents a sequence of a velar or uvular stop, followed by a sibilant. The Wanka/Jauja forms are cited in the orthography used in the standard reference works (Cerrón-Palomino 1976a, 1976b). Wanka/Jauja orthographic interpretations: {sh} = [ʂ] except adjacent to *i* and *y* where it is [ʃ]; {tr} = [č̣] (retroflex palatal).
[a] Cerrón-Palomino: "usase como imperativo para los niños y equivale a Pórtense bien" (1976b: 111).
[b] But see Santo Tomás, who cites *ticssin* (1560b: 174).
[c] Santo Tomás (1560b: 117) and Anonymous (1951 [1586]: 23) cite *caspi,* with the expected reflex.
[d] Santo Tomás (1560b) lists both *azpini* (111r) and the expected *aspini* (110r). The Anonymous *Vocabulario* cites *haspini* (1951 [1586]: 142) with epenthetic *h* reflecting ejective *p'*.
[e] Santo Tomás (1560b: 96v) agrees with Gonçález Holguín, but the *Doctrina* of the Tercer Concilio Limense, (1584: 3r), Anonymous (1951 [1586]: 21, possibly not an independent source from the former), and Aguilar (1690) all show the expected *s* reflex.
[f] The Tercer Concilio's *Sermones* (1585: 16) show the expected *asnay,* as does the Anonymous *Vocabulario* (1951 [1586]: 166).

Table 7.2. Wanka Cognates for */s/

González Holguín		Jauja	Wanka	
(*a*) González Holguín {s} : Wanka /sh/				
yscay (492)			ishkay	'two'
pissi (634)			pishi	'a few'
aslla (634)			ashlla	'a little'
pisccu (287)			pishqu	'bird'
ashuan (35)	'more'		ashwan	'on the contrary'
pussani (298)			pushay	'to lead'
kusi ~ kussi (56)			kushi	'happy'
simi (327)			shimi	'mouth'
sayani (324)			shaykay	'to stand'
suyani (516)		shuyay	—	'to wait'
sullca (331)			shullka	'younger'
soncco (330)			shunqu	'heart'
quessa (306)		qisha	qishna	'nest'
quesspi ~ quespi (59, 306)	'transparent'		qishpi	'glass'
suttuni (333)			shutuy	'to drip'
musok (359)			mushuq	'new'
massa (221)	'husband's brother'	masha		'son-in-law'
ysppay (289)			ishpay	'urine'
sullu (332)			shullu	'fetus'
huassa (515)	'back'		shaway	'to carry on the back'
			washatraw	'outside'
(*b*) González Holguín *h* < s : Wanka /sh/				
hamuni (690) ~ *şamu-[a]			shamuy	'to come'
(*c*) González Holguín {s} : Jauja /s/ : Wanka /sh/				
suti (532)		suti	shuti	'name'

Table 7.2. *(continued)*

Gonçález Holguín		Jauja	Wanka	
(*d*) Gonçález Holguín {s} : Jauja /s/ : Wanka /h/				
sallca (323)		sallqa	hallqa	'cold, arid tableland'
(e) Gonçález Holguín {s} : Jauja /h/ : Wanka /s/				
sauca (324)	'mockery'	hawtru	sawka	'bad omen'

[a] Attested as *samúsac* (first person future) in Garcilaso (1609: II, xxvii) and Guaman Poma (1615: 319).

are (*d*) and (*e*), where in one case / s / shows up in Jauja (which by a Wanka-internal sound change is / h / in Waylla and Waycha), and in the other / s / appears in Wanka. The Jauja form is possibly not cognate.

In summary, of forty-one { ç/z } (= [s̲]) stems attested in Gonçález Holguín's *Vocabulario* for early-seventeenth-century Cuzco, thirty-five show / s / or a regular reflex thereof in Wanka. Of the remaining six that do not, five have attested variation with a regular reflex in colonial Cuzco-Collao. Twenty { s } (= [ṣ]) stems in Gonçález Holguín show the expected Wanka reflex. In an additional two the correspondence is obscured by a development internal to one or the other language. There are only two outright exceptions. The regularity of the correspondences clinches the argument that the colonial sibilant distinction in Cuzco-Collao is the reflex of a parallel distinction in the Central and Northern languages, one that presumably dates back to proto-Quechua and is not a quirk of Spanish orthographic conventions.

Written Evidence

The five texts comprising the "high tradition" agree remarkably on the sibilant distinction despite inconsistency in their orthographic treatment of areas of Quechua phonology that are underdifferentiated by Spanish orthography, such as the distinction between velar and uvular consonants. Table 7.3 lists corresponding stems

Table 7.3. Orthographic {ç/z} in Five Colonial Texts

Santo Tomás	Tercer Concilio	Gonçález Holguín	Pérez Bocanegra	Aguilar	modern form	gloss
(a) Syllable-initial						
quimça (101v)	quimza (29)	quimça (684)		quimça	kinsa	'three'
çocta (95v)	zocta (209)	çocta (86)		çocta	suqta	'six'
puçac (79r)	puzac (24)			puçacc	pusaq	'eight'
maci (145v)	maci (20)	maci (455)			masi	'partner'
çapa (116r)	zapa (41)	çapa (441)	çapa (393)	çapa (19)	sapa	'each'
-çapa (125r)	-zapa (31)	-çapa (327)		-çapa (20)	-sapa	'characterized by excess'
cira- (123v)		cira- (463)		cyray (19)	siray	'to sew'
cinga (123r)	cinca- (24)	cenca (598)		cenca (20)	sinqa	'nose'
guaci (132r)	huaci- (22)	huaci (324)		huaci (58)	wasi	'house'
ricci- (165r)	ricci- (7)	ricci- (655)	recce- (395)		riqsiy	'to recognize'
cinchi (123r)	cinchi (16)	cinchi (82)	cinchi (395)		sinchi	'too much'
çuma (131r)	zumac (18)	çumak (89)	çuma (B61)		sumaq	'beautiful'
çaça (47r)		çaça (74)			sasa	'difficult'
çaro- (85v)	zaru- (16)	çaru- (79)	çaro- (394)		saruy	'to step on'
cauça- (92v)	cauza- (13)[a]	cauça- (415)	cauça- (403)		kawsay	'to live'
çacça- (112r)	zacza (171)	çacça (74)	çacça- (398)		saqsa	'full'
ciqui (132v)		ciqui (368)			siki	'buttocks'
vicça (84r)	uicza (30)	vicça (351)	vicça (405)		wiksa	'stomach'
ciça (122v)	ciza (16)	ciça (82)	ciça- (B57)		sisa	'flower'
çama- (58r)	zama- (5)	çama- (323)	çama- (403)		samay	'to rest, breathe'
çaqui- (46r)	zaque- (25)	çaqque- ~ haqque- (79)			saqi-	'to abandon'
caci- (111v)	caci- (33)	caci (60)	caci (399)		qasi	'free, quiet'
quiça- (169v)	queza (170)	qqueça- (299)	queça- (396)		qisa	'to beg, disdain'
çara (116)	zara (67)	çara (79)	çara (395)		sara	'maize'
cassa- (111v)		ccaça- (497)			qasa	'frost'
caça (49v)						

sua- (168r)	zua- (20)	çua (559)	çua (396)		suway	'to steal'
		cittuy (85)	citui (385)			'brilliance'
	zeca- (236)	cecca- (81)			siqay	'to rise, climb'
guapci- (134v)		huapci (181)	huapci (398)			'vapor'
çupay (41r)	zupay (23)	çupay (89)	çupai (397)		supay	'devil'
ñauça (154v)	ñauza (43)	ñauça (469)			ñawsa	'blind'
çuni (131r)	zuni (238)	çuni (325)			suni	'high, tall'
	uzu- (36)	uçu- (350)			usuy	'to spill'
aci- (91)	aci- (237)	aci- (14)			asiy	'to laugh'
	zipci (21)	cipci- (83)				'whisper'
	cirpa (32)	cirpa- (84)				'turn over to someone else'
	pazu (171)	paçu (273)				'luckless, unfortunate'
	llauza (33)	llauça (212)				'sticky'
ticssin (174r)	ticci (22)	ticci (687)	tecce (399)		teqsi	'beginning'
ussa (189r)		vça (632)			usa	'flea'
			(*b*) *Syllable-final*			
canchiz (96v)	*canchis* (1584: 3r)	canchiz (1607: 218)		*canchis*	qanchis	'seven'
yzcon (78v)	*yscõ* (1584: 7r)	yzccon (270)	içcon (405)	*ysccon*	isqun	'nine'
masca- (151r)	*masca*- (31)	mazca- (439)		*masca*- (18)	maskhay	'to look for'
cozñi (127r)		ccozni (70)	coçñi (399)		q'usñi	'smoke'
cazco (118v)		cazco (620)			qhasqu	'chest'
aspi- (110r) azpi- (111r)		azpi- (42)			hasp'iy	'to scratch the earth'
muzco- (984)	*mosco*- (24)	mozcco- (673)	moçco (398)		musquy	'to dream'
chazqui- (121r)	*chasqui*- (47)	chazqui (98)			chaskiy	'to receive'
azna- (66r)	*asna*- (16)	anza- (42)	açna- (434)		asnay	'to stink'
	pasca- (208)	pazca- (279)				'to untie'

[a] The Tercer Concilio's *Sermones* are inconsistent for this stem: the ç variant predominates (pp. 13, 185, and elsewhere), but an *s* variant also appears occasionally (pp. 38, 115).

with colonial */ z / (dorsal [s̲]) in the five texts, along with the modern Cuzco-Collao form for each, if there is any. The sibilants have merged unconditionally in the modern language. (Irregular or unexpected forms are italicized.)

Santo Tomás's entries for 'frost', 'steal', 'beginning', and 'flea' diverge from the other syllable-initial stem sets, in that they show { s/ss } in place of { ç/z }. It is not clear how seriously this should be taken since Santo Tomás based the lexicon on several dialects without sufficiently specifying the parameters of variation between them. The same may be said for Santo Tomás's discrepancies in the 'look for' and 'scratch' sets among the syllable-final { ç/z } stem sets. But the works of the Tercer Concilio Limense and the late-seventeenth-century *Arte* by Aguilar diverge completely from Gonçález Holguín and Pérez Bocanegra on the syllable-final sibilants. The final { ç/z } in the latter two is replaced by { s }. The Anonymous *Vocabulario* of 1586 also shows a syllable-final { s } for { ç/z }, although I have not been able to establish that it is an independent witness from the works of the Tercer Concilio.[16] Once again, there is a problem deciding whether the variation reflects the Southern Peruvian Quechua phonological system or the scribes' Spanish phonological or orthographic systems. One piece of evidence that the orthographic variation reflects variation in the Southern Peruvian Quechua phonological system is a comparison John Howland Rowe (1950: 146f.) has made between the colonial sibilants and the cognate *s* : *sh* opposition in Juan Grimm's early-nineteenth-century lexicon of the Quichua of Quito, Ecuador. The regular correspondences are { ç/z } : Quito *s* and {s} : Quito *sh*. Nine irregular cognate sets (of a total of twelve irregularities) show { s } in Gonçález Holguín's vocabulary corresponding to *s* in Quito: *añas, asta, chhasca, chuspa, chuspi, huasca, illuspi-, llustti-*, and *ñusta*. All are syllable-final. The dissolution of the s̲ : ṣ distinction might thus have begun with a shift of ṣ > s̲ at the ends of syllables. If this was the case, the dorsals and apicals were in complementary distribution before the distinction disappeared phonetically. Further work is needed before this question can be resolved.

Table 7.4 shows correspondence sets for colonial */ s /(= apical [ṣ]) in the same texts. Once again, it is the works of Domingo de Santo Tomás that contain the problematic forms. This time, though, we are dealing with a dialectal shibboleth that was attested by other colonial observers: Southern ṣ : Central and Northern ʃ, written as { x } by Santo Tomás.[17] His entries for 'name' and 'to lead' show the Central and Northern initial [ʃ] and several more entries appear in cross-referenced matched pairs, one the Southern and one the Central/Northern form. (See the entries in table 7.4 for 'mouth', 'nest', and 'truth'.) The final discrepancy here is in the form for 'missing'. The Central/Northern form, *caxa*, suggests that the Southern form *caça* was simply a mistake, since the Central/Northern form would lead us to expect *cassa*. Of the syllable-final sets, Santo Tomás's *vichu-* is an unusual rendering of an unusual form. Although the remaining colonial witnesses show [ş] at the end of the first syllable, the modern form, which first appears in the Sahuaraura codex of *Usca Paucar*, has [x] instead. The environment for the change *ş* > *x*, before a palatal ejective, *č'* (< proto-Quechua **ç̌*) is unique for syllable-final [ş], as far as I know.

Sporadic shifts of both sibilants to [h] at the beginnings of words are attested in the variant stem forms shown in table 7.5. I have already discussed the morphological reanalysis of **şamu-* and subsequent shift of the initial *ş* to *h*, in connection with the external correspondences of the colonial sibilants. The shift had already taken place by the time Santo Tomás wrote his *Lexicon* (1560b), in which the Southern and Central/Northern cognates are *hamu-* and *xamu-*, respectively. Relic forms are attested in poetry by Garcilaso (1609: II, xxvii) and Guaman Poma (1615: 319). The etymologically appropriate form for the number 'one', *suq* (compare Jauja-Wanka *suk*), is cited marginally by Gonçález Holguín.[18] Santo Tomás listed two forms, *suc* and *çuc: suc hamo*, 'de otra manera' and *çuc ximi* 'otra razón' (Santo Tomás 1560b: 168r). Santo Tomás surprisingly associated the { s } form with the Southern **şamu-* > *hamu-* area and the { ç } form with the Central/North [ʃ]-stem area. This is confirmed by Guaman Poma (1615: 611), who uses the *suc* form in his imitation of Molina "el Cuzqueño." Reflexes with an initial sibilant are found in Argentine Quechua and in a semantically narrowed cast-off in Bolivia. The regular Bolivian reflex is a zero-stem, *uj*. The verb 'to raise' is cited by Santo Tomás with initial *s*. The initial / z / cited by the others was already in variation with initial *h* in Gonçález Holguín and currently has alternate forms: *h*-stem *hoqariy* in nuclear Cuzco and zero-stem *oqariy* in the Sicuani area. *Zaqi* ~ *haqi* 'to abandon' was variable through the eighteenth century, but is now *saqi*. The word for 'bush' was also in flux between a *z* and an *h* form during the seventeenth century, but is now invariably *sach'a*.

A number of stems vary both across the textual sample and within particular works. Table 7.6 lists several such stems. Gonçález Holguín (1608: 325) described variation in the way the sibilants were pronounced in some word stems. In one entry he wrote, "*Ssecssehuanmi*. I have an itch. See *cec cec*, and *cec cihuan* with (ç), a few say it with (ss)."[19]

In addition to the stems that Gonçález explicitly pointed out were variable, a number of his entries, such as *sapsi* ~ *çapçi*, *çocco* ~ *soqos*, and *çucçu* ~ *sucsu*, silently attest to the same variability (cf. Rowe 1950: 146). Joos (1952: 222–223) has made a useful observation about the perceptibility of an apical: dorsal sibilant distinction: "the differ-

Table 7.4. Orthographic {s} in Five Colonial Texts

Santo Tomás	Tercer Concilio	Gonçález Holguín	Pérez Bocanegra	Aguilar	modern form	gloss
			(a) Syllable-initial			
suyo (168r)		suyu (134)	suyu (708)		suyu	'spatial division'
		chhusac (123)	chussac (399)		ch'usaq	
pissi- (86r)	pisi (17)	pissi (634)	pissi (398)		pisi	'a few'
llucssi- (146v)	llocsi- (201)	llocsi- (215)		lloccssi- (57)	lluqsiy	'to leave'
xuti (179r)	suti- (187)	suti (332)	suti (708)		suti	'name'
guassa (135r)	huasa (208)	huassa (185)	huasa- (405)		wasa	'back'
puxa- (109v)		pussa- (298)	pusa- (434)		pusay	'to lead'
cussi (130r)	cusi (12)	cusi (56) cussi	cusi (398)		kusi	'happy'
simi (137r) *ximi*	simi (40)	simi (327)	simi (394)		simi	'mouth'
saya- (58r)	saya- (163)	saya- (324)			sayay	'to stand'
suya- (57v)		suya- (516)	suya- (397)		suyay	'to wait'
		sallca (323)			salqa	'puna'
vssinc (66r)	ususi (20)	vsvsi (545)	usussi (435)		ususi	'daughter of a man'
sullca (168v)		sullca (331)			sullk'a	'younger'
songo- (167v)	sonco (5)	soncco (330)	sonco (393)		sunqu	'heart, essence'
vssia- (178v)	usa (49)	vsa- (333)	vssa- (396) vsa- (708)			'to accomplish, advance'

quissa	quesa- (49)	quessa (306)			q'esa	'nest, disorder'
quixa (171v)						
caxa (118r)		cassa (165)			q'asa	'missing'
caça (131v)						
sutu- (62v)		suttu- (333)	sutu- (395)		sut'uy	'drip'
mussoc (153v)	musoc (18)	musok (359)			musuq	'new'
llasa- (145v)	llasa (47)	llassa			llasa	'heavy'
		llasa (211)				
sipas (167r)	sipas (187)	sipas (326)			sipas	'unmarried woman'
massa (151r)		massa (221)				'husband's brother'
sauca (166v)	sauca- (242)	sauca (324)				'mockery'
sullull (168v)	sullull (158)	sullull (332)				'truth'
xullull						
(*b*) *Syllable-final*						
yscay (48r)	yscay (32)	yscay (493)		yscay	iskay	'two'
aslla (86r)	aslla (206)	aslla (634)		aslla (20)	aslla	'a little'
pisco (83v)	piscu (287)				pisqu	'bird'
assua (86)	ashuan- (18)	ashuan (35)	ashuan (394)		aswan	'more'
quispi- (171v)	quespi- (24)	qquespi- (59)	quespi- (396)		qispiy	'to free, save'
usca- (41r)		vsca- (358)	vsca- (406)		uskay	'to beg'
yspa- (143r)	yspa- (242)	ysppay (289)			hisp'ay	'to urinate'
vichu- (49r)	uischu- (16)	vischhu- (253)	vischu- (398)		wixch'uy	'to throw (out)'

Table 7.5. *h* Stems in Five Colonial Texts

Santo Tomás	Tercer Concilio	Gonçález Holguín	Pérez Bocanegra	Aguilar	modern form	gloss
çuc (103)	huc (31)	huc (687)			huq	'one'
suc		çuc (87)				
succari- (168)	zoccari- (233)	hoccari- (163)			(h)uqariy	'to raise'
		çoccari- (86)				
çacha (14)	hacha (233)	çacha		sacha (77)	sach'a	'bush'
		hacha (74)				
hamu- (168)	hamu- (2)	hamu (690)	hamoc- (396)	hamu (54)	hamuy	'to come'
xamu- (103r)						

Table 7.6. Variable Sibilant Stems in Five Colonial Texts

Santo Tomás	Tercer Concilio	Gonçález Holguín	Pérez Bocanegra	Aguilar	modern form	gloss
sispa- (168r)	sispa (201)	cispa- (85)	sispa- (397)		sispa	'near'
cispa- (168r)		cichpa- (85)				
çuchu- (129r)		çuchu- (87)			such'u	'lame'
	suchu (30)	suchu- (331)				
suyro (168v)		suyru (333)				'oversize clothing'
çuyro (131r)						
aposca- (109v)	apusca- (23)	apusca- (32)	apuzqui (394)			'ancestor'
çullu- (131r)		sullu (332)			sulluy	'abort, miscarry'
sullu- (179r)						
xullu-						
coça (123v)	coza (186)	coça (361)		ccossa (76)	qusa	'husband'
	cosa (49)					

ence would always be 'heard' by native speakers," he writes, "with the customary reservation applicable to all cases of small acoustic differences. . . , namely that in listening to a stranger or under bad listening conditions it would normally be the morpheme that was identified first . . . with subsequent identification (if called for) of that particular sibilant phoneme from the morpheme identity."

Identification of the sibilant depends on associating it with a particular lexical morpheme. This accounts for the unusual behavior of the sibilants. Cerrón-Palomino (1977: 62–63, 101ff.) has observed that, in modern Wanka Quechua, there is a pronounced tendency toward morpheme-internal "harmony" for the ṣ : s̲ and ç : č oppositions. Once one of the sibilants or one of the affricates has been identified in a morpheme, the other sibilant or affricate will be the same. There appears to have been a similar tendency toward morpheme-internal "sibilant harmony" in colonial Southern Peruvian Quechua. (The back stops behave in much the same way in modern Southern Peruvian Quechua: a morpheme may have two velar stops or two uvular stops, but not one of each.) Notice that in each of the four variable stems cited from Gonçález Holguín, both sibilants are affected simultaneously. The initial *z* > *s* shift in the variable stems *cispa* (table 7.6) and *çocco(s)* may be accounted for by lexical spread of syllable-final *z* > *s* and subsequent "sibilant harmony." Because there are many conditions under which identifying the sibilant depends on identifying the morpheme, the sibilants seem to function as stem-class markers; this might explain why the sibilant correspondences are inconsistent around the edges.

Some Further Problems with the Sibilants

Landerman's (1979, 1983) identification of the colonial sibilants in Quechua, Aymara, and Spanish measures up well to the colonial Southern Peruvian Quechua data presented here. It is a real breakthrough in our knowledge of colonial Native Andean philology. Among other things, the identification of the sibilants will be useful in evaluating ethnohistoric arguments when they rest on etymological evidence. Here is a brief example.

R. T. Zuidema's (1977, 1982a: 153–154) recent discussion of the colonial vocabulary of kinship draws attention to the fact that 'child of a man' is treated differently from 'child of a woman' in the earliest sources, as indeed in many contemporary Quechua-speaking communities. Gender is distinguished for the children of a man—*churi* 'son', *ususi* 'daughter' [*churiy* 'my son', *ususiy* 'my daughter' (man speaking)]—but not for a woman, who uses only *wawa* 'baby, child' [*waway* 'my child' (woman speaking)], regardless of the child's sex. Zuidema argues that this distinction is crucial to understanding how the Inka kinship system worked. The distinction, from a male point of view, makes reference to the potential loss of the daughter from the man's patri-group by marriage into another patri-group. *Ususi* 'daughter', as Zuidema observes, resembles the colonial term *uçuni* 'to be lost' (Gonçález Holguín 1608: 350; cf. *uzu-* 'to spill', Tercer Concilio Limense 1585: 36). The expression *uçuni* seems to illuminate the 'daughter' term. And what could be simpler than to find an etymological connection between the two?

But the point rests on identifying *uçu-* ~ *uzu-* with the initial portion of the daughter term: *vssinc* (Santo Tomás 1560b: 66r); *ususi* (Tercer Concilio Limense 1585: 20); *vsvsi* (Gonçález Holguín 1608: 545); *usussi* (Pérez Bocanegra 1631: 435). As we have seen, the orthographic difference, { ç ~ z } in the 'loss' stem, { s ~ ss } in 'daughter' represented two distinctive sibilants until the end of the seventeenth century. The different colonial sources are completely consistent in distinguishing the 'loss' stem from the 'daughter' stem despite the fact that no scribal tradition can be established among them. Moreover, there is no independent evidence of a deverbal derivational affix, *-*si*. *Ususi* and *uçu-* have nothing to do with one another, at least not etymologically.[20]

There are several additional problems involving the sibilants. I shall simply list them here.

(1) We have already seen that there is some evidence for lexical spread of s̠ > ṣ at the ends of syllables, followed by reassignment of the distinction to the status of allophonic variants of a single phoneme, before the phonetic difference was lost. Further work with written sources drawing upon a wider lexical sample should corroborate this and allow us to establish the chronology and structural pattern of the merger.

(2) The allophonic distribution of colonial Southern Peruvian Quechua ṣ also requires further study. Evidence from Betanzos's early *Suma y narración de los Incas* suggests that it may have had an allophonic distribution similar to modern Wanka. Betanzos frequently wrote etymological ṣ as *x* before *i* (e.g., 1987 [1551]: 101, 185), suggesting that it palatalized to [ʃ] in this context, as in Wanka. But Betanzos also shows some etymologically unexpected uses of *x* (e.g., *Caxamalca* for the place name that usually appears as *Cassamarca*, 131).

(3) A relationship needs to be established between the sibilant merger and the syllable-final weakenings and mergers that have taken place in Southern Peruvian Quechua since the European invasion (see chapters 9 and 10). The sibilant distinction was last attested at the same time as

the lenition of palatals was taking place. The expected [ʃ] reflex of the syllable-final palatals does not appear in historical texts.[21] On the other hand, dialectal evidence shows that [č] did not change directly to [s̠], since the syllable-final merger of [ʃ] and [s̠] didn't take place in stems in some dialects of Cuzco-Collao Quechua. [ʃ] is the regular syllable-final reflex of [č] in stems for many speakers living south of Cuzco. In addition, a trace of syllable-final [ʃ] appears in the form of aspiration on the following stop (even in ʃ > *s* dialects) if aspiration is permitted phonotactically. This is attested in the eighteenth-century versified dramas. Was there ever a stage in which Cuzco-Collao Quechua distinguished [s̠] and [ṣ] at the beginning of syllables, but [ṣ] (< [ṣ] and [s̠]) and [ʃ] (< [č]) at the end? Perhaps the present-day distribution of the reflexes of syllable-final [č] can provide a clue as to the dialectal spread of the merger of [s̠] and [ṣ].

(4) As we shall see in the following chapter, the sources of the Southern Peruvian Quechua ejectives are a vexing problem. Etymological [ṣ] favored ejectivity in the stem wherever ejectives were phonotactically permitted. In stems that were minimal pairs for the *ṣ* : *s̠* opposition, the distinction is now maintained by ejectivity (again, where phonotactically permitted). The *ṣ*-stem regularly acquired the ejective. Thus **qeza* 'disdained': **qeṣa* 'nest' became *qesa : q'esa* and *qaza* 'frost' : *qaṣa* 'missing, cove' became *qasa : q'asa*. The historical relationship between apical *ṣ* and ejectives requires further study in order to determine the precise conditions under which it holds.

(5) Along the same lines, Alfredo Torero noticed that "a high proportion of the roots that in proto-Quechua possessed / c / [= ç̌] in internal position are found with glottalization in Cuzco and Bolivian, either on the affricate . . . or the initial stop of the stem if there is one . . ."[22] If a relationship can be demonstrated and made more specific, it will constitute evidence that the merger of / č / and / ç̌ / followed the incorporation of ejectivity into the phonological system. Was the merger complete before the conquest or systematically missed in Spanish orthography? If the latter, might there be oblique evidence of *ç̌* in colonial texts? What was the relationship, if any, between the loss of the *č* : *ç̌* distinction and the merger of *ṣ* and *s̠*?

Assuming that the sibilant mergers, the syllable-final lenitions, and the spread of ejectives and aspirates are relatively recent innovations in Southern Quechua, the Southern Quechua prototype language has a closer affinity to the Central Quechua Junín-Wanka language than has previously been assumed. I have shown that, for the sibilant distinction, there is a point-by-point correspondence between Junín-Wanka and Southern Peruvian Quechua, once relatively recent and generally incomplete innovations in the two languages have been set aside.[23] We can no longer assume that Quechua subgrouping requires an initial division into Central (Quechua I or Quechua B) and Peripheral (Quechua II or Quechua A) branches (cf. Bird, Browman, and Durbin 1984: 189–193). The answers to many of the larger questions of Quechua genetic subgrouping and linguistic history are to be found in the fine detail of written evidence.

8 The Ejectives and Aspirates

In the synchronic grammar of Southern Quechua, the ejective (glottalization) and aspirate features are functionally different from the other segmental features in that they are *culminative.* (In this chapter, as elsewhere in the book, I use *glottalization* to refer to the phonological feature and *ejective* to refer to the class of sounds so produced.)[1] They occur only once per word; they are restricted to the first oral stop in the word, to syllable-initial position, and to lexical stems. One manifestation of the once-per-word restriction is the "epenthetic-*h*." Quechua word stems that begin with vowels are normally preceded by a glottal catch.[2] But if the word contains an ejective, the glottal catch would violate the once-per-word restriction. Such words have an initial *h* instead. Thus, in the modern language we observe doublets like *'allpa* ~ *hallp'a* 'land' and *'irqi* ~ *hirq'i* 'child'. (I include the glottal catch for clarity.) The segmental features other than glottalization and aspiration are relatively freer in their distribution. They can occur more than once per word and are found both in stems and suffixes. Apart from the weakenings and mergers at the ends of syllables (and this is a large exception) they can occur anyplace in the syllable as well.

From a genetic point of view, the ejectives and aspirates are a mystery. Their distribution in the Quechua family is summarized in figure 8.1. Ejectives and aspirates appear only in the Southern Quechua languages, including Southern Peruvian Quechua, although there are reflexes of aspirates in some Ecuadorian (Northern) varieties (Cerrón-Palomino 1987a: 187–188). There are no reflexes of either feature in the Central Quechua languages. Even in Southern Quechua they are quite irregular. Thus, for stems in which Cuzco-Collao Quechua has an aspirate, Bolivian might have the corresponding ejective or plain stop (Parker 1969c: 84f.; Carenko 1972: 100, 1975 [1972]: 10; Stark 1975: 214–218),

Figure 8.1

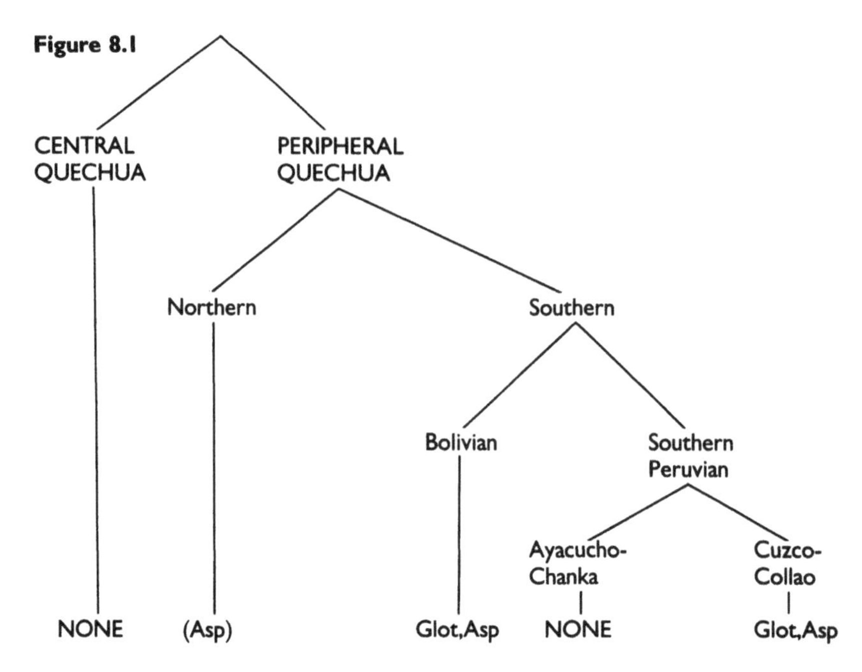

as in Cuz. *phusuqu* ~ Bol. *pusuqu* 'foam'; Cuz. *wathiya* ~ Bol. *wat'iya* 'earth oven'; Cuz. *khaya* ~ Bol. *kaya* 'freeze-dried oca (*Oxalis tuberosa*)' (Stark 1975: 214–215). Likewise, within Cuzco-Collao Quechua, there are dialect variants of the same stems that differ only in the ejective and aspirate features, such as *k'ullpi* ~ *khullpi* 'pieces of a material used for fuel' and *llusk'a* ~ *lluskha* 'slippery'. Modern Southern Peruvian Quechua is split between two major dialects, Cuzco-Collao Quechua, which has ejective and aspirate stops, and Ayacucho-Chanka Quechua, which lacks them (see chapters 1 and 5). The evidence that Ayacucho-Chanka Quechua ever had these features is slim (chapter 5). The ejectives and aspirates are irregular even *within* Cuzco-Collao Quechua. However shallow the historical perspective, reconstruction of the ejectives and aspirates is problematic; the problems increase in proportion to the number of dialect witnesses used.

As we saw in chapter 2, there are good reasons to believe that glottalization and aspiration are areal features that entered Southern Quechua as a result of long-term, intimate contact with neighboring languages in the Jaqi/Aru family, including Aymara. The Ecuadorian aspirates aside, ejectives and aspirates only appear in a contiguous area from southernmost Peru through Bolivia; the Ecuadorian aspirates are thought to reflect the influence of the Inka lingua franca, which was also Southern Quechua. The territorial range of glottalization and aspiration includes areas in which Aymara was spoken at the time of the European invasion that are contiguous with the modern Aymara territory. It also includes the heartland of the Inka state, which might have been a vehicle for diffusion of an Aymara vocabulary stratum. Sixteenth-century missionary priests observed the strong inclination on the part of the Inka court in Cuzco to borrow foreign and unusual lexical items, "introducing words that by chance were used earlier, but no longer are, or taking advantage of the words used by the Inkas and lords, or taking them from other nations with which they were in contact" (Tercer Concilio Limense 1584: 74r.)[3]

It is striking that the Southern Quechua and Jaqi/Aru languages have influenced each other so intimately, when the more recent (though also long-term) influence of Spanish on Southern Peruvian Quechua has been so much more superficial (chapter 4). This difference reflects the nature of the contact situation. Thomason and Kaufman (1976) distinguish stable contact with widespread borrowing (such as the pre-Columbian contact between Quechua and the Jaqi/Aru languages) from language shift (such as the post-conquest contact between Quechua and Spanish) and observe that the structural effects of the two types of contact differ. Such nonlinguistic features as the degree of bilingualism, the relationship between the speech communities in contact, and the presence or absence of language shift play an important role in determining the effects of language contact. As I reconstructed the preconquest social setting (chapter 2), Southern Quechua was intimately intermeshed with Puquina and Jaqi/Aru languages, without a tendency for speakers to shift from one language to another. In stable multilingual settings such as this, speakers tend to borrow individual forms from the other languages. They also accommodate to the phonological and syntactic patterns of the speakers with whom they are in contact, resulting in gradual structural convergence between the respective languages.

The scenario of intimate contact, massive borrowing and structural convergence between Southern Peruvian Quechua and Jaqi/Aru is especially pronounced for the ejectives and aspirates. A disproportionate number of stems with ejectives or aspirates are similar in Southern Peruvian Quechua and Aymara: 67 percent of the Southern Peruvian Quechua stems with these features are shared with Aymara, as opposed to 20 percent without either feature (Stark 1975: 212–213). The disproportionate number of similar stems with the features suggests that a word was more likely to be borrowed if it had an ejective or aspirate stop, for aesthetic reasons. It is also possible that Quechua speakers initially perceived glottalization and aspiration as "foreign" features and that loanwords were more likely than native vocabulary to acquire glottalization and aspiration even after they were borrowed, as signs of their foreign status.

Both features, however, are well integrated into the segmental phonology of modern Cuzco-Collao Quechua. There are five historical sources for the modern ejectives and aspirates.

(1) A core set of words with ejectives and aspirates was undoubtedly introduced into Southern Quechua from the Jaqi/Aru family; the process of borrowing tended to favor stems that were phonologically marked by glottalization and aspiration.

(2) Glottalization and aspiration spread through the lexicon by means of "sound imagery" (or "primary sound symbolism"), in which the form of a word comes to mirror its use or meaning.

(3) They also spread by means of "associative lexical influence" (or "secondary sound symbolism"), in which the features spread from one lexical stem to other stems that are cognitively associated with the first (Parker 1969c: 85; Proulx 1972: 143–144).

(4) As we saw in chapter 7, the retracted sibilant ṣ and the retracted palatal stop č̣ are possible genetic sources of glottalization. For both, phonetic retractedness was reinterpreted as glottalization and moved to a position consistent with the constraints on glottalization mentioned at the beginning of the chapter.

(5) Aspiration appears as a reflex of syllable-final palatal stops, which weakened and caused the stop immediately following to aspirate, again consistent with the constraints discussed in the first paragraph of this chapter.

This chapter concentrates on the modern results of the second and third of the five sources of glottalization and aspiration, namely, sound imagery and associative lexical influence. A detailed study of the massive lexical borrowing from the Jaqi/Aru languages is outside the scope of this book. (See Hardman-de-Bautista [1985], Adelaar [1986 and 1987], and Cerrón-Palomino [1986] for preliminary discussions of the problem.) The fourth and fifth are relatively minor genetic sources of glottalization and aspiration, respectively. In order that either could be represented in the speakers' mental lexicons, ejectives and aspirates would already have to have been integrated into the sound system of Cuzco-Collao Quechua. The fourth was discussed in chapter 7, along with the sibilants; the fifth is discussed in chapter 10, along with the syllable-final weakenings.

Iconicity, Double Articulation, and Sound Change

In order to understand the roles of sound imagery and associative lexical influence in the spread of aspiration and glottalization in Cuzco-Collao Quechua, we must first consider their place in the repertoire of linguistic changes. The classic nineteenth-century handbooks of historical linguistics, such as Hermann Paul's *Principles of the History of Language* (1880), distinguished regular sound changes, or *Lautgesetze,* from other types of change, such as analogy and contamination. The crux of the distinction is that regular sound changes (*Lautgesetze*) are mechanical, in that they involve involuntary changes in the articulatory habits of a community of speakers. Insofar as they are mechanical, they are also exceptionless (Osthoff and Brugmann 1878). That is to say, given a change in which sound *X* becomes *Y,* for any given context in which that change takes place, every *X* will become *Y,* regardless of other factors. Meaning, use, semantic word-class, and syntactic category do not have any role in determining the progress of a regular sound change. The Neogrammarian doctrine of exceptionless sound change remains one of the cornerstones of historical linguistics.

Other types of change, such as analogy and contamination, are motivated conceptually. In analogical change, speakers set up a conceptual proportion between two forms or two grammatical markers and restructure the more complex of the forms on the model of the simpler one. For example, it is common for English speakers to pluralize *fish* as *fishes,* discarding the irregular zero-plural *fish* in favor of the more frequent *-es* plural. In contamination, speakers associate two words mentally and make them similar to one another in form. To take another example from American English, many speakers use *irregardless* in place of *regardless,* by association with *irrespective.*

Analogy and contamination provide explanations for forms that would otherwise appear to be exceptions to regular sound changes. The critical difference between these types of change and exceptionless sound change is that analogy and contamination are motivated by meaning, whereas meaning could play no role whatsoever in exceptionless sound changes. The crucial assumption behind this distinction (and behind the doctrine of the exceptionless sound change) is that it is possible for sound to change autonomously from the rest of language.

Ferdinand de Saussure (1971 [1915]: 110, 208) argued that the autonomy of sound change followed from the arbitrary nature of the linguistic sign; similar points were made by Whitney (1875: 106) and Meillet (1967 [1924]: 2). Saussure's doctrine of the "arbitrariness of the sign," which posits a radical separation between linguistic form and meaning, has been challenged on a number of grounds—epistemological, methodological, and empirical—to the point that it is no longer viable as a working principle of linguistics (Benveniste 1939; Jakobson 1965; Williams 1977: 168; Friedrich 1979a; Waugh 1984). Friedrich (1979a) refers to it as a "debilitating premise" in that it has discouraged investigation into the relationships between linguistic form and meaning. For the purposes of the present discussion, it need only be said that the Saussurean doctrine is too powerful. Although it posits a radical disjunction between form and meaning, much linguistic change is motivated in a positive way by form-meaning or form-function relationships, as scholars such as Malkiel (1962, 1964, 1982), Kuryłowicz (1949), Andersen (1980), Anttila (1977b), Watkins (1962), and Haiman (1985) have demonstrated for lexical, morphological, and syntactic change. The doctrine of arbitrariness incorrectly predicts that morphological, syntactic, and lexical changes should be as arbitrary and as regular as sound change.

The relative autonomy of sound change and the principle of regularity also follow from another "design feature" of language, the principle of "double articulation," also known as "duality of patterning".[4] "Double articulation" was first observed by Aristotle, who wrote in the *Poetics* (§20) that "the Letter is an indivisible sound of a particular kind, one that may become a factor in an intelligible sound."

Language is structured (or *articulated* or *patterned*) in terms of two relatively autonomous sets of conventions: (1) a set of conventions for meaningful elements (intonation contours, morphemes, words, phrases, clauses, interactional routines, and so forth), in which form and meaning co-vary directly; and (2) a set of conventions for elements that are meaningless in themselves (phonological features) but serve to distinguish the meaningful elements (Hockett 1960: 152; Martinet 1964 [1960]: 22–24; Jakobson and Waugh 1979: 43–44, 177; Shapiro 1983: 13). Duality of patterning (or "double articulation") allows a small number of meaningless phonological elements to be combined to distinguish an infinite set of meaningful utterances. The relationship between levels of patterning is very specific: the second (nonmeaningful) level is made up of those aspects of phonology that can distinguish meaningful elements (segmental features and certain prosodic features); it does not consist of sound in general, nor of form in general.[5] This formulation of "duality of patterning" correctly predicts the scope of exceptionless sound changes. Changes are regular and independent of meaning only insofar as they occur within the second, nonmeaningful level of patterning.

The fact that the two levels of patterning are relatively autonomous does not prevent speech sounds from being motivated by (or *iconic* of) meaning. For speakers of a language, the relationships between forms and meanings are completely natural and necessary (Benveniste 1939; Friedrich 1979a). Speakers have an intuitive sense of the ways in which sounds are used in the language, a sense that may come into play in linguistic change. The speaker's intuitive feel for the language might suggest that a newly coined word should have a certain shape reflecting other words, as when Southern Peruvian Quechua speakers formed *qutiy* 'to give something back' from the verb *quy* 'to give' and *kutiy* 'to return', or when English speakers extend *-oholic* from *alcoholic* 'one who is addicted to alcohol' to form *jazzoholic* 'one who is addicted to jazz'. Similarly, the English words beginning with *fl*, such as *flicker, fly, flip, flop, flap, flit,* and *flute* are all words of breath and erratic motion. As English speakers, our intuitive sense of the language would suggest that an unfamiliar word beginning with *fl* should be a semantic relative of the other *fl* words. Conversely, we might vaguely grasp for a concept that we intuitively know *should* begin with *fl* and coin a new word. Thus, although the two levels of patterning are autonomous, the inner sense that speakers have of their language tends toward motivating the sound shape of words. The natural feel that such words have is culture-specific and conventionalized (Empson 1947 [1930]: 9–15). Moreover, the extent to which linguistic forms are motivated iconically also varies across cultures. Quechua culture, as we shall see, places a premium on iconicity in language.

To say that the levels of patterning are autonomous is not the same as saying that they are unrelated *in principle.* The phonological forms of words are better thought of along a gradient of motivation from the most iconic and motivated to the most symbolic and unmotivated (Saussure 1971 [1915]: 181–183; Friedrich 1979a). The types of motivation are multiple. The feel that speakers have for their language allows forms to be motivated by cultural-linguistic perceptions of the world (onomatopoeia, primary sound symbolism, or sound imagery),[6] by other linguistic forms (secondary sound symbolism, associative lexical influence, phonetic associative interference, or metaphoric iconicity), or by the relationships between patterns of forms (diagrammatic iconicity). The first two types of motivation, sound imagery and associative lexical influence, are the most significant for understanding the patterning of Quechua glottalization and aspiration. (Diagrammatic iconicity, the third type, figures in the discussion of the spread of sound change in chapter 10.) Because the historical data are so difficult to interpret, I rely on the modern distributions of these features to reconstruct a plausible scenario for their entry into the Cuzco-Collao sound system. I should add that partly due to the nature of the phenomenon, and partly due to the lack of a well-established tradition of Quechua historical philology, my treatment of associative lexical influence is speculative, a first attempt to measure the compass of the problem and to set out an approach that will account for the peculiar historical and lexical distributions of the ejectives and aspirates.

Cultural Identification of Word and Object

Sound imagery (onomatopoeia) and associative groups (like the English *fl-* set) are common enough in languages of the world, but they assume a special importance in Southern Peruvian Quechua, where they pervade the lexicon. The Quechua fondness for iconicity corresponds to their orientation toward language in general. For Quechua speakers, language is part and parcel of the natural world. Words are consubstantial with their objects in a deeper sense than in the Western tradition: we have a long-standing tradition, reflected in folk and learned theories of language, that words stand for their objects and that language is (or at least should be) a mirror of the world. In Quechua culture, words are consubstantial with their objects in the same sense in which the Trinity is consubstantial. Language is both in and of the natural world. This naturally led to confusion when the first missionaries introduced Roman Catholic saints and symbols; in their sermons, they were forced to explain not only that the objects that they appeared to adore were signs rather than idols but also that there were such things as signs in the first place. The Quechua identification of word and object helps explain why practical knowledge of the everyday world is identified with knowledge of language and ability to speak and is designated with a single verb stem, *yachay,* which is usually translated as 'to know', but also can be used to mean 'to know Quechua' without any modification and without mentioning the language.

The pervasive cultural identification of word and object is reflected in the extent to which the lexicon is shot through with nonsystematic similarities of sound reflecting—and creating—similarities of meaning. The kinship of sound and meaning is beautifully evoked by José María Arguedas (1982 [1958]: 64–65) in his novel *Deep Rivers,* in which he reflects upon an associative set in Ayacucho Quechua:[7]

> The Quechua ending *yllu* is onomatopoeic. *Yllu,* in one form, means the music of tiny wings in flight, music created by the movement of light objects. This term is similar to another broader one—*illa. Illa* is the name used for a certain kind of light, also for monsters with birth defects caused by moonbeams. *Illa* is a two-headed child, or a headless calf, or a giant pinnacle, all black and shining, with a surface caused by a stream of white rock, of opaque light. An ear of corn with rows of kernels that cross or form whorls is also *illa; illas* are mythical bulls that live at the bottom of solitary lakes, of highland ponds ringed with cattail reeds, where black ducks dwell. All *illas* bring good or bad luck, always to the nth degree. To touch an *illa,* and to either die or be resurrected, is possible. The term *illa* has a phonetic relationship and, to a certain extent, shares a common meaning with the suffix *yllu.*

Arguedas goes on to speak of the *tankayllu,* a humming insect; *pinkuyllu,* a heroic, giant flute; *zumbayllu,* a whirring top; *illa,* 'the diffusion of nonsolar light'; *illapa,* lightning; and *illariy* 'the light of dawn'. According to Arguedas, "*Illa* is not the term for fixed light, like the resplendent, supernatural light of the sun. It represents a lesser light—a radiance, the lightning flash, the rays of the sun, all light that vibrates."

Arguedas's insight is that the (submorphemic) sequence *yll* or *ill* ([ιλ]) is "onomatopoeic" in a sense beyond the usual one in which the combination of a high, compressed vowel and consonant would be said to evoke 'lightness'; the words in his passage evoke and interanimate each other. The sound sequence stitches together an open network of lexical stems whose forms evoke one another, and whose meanings interpenetrate, making each one a stem in which "the sound must seem an echo to the sense" (Pope 1711: 419).

Rarely are lexical networks as closed and compact as the following lexical diagram, in which consonant gradation reflects the semantic organization of the set. (The word-stems are not related derivationally to each other.)

Pampa is a 'flat plain or surface that is conceptually unbounded'; *pata* 'a floor, agricultural terrace, or restricted two-dimensional space'; *pacha* an 'enclosed three-dimensional space, a state-of-affairs or world, a moment of time'; *pakay* 'to hide within a three-dimensional space'; and *paqa-riy* 'to give birth, or to emerge from a three-dimensional space'. The derivational suffix on the last form aside, the stems differ by the place of articulation of the medial stop. The successive backing of the stop is isomorphic to a series of spatial and dimensional restrictions in the conceptual succession of the denotata. The first stem, *pampa,* is a flat plain or a two-dimensional surface that is conceptually unbounded. The nasal preceding the internal stop makes this example exceptional in terms of the formal structure of the set. But the exception is motivated by the fact that the expected form *papa* is taken up with the meaning 'potato'. The second, *pata,* is a restricted version of *pampa,* a bounded two-dimensional space such as the floor of a room or an agricultural terrace. A further conceptual development is shown in the next member of the set, *pacha,* which refers to a three-dimensional enclosed area in space (the referent 'world') or in time ('moment of time'). The next semantic step through this diagrammatic set, to *pakay,* includes a perceptual focus on something lying within the dimensions set up by *pacha,* and the resultant denotatum, in verbal form (with final suffix *-y*), is 'to hide' (within a three-dimensional space). The last item of the set involves the restriction of the previous step by the explicit cancellation

Figure 8.2

chanlalan	'sound of breaking glass or jingling coins'
akhakáw	'ouch' (reaction to being burned)
k'ichichichiy	'to creak, gnash one's teeth, to make a squishing noise'
ch'allallalla	'cry baby'
qhurururuy	'to snore'
	(cf. *qhurquy*, 'to snore')
ruqhuququy	'to thunder'
q'aqraray	'to thunder'
t'uqraray	'to thunder'
q'ulululuy	'to growl' (stomach)
	'to mate' (llamas and alpacas)
thinininiy	'to giggle'
ixixixiy	'to laugh'

of what was represented by *pakay*. The meaning of *paqa-riy*—stem *paqa-* modified by the (productive) inceptive suffix *-ri-* 'to emerge from a three dimensional space' (contextually, 'to give birth')—presupposes the existence of that space and the previous location of the associated noun adjunct within its dimensions.

Sound Images

Charles Sanders Peirce (1940 [1902]: 105) defined *images* as signs that "partake of the simple qualities" of their objects. They may be graphic, optical, perceptual, mental, or verbal (Mitchell 1984), but what they have in common is that the form of the sign reflects its object directly and concretely. Sound images include verbal signs that are sometimes referred to as "sound symbolic" or "onomatopoeic." Consider the following Southern Peruvian Quechua stems for types of sounds in figure 8.2 (cf. Solá and Cusihuamán 1967a, ch. 12: 10, 1967b: ch. 6: 10; Cusihuamán 1976a: 216–218).

All use reduplication; the class is open, which means that Quechua speakers can productively create new reduplicated stems, especially verbs, for sounds. These stems may be formed either directly on the basis of a sound or by building on a monosyllabic onomatopoeic word denoting a sound or other quality. They may take any of the grammatical morphology other stems take, although they are distinctive in that they are three or four syllables long, as opposed to the two-syllable norm for Southern Peruvian Quechua word stems.

In an image, the information provided by the form about the meaning depends on the acoustic quality of the signal. Many examples of sound imagery involve words that stand for types of sounds. In such words, the pronunciations are similar to the sounds they represent. There are also more abstract examples in which an understanding of the similarity between form and meaning depends on a more exact knowledge of the acoustic properties of a particular sound. This is particularly true of the ejectives and aspirates.

Ejective and aspirated stops are marked in relation to their nonejective or nonaspirated counterparts, that is, they provide additional acoustic information beyond the corresponding unmarked stops. Both features delay the onset of voicing in the following vowel; they are also characterized by a greater discharge of energy as compared to the unmarked stop. In an aspirated stop, the acoustic energy is spread over a relatively longer time interval in which the vocal organs deviate from a rest position; in an ejective stop, the acoustic energy is compressed into a relatively shorter time interval corresponding to the relatively shorter duration of the actual occlusion (Jakobson and Halle 1956: 42f.; Jakobson and Waugh 1979: 145). The acoustic properties of glottalization and aspiration are used in the sound images listed in figures 8.3 and 8.4. Aspiration reflects the expulsion of air in the denotata; glottalization, sharpness or violence.

Such sound images are especially appropriate for the words that describe body functions and body emissions. The first five stems in figure 8.3 have aspirated stops; these reflect the expulsion of air in the actions of sneezing, spitting, belching, and farting. Other sounds in these words also contribute to the images. Notice that the words for spitting, *thuqay* and *qhutu,* have uvular (*q*) and alveolar (*t*) stops. The palatal stop (*ch*) in the words for sneezing is likewise significant, whether it is aspirated as in *achhiw* or ejective as in *hach'iy.* Both ejective and aspirate are equally appropriate to the image function for 'sneeze' but represent different aspects of the action: air expulsion for the aspirate versus a sharp, violent sound for the ejective. Aside from the alternation of aspirated and glottalized consonants, the differences between these two stems for 'sneeze' result from the fact that all Quechua verb stems end in a vowel, with the final *y* marking the infinitive, and from the automatic addition of an epenthetic *h* to any vowel-initial stem containing an ejective: *hach'iy.*

This set includes several loanwords from Spanish in which a stop has been glottalized. In *hach'a* 'ax' and *hasut'i* 'whip', the ejectives reflect the sharp sounds made by these instruments. Once again, the initial *h* in these words is epenthetic and reflects the presence of glottalization elsewhere in the word. In both native Quechua word stems and Spanish loans, the compressed energy discharge of the ejectives reproduces the sharpness or violence of the action referred to by the word, as in *saq'ay* 'to take out'; *wikch'uy* 'to expel violently, to vomit' (compare the words

Figure 8.3

thuqay	'to spit'
qhutu	'spit' (n.)
khasay	'to belch'
khapay	'to fart'
achhiw	sound made when sneezing
hach'iy	'to sneeze'

Figure 8.4

hach'a	[< Sp. *hacha*] 'ax'
hasut'i	[< Sp. *azote*] 'whip'
wikch'uy	'to expel violently, to vomit'
sik'iy	'to take or pull out violently'
hayt'ay	'to kick'
hich'ay	'to throw out'
saq'ay	[< Sp. *sacar?*] 'to take out'
t'ira-	'to pull out'
t'inkay	'to flick with the finger'

for body emissions in fig. 8.3), *sik'iy* 'to take or pull out violently', as when a plant is uprooted; and *hayt'ay* 'to kick'.

Associative Influence

Peirce (1940 [1902]: 105) identified a second type of iconic signs, which he called *metaphors* and defined (cryptically) as signs that "represent the representative [i.e., sign-like] character of a representamen [the form of a sign] by representing a parallel in something else." Metaphoric icons are motivated in ways that do not necessarily involve direct resemblance of sound and meaning, but rather resemblance of words to each other by a vaguely sensed affinity: similarity of meaning, similarity of referent, or frequent association with another stem (Firth 1935: 44–45; Bolinger 1940; Mannheim and Newfield 1982: 215). Quechua word-stems are often organized as open and fluid networks of associations, whose similarity is indicated by partial similarity of form. The passage from Arguedas on the meanings of *illa* and associated words is a good example of a metaphoric or associative set. In traditional handbooks of historical linguistics, the process by which associated words influence one another formally is known as "contamination." Hermann Paul (1889 [1880]: 160) defined it as "the process by which two synonymous forms of expression force themselves simultaneously into the consciousness, so that neither of the two makes its influence felt purely and simply: a new form arises in which elements of one mingle with elements of the other." The forms that are brought together are etymologically unrelated, but associated in the speaker's intuitive sense of the language. In order to avoid the pejorative connotation of "contamination," I use the phrase *associative lexical influence,* from Malkiel's "associative interference" (1968b: 13).

In Southern Quechua, glottalization and aspiration can only occur once in each word. This makes them ideal markers of associative sets, since the features in effect become properties of the entire stem (cf. Williams 1968: 56–57; Dent 1981: 81–83). An important aspect of such associative lexical sets is the fluidity and variability of their membership (Paul 1889 [1880]: 160; Bolinger 1940: 122; Samuels 1972: 46–48; Anttila 1977a, 1977b: 118–120; Rhodes and Lawler 1981; Lawler 1989; Waugh and Newfield 1989; Waugh 1990). It is impossible to establish categorical relationships between particular meanings and their formal expressions.[8] Metaphoric correlations are tendencies or potentialities built into the linguistic system; the perception of these relationships and their deployment in associative influence vary among language users; even individual speakers perceive different relationships from time to time. The associative sets presented here synthesize modern written and field evidence from several parts of the Department of Cuzco. A sample composite list of eighty stems was reviewed with a Cuzco-Collao Quechua speaker who confirmed that fifty-four were present in her own speech, accepted ten more with a different meaning, and rejected sixteen as forms with which she was not familiar. Importantly, many of the rejections and replacements were themselves patterned into associative sets.

Several associative sets varying in size and complexity are presented below as illustrations. The stems in each group share either glottalization or aspiration. I also included semantically related stems without glottalization and aspiration when the stems could not carry glottalization and aspiration for independent phonotactic reasons (e.g., they lacked oral stops). As a first set, consider the words for different ways of swallowing and sucking: *ch'uqchuy* 'to suck out', *ch'unqay* 'to suck, to absorb', *suq'uy* 'to drink through a cylindrical tube', *suqsuy* 'to swallow drops or particles', *wilq'uy* 'to gulp down', *winq'uy* 'to consume in large gulps' (after Mannheim and Newfield 1982).

Ch'uqchuy may be translated as 'to suck out', as when a raw egg is extracted from its shell. It presupposes a liquid material held by a solid container. In a variant meaning, *ch'uqchuy* refers to the manner in which pigs eat food, particularly liquids, making the sound *ch'uq, ch'uq*.

Ch'unqay is used to describe the sucking action in eating a very ripe, mushy fruit, or the tenacity of muddy ground. In contrast to *ch'uqchuy*, it implies a spongy, semisolid mass of material that acts as a medium through which a liquid is transferred. *Ch'unqay* is used to describe eating soft candy or an orange. It also refers to the action of dry ground absorbing rainwater. In the context of ritual mediation between people and the earth, *ch'unqay* would be used when the earth is 'open' and absorbs a spirit through porous ground.

Suq'uy refers to the action of sucking or drinking a liquid in a continuous gulp through a cylindrical tube, as in opening one's throat to quaff a shot of liquor. The key distinguishing features of *suq'uy* is that the mediating structure is cylindrical, and the activity is silent. In contrast with the preceding ritual context, when the earth is not 'open', spiritual exchange between people and the earth must proceed through an *usñu*, a cylindrical hole made in the ground for this purpose (Zuidema 1980). *Suq'u* has a further morphological affinity relation. The word *suqu*, differing only by the absence of glottalization from the uvular consonant, denotes 'reed'; it also correlates with a cylindrical shape. Both *suq'u* and *suqu* are descended from Common Southern Peruvian **zuqu*, a form that can be reconstructed to a period earlier than the adoption of glottalization into the phonological system; ultimately it can be reconstructed to proto-Quechua. Both senses are cited with initial *c* in Gonçález Holguín's *Vocabulario.* There is no orthographic evidence that *suq'u* had yet acquired glottalization. Gonçález Holguín (1608: 86) also lists a cast-off version of the 'reed' stem, *soqos*. Presumably, the formal split between *suqu* and *suq'u* was prompted by the associative significance of glottalization for this semantic set.

Suqsuy, which lacks a syllable-initial stop to carry glottalization, is semantically a quantized version of *suq'uy:* 'to consume individual units, swallowing them (sucking them up) without chewing them', as a chicken eats grain or one might let drops of liquid go straight down one's throat.

The remaining two members of this set, *wilq'uy* and *winq'uy*, represent differing senses of English 'gulp' and reflect this semantic closeness with an obvious phonological similarity. *Wilq'uy* denotes 'to gulp something down', and *winq'uy* 'to consume in large gulps'. The speaker with whom I reviewed the associative sets rejected both with these meanings, but heard *wilq'uy* with a completely different meaning, 'to insert something in order to take something else out, as one takes a parasite out of a cow's ear'.

The following associative set is also a useful illustration of the variability of such sets. The first two columns in figure 8.5 list forms from the composite list, along with their meanings. The last two columns list responses of the speaker along with alternative forms ("=" indicates that the form is the same as the first; a blank in the last column indicates that the meaning is the same; and "*" indicates that the form was rejected).

As the translations show, the basic semantic unity of this set revolves around the notion of a planar or regular two-dimensional surface, 'flatness' or 'smoothness'. These two semantic aspects are differentiated by phonological factors other than glottalization. The first four stems, which focus on the planar aspect ('flatness'), share the initial stop, as well as a predominance of compact vowels. In contrast, the seven forms

Figure 8.5

(1)	*p'aqpa*	'flat'	*	
(2)	*p'altu*	'flat'	*	
(3)	*p'arpakuy*	'to become flat'	*	
(4)	*p'aqla*	'bald, skinned'	*p'aqla mat'i*	'receding hairline'
(5)	*t'aqtay*	'to flatten'	*	
(6a)	*last'ay*	'to make thin, stretch out'	=	'to extend'
(6b)	*t'aslay*		=	'to flatten'
(7a)	*llamp'u*	'smooth, soft' (liquid, skin)		
(7b)	*llamp'uy*	'to put sheets on a bed'	=	'to smooth'
(8a)	*llusp'a*	'smooth, polished' 'slippery'	=	'extremely slippery'
(8b)	*llusk'a*		*llushk'a*	'slippery'
(8c)	*lluskha*		*	
(8d)	*llusp'iy*	'to slip a needle'	=	'to grab something slippery' (as a fish)
(8e)	*lluskhay*	'to slip and fall'	*llushk'ay*	
(9a)	*rahk'a*	'thick' (for flat objects)	*raφt'a*	
(9b)	*raht'a*		*raφt'ay*	

listed as 7 and 8 share an initial liquid and emphasize the regularity and smoothness of the surface, extending this by contiguity to *llusp'iy* 'to slip a needle' and *lluskha* 'to slip and fall'. *Lluskha* (8c/8e) has an aspirate rather than ejective for etymological reasons. It is derived historically from **lluchka* (attested as *lluchca* by Gonçález Holguín 1608: 216), and aspiration is the regular reflex of a syllable-final palatal stop. But the variant pronunciation, *llusk'a* ~ *llushk'a* (8b), has the characteristic ejective in spite of the etymological source. The most likely starting point for this set was *llusp'iy*, 'to slip a needle' (8d), which was attested with glottalization in the early seventeenth century (Gonçález Holguín 1608: 219). The metathesis of *last'ay* ~ *t'aslay* (6) allows it to cross-cut the formal contrast between the 'smooth' and 'flat' sets, but this is semantically appropriate because the word is used especially for the process of metal lamination, which puts the material into a form that is both flat and smooth. Undoubtedly, *last'ay* was the older of the two, since *l*, which is exceedingly rare in Quechua, normally occurs only word-initially.

Consider the vocabulary of twists and bends, which also is marked by glottalization (after Mannheim and Newfield 1982: 217–219). *Q'iwi* (1) is a crook or bend, with its derivatives *q'iwiy* 'to twist, to turn aside' and *q'iwi-q'iwi* 'zigzag'. *T'iksu* (2) is 'twisted, inclined'. *T'ikray* 'to re-

Figure 8.6

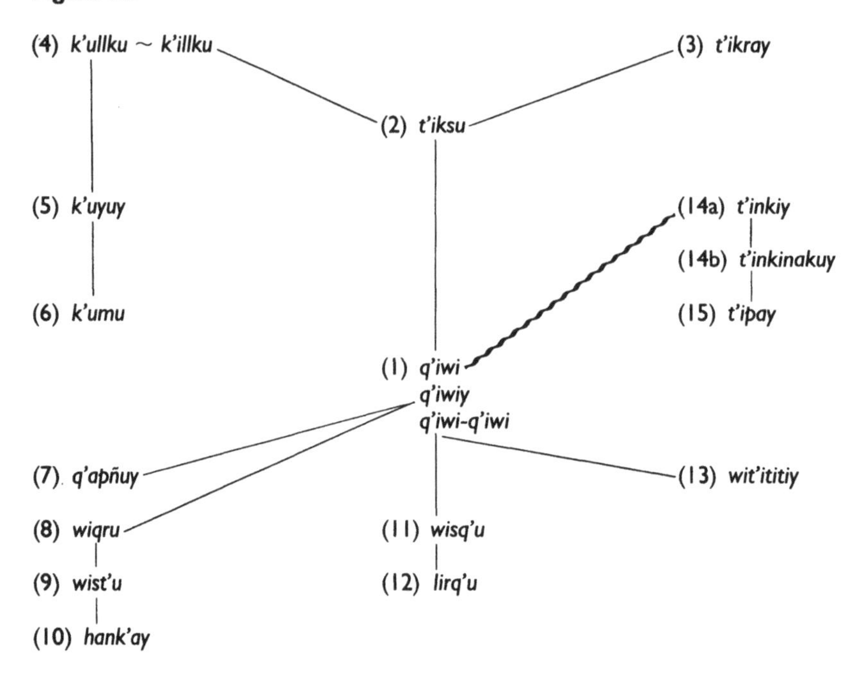

verse, to turn inside out, to change' (3) extends 'twist' or 'turn' to a complete reversal. In Quechua culture, change is perceived as occurring through a process of inversion. *K'ullku* ~ *k'illku* 'very twisted' (4) denotes the twist in spun yarn or thread. *K'uyuy* 'to twist, to roll up' (as a belt, or a coiled rope) (5) reframes twistedness as circularity. (Notice that *k'uyuy* is also metaphorically iconic of *muyuy* 'to go around in a circle'.) *K'umu* (6) restricts the notion of 'rolling' to a single bend as 'bent over'. Another chain of traces extend the constellation into twistedness in a particular medium or context. *Q'apñuy* 'dent' (7) is a bend in a surface. The stems of the chains from (8) to (10) denote crookedness in the legs: *wiqru* 'crooked-legged' (8) cannot receive glottalization for phonotactic reasons, but *wist'u* 'lame, bowlegged' (9), *wist'uy* 'to limp', and *hank'ay* 'unequal limp' (10) do. *Wisq'u* (11) and *lirq'u* (12) both denote 'cross-eyed', *wisq'u* (pronounced [wisq'o]) as a loanword from Spanish *bizco*. *Wit'ititiy* (13) denotes 'to flip around, to convulse, to thrash'. Stems (14) to (15) are the twists that bind: *t'inkiy* 'to tie together or twist in order to connect' (14a) and *t'ipay* 'to join together with a nail or needle' (15). And *t'inkinakuy*, the reciprocal form of (14a), denotes two bodies, twisted around and through one another, intertwined in mutual desire.

The fourth associative set, in figure 8.7, also involving ejectives, is larger than the others and consequently more diverse semantically. The central semantic themes are smallness, narrowness, and tightness (1–4 and 15–16); the ejectives in these stems are also acoustic images in that ejectives concentrate their energy discharge in a reduced interval of time. But the sound images are linked into a chain of associations that at the far extreme are removed from the image. To trace the intervening associations in more detail, treat the figure as forming a large *C* and begin at the center with *q'iqi* 'tight' (1). *Mat'i* (4), denoting 'a large amount of material packed into a small space' as well as 'forehead', leads to *siq'u* (5), 'a hard substance', and as a verb *siq'uy*, 'to strangle, or to tighten'; to the transitive actions of compressing and squeezing, *q'apñuy* 'to squeeze, crush, or crumble' (6) and *ñit'iy* 'to compress, to squash' (7); and to the intransitive actions of shrinking, contracting, and closing, as in *k'uytuy* 'to shrink the body, to squat' (8), *q'intiy* 'to shrink, contract' (9), *ch'uka* 'closed or squinting eyes' (10a), or as a verb, *ch'ukay* 'to close by sewing'.

In turn, these tie into other associated qualities, such as thinness, narrowness, and small size. Glottalization is represented both in words that describe these qualities and in the words for objects that exemplify them, such as *sit'i* 'small child' (11), *ch'ini-challwa* 'small fish' (12), *q'awti* 'skinny' (13; also *q'awti wiksa* 'narrow stomach', *q'awti kunka* 'skinny throat', *q'awti siki* 'skinny ass'), and *p'itita* 'small room, alcove' (17). By considering these qualities and objects relationally, an implicit comparison is made between smaller entities and larger ones from which they might be taken, leading to the notion of 'pieces' and the actions of cutting or breaking them off, including *lliφch'i* 'nip off' (21), *t'ipiy* 'to pinch, or nip' (22), *ch'aφchi* 'piece' (23), *ch'iφtiy* 'to break into pieces' (24), *p'akiy* 'to break' (bones, pots) (25), *aqnu* 'piece' or as a verb *aqnuy* 'to chip, break off' (26), and *t'aqay* 'to separate or divide' (29). Two nouns related to these notions are *k'ullpi* ~ *khullpi* (27), which refers to materials, such as wood or dung, broken up to be used as fuel, and *k'ukmu* (28), beard stubble, or the stubble that remains as a result of cutting or breaking stalks of grain. The final link in this chain of lexical associations takes us from the creation of these solid or liquid entities of reduced size to the action of dispersing them by sprinkling or scattering: *ch'aqchuy* 'to sprinkle, to wet down' (30), *t'inkay* 'to sprinkle liquid in ritual' (31), *ch'allay* 'to sprinkle, to scatter', or 'to sprinkle water' as in a baptism (32), *wisniy* ~ *wisñiy* ~ *wishñiy* 'to scatter, to spill unintentionally' (33), *ch'iqi* 'dispersed, scattered' (34), *t'akay* 'to seed, spill' (35). Stem (33), *wisñiy*, is another that cannot receive glottalization for phonotactic reasons.

The stems in associative set figure 8.7 were included in the composite list. This set fared only slightly better than figure 8.5 in the test.

Figure 8.7

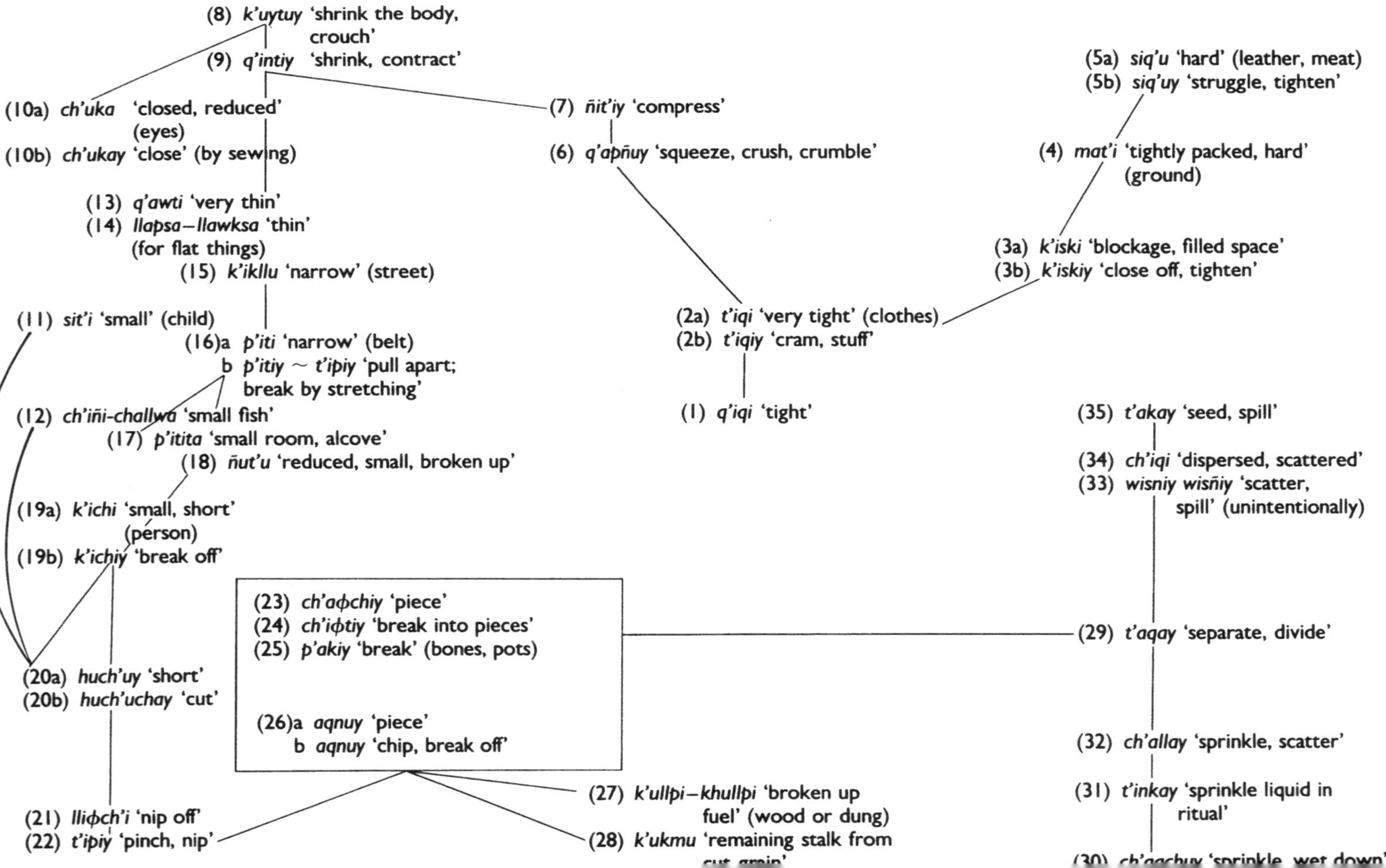

(8) *k'uytuy* 'shrink the body, crouch'
(9) *q'intiy* 'shrink, contract'
(10a) *ch'uka* 'closed, reduced' (eyes)
(10b) *ch'ukay* 'close' (by sewing)
(7) *ñit'iy* 'compress'
(6) *q'apñuy* 'squeeze, crush, crumble'
(5a) *siq'u* 'hard' (leather, meat)
(5b) *siq'uy* 'struggle, tighten'
(4) *mat'i* 'tightly packed, hard' (ground)
(3a) *k'iski* 'blockage, filled space'
(3b) *k'iskiy* 'close off, tighten'
(13) *q'awti* 'very thin'
(14) *llapsa–llawksa* 'thin' (for flat things)
(15) *k'ikllu* 'narrow' (street)
(11) *sit'i* 'small' (child)
(16)a *p'iti* 'narrow' (belt)
b *p'itiy* ~ *t'ipiy* 'pull apart; break by stretching'
(2a) *t'iqi* 'very tight' (clothes)
(2b) *t'iqiy* 'cram, stuff'
(1) *q'iqi* 'tight'
(12) *ch'iñi-challwa* 'small fish'
(17) *p'itita* 'small room, alcove'
(18) *ñut'u* 'reduced, small, broken up'
(35) *t'akay* 'seed, spill'
(34) *ch'iqi* 'dispersed, scattered'
(33) *wisniy wisñiy* 'scatter, spill' (unintentionally)
(19a) *k'ichi* 'small, short' (person)
(19b) *k'ichiy* 'break off'
(23) *ch'aφchiy* 'piece'
(24) *ch'iφtiy* 'break into pieces'
(25) *p'akiy* 'break' (bones, pots)
(26)a *aqnuy* 'piece'
b *aqnuy* 'chip, break off'
(29) *t'aqay* 'separate, divide'
(20a) *huch'uy* 'short'
(20b) *huch'uchay* 'cut'
(32) *ch'allay* 'sprinkle, scatter'
(27) *k'ullpi–khullpi* 'broken up fuel' (wood or dung)
(28) *k'ukmu* 'remaining stalk from cut grain'
(31) *t'inkay* 'sprinkle liquid in ritual'
(21) *lliφch'i* 'nip off'
(22) *t'ipiy* 'pinch, nip'
(30) *ch'aqchuy* 'sprinkle, wet down'

The speaker did not recognize *q'iqi* (1), *siq'u* (5a, as a substantive only), *q'inti* (9, though it was used as an unrelated term for a species of bird), *sit'i* (11), *q'awti* (13), *p'iti* (16, as either a substantive or a verb), *p'itita* (17), *lliφch'i* (21), *ch'aφchi* (23), or *aqnu* (26, as either a substantive or a verb). *P'itiy* (16b, as a verb only) was replaced with *t'ipiy*, by metathesis. *K'ikllu* (15) was replaced with *k'illku* (again by metathesis), although for other speakers, *k'illku* had the meaning 'twisted thread' (see fig. 8.6). *K'iski* (3a) was narrowed semantically to 'constipation' and 'blocked nasal passages'; *mat'i* (4) had only its body part meaning; *siq'uy* (5b, in verbal form only) was semantically narrowed to its 'strangle' meaning; *k'ichi* 'small or short' (19a) was not used to refer to people, but rather to grass eaten down to stubble by animals at the beginning of the spring. Along with *ch'iφtiy* (24) 'to break something into pieces', there is a verb *ch'iφtay*, for a chicken to do the same with its beak.

Now consider several associative sets marked by aspiration. One of the ways the aspirates and ejectives differ is in the duration of their energy discharge; it is understandable, then, that they would be used as images of opposing semantic qualities. The semantic core of the last associative set was smallness, narrowness, and thinness; glottalization, which involves a reduced duration for the acoustic discharge, functioned as both a sound image and a marker of the associative set. In contrast with the last set, there is a much smaller associative set for large size or quantity in figure 8.8, which is marked by aspiration.

The alternation between *hathun* and *hatun*, the first aspirated and the second unaspirated, is partly dialectal and partly emphatic. There are some individuals who use both variants and save the aspirated form *hathun* for emphasis. This fits well with the iconic association between aspiration and largeness. In figure 8.8, I list several stems that fit semantically but cannot receive aspiration because they lack a syllable-initial oral stop. *Ukhu* 'deep, inside' has undergone fricativization of the consonant in many dialects of Cuzco-Collao, to *uxu*. This is a common fate for the aspirated *kh* between vowels.

Figure 8.9 includes words that are associated semantically with 'filth'. There is little to say about this set other than that *qhuña* is culturally the very epitome of disgusting and dirty, and the insult *qhuñasapa* 'snotface' appears in several colonial texts.

Aspiration also marks stems denoting sorrow and pain, as in figure 8.10.

A final complex constellation of affinities among stems with aspiration, especially those beginning with *ph*, is presented in figure 8.11. The set does not have the semantic unity of the earlier ones; keep in mind that associative lexical influence is a relationship between individual items and not a hard-and-fast relationship between a formal feature and

Figure 8.8

hathun ~ *hatun*	'large'
althu	[< Sp. *alto*] 'high'
suni	'large, gigantic'
ukhu	'deep, inside'
rakhu	'thick' (cylindrical objects)
runkhi	'thick' (vessels and tools)
ramphu	'thick' (thread)
raktha ~ *rakt'a* ~ *rakk'a*[a]	'thick' (flat objects)
askha	'a lot, many' (measurable things)
khuway	'much'
waliq	'abundant'
llasa	'weighty, heavy'
llasaq	'sufficient, enough'

[a] Syllable-final k̲ is pronounced as velar fricative [x].

Figure 8.9

thanta	'worn out, old' (clothes, tools)
chhachu	'ragged'
mullpha	'very old, decaying'
qhilli	'dirty' (hands, clothes)
kharka	'dirty, filthy'
khanka	'muddy, scaly'
saqsa	'muddy, stained'
qhuña	'snotty'
khacha	'crusty dirt or mud, dirty and calloused skin'
qhanra	'filthy, greasy dirt'
qhuspay	'to wallow in filth'

Figure 8.10

phuti	'pain'
phiña	'anger'
phiru	'harmful'
qhiwi	'sad'
qhisti	'constantly crying'
usphu ~ *unphu*	'crestfallen'
khuyay	'sad, pained, bitter'

a semantic notion shared by the members of the set. (This is also a much more speculative constellation of associations than the others.) The relationships traced out here are of two kinds. First, there are relationships of similarity, such as between *phusuqu* 'foam, bubble' (20) and *phuyu* 'cloud, fog' (35). Relationships of similarity are indicated by a solid line. Second, the referents of two stems might be found in frequent association with one another, as *phusuqu* 'foam' (20) and *phuspuy* 'cooked beans' (26). Relationships of contiguity between the referents of the stems are indicated by wavy lines.

Generally speaking, those items below the center and to the right have to do with liquid materials, and those above and to the left of center have to do with air. The order of example numbers follows the semantic associations in a general way. But it is testimony to the inherent complexity of the various interrelations that there are also several occasional connections that jump across the chain to interweave diverse areas in a web of affinity relations.

As in the earlier sets, a number of stems are also sound images; this is especially so for the words having to do with 'blowing', such as *phukuy* 'to blow, to blow out' (17), *phusa* 'panpipe' (14), *phullchu* 'puffed, puckered' (16), all of which begin with a bilabial aspirate. (Compare the labial aspirates and fricatives in English *puff, poof,* and *pant.*) Other sound images include *thasnuy* ~ *thasniy* (40), which mimics the sound of liquid hitting a hot surface or a fire, and the reduplicated stems, *raphapapay* 'to flicker, to flutter' (6b), *phapapapay* 'to flap wings silently' (7), *pharara, ray* 'to flap wings violently' (8), *wararaay* 'to create a din' (12), *phatatatay* 'to convulse, to palpitate' (46b).

Several of the stems have regular etymological sources for the aspiration. In *uspha* 'ash' (1), the sequence of *s* plus aspiration on the following stop is a normal reflex of an older syllable-final palatal stop (*uchpa,* attested by Gonçález Holguín [1608: 468] as *Vchpa;* see chapter 9, sound change ii). In *phuspuru* 'match' (4), from Spanish *fósforo,* the aspirated *ph* is a normal Quechua adaptation of Spanish *f,* and the second *p* has been deaspirated to conform to the "once per word" restriction. But I also elicited *phuspuru* from a speaker who spoke a dialect of Cuzco-Collao Quechua with a phonemic bilabial fricative, *ϕ*. Speakers of this dialect do not normally convert the Spanish *f* to *ph* but rather convert it to *ϕ*. For this speaker, the change of Spanish *f* to *ph* was exceptional. Presumably, it was motivated by association of *phuspuru* with others denoting 'heat' or 'flame' such as *rapha* 'flame' (6a), and *ruphay* 'to be hot, to burn' (5). If indeed the presence of aspiration in words like *uspha* and *phuspuru* cannot be causally linked to associative lexical influence, the presence of independently developed aspiration draws the stem into the associative set.

To discuss each associative pathway through figure 8.11 would be prohibitively long and involved, but let me provide a "road map" through the basic conceptual subgroups. Beginning at the left side of figure 8.11, stems (1–6) deal in a general way with 'fire': *rapha* 'flame', *ruphay* 'to be hot, to burn', *phuspuru* 'match', *rawray* ~ *yawray* 'to catch fire, to burn', *nina* 'flame', *uspha* 'ash'. Mediated by *raphapapay* 'to flicker,

Figure 8.11

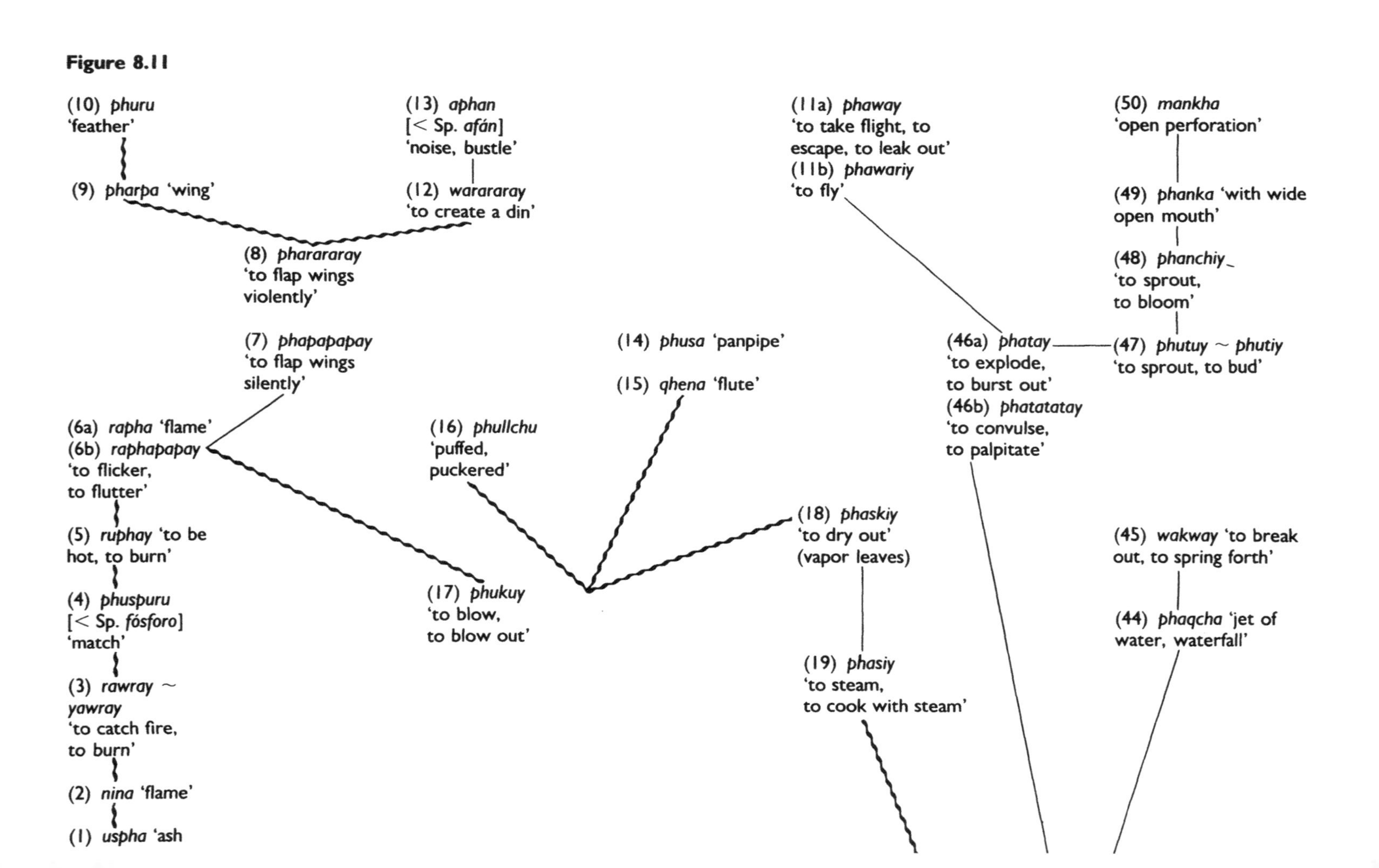
(10) phuru
'feather'
(9) pharpa 'wing'
(13) aphan
[< Sp. afán]
'noise, bustle'
(12) wararaway
'to create a din'
(8) phararaway
'to flap wings
violently'
(7) phapapapay
'to flap wings
silently'
(6a) rapha 'flame'
(6b) raphapapay
'to flicker,
to flutter'
(5) ruphay 'to be
hot, to burn'
(4) phuspuru
[< Sp. fósforo]
'match'
(3) rawray ~
yawray
'to catch fire,
to burn'
(2) nina 'flame'
(1) uspha 'ash
(16) phullchu
'puffed,
puckered'
(17) phukuy
'to blow,
to blow out'
(14) phusa 'panpipe'
(15) qhena 'flute'
(11a) phaway
'to take flight, to
escape, to leak out'
(11b) phawariy
'to fly'
(18) phaskiy
'to dry out'
(vapor leaves)
(19) phasiy
'to steam,
to cook with steam'
(46a) phatay
'to explode,
to burst out'
(46b) phatatatay
'to convulse,
to palpitate'
(50) mankha
'open perforation'
(49) phanka 'with wide
open mouth'
(48) phanchiy
'to sprout,
to bloom'
(47) phutuy ~ phutiy
'to sprout, to bud'
(45) wakway 'to break
out, to spring forth'
(44) phaqcha 'jet of
water, waterfall'

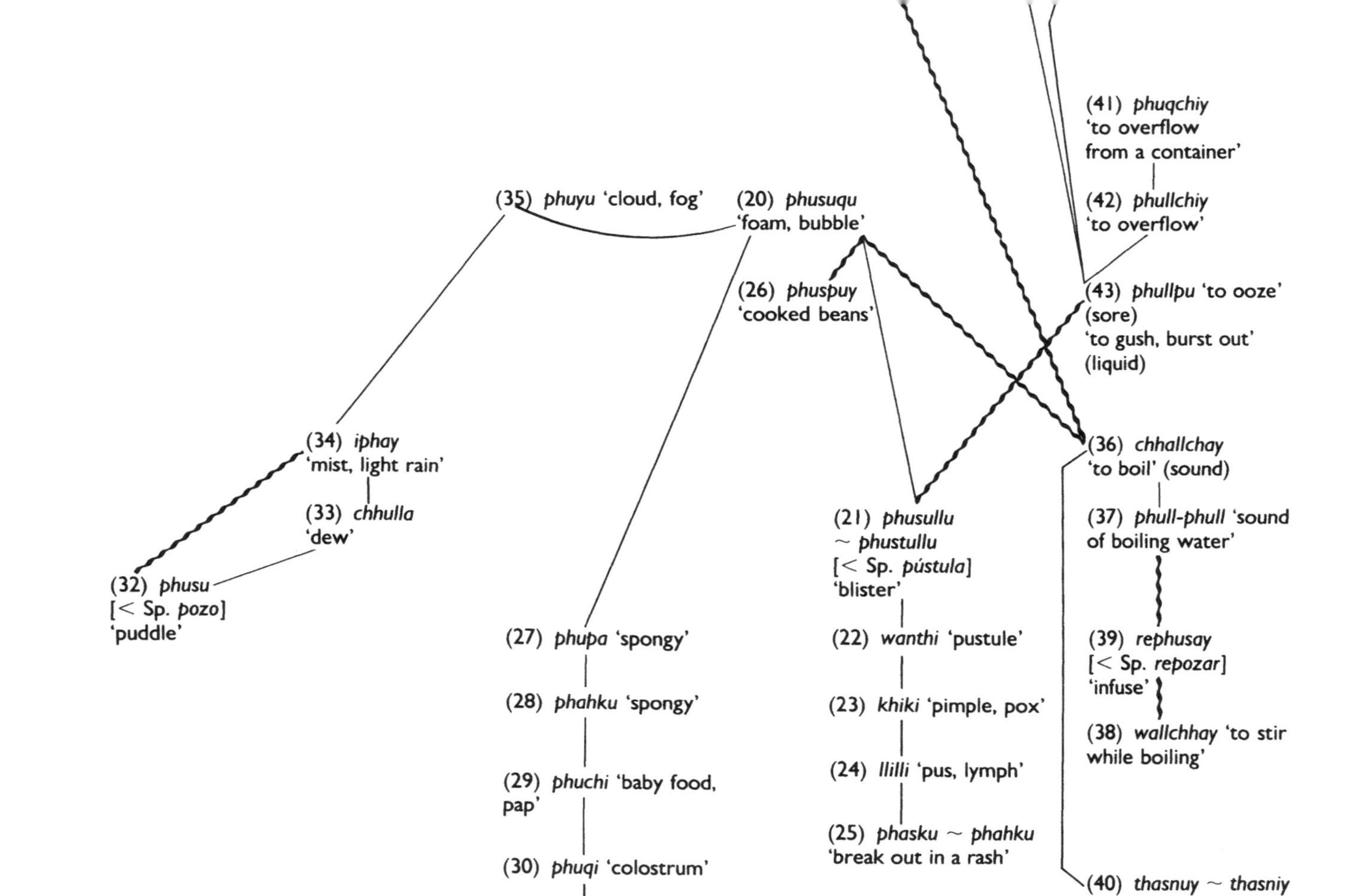
(41) phuqchiy
'to overflow
from a container'
(42) phullchiy
'to overflow'
(35) phuyu 'cloud, fog'
(20) phusuqu
'foam, bubble'
(26) phuspuy
'cooked beans'
(43) phullpu 'to ooze'
(sore)
'to gush, burst out'
(liquid)
(34) iphay
'mist, light rain'
(33) chhulla
'dew'
(32) phusu
[< Sp. pozo]
'puddle'
(36) chhallchay
'to boil' (sound)
(37) phull-phull 'sound
of boiling water'
(21) phusullu
~ phustullu
[< Sp. pústula]
'blister'
(27) phupa 'spongy'
(22) wanthi 'pustule'
(39) rephusay
[< Sp. repozar]
'infuse'
(28) phahku 'spongy'
(23) khiki 'pimple, pox'
(38) wallchhay 'to stir
while boiling'
(24) llilli 'pus, lymph'
(29) phuchi 'baby food,
pap'
(25) phasku ~ phahku
'break out in a rash'
(30) phuqi 'colostrum'
(40) thasnuy ~ thasniy
'to sizzle,
to extinguish'
(31) phiwi 'first-born'

to flutter', they give way to air movement and airborne motion: *phapapapay* 'to flap wings silently', *phararaway* 'to flap wings violently' (7–8); and to the contiguous notions of 'wings, feathers, and flight', *pharpa* 'wing' (*phar* is the sound of flapping wings and the sound that announces the arrival of a mountain deity during a shaman's trance), *phuru* 'feather', *phaway* 'to take flight, escape, or leak out', *phawariy* 'to fly' (9–11); and 'noise': *wararaway* 'to create a din', *aphan* 'noise, bustle' (12–13). The 'air' connection continues through *phusa* 'panpipe', *qhena* 'flute', *phullchu* 'puffed, puckered', *phukuy* 'to blow, to blow out' (14–17) and ties in with *phaskiy* 'to dry out' (18), which is a pivot involving both the causative influence of air and the perception of vapor evaporating or steam rising off something in the sun.

From *phaskiy*, cross to *phasiy* 'to steam, to cook with steam' and *phusuqu* 'foam, bubble' (19–20). In turn, these lead in several directions, to the stems for various types of bubbles on the skin—blisters and rashes (21–25, also by contiguity 43); to (26) *phuspuy* 'cooked beans', because of the foaming that occurs when beans are being cooked; to the quality of spongy texture in *phuchi* 'baby food, pap' (29), leading to a metonymic connection through the notion of birth to (31) *phiwi* 'firstborn'; also from 'foam' to (35) *phuyu* 'cloud, fog' and from there to stems involving water in nature, such as *phusu* [< Sp. *pozo*] 'puddle', *chhulla* 'dew', and *iphay* 'mist, light rain' (32–34).

Returning to 'steam' and 'foam' (19–20), we can follow another set of links to the subgroup having to do with boiling: *chhallchay* 'to boil', the sound of boiling; *wallchhay* 'to stir something that is boiling' (notice that the aspiration here is on the second syllable); and *phull-phull*, the sound of boiling water (36–38). In *phull-phull*, the bilabial aspirate also functions as a sound image. The second syllable was aspirated clearly, although normally aspiration is eliminated on the second part of the reduplicated stem. Another associated path leads from overflowing—in *phuqchiy* 'to overflow from a container', *phullchiy* 'to overflow', *phullpu* 'for a sore to ooze or a liquid to gush out' (41–43)—to more specialized forms of bursting forth: plants sprouting and blooming, as *phutuy* ~ *phutiy* 'to sprout, to bud', *phanchiy* 'to sprout, to bloom'; and finally to more general notions of 'open': *phanka* 'something with a wide open mouth', *mankha* 'open perforation' (47–50).

These examples are far from exhausting what appears to be an endless supply of lexical associations in Cuzco-Collao Quechua, especially involving ejectives and aspirates. The aspirated *ph*, which was amply represented in the last set, seems to be particularly prone to associative influence. Approximately half of the stems beginning with *ph* in the abridged edition of Jorge Lira's massive Quechua dictionary (1973) can be tied into associative lexical sets.

Lexical Association, Sound Imagery, and Sound Change

In this chapter, I have explored two forms of iconicity in the Southern Quechua lexicon, sound imagery and associative lexical influence. For cultural reasons, Southern Quechua is especially prone to making sound "seem an echo to the sense." The tendency toward iconicity is most pronounced for the ejectives and aspirates, and I have suggested that attention to the nature of sound imagery and associative lexical influence in Southern Quechua would enable us to understand the process by which glottalization and aspiration developed into full-blown features of Southern Quechua phonology.

As a result of intensive, interspersed contact with Jaqi/Aru languages, Southern Quechua borrowed large numbers of stems with ejectives and aspirates. Among the lexical stems that could potentially be borrowed into Southern Quechua, those stems that were marked phonologically by glottalization and aspiration were favored. Both features spread through the native Quechua lexicon as sound images and through associative lexical influence, in which the features spread from one lexical stem to other cognitively associated lexical stems, on a massive scale. There are several minor genetic sources for ejectives and aspirates as well, but they suppose that glottalization and aspiration were already cognitively salient features of the Southern Quechua phonological system.

At this point, the roles of sound imagery and associative lexical influence in the spread of the Southern Quechua ejectives and aspirates can only be observed through their distribution in the modern language. Their distribution is consistent with the hypothesis that glottalization and aspiration spread by sound imagery and associative influence in two senses. First, sound imagery and associative influence explain the nonrandom distribution of ejectives and aspirates in the lexicon. Second, both processes are stochastic, rather than regular, and their stochastic nature accounts for the genetic irregularities of glottalization and aspiration among Southern Quechua dialects and speakers. These observations are very preliminary; systematic philological work on these issues is needed in order to elaborate the process of expansion of glottalization and aspiration in detail.

Before I turn to the related matter of the restrictions on ejectives and aspirates, there are several general points that bear discussion in a preliminary way.

(1) Although my Peirce-inspired definitions of sound image and lexical association suggest a sharp dichotomy between them, we have seen in each of the associative sets that it is possible for a stem to be a sound

image and part of an associative set at one and the same time. Sound imagery and associative lexical influence are not mutually exclusive. For example, the associative set for small and thin objects is marked by glottalization, and the set for large and thick objects by aspiration; in this case they are both markers of the associative sets and sound images. Similarly, in modern Egyptian Arabic, phonetic "emphasis" (*mufaxxam* 'honored') is distributed lexically by associative influence, but has a general connotation of maleness. Insofar as it does, it is a sound image as well, since one acoustic signal of emphasis is lowered pitch, especially on the second formant (Harrell 1957: ch. 8; Robert Hoberman, letter, 4 May 1981).

(2) How are sound imagery and associative lexical influence related to exceptionless sound laws (*Lautgesetze*)? In a very general methodological sense, sound imagery and associative lexical influence are supplements to, not replacements for, exceptionless sound laws. Sound images and associative lexical influence depend upon the speakers of a language making an association between the phonological form of a sign and its meaning, or between the phonological forms of two signs. Both of these are therefore stochastic rather than categorical. This means that, for methodological reasons, sound images and associative lexical influence, like other kinds of "weak phonological change" (Malkiel 1964; Hoenigswald 1964), can only be identified against the background of exceptionless sound laws. Exceptionless sound laws make a stronger claim on the data; weak phonological changes, including sound imagery and associative influence, turn up at their ragged edges. In this sense they are "subsidiary" to regular sound laws. The subsidiary methodological status of sound imagery and associative lexical influence does not mean that they can be dismissed. Linguistic history does not conform to the neat methodological prescriptions of the comparative method. Empirically speaking, sound imagery, associative lexical influence, and other minor changes are facts of life; methodologically, they permit an orderly account of otherwise unaccountable data.

The traditional, Neogrammarian view of sound change holds that it is regular and takes place across the board in all relevant phonological contexts. The Neogrammarian doctrine of exceptionless sound laws was challenged in the 1970s by William S-Y. Wang and his associates, who have argued that "a phonological rule gradually extends its scope of operation to a larger and larger portion of the lexicon until all relevant items have been transformed by the process" (Chen and Wang 1975: 256; cf. Wang 1969; Chen 1972), a process they call "lexical diffusion." According to Wang and Chen, it is possible for a phonological innovation to give out before it runs its course through the lexicon, leaving a residue of unaffected forms. Wang and Chen base their proposal on an analysis of tonal splits between Middle Chinese and twenty-one modern Chinese dialects. They demonstrate that it is not possible to account for these data in terms of phonological conditioning or dialect borrowing. With respect to one such case, the split of four Middle Chinese tones to eight distinctive tones in modern Cháozhōu, they conclude that "the tone change in question must be a system-internal development that is . . . caught in 'mid-stream'" (Chen and Wang 1975: 259). Similar observations have been made in other contexts: the displacement of apical consonants to word-initial position in seven South-Central Dravidian languages (Krishnamurti 1978); the tensing of *æ* in Philadelphia English in words like *planet* and *damage*, in which tensing is in the process of spreading from word to word (in the speech community, not the individual: Labov 1981: 293–298); and the shift of *a* to *o* before nasals in early Old English (Toon 1976).

Labov (1981: 299) observes that lexical diffusion might take place under circumstances different from regular sound change. Thus, he proposes that "Neogrammarian regularity [is located] in low-level output rules, and lexical diffusion in the redistribution of an abstract word-class into other abstract classes" (1981: 304). If Labov is correct, lexical diffusion is not a mechanism by which regular sound change takes place, but rather a different type of change. I concur, because many apparent cases of lexical diffusion involve assignment of lexical stems into word classes that are marked by a single phonological feature (contrastive tone, vowel quality, the place of articulation of a consonant); the sound changes involve splits in the word classes or reassignment of word stems between classes. What is the relationship between lexical diffusion, in this narrower sense, and associative lexical influence? Might they be special cases of a single, more general process of change? If not, what are the circumstances—linguistic, cultural, and social—that determine which of the two, lexical diffusion or associative lexical influence, takes place? What are the semantic principles, if any, involved in determining the direction of lexical diffusion?

(3) These questions can only be resolved by more systematic work on associative lexical influence in individual speech communities, as well as systematic cross-cultural work on lexical association. Although associative lexical influence (or metaphoric iconicity) has been described in several languages by some of the finest empirical linguists of our time, such as Stern (1964 [1931]), Bolinger (1940), Harrell (1957), Diffloth (1976: 260–261), and Malkiel (1964, 1985), its principles are still poorly understood.[9]

(4) There are some cross-cultural regularities in the kinds of semantic domains that are most prone to associative lexical influence. For example, there is some overlap between the English *fl* words such as *fly*,

flutter, and *flicker*, and the Cuzco-Collao Quechua words beginning with *ph* in figure 8.11.[10] Many of the Cuzco-Collao Quechua stems expressing physical defects contain ejectives (fig. 8.6). The vocabulary of physical defects is also the basis of associative lexical sets in Romance (Meillet 1966 [1931]: 169; Malkiel 1982: 138–143, 1985: 3–4), and Indic.

Restrictions on Ejectives and Aspirates

I have already mentioned that the Southern Quechua languages that have distinctive glottalization and aspiration restrict these features to the first syllable-initial stop in a stem. From a functional point of view, these features are culminative, in that they "signal the division of the utterance into grammatical units of different degrees of complexity, particularly into sentences and words, . . . by signaling out these units and indicating their hierarchy . . ." (Jakobson and Halle 1956: 20).

In the Southern Quechua dialects with glottalization and aspiration, the ejectives and aspirates tacitly mark the word (the long-word, that is, a stem with all of its affixes) as a unit, in that these features are restricted to one occurrence in each word. Within the word, they tacitly mark the hierarchy of the word-stem, which may be marked by glottalization or aspiration, versus the suffixes, which may not.[11] These restrictions may be stated as a constraint on the structure of words:

(i)

$$[\quad] \longrightarrow \begin{bmatrix} -\text{ASPIRATE} \\ -\text{GLOTTALIZED} \end{bmatrix} / \text{ X [STOP] Y } \_\_$$

in which *X* and *Y* are variable sequences of segments. Informally it reads, "No segment may be aspirated or glottalized if it is preceded by a stop."

To what extent is the word structure constraint stated in (i) conceptually real to speakers of Cuzco-Collao Quechua? To what extent does it correspond to their tacit grammatical knowledge and to what extent is it merely a statement describing some regularities in their language? Historically, the constraint on ejectives and aspirates is the outcome of several minor, structurally disjoint changes. But it also restricts the operation of regular sound laws and constrains sound imagery, associative lexical influence, and sporadic sound changes. To the extent that it is a constraint on linguistic change, and not simply the outcome of change, I am tempted to say that it is part of the speakers' tacit grammar. That it has constrained phonological changes over the course of centuries suggests that it is an enduring part of their grammar.

To see how it operates as a constraint, consider the following sporadic sound change. Gonçález Holguín (1608: 289) lists the verb *ppitini*, 'to stretch something pliant until it breaks'; the same verb, *p'itiy*, is used with the same meaning by modern Quechua speakers. But for some, *p'itiy* has undergone a metathesis to *t'ipiy* (see fig. 8.7). (There is also a verb *t'ipiy* 'to pinch', but not for speakers with the metathesis; *t'ipiy* was attested with the meaning 'to pinch' by Gonçález Holguín [1608].) When words undergo consonant metathesis in Quechua, the manner feature usually accompanies the segment that is moved, even when the manner of articulation is phonologically inappropriate in the new context. For example, the dialectal change of *raϕra* > *ϕarϕa* 'wing' results in a unique phonemic syllable-initial [ϕ]. But were glottalization to move along with the consonants in *p'iti*, it would become **tip'i*, which is ruled out by the restrictions on glottalization. Thus glottalization remains in the initial position.[12]

By regular sound change (chapter 9), *ch* weakened to *s* (or dialectally to *sh*) at the ends of syllables. If the change took place before a stop, the stop was aspirated, as in *achka* > *askha* 'many' and *uchpa* > *uspha* 'ash'. But aspiration was not introduced in the following changes: *kichka* (*quichca*, Gonçález Holguín 1608: 308) > *kiska*, 'thorn'; **quchpay* (*cuchpani*, Gonçález Holguín 1608: 653) > *qhuspay* 'to wallow'; *-chka-* > *-ska-* ~ *-sha-* ~ *-sa-*, 'durative aspect'. Aspiration is missing in exactly those cases in which its presence would violate the word structure constraint.[13] There is no reason why the restrictions on the introduction of aspiration by the sound change should be treated as an idiosyncratic restriction on the sound change, and not as a consequence of the word structure constraint. Glottalization and aspiration can appear as late as the third syllable in the word; the main stress is penultimate and the most prominent secondary stress is word-initial, so that stress does not condition the restriction on ejectives and aspirates.

The restrictions on glottalization came about in the following ways:

—*h*-epenthesis: words that begin with vowels are preceded by a predictable glottal catch. But if the word contains an ejective, the glottal catch is replaced by an initial *h* (ii). Gonçález Holguín (1608) provides uneven evidence of *h*-epenthesis; further study is required to determine whether there is significant patterning to the variability.[14] In modern Southern Quechua dialects, *h*-epenthesis continues to be productive, in dialect variation (e.g., *allpa* ~ *hallp'a*) and in borrowing (e.g., *hasut'i* < *azote* 'whip', attested by Gonçález Holguín without epenthetic *h*). That it is productive suggests that it is a rule in the synchronic grammar, as in (ii).

Figure 8.12

source form	azote (Spanish)	*iṣpay (CSPQ)	*as̲piy (CSPQ)	*amawta (CSPQ < Aymara)
ejectivity acquired	as̲ut'i[a]	iṣp'ay[b]	*as̲p'iy[c]	*amawt'a[d]
ṣ > s̲		is̲p'ay		
h̲-epenthesis	has̲ut'i	his̲p'ay	has̲p'i	hamawt'a
	'to whip'	'urine'	'to scratch the earth'	'learned person'

[a]Gonçález Holguín (1608: 388) as *açuttacuni.*
[b]Gonçález Holguín (1608: 370) as *ysppay.*
[c]Gonçález Holguín (1608: 42) *azpini* shows no evidence of ejectivity.
[d]Gonçález Holguín (1608: 24) *amauta* shows no evidence of ejectivity.

Figure 8.13

source form	*piṣtuy (CSPQ)[a]	p'amp'ay (Ay. loan)[b]	*uṣuta (CSPQ)
(2)	*p'iṣtuy	—	*uṣut'a
(3)	—	p'ampay	—
(4)	*ϕiṣt'uy	—	—
(5)	*miṣt'uy	—	—
ṣ > s̲	p'is̲tuy ~ ϕis̲t'uy ~ mis̲t'uy	—	*us̲ut'a
(1)	—	—	hus̲ut'a
	'to cover'	'to bury'	'sandal'

[a]I am in doubt as to whether the sibilant was apical or dorsal.
[b]Gonçález Holguín (1608: 276, 465, 582, 677) cites both *pamppani* and *ppampani,* perhaps reflecting variation in which stop lost glottalization.

(ii)

$\phi \rightarrow$ h / #__VX [EJECTIVE]

in which X is a variable. Informally, rule (ii) reads, "An *h* appears before a vowel at the beginning of a word containing an ejective stop."

Figure 8.12 contains some examples of *h*-epenthesis, beginning with the Common Southern Peruvian Quechua form (CSPQ) or a loanword source.

—glottalization was placed directly on the first stop in the word by associative lexical influence or was already there when the word was borrowed.

—loanwords with more than one ejective eliminate all but the first. Loanwords with glottalization later than the first stop shifted it to the first stop. Presumably this also affected stems in which the former apicals (ş and ç̌) were reinterpreted as glottalization. According to the phonetician John Ohala (1981: 189), glottalization colors the voice quality of adjacent vowels. Laryngeal coloration of the intervening vowels could have been perceived as having its source in the earlier rather than the later stop.

—oral stops that occurred before an ejective sporadically weakened to fricatives at the beginnings of syllables. This process might also account for the beginnings of the weakenings of stops at the ends of syllables described in chapter 9.

—oral stops that occurred before an ejective sporadically nasalized in syllable-initial position.

Examples of each of these changes appear in figure 8.13. Each of the forms listed for **pistuy* is a modern dialect variant. The restrictions on aspirates came about in similar ways to the restrictions on ejectives. There is no aspirate counterpart to the *h*-epenthesis for ejectives. It is perfectly acceptable to have aspiration in a stem that begins with *h;* aspiration is not identified structurally with the *h* phoneme. Otherwise, the constraints on aspirates are structurally isomorphic with the constraints on ejectives and came about in similar ways. In addition to these changes, aspiration that would otherwise have been introduced by the weakening of palatals (see above) fails to be introduced under just those circumstances when it is ruled out by the word structure constraint.

9 Syllable-Final Weakenings

As we have seen, Southern Peruvian Quechua is split into two main dialect areas, according to two phonological traits: (1) the presence of ejective and aspirate stops in the phonological system and (2) the status of the consonants at the ends of syllables. In the dialect that possesses ejective and aspirate stops, Cuzco-Collao Quechua, there have also been a series of weakenings and mergers of syllable-final consonants. The dialect that lacks ejectives and aspirates, Ayacucho-Chanka Quechua, has maintained the finals of syllables intact. On the face of it, the two isoglosses are connected. In any case, the weakenings and mergers have left a strong mark on the synchronic phonology of Cuzco-Collao Quechua. Most of the phonological rules affecting consonants are consequences of the weakenings and mergers of syllable-finals. For example, the genitive suffix in Ayacucho-Chanka is *-pa* after a consonant and *-p* after a vowel. In contrast, the same morphological alternation in Cuzco-Collao Quechua is *-pa* after a consonant (as in Ayacucho-Chanka) but [x̣], a uvular fricative, after a vowel! These changes are also responsible for most of the phonological dialect variation in modern Cuzco-Collao Quechua. Local dialects differ in the extent to which the weakenings and mergers have taken place, and in the progress of a particular change through the word (chapter 10). For example, the palatal stop *ch* weakened to a fricative *sh* at the ends of syllables; for some local dialects (especially those to the north and east of the Vilcanota River), the *sh* depalatalized and merged with *s*; in others (especially those to the south and west of the Vilcanota) it remained a palatal. Similarly, the labial stop, *p*, weakened to a labial fricative, *ϕ*, at the end of syllables. The resulting labial fricative merged with the uvular fricative x̣ in suffixes, in the entire Department of Cuzco. But in word-stems, there are some dialects in which the weakened stop is still pronounced as a labial, *ɸ*; some in which it has become a uvular but has labialized the preceding vowel, ʷx̣; and some in which it has become a uvular fricative, x̣.

The purpose of this chapter is to describe the weakenings and mergers of syllable-final consonants in Cuzco-Collao Quechua, their relative order, and some of the consequences of each for local dialectology. For each of the changes, I use a standard formulaic notation, followed by a verbal restatement of the same change for readers who are unfamiliar with the notation.

Here is a brief but dense summary of the weakenings and mergers, all of which took place at the ends of syllables. Stops weakened along an acoustic gradient, from those that concentrated acoustic energy in relatively higher portions of the auditory spectrum (*acute*) to those that concentrated acoustic energy in the lower portion (*grave*), in order of increasing gravity. The stops have merged into the fricatives *s* and x̣. Tap *r* has weakened to [ɹ]; the frequency of *r* has also been reduced by restructuring individual lexical and grammatical morphemes. The frequency of sibilants at the ends of syllables has been reduced in inflectional morphemes, although these changes continue to show dialectal variability. Nasals have assimilated to the place of articulation of the following obstruent and are velarized elsewhere. The nasality feature is in the process of shifting from the consonantal ends of syllables to vocalic nuclei. This change is also dialectally variable. The contrast between the laterals *l* and *ll* [ʎ] has been largely neutralized. Vowel-glide sequences are dialectally in the process of reanalysis as single vowels.

There are several general issues that emerge from this description. First, although the changes are structurally independent of one another and occurred at different times, their organization and sequence follow a definite pattern. The sequence is partly determined by the acoustic and perceptual properties of the affected sounds. The attrition of syllable-final (oral) stops proceeds at a faster pace than that of the nasals. Stops are less salient than nasals. Nasals are identifiable on the basis of a clear, vowel-like formant structure; (oral) stops, on the other hand, are characterized by a period of silence and are identified acoustically by the formant transitions to adjacent segments (Chen and Wang 1975: 266–271). When the following segment is another stop, as is frequently the case at the ends of syllables, the perceptual salience is minimal. The relative perceptual salience among the stops also determines the order of their erosion. As I have already observed, the stops that concentrate acoustic energy in relatively higher portions of the auditory spectrum weakened before those that concentrated acoustic energy in the lower portion.

Second, most of the changes are regular sound changes (*Lautgesetze*). In the Neogrammarian tradition, regular sound changes are expected to take place in every relevant phonological environment, regardless of other factors, such as morphological category, semantic word class, or meaning (see chapter 8). But these changes do not take place all at once; rather, they follow a regular trajectory that follows the internal grammatical structure of the Quechua word, from suffixes into stems. The syllable-final weakenings and mergers are subject to several general conditions. If a particular change has taken place in stems, then it has taken place in the derivational morphology; if in the derivational morphology, then in the inflectional and discourse-level morphology, providing, of course, that the appropriate structural requirements for the change are met. If a change has taken place inside the word, then it has taken place at the ends of the words, but not vice versa. Likewise, if a change has taken place inside of word-stems, then it has taken place at the ends of word-stems, but not vice versa. These general conditions are discussed in detail in chapter 10.

Lenition of syllable-final palatals and to a limited extent of alveolars is attested as early as 1560 by Domingo de Santo Tomás. But the difficulties with establishing dialect provenience for Santo Tomás make it unclear whether we are witnessing the same sound changes as those reported by others a century and a half later (perhaps because the others were reporting conservative speech) or a different basic variety of Quechua altogether. But there is a good reason to discard the possibility that later texts reported more conservative speech forms than Santo Tomás did. Quechua texts were always written in Spanish orthography, almost always by non-native speakers. The political oppression of Quechua speakers and legal maneuvers to prevent the establishment of an indigenous literate class prevented language standardization and the growth of literary and orthographic traditions. Since there was no consistent scribal practice, it is unlikely that the later texts reported more conservative forms than Santo Tomás did. Apart from Santo Tomás and besides archaic and very sporadic variation of syllable-finals (e.g., *cichpa* ~ *cispa* in Gonçález Holguín's *Vocabulario*, *huaynacauri* ~ *huaynacapri* in Santa Cruz Pachacuti Yamqui's *Relación*), we do not find evidence of regular syllable-final lenitions until Juan de Aguilar's *Arte* of 1690. Aguilar reports variable lenition of the final palatals in inflectional morphology but not in stems.

Syllable-final *č*, the least grave of all the stops (in a scalar sense of grave), weakened to [ʃ] at the ends of syllables (change i). This established a syllable-final [s] : [ʃ] contrast, which has reflexes in all modern varieties of Cuzco-Collao Quechua.

(i)

č > [ʃ] /__$

Palatal stops become fricatives at the ends of syllables.

The syllable-final [s] : [ʃ] distinction has been eliminated entirely in suffixes and stem-finally; north of Cuzco and east of the Vilcanota River, it has also been eliminated in stems (sound change iii). The palatal fricative has a regular aspiration reflex by sound change (ii) in the following stop if the following stop is the first one in the word.[1] For examples, see figure 9.1. Notice that in the third example *pishqa* ~ *pisqa* does not have an aspirated *q* because it is not the first stop in the word.

(ii)

[STOP] > [ASPIRATE] / { ʃ / č } __

Palatal stops or fricatives induce aspiration on the following stop.

(iii)

ʃ > s /__$

Palatal fricatives depalatalize at the ends of syllables.

The fourth change in this group occurs in a rare environment. Jointly with (i) and (iii), it accounts for (as far as I know) two forms, the stem *inchik* > *inchis* 'peanut' and the inclusive plural *-chik* > *-chis*. Although the output of (iv) created new contexts for (i) and (iii), there are no historically attested examples of forms that have undergone (iv) but not (i) and (iii).

(iv)

k > č /i__

Velar stops become palatals at the ends of words, following *i*.

Juan de Aguilar's *Arte de la lengua quichua* (1690) showed (i) and (iii) to vary as a single unit in suffixes. Thus the enclitic *-chuch* 'perhaps' also appeared as *-chus*, but never as **-chush*. Changes (i) and (iii) must nonetheless be formulated as separate changes in order to account for modern dialect differences. Many speakers of Cuzco-Collao Quechua have a palatal fricative in stems as a reflex of the older palatal stop. For such speakers, sound change (iii) did not take place in word-stems.

Figure 9.1

source	changes (i)–(iii)	
achka	ashkha ~ askha	'many'
uchpa	ushpha ~ ushpa	'ash'
pichqa	pishqa ~ pisqa	'five'

In Aguilar's *Arte,* durative *-chka* also appears as *-ʃa.* But Aguilar lacked sound change (iv) so there is no corresponding *-chis* 'inclusive' attested. Centeno's *auto sacramental, El pobre más rico,* shows the palatal lenition rule jointly with the ʃ > *s* merger having gone to completion except for the postvocalic variant of the dubitative enclitic *-cha,* which regularly appears as *-ch,* always in word-final position. The enclitic *-cha* was a member of a class of enclitics that alternated between a postconsonantal consonant-vowel form and a postvocalic consonant form, including *-mi* → *-m* /V___ for the enclitic that marks witnessed events, and *-si* → *-s* / V___ for the reportive. According to sound changes (i) and (iii), the postvocalic form of *-cha* should have been either *-s* or *-ʃ;* but the post vocalic *-ch* form was analogically restored on the model of *-cha.* In the *chu* + *ch* sequence, on the other hand, the dubitative never alternated between *-ch* and *-cha.* In this context, *-ch* (< *-cha*) followed the normal course of change to *s.* The resulting form, *-chus,* was reanalyzed as a single morpheme. Ultimately the alternation was dropped, thereby avoiding homophony with the reportive *-s* in the more frequent postvocalic environment. The enclitic *-cha* was reassigned from the class of alternating enclitics (*-mi, -si*) to the nonalternating set (negative/ yes-no question *-chu,* emphatic *-ya,* and so forth). Regularization of *-cha* is attested in the Sahuaraura codex of *Usca Paucar.* The *-chis* form of the inclusive plural (< *-chik* by [iv], [i], and [ii]) appears in *El pobre más rico* in word-final position only, that is, just the condition under which palatalization of *k* is regular. Word-internally it appears as *-chik.* In the Sahuaraura *Usca Paucar* manuscript the alternation between *-chik* and *-chis* was leveled to *-chis.* The aspiration reflex of the syllable-final palatals is first attested in an unequivocal form in *Usca Paucar.* By this time the change was complete.

Syllable-final *t* did not occur in the suffix system. In stems it regularly weakened to *s* (sound change v, see examples in figure 9.2),[2] except idiosyncratically in a single place name, *Ccatca* [q'aθqa] ~ [q'asqa]. I suspect that the variant with *θ* began as a spelling pronunciation by

Figure 9.2

source	t > s	
mutki-	muskhi-	'to smell'
mitka-	misk'a-	'to trip'
utqay	usqhay	'quickly'

mestizo first-language speakers of Spanish. Lenition of syllable-final *t* did not become regular in stems until the nineteenth century at the earliest.

(v)

t > s /__$

Alveolar stops became fricatives at the ends of syllables.

Upon weakening, the syllable-final [grave] stops have gradually been converging upon [x̣]. The modern synchronic reflex of these changes is a phonological rule that realizes all nonstrident occlusives as [x̣]; it is widespread in the Department of Cuzco. Sound changes (vi), (vii), and (viii) represent three stages in the lenition and uvularization of syllable-final *p*. Stage (viii) has regularized in suffixes; all three are dialectally and lexically attested in stems in present-day Cuzco.

(vi)

p > ϕ /__$

Labial stops became fricatives at the ends of syllables.

(vii)

ap > a^wx̣ /__$

Following *a* and at the ends of syllables, labial stops became uvular fricatives and labialize the *a*.

(viii)

ϕ > x̣ /__$

Labial fricatives became uvular at the ends of syllables.

Stages (vi) and (vii) are in competition in the more conservative dialects. Stage (viii) has been reached in suffixes and is currently diffusing across the lexicon, where its progress slows to avoid homonymy. For example, one of the most resistant words is *raϕra* 'wing', which would fall together with *raqra* 'split, to split'. But stage (viii) is further advanced in casual than in careful speech: a speaker who used the form *ch'ax̣ra* 'plant' in an unguarded moment denied it when the word was elicited later in the day in a more formal setting as *ch'aϕra.*

Regular expansion of (viii) may be sidetracked by other sound changes that otherwise bear no relation to the sequence of syllable-final lenitions and mergers. In the district center of Andahuaylillas (Quispicanchi), the aspirated labial [p^h] has become fricative [ϕ]: Speakers from the center say *ϕiñakuy* 'to get angry' as opposed to *p^hiñakuy* heard in the outlying communities in the district. The new initial [ϕ] has been supported by other changes, such as the metathesis of *raϕra* to *ϕarϕa.* Uvularization of the syllable-final bilabials has stagnated at the same time as more recent changes (such as *uy* > *i*) have entered the grammar. For these speakers, syllable-final [ϕ] has been held in place by the establishment of a / ϕ / phoneme.

Neither stage (vi) nor stage (vii) is independently attested for suffixes in the older texts, although in the case of (vi) this may be an accident of orthography. Uvularization (stage viii) first appears in the Sahuaraura codex of *Usca Paucar,* where it is attested variably, and then only in suffixes. Sahuaraura's *Ollanta* manuscript shows regular uvularization of the postvocalic genitive and frequent uvularization in switch-reference *-pti.* There is no change whatever in the stems. By the time of the Justiniani codex of *Ollanta,* uvularization was complete in suffixes. Uvularization presupposes fricativization of the labial and so also presupposes fricativization of the uvular. The gap between *El pobre más rico* and the two Sahuaraura manuscripts, regardless of whether it is historical or orthographic, is too large to establish the sequence of these changes on other than internal implicational grounds. It is possible (though it is not attested) that the grave stops simultaneously became fricatives, that is, that (vi) was actually a part of the more general sound change (ix).[3] Examples of (ix) appear in figure 9.3.

(ix)

[+ GRAVE] > [+ CONTINUANT] /___$

Grave segments (labials, velars, and uvulars) became fricatives at the ends of syllables.

Assimilation of syllable-final nasals to the following stop is attested variably in stems throughout the written sample. Assimilation of *n* →

Figure 9.3

source	(ix)	x > x̣	(vii)	(viii)	
-q	-x̣	—	—	—	'agentive nominalizer'
-pti	*-ϕti	—	—	-x̣ti	'subordinating suffix'
maqch'iy[a]	max̣ch'iy	—	—	—	'to wash'
wakcha[b]	waxcha	—	—	—	'orphan'
*hapq'iy	haϕq'iy	—	ha^{w}x̣q'iy	hax̣q'iy	'dig up'
q'apñusqa[c]	q'aϕñusqa	—	q'a^{w}x̣ñusqa	q'ax̣ñusqa	'dented'
rapra[d]	raϕra	—	—	rax̣ra	'wing'
wak	wax	wax̣	—	—	'several'

[a]Gonçález Holguín (1608: 223) *macchhini* ~ *macchini.*
[b]Gonçález Holguín (1608: 167) *huaccha.*
[c]Gonçález Holguín (1608: 135) *kapñuscca.*
[d]Gonçález Holguín (1608: 313) *rapra* as *rama de arbol o ramo.*

m /__*p,* is widespread in *El pobre más rico* and probably led to a reanalysis of other occurrences of syllable-final *m* that were not involved in an alternation as underlying / n /. By the time of the *Usca Paucar* manuscript, the postvocalic form of the enclitic that marks witnessed events, *-mi,* was also *-n.* Ultimately, the nasal neutralization rule was generalized to environments before a continuant. This final expansion occurred by the time the Sahuaraura codex of *Ollanta* was written.

Fricativization of tap *r* began word-finally; this is a regular stage in the lenition process. The rule was generalized to "adjacent to a word-boundary," perhaps under the influence of a parallel rule affecting Spanish *r,* which in much of the Americas, including highland Peru, also undergoes fricativization. The *r* is currently weakening before consonants as well. The history of the *r* lenition (which has a direct counterpart in the synchronic grammar) demonstrates the dialectic between form and function in the evolution of grammatical rules. Like the other fricativization processes, it appears to have begun at the ends of words and then of stems. The structural description of the rule was generalized from "before" to "adjacent to" word and stem boundaries under the influence of a formally identical rule in language contact. This obscured the relationship between the form of the rule and its concomitant function. Further generalization of the rule to "before a syllable boundary"—which was the functionally consistent natural next step for the rule to take—became quite complicated from a formal point of view. With time, however, the functional motivation is coming to be reflected in the form of the rule, even at the cost of considerable formal complication.

Three processes have contributed to simplification of vowel-glide sequences. (1) Back glides have fronted at the ends of syllables, following the regular pattern of change from derivational morphology to stems and from the ends of words and stems to stem-internally; (2) / ay / diphthongs have coalesced into high vowels; and (3) / uy / diphthongs have simplified to [u]. The first of the changes is widespread, although still variable within stems, while the second and third are both changes in progress.

(x)

w > y /__$

w became *y* at the ends of syllables.

(xi)

ay > e: > i /__$ except after a uvular

Sequences of *ay* became long *e*, and finally *i*, at the ends of syllables.

(xii)

uy > u /__#

After *u*, *y* dropped, at the ends of words only.

The shift of *w* to *y* is attested in the derivational suffix *-wsi-* 'to assist to' in the Sahuaraura manuscript of *Ollanta*. (The suffix *-wsi-* is the only one in which it occurred.) The Justiniani manuscript, on the other hand, shows the change stem-finally as well. It is now complete in suffixes and stem-finally; it is variable, lexically and dialectally, inside stems, as in figure 9.4.

Cuzco-Collao vowels are raised phonetically before a high, front glide, *y*; for / a /, this is *æ* → ε. Phonetic raising, like many coarticulatory effects, is normally attributed to the segment that induces the effect, in this case the *y*. But many speakers are no longer attributing the effect to the adjacent *y* and are treating the raised ε as basic and unmodified. In turn, the diphthong is coalescing (monophthongizing) around ε. Coalescence does not appear to be taking place in the suffix system. Moreover, in the sequence *-sqayki* 'I to you, future', the uvular prevents raising from taking place. The sequence is currently in the process of dropping the uvular; but, even without the uvular, raising and coalescence do not take place. Rather, there is a competing change in which the *y* is lost

Figure 9.4

source	w > y	
-wsi-	-ysi-	'to assist to'
p'unchaw	p'unchay	'daylight'
wawqi	wayqi	'brother of a male'

regardless of whether the uvular is then dropped. This change, which is present only in suffixes, also affects the second person nominal form, *-yki*. But there is no evidence that the second person nominal form is being leveled to **-ki*.

One of the critical points for establishing a relative chronology of the written sources is that the syllable-final weakenings and mergers spread from one morphosyntactic context to another, in a regular way. In the following chapter, I discuss the morphosyntactic conditions governing these changes and show how the conditions fit broader patterns in the grammar of Southern Peruvian Quechua.

10 Conditions on Sound Change

The weakenings and mergers of consonants at the ends of syllables are clearly related to one another, although that relationship is not a *formal* one. From the standpoint of the structural form of the processes, they reflect separate innovations, that is to say, separate historical events. The written sources bear this out. Since many of the correspondences are quite systematic, they could be subsumed by a few general statements, such as that all stops at the ends of syllables correspond to fricatives in the modern Cuzco-Collao dialect. Nonetheless, the written sources show that the changes took place separately at each point of articulation. Once we discard the possibility of collapsing these changes into more general statements of sound correspondences, at a formal level they appear to be unrelated to each other. But the overall organization and sequence of these changes suggests that there is an underlying functional unity to them. They occur in an orderly, implicational sequence. Within the stops, the order of the weakenings is predictable from their acoustic characteristics. The more acute stops, which concentrate acoustic energy higher in the spectrum and have a smaller overall energy packet, weakened first. The more grave stops, which concentrate acoustic energy lower in the spectrum, weakened later. The weakenings have also left a strong mark on the synchronic phonology of the language in the form of a clear unifying orientation to a number of structurally discrete rules.

The syllable-final weakenings also show another kind of unity. The changes do not take place equally in all morphological classes. Rather, they spread across the word, from morphological class to morphological class, and from narrower phonological environments to more inclusive ones.

The traditional and still dominant view of phonological change excludes the possibility that sound change might be morphologically conditioned. Leonard Bloomfield (1933a: 354) put the traditional view very simply: "Phonemes change." By this he meant that instances of a phonological segment change equally in all nonphonological linguistic contexts. Studies of sound change in progress and of lexical diffusion of phonological changes show that, even if the slogan is a good working assumption, it is an oversimplification (Wang 1969; Chen 1972; Krishnamurti 1978; Labov 1981). In tracing the history of the syllable-final weakenings and mergers in Southern Peruvian Quechua, we found that regular principles govern the spread of innovations from environment to environment. These principles constrain the set of possible transitions between any two grammars that are related by a single historical process. The principles bear up equally well against the written evidence (in which they constrain variation in time), dialectological evidence (in which they constrain variation in social space), and internal reconstruction (in which they constrain variation in tendencies toward change that are internal to the speaker's cognitive grammar). Here are informal statements of the principles. First, the syllable-final weakenings and mergers begin at the ends of words and word-stems and spread to word- and stem-internally. This has a straightforward phonological basis, as I show below. Second, the syllable-final weakenings and mergers begin in the suffix system and spread into word-stems. This seems to have a morphosyntactic motivation. The Southern Peruvian Quechua word consists of a stem followed by an ordered sequence of suffixes. Suffix-classes have the following order: derivation ˆ inflection ˆ discourse-level. With the relatively minor exception of stem-reduplication, suffixation is the only productive morphological process in Southern Peruvian Quechua. I elaborate below on the morphosyntactic nature of the Southern Peruvian Quechua word in the course of explaining the significance of the second principle.

The principles may be stated as implicational relationships that constrain the class of possible language states relative to the output of a particular change. Linguists traditionally have used implicational hierarchies to demonstrate that superficially diverse phenomena have a deep-seated structural unity, as when Jakobson used implicational hierarchies to demonstrate that the child's acquisition of phonology represents a process of structural genesis rather than acquisition of a collection of unrelated sounds (Jakobson 1962 [1941]: 357f.; Jakobson and Halle 1956), or when Greenberg demonstrated that apparently unrelated morphosyntactic phenomena covary in a predictable way (Greenberg 1963; Jakobson 1963). More recently, sociolinguists have used implicational hierarchies to demonstrate the underlying unity of a set of grammatical variables, such as the degree of self-monitoring of the speech event by the speaker (Labov 1972 [1970]: 208). In cases such as the latter, in which linguistic variables are interpreted socially as part of an overarching, intersubjective system of status evaluation, the linguistic phenomena that pattern along an implicational scale can be unconnected to one another formally (Albó 1970; DeCamp 1971, 1973). In the case we are considering here, the implicational hierarchies are of the first, structurally motivated type. They demonstrate that we are dealing with conditions on the spread of unitary linguistic changes, not with a series of accidentally related individual sound changes.[1]

To repeat, the implicational hierarchies constrain the class of possible language states relative to the output of a particular change. In other words, they permit sound changes to expand in certain ways only. Thus they restrict possible transitions between two historical or dialectal states.

(i)

1. **If a sound change takes place word-internally, then it takes place word-finally.**[2]
2. **If a sound change takes place stem-internally, then it takes place stem-finally.**

The first clause of condition (i) follows straightforwardly from the nature of the syllable. The changes in question occur at the ends of syllables. A phonological word must contain an integral number of syllables. The environment "word-finally" is therefore a proper subset of the environment "syllable-finally." Southern Peruvian Quechua does not resyllabify at word boundaries. For the syllable-final changes in Southern Peruvian Quechua, the environment "stem-finally" is also a proper subset of "syllable-finally." All verbs and some substantives end in vowels, and the addition of a suffix often adds a final consonant to the last syllable in a stem. Verbs are bound forms. But nouns that act as lexical stems are free, that is, they may occur without suffixes. Many of these end in a consonant. Condition (i) may be captured formally by assigning the #-boundary to stems and the ##-boundary to words. The # (stem) boundary is independently required by other phonotactic constraints; the ## (word) boundary also marks the domain of other phonological processes, including stress assignment. The ## boundary is a proper subset of the $ (syllable) boundary.

The second part of condition (i) accounts for the spread of the weakenings and mergers from /__# (at the end of stems) to /__$ (at the end of syllables).[3] This may be attributed to analogical leveling of suffixed stems to their nonsuffixed counterparts. In Southern Peruvian Quechua, there is a strong tendency for morphemes to have an invariable phonological shape. Very few grammatical morphemes and almost *no* lexical or stem morphemes are involved in regular, phonologically motivated

Figure 10.1

	all syllable-final contexts	stem-finally	word-finally
a	−	−	−
b	−	−	+
c	−	+	+
d	+	+	+
*e	−	+	−
*f	+	+	−
*g	+	−	−
*h	+	−	+

alternations. The few exceptions among lexical morphemes involve reduplication, for example, *haqay* 'there' (deictic) / *Hax̣-hax̣-haqay* 'over there!' (as a warning); *wich'is* 'pig cry' / *wich'*ich*ichiy* 'to cry sharply' (Cusihuamán 1976a: 217). The second part of the condition contributes to the preservation of stem invariance.

The implicational hierarchies in (i) are consistent with the states summarized in rows *a–d* of figure 10.1, but not consistent with *e–h.* Here "+" means that the change has taken place in a particular environment and "−" that it has not ("+" includes cases in which the structural description of the change is not met in the environment). The inconsistent cases are marked with an asterisk (*).

Here is an example: the shift of syllable-final *w* to *y* (chapter 9, change x) took place in the derivational suffix *-wsi-* > *-ysi-* 'to assist to VERB' prior to its spread into stems, where there is still dialectal variation in the modern language (see fig. 10.2). The shift has been completed in final position in stems, as in *p'unchaw* > *p'unchay* (invariably) 'day(light)', but not internal to stems, where the older form *wawqi* varies with a newer *wayqi* 'brother of a male'. The two *Ollanta* codices—which reflect similar but not identical states of the language—provide a useful comparison. In the Sahuaraura text, *-wsi-* > *-ysi-* is complete, but both *punchau* and *punchai* appear for 'day(light)'. In the Justiniani manuscript, it has gone to completion stem-finally.

Notice that (i), the phonologically motivated condition on sound change, accounts for the relationship between the stem-final and stem-internal environments, but does not correctly account for the initiation of the change in suffixes. The *-wsi-* > *-ysi-* shift precedes any change in stem-final position, even though it occurs word-internally. Were the expansion of the sound change motivated entirely on phonological grounds,

Figure 10.2

	Gonçález Holguín	Anon., *Usca Paucar* (Sahuaraura)	Anon., *Ollanta* (Sahuaraura)	Anon., *Ollanta* (Justiniani)	modern dialects	
w > y (suf)	–	–	+	+	+	+
w > y (stem-final)	–	–	%	+	+	+
w > y (stem)	–	–	–	%	%	+

(suf) = in suffixes.
(stem) = in stems.
\+ = regularly attested.
% = variably attested.
– = not attested.

we would expect rather that the stem-final change (with concomitant leveling of the variant forms to the newer one) would precede the word-internal change in the suffix system. Moreover, these data are consistent with others in the written and dialectological data sets and with the application of synchronic phonological processes.

Consider the fricativization of syllable-final labials and their merger with the uvular fricative (uvularization) (chapter 9, sound changes [vi] and [viii]; see fig. 10.3). There are three instances in which the appropriate structural description is met: in the postvocalic form of the genitive, *-p;* in the switch-reference subordinator *-pti-;* and in numerous stems (for example *hapt'ay* 'handful' or *q'apnuy* 'to dent'). The syllable-final bilabial merged with the uvular fricative first in the genitive, then in the switch-reference subordinator (both in the eighteenth century), and is currently shifting in stems. (The extant textual data show uvularization together with fricativization in the suffixes, but as independent of one another in stems. Dialectological evidence supports their separateness in stems.) Uvularization of the genitive is complete in the Sahuaraura codex of *Ollanta,* but switch-reference uvularization is variable, and there is none in stems. By the time of the Justiniani codex of *Ollanta,* uvularization was complete in the suffixes. At the present time, uvularization in stems is a major dialectological variable in the Department of Cuzco.

The weakening of syllable-final palatals (chapter 9, sound change i) resulted in a ʃ : *s* contrast in that position. Syllable-final ʃ in turn con-

Figure 10.3

	Centeno	Anon., *Usca Paucar* (Sahuaraura)	Anon., *Ollanta* (Sahuaraura)	Anon., *Ollanta* (Justiniani)	modern dialects	
$p > \phi$ (suf)	–	%	%	+	+	+
$p > \phi$ (stem)	–	–	–	%	+	+
$\phi > \underset{.}{x}$ (suf)	–	%	%	+	+	+
$\phi > \underset{.}{x}$ (stem)	–	–	–	–	–	%

(suf) = in suffixes.
(stem) = in stems.
+ = regularly attested.
% = variably attested.
– = not attested.

ditioned aspiration on the following stop, provided that the context met other restrictions on aspiration, namely, that it can only occur in stems and on the first oral stop in a word (chapter 9, sound change ii). The *ʃ* : *s* contrast has since been eliminated in suffixes by the sound change *ʃ* > *s* (chapter 9, sound change iii). The change has spread to stems in Cuzco and the area north and east of the Vilcanota River, where aspiration (from sound change [ii]) is the only remaining trace of the former contrast between palatal and nonpalatal sibilants. (The only syllable-*initial* *ʃ* is in the durative suffix as a result of other changes. But in the Urubamba valley the *ʃ* > *s* merger is in the process of being generalized to eliminate the unique syllable-initial *ʃ* as well.) South and west of the Vilcanota River, the merger of final sibilants (iii) is restricted to suffixes, leaving the *ʃ* : *s* contrast intact in stems. The contrast is reinforced by syllable-*initial* variable palatalization, *s* > *ʃ*, before front vowels and (in loanwords) before palatal glides. The *ʃ* : *s* contrast is one of the principal parameters of dialectal variation in modern-day Cuzco-Collao Quechua.

In the historical texts, *ʃ* > *s* was first attested in Aguilar's *Arte*, where it had taken place in suffixes. It was complete in stems in Centeno and in the two dramas recorded by Sahuaraura (see fig. 10.4). The dramas evidently belong to the dialect area that includes the city of Cuzco and the area to its north and east. The association of the drama *Ollanta* with the village of Tinta (southwest of Cuzco) is not supported for either the Sahuaraura or the Justiniani manuscripts of *Ollanta*.

Figure 10.4

	Gonçález Holguín	Aguilar	Centeno	Anon., *Usca Paucar* (Sahuaraura)	Anon., *Ollanta* (Sahuaraura)	Anon., *Ollanta* (Justiniani)
(iii) ʃ > s (suf)	–	+	+	+	+	+
(iii) ʃ > s (stem)	–	–	+	+	+	+

(suf) = in suffixes.
(stem) = in stems.
\+ = regularly attested.
% = variably attested.
– = not attested.

The morphosyntactic condition on the syllable-final changes is stated in (ii). It is a condition on the output of changes, including morphological changes as well as sound changes. The preterite tense suffix is restructuring from *-rqa-* to *-ra-*; this is a morphological change in progress that eliminates syllable final *r* from a very common inflectional context. The 'urgency' suffix, a derivational suffix, is undergoing a comparable morphological change, *-rqu-* ~ *-rqa-* > *-ru-* ~ *-ra-*. The inflectional change is a precondition for the derivational.

(ii)

If a change takes place in stems, then it takes place in derivational morphemes; if in derivational morphemes, then in inflectional and discourse-level morphemes,[4] provided that the structural description of the change is met.

The implicational hierarchy in (ii) is consistent with the cases summarized in rows *a–d* of figure 10.5, but not consistent with *e–h*.

Conditions (i) and (ii) are constraints on the expansion of the changes. Thus (i) does not stipulate that sound changes must expand from the word-final environment to the syllable-final; rather, they can only expand consistent with the condition. Simultaneous actualization of the change throughout the word, for example, would be consistent with case *d* of figure 10.1. Nor does (ii) stipulate that a sound change in the suffix system must precede the same change in the stem. Condition (i) permits the cases listed in rows *a–d* of figure 10.1 and rules out those starred in *e–h*. Similarly, (ii) rules out the cases starred in figure 10.5.

Figure 10.5

	stem	derivation	inflection/ discourse
a	−	−	−
b	−	−	+
c	−	+	+
d	+	+	+
*e	−	+	−
*f	+	+	−
*g	+	−	−
*h	+	−	+

But there is a violation of these conditions in the written corpus. Centeno's drama *El pobre más rico* shows completed lenition of syllable-final palatals except for the postvocalic form of the dubitative *-cha* which regularly appears as *-ch*. Worse still *-cha* ~ *-ch* is always the last suffix in the word. It contradicts both conditions (i) and (ii) by realizing case *f* of figures 10.1 and 10.5. But the source of the retention of the *-ch* form is clear. The postconsonantal long form of the dubitative *-cha* provides a model for speakers to restore the palatal stop in the postvocalic short form *-ch*. The alternation was parallel to *-mi* ~ *-m* 'scope of affirmation, witness' and *-si* ~ *-s* 'scope of affirmation, reported'. We must therefore weaken conditions (i) and (ii) with a third condition, (iii), which allows conditions (i) and (ii) to be overridden in the event that a morpheme alternation in a regular paradigm provides a model for restoring the phonetics of the final stop.

(iii)

The expansion of a sound change may be delayed for a morpheme that otherwise meets the structural description, if the morpheme is involved in a phonologically determined alternation from which the original form can be restored.

Final *č* was restored in the *-ch* suffix, which alternated with a longer *-cha* form. In the sequence *-chu* + *ch,* in which it never alternated, it was not restored; the resulting *-chu* + *s* was reanalyzed as a single morpheme. By the time of the Sahuaraura manuscript of *Usca Paucar,* the *-cha* suffix had been reassigned from the class of alternating enclitics to the nonalternating class. It invariably appears there as *-cha,* just as it does in the modern language.

The Word as Diagram, Diagrams of the Word

The first part of condition (i) has a clear phonological motivation. The sound system of language is organized into a hierarchy of nested constituents. Below the level of the word, there are features nested into segments, segments nested into syllabic onset and rhyme, onset and rhyme nested into syllables, syllables nested into feet, and feet nested into words. The weakenings and mergers occur at the level of the syllabic rhyme; in Southern Peruvian Quechua, a rhyme consists of a vocalic nucleus followed by a consonantal adjunct. Rhymes are defined by their role in the organization of the syllable. The next larger constituent, the foot, plays a role in the distribution of stress in Southern Peruvian Quechua, but does not seem to be relevant at all to the weakenings and mergers. Finally, there is the word, which is composed of an integral number of syllables and feet. Both "word" and "syllable" are relevant contexts for the changes. Any sound change that takes place at the ends of syllables perforce takes place at the ends of words, but not all sound changes that take place at the ends of words also take place at the ends of syllables internal to the word. If __$, then __# (see clause 1 of [i]). Condition (iii) and the second clause of condition (i) appear to be consequences of the strong orientation of Southern Peruvian Quechua to agglutinative, transparent morphology, in other words to a condition in which every morpheme has one and only one surface manifestation. Southern Peruvian Quechua has few morphological alternations and very few obvious morphophonemic processes. There are exceptions, but they are relatively rare. Thus in the case of the second clause of condition (i), word-internal but stem-final consonants are leveled to word-final variants. Conversely, in the case accounted for by (iii), an alternation was used to restore the older phonetic form and prevent allomorphy, until *-cha* was reassigned from the class of alternating enclitics to the nonalternating class.

Condition (ii) is another matter; it allows for the spread of sound changes from discourse and inflectional morphemes to derivational morphemes to word-stems. The Neogrammarian position that "sound-laws, inasmuch as they are mechanical, hold without exception" has been so productive that we are often loath to accept the possibility of nonphonological conditioning of what are otherwise regular sound changes; Hockett (1965) is correct in referring to the Neogrammarian axiom as one of the few "great discoveries" in linguistics. This is not to say that all phonological changes are sound laws (*Lautgesetze*). The Neogrammarians recognized analogy and contamination (associative lexical influence; see chapter 8) as valid mechanisms of phonological change; Whitney (1875: 106) and Meillet (1967 [1924]: 14), among others, recognized that primary sound symbolism (sound imagery) works in other ways, and Wang, Chen, and Labov (also among others) have shown the importance of phonetically defined word classes to the phonological histories of Middle Chinese and Modern American English. But the syllable-final weakenings and mergers are garden variety sound laws, *Lautgesetze*, exactly the kind of change to which the Neogrammarian axiom applies. And condition (ii) *does* hold for these changes, as well as other, more properly morphological innovations. Nor is it an isolated set of coincidences. Cerrón-Palomino (1974) has observed similar conditioning of sound change in Wanka, a Central Quechua language. He suggests that (ii) is a type of conditioning of sound change that is characteristic of the Quechua family. Adelaar (1982: 62–66) has likewise observed that the Quechua suffixes have been more susceptible than stems to sound change, morphologically and semantically motivated changes aside. Inflectional lead in sound change has also been observed in Indo-European by Turner (1927, 1937; for Indic) and Malkiel (1968a; for Romance).

Although there are parallels elsewhere in the Quechua family, and in other, unrelated genetic groupings, I propose to account for condition (ii) in terms that are specific to the grammar of Southern Peruvian Quechua. To do so, I draw upon the notion of *diagram*, a type of icon in which the arrangement of parts of the signifier is isomorphic with the arrangement of parts of its object (Peirce 1940 [1902]: 105). According to Peirce, diagrams are signs "which represent the relations, mainly dyadic, or so regarded, of the parts of one thing by analogous relationships in their own parts . . ." Briefly, in the syllable-final weakenings and mergers, the spread of the changes diagramed the internal structure of the word. As any iconicity in language, it is a product of cultural apprehension, rather than of natural compulsion. Iconicity in language does not have a lawlike character in the sense that the form of a sign is predictable from its object. Rather, cultural perception of the motivation of a sign favors its retention by speakers and its persistence over time. In this case the signifier is the implicational hierarchy specified in condition (ii). Its object is the internal structure of the word, which in Southern Peruvian Quechua is itself a complex and layered morphological, syntactic, and semantic diagram. In order to explain how this is so, let me sketch some basic typological properties of the Quechua word.

The critical relationship for word and morpheme order typology is the verb-object pivot. Broadly speaking, languages in which the verb precedes its direct object (verb^object languages) are strikingly different from languages in which the verb follows it (object^verb languages). Southern Peruvian Quechua is an extremely consistent object^verb language with all that that implies typologically: relative clauses precede the nouns they modify, other subordinate clauses precede main clauses in the stylistically most neutral circumstances, adjectives and genitives precede nouns, and word order outside of main clauses is virtually fixed as subject^object^verb (cf. Greenberg 1963). Apart from limited reduplication (as an intensifier and in onomatopoetic stems), Southern Peruvian Quechua exclusively uses suffixing as a morphological process. Consider the structure of the verb. Each suffix modifies the sister constituent that immediately precedes it, in the asymmetrical primacy relationship diagramed in (iv). Node B and C are both daughter constituents of A. B modifies C but not vice versa. B is a semantic function from C to A.

(iv)

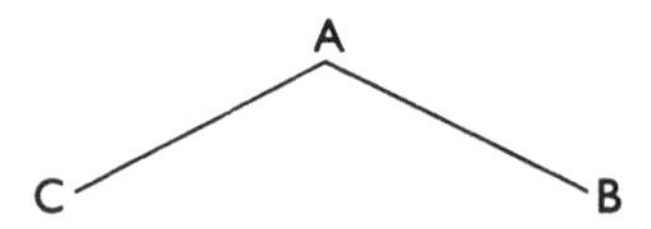

In the verb, modification structures are compositionally built up into a left-branching hierarchy of the kind represented in (v) and (vi), in which every suffix modifies the expression dominated by its sister node.[5]

Each suffix has its (left-adjoined) sister constituent within its syntactic domain. Derivational suffixes potentially change the syntactic category of the larger constituent; inflectional suffixes map the category of the sister node onto the next higher node; discourse-level suffixes mark entire main-clause constituents without regard to syntactic category. Semantically, each suffix is a function that takes its sister expression as its argument (cf. Weber 1976). If we regard deixis as a gradient property (relative subjectivity), no suffix may be contained within the semantic scope of another suffix that is less deictic but a member of the same suffix class (derivational, inflectional, discourse-level). The semantic domain of derivational suffixes is the sister constituent, at most a phrase. The semantic domain of inflectional suffixes is larger than a single phrase and is often a clause. Discourse-level suffixes syntactically modify phrasal constituents but contain whole sentences within their semantic scope and are subject to constraints that operate above the level of the sentence. The distinction between suffix classes is marked categorically by the order of affixes. For the verb, the boundary between derivational and inflectional suffixes marks the outermost point at which the verb may be nominalized, and the innermost point at which the restrictive quantifier *-lla-* may appear. (The same suffix precedes

(v)

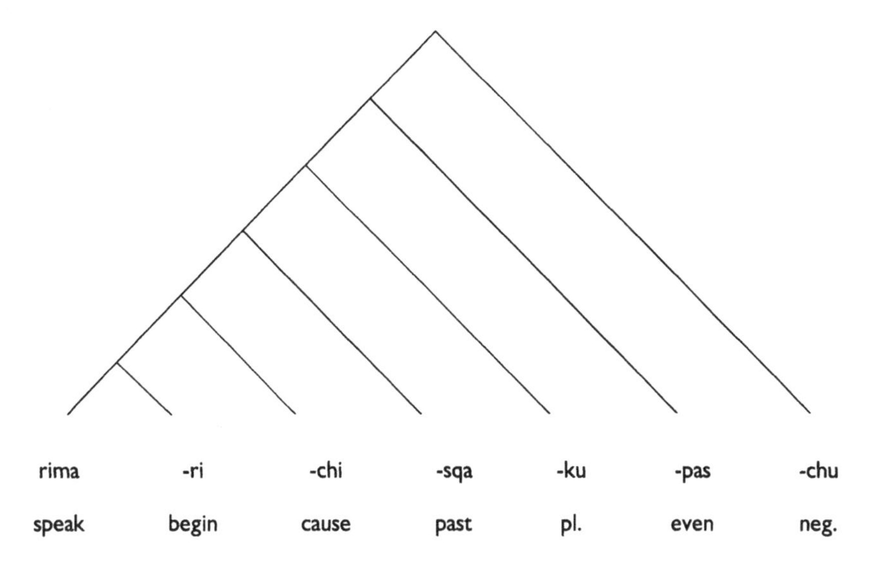

[Manas] rimarichisqakupaschu.
'It is said that they didn't even let him speak' (cf. Cusihuamán 1976a: 89)

(vi)

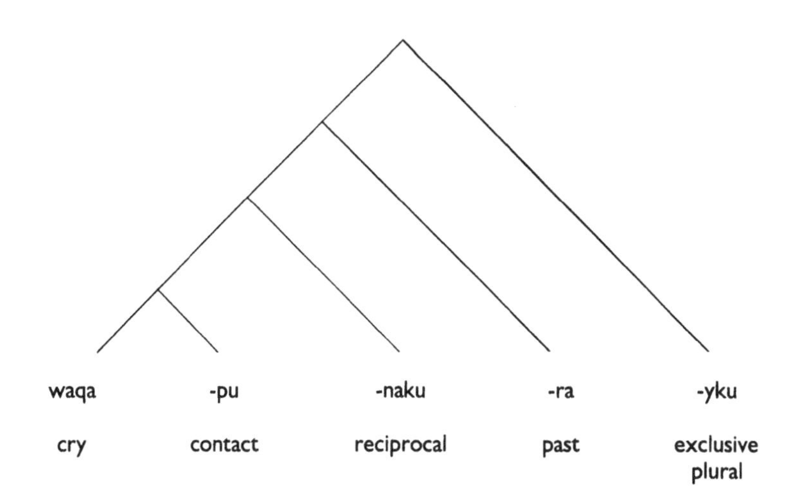

Waqapunakurayku.
'We looked at each other and cried'

nominal inflection.) The major suffix classes mark the domains of virtually all morphological processes: fusion and asymmetric morphological vowel gradation within derivation, syncretism within inflection, and clisis within the discourse-level.

The linear order of suffixes on the verb reflects their hierarchy in a consistently left-branching geometric structure and this in turn diagrams the nested semantic hierarchy among the semantic units that these suffixes represent. The order of the major suffix classes diagrams the relative breadth of their syntactic domains and, within suffix classes, diagrams their relative deixis.[6] The following order thus obtains among major verbal categories: the stem is followed by a series of extremely concrete modifiers, which are in turn followed by voice, directionals, aspect, tense, person, number, mood, and then a series of wider domain functions that indicate such discourse-sensitive notions as scope of affirmation, speaker's evaluation of the narrated events, emphasis, and so forth.[7] For present purposes, it is sufficient to observe that in gross terms the following hierarchy and left-to-right order obtain:[8]

(vii)

[[[[stem] derivation] inflection] discourse-level]

In each case in which the structural description for a sound change was met, it began in discourse-level suffixes and the inflectional system, spread into the derivational system, then finally moved into the stem. The progress of the changes diagrams the internal structure of the word, marking the distinctions between the word-stem and the derivational, inflectional, and discourse-level suffixes. There can be a considerable time lag between the initial change in inflectional morphemes and its completion in the stem. For example, for those registers in which uvularization has gone to completion, there has been a two-century lag since its inception in the inflectional machinery.

Condition (ii) then, does not predict changes; it predicts a set of possible paths that the changes can take. To borrow an analogy from the Indo-Europeanist Jerzy Kuryłowicz (1966 [1949]: 174), condition (ii) is like a rain gutter: it will not predict rain, but once it does rain, we know which way the water will flow.

Let us consider some alternative ways to account for condition (ii). A first strategy would be to replace it with an expanded version of the phonologically motivated condition, (i), in which sound changes mechanically spread from the ends of words to the beginnings. But that alternative is not viable, since, as we saw with the sound changes summarized in figures 10.2, 10.3, and 10.4, sound changes affect one suffiix class before they enter another. Within a speech register, there is no change in stems unless the change has been completed in suffixes. Nor is the condition restricted to sound change. It also governs the output of morphological change. The regularity of the implicational relationship suggests that it is structural and not simply a matter of mechanical penetration of the word as a domain.

A second alternative would be to treat the implicational relationships in (i) and (ii) in terms of frequency. It is often suggested that susceptibility to sound change is a function of the frequency of a morpheme in running text. Inflectional and derivational morphemes should therefore be expected to undergo a particular change prior to lexical morphemes. But this alternative is not viable either. Where we have an infrequent derivational morpheme and frequent lexical formative (as in the case above of *-wsi-* and *p'unchaw*), it is the morpheme hierarchy and not textual frequency that determines the order in which they undergo the sound change.[9]

As a final alternative, consider the observation by Roman Jakobson (1987 [1965]: 420) that "affixes, particularly inflectional suffixes, in languages where they exist, habitually differ from other morphemes by a restricted and selected use of phonemes and their combinations. Thus the only consonants utilized in the productive inflectional suffixes of English are the dental continuant and stop, and their cluster *-st*. Of the 24 obstruents of the Russian consonantal pattern, only four phonemes, saliently opposed to each other, function in the inflectional suffixes."

To follow the logic of Jakobson's observation, the suffixes would be expected to have a restricted segmental inventory in comparison to word-stems. Thus the directionality phenomenon should result from the fact that the changes with which we are concerned are mergers. But since they only affect the finals of syllables, they do not reduce the segmental inventory in grammatical morphemes; in one case, the *-ʃa-* variant of the durative, a distinctive segment has actually been created in a grammatical formative that is not distinctive anywhere else. Although it is intuitively appealing to seek a motivation for conditions (i)–(iii) in more general principles of linguistic structure, Jakobson's principle is not applicable.

The conditions on phonological change provide a restrictive account of the relationships that may hold between any two successive, dialectal or historical, grammars. As such, they are testable against two kinds of evidence, dialect variation and philologically attested historical systems, which is to say, diachronic variation. Together with the motivated relative chronology of the sound changes (e.g., the role of relative acoustic gravity in determining the sequence), they establish both a set of consistent (or "lawful") variant phonological systems and a partial diachronic ordering (or relative chronology) among them. They draw attention to a significant type of covariation between form and meaning in Southern Peruvian Quechua, in which the relative domains of the synchronic reflexes of the changes reflect the internal structure of the word; thus they shed light on the nature of form/meaning covariation in language, more generally. The observations by Adelaar, Cerrón-Palomino, Lastra and Horcasitas, Malkiel, and Turner demonstrate that the Southern Peruvian Quechua conditions on phonological change are instances of a phenomenon of more general applicability and demonstrates the need for a general theoretical account of these principles.

In this chapter, I have shown that the syllable-final weakenings and mergers follow a set of general principles that govern their spread through the word. These involve both phonological and nonphonological conditioning, which can be formulated as three very general conditions on phonological change (including, but not restricted to regular sound changes [*Lautgesetze*]). These are restated as the primes of (i) to (iii).

(i′)

1. If a sound change takes place word-internally, then it takes place word-finally.
2. If a sound change takes place stem-internally, then it takes place stem-finally.

(ii′)

If a change takes place in stems, then it takes place in derivational morphemes; if in derivational morphemes, then in inflectional and discourse-level morphemes, provided that the structural description of the change is met.

(iii′)

The expansion of a sound change may be retarded for a morpheme that otherwise meets the structural description if it is involved in a phonologically determined alternation from which the original form can be restored.

The first condition, (i′), has a phonological motivation, in that in Southern Peruvian Quechua, the environments "word-finally" and "stem-finally" are proper subsets of the environment "syllable-finally" for the consonant weakenings. The second, (ii′), accounts for the spread of phonological changes from discourse and inflectional morphemes to derivation morphemes to word-stems. According to (ii′), phonological changes are conditioned by nonphonological factors, in this case by the morphological class of the formative in which they take place. If a phonological change has taken place in stems, then it has taken place in suffixes; if it has taken place in derivational suffixes, then it has taken place in inflectional suffixes; if it has taken place in inflectional suffixes, then it has taken place in discourse-level suffixes (enclitics). The progress of phonological changes through the word is a diagrammatic icon of the internal structure of the word. In this respect, phonological changes may contribute to the perceptual salience of the hierarchy of morpho-syntactic elements in the word. The third condition, (iii'), is a diachronic consequence of the overall tendency of Southern Peruvian Quechua morphology toward nonallomorphic agglutination. The first condition can be accounted for in a straightforwardly mechanical way. The second and third conditions, on the other hand, seem to be due to pattern consistency, that is, the speaker's intuitive feel for formal patterning in the language (Sapir 1949 [1925]: 44, 1949 [1933]: 23).

In the last chapter, I observed that, at a structural level, the syllable-final weakenings and mergers appear to be independent of each other. But when they are viewed as a whole, in the perspective of a longer time frame, their organization and sequence follow a definite pattern. First, the sequence of the changes is partly determined by the acoustic and perceptual properties of the affected sounds. There is a definite hierarchical and sequential order among the changes. Second, the erosion of syllable endings follows a predictable course that reflects the internal grammatical structure of the Quechua word, from suffixes into stems. The syllable-final weakenings and mergers are subject to several general conditions that I have discussed in this chapter. These patterns are not evident if historical reconstruction is limited to statements of correspondences between cognate dialects and languages. Paradoxically, they emerge only when language change is viewed in a perspective that is both more fine-grained and more holistic; more fine-grained, in that a variety of evidence—especially philological and dialectological—is used to reconstruct the precise course followed by the erosions of syllable endings over five hundred years; more holistic in that the course of these changes has been constant from change to change over the entire period; and more holistic in that the hierarchy among the weakenings and mergers is only evident in what the historian Fernand Braudel (1958) calls *la longue durée,* in this case, in the perspective of five hundred years.

The forte of historical linguists is to account for the individual change, as a single event, at a single point in time, and in a single place. Phonological innovation can be approached in many different ways: acoustically, as the reinterpretation of the speech signal by the hearer; articulatorily, in terms of the influence of one motor gesture on another; cognitively, as the acquisition or simplification of a rule schema; sociolinguistically, as an index of status or affiliation in a complexly stratified speech community; and developmentally, as a reflection of the child's acquisition strategies. Each of these is a common explanatory strategy in modern historical linguistics. What they have in common is that they focus on the single innovation as their object of scrutiny and propose to explain it by identifying a single efficient cause. Each of these strategies has been fruitful, insofar as we now know a great deal about how these factors contribute to sound change. But consider for a moment that each of these explanatory strategies has a built-in limitation in historical perspective: histories are made up of sequences of events, individual and unconnected. The narrowness of this perspective creates the illusion that linguistic changes are merely shifts in the sands of time.

The broader patterns observed here suggest that linguistic change must be observed within multiple time frames if historical linguistics is to be more than a collection of observations of events (cf. Sapir 1921: 147–170; Polivanov 1928; Jakobson 1929; Martinet 1955; McQuown 1956; Labov 1966a: 566–569; Lakoff 1972; Stockwell 1979; Eckert 1980). Contemporary historical linguistics has suffered a continuous tension between the atomism inherent in its analytical techniques and the holism inherent in its search for pattern. We will make significant advances in understanding individual changes, such as the Southern Peruvian Quechua consonant attritions, or even understanding the processes of linguistic diversification and change more broadly, only if we are willing to hammer analytically at the broader patterns. For, as Sapir (1921: 150) has observed, "language is not merely something that is spread out in space, as it were—a series of reflections in individual minds of one and the same timeless picture. Language moves down time in a current of its own making."

Appendix 1. Southern Peruvian Quechua Practical Orthography

In this book, I have for the most part followed the standardized alphabet for the Quechua languages spoken in Peru, adopted by the Peruvian government in 1975, and amended in 1985 (*Resolución Ministerial* 4023–75–ED, 16-x-75; *Resolución Ministerial* 1218–85–ED, 18-xi-85; see Montoya, Montoya, and Montoya 1987: 679–686 and Cerrón-Palomino 1987a: 380, 396). It is appropriate for most practical purposes and reasonably approximates the inner structure of the Southern Peruvian Quechua sound system. There are two main exceptions to my adoption of the standardized alphabet: I have cited all written sources in the original orthographies, without any attempt to transliterate them into the official alphabet, in order to maintain their value as phonological witnesses. I have also used a small number of phonetic symbols when a more precise transcription than that offered by the official alphabet was required to make a specific phonetic or dialectological point; these are listed under "special characters."

In Cuzco-Collao Quechua, the official alphabet underdifferentiates a dialectally variable phonological opposition of extremely low productivity, namely, the difference between the velar fricative / x / and the uvular fricative / x̣ / between vowels, representing both as *h*. In those cases the phonetic value of *h* is usually clear from the context. In the 1975 alphabet, the vowels were overdifferentiated in order to approximate use of the alphabet by bilinguals who often associate lowered phonetic variants of the high vowels with Spanish mid vowels. This has been a bone of contention, especially for educators in Quechua-Spanish bilingual programs, where it has been found that introducing a five-vowel Quechua orthography in primary education may be the source of later reading problems in Spanish. (See Albó 1987; Jung and López 1987; Zúñiga 1987; and the debate published in *Allpanchis* 29/30 [1987] for

Table A.1. Practical Orthography: Vowels and Glides

Vowels

a	/a/	pampa	'plane'
		ima	'what'
i[a]	/i/	riqsiy	'to know a person'
		siqi	'straight line'
		kiki	'oneself'
		wasi	'house'
u[a]	/u/	quy	'to give'
		sunqu	'heart, essence'
		tuta	'darkness, night'
		tukuy	'to finish, to change form'

Glides

h	/h/	huq	'one'
y	/i/	yachay	'to know, to learn'
		may	'where'
w	/u/	wasi	'house'
		chawpi	'center'

[a]In the 1975 alphabet, the *i* and *u* were written as e and o, respectively, in certain contexts. The high vowels *i* and *u* are always lowered adjacent to a uvular. (Additionally, certain segments may intervene before a uvular.) High vowels also tend to be lowered and centralized toward the end of a word by a variable prosodic rule. In either of these cases, they were written as mid vowels (e, o) in the 1975 alphabet since to the Spanish ear they correspond to the Spanish mid vowels, provided that this does not lead to orthographic alternations of a word or suffix (e.g., *takiq* 'singer' from *taki* + *q* is not written **takeq*). Quechua first-language speakers often use e and *o* to represent the lax variants of the high vowels and *i* and *u* the tense alternates, respectively. In the 1985 alphabet, they are written as *i* and *u* regardless of phonetic and morphological context.

representative positions.) The 1985 alphabet uses a three-vowel system to represent the vowels, I believe appropriately so.

Vowels and glides are presented in table A.1. The letters appear in the leftmost column, followed by the underlying segment they represent between slashes. Examples of each appear in the columns on the right. Consonants are presented in table A.2. As we have seen earlier in this work, the consonant systems of Ayacucho-Chanka Quechua varieties and Cuzco-Collao Quechua diverge from each other in the inventory and distribution of most of the consonants. The presentation of the consonants therefore includes (from the left to right) the letter, the most

Table A.2. Practical Orthography: Consonants

	Cuzco-Collao			Ayacucho-Chanka		
p	[p]	tu*p*u		[p]	tu*p*u	'measure of land'
	[ɸ][a]	lli*p*t'a		[p]	lli*p*ta	'paste chewed with coca'
p'	[p']	*p'*acha	'clothing'	*[b]		
ph	[pʰ]	*ph*away	'to run, to fly'	*[b]		
t	[t]	*t*apuy		[t]	*t*apuy	'to ask'
	*[c]			[t]	u*t*qay	'to hurry'
t'	[t']	*t'*anta	'bread'	*[b]		
th	[tʰ]	*th*anta	'rag, worn out'	*[b]		
ch	[č]	*ch*aki		[č]	*ch*aki	'foot'
	*[c]			[č]	u*ch*pa	'ash'
ch'	[č']	*ch'*aki	'dry'	*[b]		
chh	[čʰ]	*chh*achu	'baby donkey'	*[b]		
k	[k]	*k*usi		[k]	*k*usi	'happy'
	[x]	wa*k*cha		[k]	wa*k*cha	'poor, orphan'
k'	[k']	*k'*uychi	'rainbow'	*[b]		
kh	[k~x]	*kh*uru	'insect, worm'	*[b]		
q	[q]	*q*osa		[x̣]	*q*osa	'husband'
	[x̣]	lla*q*ta		[x̣]	lla*q*ta	'home place, village'
q'	[q']	*q'*ero	'ritual drinking vessel'	*[b]		
qh	[qʰ]	*qh*ata	'incline'	*[b]		
r	[ɾ]	ki*r*u		[ɾ]	ki*r*u	'tooth'
	[ɹ]	yawa*r*		[ɹ]	yawa*r*	'blood'
m	[m]	war*m*i		[m]	war*m*i	'woman'
n	[n]	*n*i*n*a		[n]	*n*i*n*a	'fire'
ñ	[ñ]	wa*ñ*uy		[ñ]	wa*ñ*uy	'to die'
l	[l]	*l*ayqa		[l]	*l*ayqa	'witch'
ll	[ʎ]	ki*ll*a		[ʎ]	ki*ll*a	'moon'
s	[s]	*s*apa		[s]	*s*apa	'each'
sh	[ʃ][d]	a*sh*ka	'many'			
h	[x̣][e]	a*h*a	'chicha'			
	[x][f]	u*h*u	'inside'			

[a] Bilabial fricatives [ɸ] may also be written *f*.
[b] Ejective and aspirate stops do not exist in Ayacucho-Chanka Quechua.
[c] Fricativizes syllable-finally and merges with another segment in Cuzco-Collao Quechua.
[d] *sh* is a geographically-circumscribed, dialectally distinctive sound of low-yield in Cuzco-Collao. Both examples also have variants without *sh* in other areas.
[e] In Ayacucho-Chanka Quechua, [x̣] is represented only by *q*. In Cuzco-Collao Quechua [x̣] is dialectally distinctive between vowels and represented by *h*.
[f] [x] is dialectally distinctive in Cuzco-Collao Quechua. In syllable-initial position it may, along with [x̣], be represented by the *h* graph.

important phonetic variants (between square brackets), and examples of each in syllable-initial and syllable-final position for both Cuzco-Collao and Ayacucho-Chanka Quechua. When the segment is not found in syllable-final position (in Cuzco-Collao) or at all (in Ayacucho-Chanka), an asterisk appears in the appropriate column.

In addition to the consonant symbols listed in table A.2, I use *z* for the sixteenth and seventeenth-century dorsal sibilant / s̲ / (pronounced like the *s* of Modern American English), in contrast to *s*, which represents the apical sibilant / ş / (pronounced like the *s* of Madrid Spanish).

Unassimilated loanwords from Spanish are written in Spanish orthography. For more details on the official alphabet and examples of its use, see Cusihuamán 1976a and 1976b, Soto 1976a and 1976b (with very minor modifications), Cerrón-Palomino 1987a, and Montoya, Montoya, and Montoya 1987.

Appendix 2. **Special Characters and Other Special Symbols**

*	hypothetical, reconstructed form
:	(between sounds or words) contrasts with, is opposed to
<	is historically derived from
>	becomes (historically)
→	is (synchronically)
/	in the context
A___B	after A and before B
⊃	conditional (if, then)
{ }	either, or (in a conditional statement or a rule)
{ }	orthographic unit (for sounds)
[ ]	phonetic representation
/ /	phonological (phonemic) representation
C	any consonant
V	any vowel
X	any segment
[ɸ]	bilabial fricative (like English *f*, but pronounced with both lips)
[s̺]	apical sibilant (like the *s* of Madrid Spanish)
[s̲]	dorsal sibilant (like the *s* of English)
[ʃ]	palatal fricative (like English *sh*)
[x]	velar fricative (like the Spanish *jota*)
[x̣]	uvular fricative (like the *ch* of German *Ach*, but deeper in mouth)
[ɾ]	retracted tap *r*
[ɹ]	retracted fricative *r*
[ʎ]	palatal lateral
[a^w]	labialized *a*
[ŋ]	velar nasal (like the *ng* in *sing*)
#	word boundary
/___#	at the end of a word
$	syllable boundary
/___$	at the end of a syllable

Appendix 3. **Abbreviations**

Aya.	Ayacucho-Chanka Quechua
Bol.	Bolivian Quechua
Cuz.	Cuzco-Collao Quechua
Lat.	Latin
Sp.	Spanish

Appendix 4. **Glossary**

Diachronic Processes

lenition: process by which the manner of articulation of a sound becomes weaker. In Quechua, the process of *fricativization,* in which a stop becomes a fricative or spirant, is especially relevant.

merger: process by which a phonemic distinction is lost, either in a specific context or in the system as a whole.

palatalization: process by which the place of articulation of a sound shifts to the palate, for example, *s* > *sh* [ʃ].

Phonological Units

affricate: a consonant produced with complete closure of the vocal cavity (like a stop) and released with friction (like a fricative). In Southern Peruvian Quechua, *ch, ch',* and *chh* are affricated, but function as palatal stops. Their counterparts in Central Quechua languages, *ch* [č] and *tr* [ç̌], function as affricates.

aspirate: a consonant that produces a delayed onset of voicing in the following vowel. In Quechua, a puff of air is audible following the release of the consonant.

ejective or glottalized consonant: a consonant that is produced using glottalic air rather than pulmonic air, resulting in a sharper release of the consonant. The force of ejective consonants varies dialectally in the Southern Peruvian Quechua varieties that have this feature.

fricative or spirant: a consonant for which the oral cavity is constricted to produce friction with the passage of air through it.

glide: a vowel that functions in a consonantal position in the syllable; in Southern Peruvian Quechua, *y, w,* and initial *h.*

glottalized: see ejective.

obstruent: consonant class including stops, fricatives, and affricates.

spirant: see fricative.
stop, or plosive: a consonant produced by complete closure of the oral cavity.
syllable: the basic unit of phonological perception, production, and timing. In Southern Peruvian Quechua, a syllable consists of a vowel nucleus, preceded by a consonantal *onset* and followed by a consonantal *coda.* The onset and coda are also called *margins.* A syllable may lack either or both margins. The changes described in chapters 9 and 10 affect the postvocalic margin (or coda) of the syllable or affect the nucleus and coda simultaneously.

Morphosyntactic Classes

derivational suffix: derivational suffixes change the meaning of the stem to which they are attached in a concrete way. The derived form has the syntactic category of the suffix. The semantic scope of the suffix is the maximal projection of its category. Derivational suffixes follow the word-stem and precede inflectional and discourse-level suffixes.
discourse-level or enclitic: Cusihuamán (1976a: 295) defines it as a "suffix that may be added to any word class, be it a noun, verb or particle . . . with the goal of signalling the topic or focus of an utterance, or its relationship to another utterance, and also to [mark] . . . utterance-type, such as declarative, imperative, and interrogative" (translation mine). Discourse-level suffixes contain clause-level or larger constituents within their semantic scope. Discourse-level suffixes are added at the end of a phrase.
inflectional suffix: inflectional suffixes express obligatory grammatical categories, grammatical relationships, and functions. Inflectional suffixes follow derivational suffixes and precede discourse-level suffixes. In Southern Peruvian Quechua, inflectional categories for the noun (or noun phrase) include person and case, and for the verb (or verb phrase) aspect, tense, person, number, and mood.

Morphosyntactic Categories

nominalizer: in Quechua, a suffix that converts another part of speech into a noun.

subordinator: derivational suffix that marks a clause as subordinate. In Southern Peruvian Quechua, all subordinators are deverbal nominalizers; they mark the verb of the subordinate clause and turn it into a noun.

switch reference: a subordinator that marks the subordinate action as having an agent different from the main verb.

For additional discussion of linguistic terminology with examples from Quechua languages, see Cusihuamán (1976a: 293–239) and Cerrón-Palomino (1976a: 272–279, 1987a: 17–20). For a general guide to phonetic symbols, see Pullum and Ladusaw (1986).

Appendix 5. **Political Chronology**

	Spain and Spanish Peru	**Native Andeans**	**Language & Literature**
15th century		Rise of the Inka State	
1492	Fall of Granada to the Kingdom of Castile		Nebrija's grammar of Spanish published
	Expulsion of Jews from Spain		
	Columbus's first voyage		
1519	Charles V becomes King of Castile and Aragon		
1532	Spaniards invade Peru		
	Atawallpa Inka captured and executed		
1533	Spaniards capture Cuzco	Neo-Inka State resists Spaniards	
1537–1544	Civil war among Spanish settlers		
1545–1563	Council of Trent		Church promotes vernacular
1551	First Council of Lima		Betanzos, *Suma y narración*
1555	Philip II becomes King of Spain		
1560			Santo Tomás, *Grammatica* and *Lexicon*
1560s		Taki Onqoy millenarian movement	
1567	Second Council of Lima		
1569	Francisco de Toledo, Fifth Viceroy, arrives and begins reorganization of colony		
1572	Forced consolidations of Native Andean settlements	Neo-Inka resistance defeated, Thupa Amaru Inka executed	
1574			Molina, *Fábulas y ritos*
1583	Third Council of Lima		Tercer Concilio Limense, *Doctrina* and *Cathecismo;* Anonymous, *Arte y vocabulario*

1586	Administrative survey of the colonies		Relaciones geográficas
1598	King Philip II dies, succeeded by Philip III		
early 17th century	Campaigns against native religion		Anonymous, Huarochirí manuscript
1607			Gonçález Holguín, *Gramática* and *Vocabulario*
1609			Garcilaso, *Commentarios*
1615			Santa Cruz Pachacuti Yamqui, *Relación;* Guaman Poma, *Nueva corónica*
1631			Pérez Bocanegra, *Ritual formulario*
mid 17th century	Codifications of colonial law		Hispanization of Native Andeans promoted, decline of religious literature in Quechua
1690			Aguilar, *Arte*
1700	Charles V (Bourbon) succeeds to Spanish throne		
1701	War of Spanish succession		
mid 18th century	Growing nationalist sentiment Provincial landowners identify with Inkas	Local uprisings	Versified dramas: *Ollanta, Usca Paucar, El pobre más rico*
1767	Expulsion of Jesuits		
1780		Rebellion of Thupa Amaru	
1781	Bourbon reorganization of colonies	Rebellion defeated	Areche bans Quechua literature and language
1814	Nationalist rebellion in Cuzco		
1821	Peruvian independence declared by San Martín		
1824	Battle of Ayacucho, Spanish capitulate		
mid–late 19th century			Interest in Quechua studies by provincial elites and foreigners Markham, Middendorf, Pacheco, Tschudi

	Spain and Spanish Peru	Native Andeans	Language & Literature
1879–1883	War of the Pacific		
1920s	Indigenist movements, indigenous communities achieve legal status	Agrarian unrest in the Andes	Increased interest in Native Andean history and anthropology
1940s–1965			J. M. Arguedas: novels, Quechua poetry
1965		Agrarian unrest in the Andes	
1968–1975	Nationalist military government of Juan Velasco Alvarado		Pilot bilingual education programs
1969	Agrarian Reform		
1975			Quechua declared "official" language
mid 1970s			Ministerio de Educación reference grammars (Cerrón-Palomino, Cusihuamán, Soto, et al.) Native testimonies published in Andean languages: Condori, Gow and Condori; growth of national anthropology and linguistics
1975	Velasco government falls in coup		
1979	New constitution		Spanish literacy dropped as criterion for voting
1980s	Economic chaos	Shining path insurgency	Colonial works in Quechua reprinted, Montoya, *Urqukunapa yawarnin*

Notes

1. Introduction

1. Cerrón-Palomino (1987c) identifies the *lengua general del ynga* with the Quechua described by Fray Domingo de Santo Tomás (1560a, 1560b) rather than with the language of Cuzco. But there is good reason to believe that Santo Tomás worked with speakers of several different Quechua dialects and was not describing a single, consistent variety of Quechua (see chapter 6).

2. ". . . tratando de la lengua deste reino, hablo solamente de la quichua, como general y común a todos los naturales y moradores dél . . . ; que la tenían propia y de donde se derivó á los demás, que son los quichuas; como á la castellana le llamaron así, por ser la materna que hablabamos los castellanos."

3. The word *Runa* has a positive connotation in Southern Peru, although I understand that it is pejorative in some other parts of the Andes, including Argentina (Cerrón-Palomino 1987a: 36) and parts of highland Ecuador (Barry Lyons, personal communication, 1988). I use it here in part because there is no general term that would be acceptable in some part of the Andes that does not have negative connotations elsewhere, and *Runa* is positively valued for the people about whom I am writing.

4. Needless to say, this summary skims over geographic and cultural variation in Tawantinsuyu and significant differences in the ways in which the colonial sources are interpreted by modern scholars. Almost every single generalization presented here should be qualified in one way or another, but that would fall outside of the scope of a background survey like the present one. I recommend Rowe (1946), Murra (1980 [1956], 1975), and Murra, Wachtel, and Revel (1986) to the reader interested in reading further on the Inkas. The ceremonial and social organization of Cuzco is discussed in Zuidema (1964, 1986); the astronomical uses of the *ziqi* system in Zuidema (1982c); and its role in organizing the irrigation of Inka Cuzco in Sherbondy (1986).

5. There are a number of excellent book-length studies of Runa life in the Southern Peruvian Quechua–speaking area from which to approach the current diversity in Quechua social and economic forms. Isbell (1978) is a study of a mixed agricultural/herding municipality in the Department of Ayacucho, in an area that has recently hosted the guerrilla activity by the Partido Comunista

del Perú—Sendero Luminoso. Isbell's book is an excellent general introduction to the relationship between agricultural and herding practices and ritual. Quispe (1969) and Palomino (1970) are important community studies from the same region. José María Arguedas has documented the provincial center of Puquio (Ayacucho) in novels (1941, 1958) and ethnography (1964). His complexly textured novels capture the polyphony of cultural voices and consciousnesses in a much more stark way than is possible for an ethnographer. Montoya (1980) and Montoya et al. (1979) are outstanding studies of the articulation of the southern Peruvian countryside and the encompassing capitalist economy and of the ideological forms through which this encompassment is expressed, for the same region in which Arguedas's novels are set. Allen (1978, 1988) describes the ways in which Runa social forms are emergent from etiquette and ritual practices in a small mixed agricultural-herding *puna* community in the Province of Paucartambo, Department of Cuzco. Molinié (1982) approaches interactions among communities, economic activities, and micro-ecological zones in the Urubamba valley, where settlements have a much more restricted direct access to multiple zones than elsewhere in Cuzco. Urton (1981) is a study of the formal cosmology of a community in the Urubamba region. Orlove (1977) discusses the articulation of a herding-wool production on the edge of the *altiplano* with regional and world markets. Flores (1979 [1968]) is a study of an *altiplano* herding community. Finally, the impact of recent transformations of the agrarian sector on rural southern Peru is approached by Guillet (1979), Skar (1982), and Hopkins (1985).

2. The Ecology of Language Contact before the European Invasion

1. For the purpose of this discussion, I have simplified the examples considerably.

2. ". . . son tantas y tan diferentes las lenguas que ablan . . . que creo faltaran letras en la Arichmetica para numerarlas segun son muchas, y en esto en tan notable manera que en muchas Prouincias no se andara legua que no se alle lengua diferente, y tan remota, y distinta la una de la otra como la Castellana de la Vizcayna, ó de la Ynglesa ó de la Aphricana en unas lagunas que hace un brazo de el Rio grande de la Magdalena llamado Cesare . . . ay ciertas Ysletas pobladas á vista las unas de las otras, y en cada Ysla de estas se abla muy diferente lengua. En otras partes de estas Yndias sucede aquesto con tanto estremo que en un pueblo mismo se hablan dos, y tres lenguas diferentes y en una casa acontece hablar la muger, y las hijas una lengua, y el marido y los hijos otra muy diferente, y en partes se tiene por deshonestidad en la muger hablar la lengua de el varon, y en el varon se tiene por menosprecio, y infamia ablar la lengua, y terminos de la muger . . ."

3. Keep in mind that, when the two language families are grouped together in bibliographic essays on the languages of South America, it is really not a stand on genetic relationships at all, but a convenient classificatory device.

4. Both *Jaqi* and *Aru* are used by reputable scholars as the name for the family, largely as a matter of personal preference. I use *Jaqi/Aru* here to avoid misunderstanding, although *Aru* is used by most scholars outside of the United States.

Note that *Jaqi/Aru* is used here only for the language family and not for any of the individual languages within it.

Greenberg (1987: 99–106) places both Quechua and Aymara within his "Andean" grouping, including Catacao, Cholona, Culli, Leco, and Sechura in a Northern subgroup; Alakaluf, Araucanian, Pehuelche, Tehuelche, and Yahgan in a Southern subgroup; and Auca, Aymara, Itucale (Simacu), Mayna, Quechua, and Zaparo without any clear subgrouping within Andean. Greenberg suggests that Aymara and Quechua do not have a special relationship—that is, do not form a subgroup—within Andean, and that Aymara appears to be relatively isolated among these languages. Greenberg intends his work to be a "genetic classification" rather than a fully articulated linguistic history (see 1987: 1–37); the groupings are, therefore, more secure at higher levels of generality rather than at lower levels (exactly the reverse of a linguistic history). I have not yet been able to work through Greenberg's *Language in the Americas* in sufficient detail to assess his classification of Quechua, either within his "Andean" grouping or in a broader South American context.

5. " . . . las dos lenguas quichua y aimara . . . por ser de dos naciones vecinas y cotérminas, tienen tanta similitud en los vocablos y construcción, que cualquiera que supiese lo poco que yo dellas, no podrá negar haberse originado ambas de un principio, al modo que la española e italiana nacieron de la latina."

6. See Stark (1975) for counterexamples to Orr and Longacre's correspondences.

7. In writing this section, I have reviewed most major discussions of this point since the nineteenth century and followed up their references. First, I eliminated references that were not directly relevant to southern Peru but were used to support the author's conjectures. Second, I eliminated conjectures based on the personal authority of the author. Third, I eliminated references that were copied from older, more specific reports. (For example, the *Decadas* of Antonio de Herrera borrowed from some of the unpublished reports later included in the *Relaciones geográficas de Indias.*) And fourth, I disambiguated every use of the name *Aymara* in colonial sources. The word *Aymara* was used for: (1) Aymaraes, a pre-Colombian local polity located in modern-day Apurímac, (2) *mitmaq* from Aymaraes, and (3) the language. (Markham [1871a] suggests that the language name resulted from a Spanish error and had nothing whatever to do with the province or its people.) This left the residue that is reported here.

Bouysse-Cassagne (1977), Espinoza (1983), and Torero (1987) have written about the social geography of language in the Audiencia de Charcas, south of the area that I am discussing here. Torero's survey of evidence on the colonial distribution of the Jaqi/Aru languages is excellent (1972 [1970]: 66–75) and can also be consulted with profit. I have followed some of the same references as Torero (1972 [1970]), but I disagree with many of his interpretations. I disagree especially with the ways in which Torero uses evidence of local language use to postulate pristine, geographically contiguous speech communities in prehistory without any other evidence for them. For instance, he uses sixteenth-century reports of local interspersion of Aymara with Quechua in the Río Pampas region of Ayacucho to argue: (1) that the Río Pampas region was originally Aymara-speaking, and (2) that it was the Aymara homeland. Given the extraordinary complexity of the sociolinguistics of the Andean region at the time of the European invasion, it is important to put historical interpretations in the particular social and historical circumstances of each place for which there is evidence. It is especially important not to confuse speech communities and historical (or mytho-historical) polities, and not to mistake either of these for "nations" in the eighteenth- and nineteenth-century European sense of the word.

8. " . . . hablan algunos dellos la lengua aymará y otros la lengua general del inga . . ."

9. For a useful synthesis of the ethnic symbiosis between the Collaguas and the Cavanas in the context of the local history of the Colca Valley of Arequipa, see Manrique (1985). Modern ethnographers (Carmen Escalante, Paul Gelles, and Ricardo Valderrama) report that the descendants of the Cavanas continue to maintain their distinctiveness linguistically, by speaking a different variety of the local Southern Peruvian Quechua from the modern descendants of the Collaguas (Manrique 1985: 33; Gelles, personal communication 1989).

10. " . . . Cuzco . . . tiene pueblos de indios quichuas, aymaraes y puquinas, la cual diversidad se halla también en este obispado de Arequipa . . ."

11. "la mayor parte tienen diferentes lenguas, pero la que hablan es la general."

12. Archivo Departmental del Cuzco, Archivo del Ilustre Cabildo del Cuzco, top. 14, sig. 3–31, caja 9.

13. "Tienen diferentes lenguas, porque cada parcialidad habla su lengua diferente, aunque todos hablan la general del Cuzco, que les mandaron hablar generalmente los Ingas, y se han quedado en este uso, que es muy necesario, usando la suya y la natural entre si."

14. "al presente hablan la lengua general quichua del Inga. Tienen otra lengua natural suya, que es la lengua aymara, y tienen otras lenguas en que se hablan y se entienden, que se llama *hahuasimi*, que quiere decir lengua fuera de la general."

15. "en este repartimiento hay muchas diferencias de lenguas porque casi cada cacique tiene su lengua, aunque todos hablan y entienden en la del Inga; y a las lenguas diferentes de la del Inga en que se hablan y entienden la llaman *hahua simi*, que quiere decir lengua fuera de la general, que es del Inga, y en la que tratan y hablan con los españoles y se entienden con los indios."

16. "Hay en este repartimiento mucha diferencia de lenguas; porque, los de la parcialidad de Antamarca tienen una de por sí antiquísima, y los de Apcaraes otra, y otra los Omapachas, otra los Huchucayllos, y estas lenguas no tienen nombre cada una por sí, mas que todos ellos dicen a su propia lengua *hahuasimi*, que quiere decir lengua fuera de la general, que es la del Inga, que en común usan della . . . y en que todos se entienden y hablan."

17. Torero asserts that my account "es totalmente inválida porque la iglesia fue hecha construir en los ultimos años del siglo xvi por los dominicanos, quienes continuaron en ella durante la primera mitad del siglo xvii, siendo reemplazados después por sacerdotes seculares. Los jesuitas la tienen a su cargo sólo desde 1968, hace menos de veinte años" (1987: 399). But, by all evidence, Pérez Bocanegra, a third-order Franciscan (not a Dominican!) was assigned to Andahuaylillas as *párroco* by the Diocese (not by an order) during the first half of the seventeenth century, until his death in 1645 (Pérez Bocanegra 1631: title page;

Ocón de Contreras 1649; Mendoza 1665: 551). The church was constructed in the early seventeenth century: Pérez Bocanegra's name appears on the cornerstone of the church, with the date 1626. Early in the seventeenth century, the Jesuits expressed interest in taking over a parish to train priests in Quechua. In response to a request from Gregorio de Cisneros (1601) for a language training *doctrina* (or native parish) in "Andahuaylas," Jesuit General Aquaviva (1603) authorized a "seminario de lenguas quichuas, como Julli lo es de los aymaraes." In Cisneros's letter, the place name "Andahuaylas" is ambiguous, since there were two places known by the same name in colonial times, Andahuaylas (or Andaguailas, or Antahuaylla), the capital of the province of the same name in modern-day Apurímac, and Andahuaylillas (or Andaguailas la chica, or Antahuaylla la chica), located in the modern Province of Quispicanchi in the Department of Cuzco. Cisneros estimated that "Andaguaylas" was "four or five leagues from Cuzco" (1601: 285). This could only have been Andahuaylillas (Quispicanchi) and not Andahuaylas (Abancay). The Jesuits were granted Andahuaylillas (Quispicanchi) by a *provisión* from the viceroy, prince of Esquilache (10-iii-1621, authorized by a letter from the king, 16-iv-1618), but did not take possession of the parish from the diocese until 1628 (Archivo del Gesú 1407, cited by Vargas Ugarte 1947: 178). The eight-year Jesuit presence in Andahuaylillas provoked litigation on the part of the diocese (Vargas Ugarte 1960: 368–369; Hopkins 1983: 186–190). According to the Jesuit historian Vargas Ugarte (1960: 368), "El cabildo eclesiástico, al saberlo, escribió a S.M. una carta de 10 de Abril de 1621, quejándose de que se quitara esa doctrina al Lic. Juan Pérez Bocanegra, que la servia, para darle a los PP. de la Compañia, bajo pretexto de aprender la lengua. Según ellos afirman, la razón era otra, o sea, 'servirse de los indios de dicha doctrina en unas haciendas y molinos que tienen junto al pueblo de Quiquixana, unas dos o tres leguas distantes de Andahuailillas . . .'"

Torero does not offer any evidence for his account. But a neighboring parish, Quiguares (in the modern district of Rondoccán, Province of Acomayo), was granted to the Dominicans, who held it at least into the late seventeenth century (Lira 1689).

18. For comparable cases from India of the use of linguistic differences to mark stable, ascriptive hierarchies, see Gumperz (1958) and Ramanujan (1968: 471).

19. Dialect differences among modern Quechua speakers are like the pre-Columbian system. The differences are not the subject of conscious evaluation, except for lexical differences, in which the local form (whatever it may be) is the most highly valued.

20. Cerrón-Palomino has pointed out to me, though, that Southern Peruvian Quechua *hich'ay* has regular cognates in Wanka *hitray* [hiçay] ~ *sitray* [siçay]. The correspondence would allow a proto-Quechua source to be reconstructed for the 'throw out' set, and consequently rule out a Spanish source. But the evidence is not unequivocal; correspondences of this kind may arise by means of loans across dialectal shibboleths, as Leonard Bloomfield's (1946: 107) reconstruction of the proto-Algonquin compound for 'whiskey'—which clearly *was* a borrowed form—showed.

21. Jakobson, Cherry, and Halle (1953) and Cherry (1957) have discussed the probabilities of synchronic sequential transitions between segments in informa-

tional terms. It has subsequently been found that sequential transitions could be accounted for more rigorously in terms of formal phonological rules. Van Wijk (1938) and Martinet (1938) discuss the probability of sound change in terms of maximization of acoustic distance and functional load. These proposals were never made precise enough to be testable (King 1967; Lass 1980: 91ff.).

22. One of his restrictions, "if the root begins with *h*, the next stop in the root must be glottalized," (Campbell 1976: 191) is incorrect: there are many roots with initial *h* in which the following stop is not an ejective. The relationship he alludes to is a diachronic process of *h* epenthesis, $\phi \rightarrow$ h / #__[VOWEL] X[EJECTIVE], in which epenthesis is one, but not the only, historical source of initial *h*. Synchronically, the epenthetic *h* prevents the occurrence of a predictable glottal catch that would violate a constraint that prohibits the occurrence of two glottalized segments in a word (chapter 8).

3. Language and Colonialism

1. The concept of "oppressed" or "dominated" language also figures importantly in the work of Bareiro (1975), Cerrón-Palomino (1975, 1983), and Taylor (1978).

2. Both models suppose a similar relationship among language, culture, and territory, as Rouse (1988) argues. For the dual society model, Quechua and Spanish belong to spatially distinct communities, Quechua as the language of highland Andean villages, Spanish as the language of urban Peru. The imagery of autonomous, culturally and territorially distinct communities has persisted in Peru since the early colonial debate about the legal status of the newly conquered native populations. Jurists such as Matienzo (1567) argued that the cultural distinctiveness of the "República de los Españoles" and the "República de los Indios" should be recognized legally by means of strict administrative and territorial separation.

For the internal colonialism model, the urban "center" has a hold on the colonized rural "periphery." Urban center and rural periphery have the same territorial and cultural referents as in the dual society model, but assume a different polarity. While the dual society model supposes that the spatial differentiation of Spanish and Quechua Peru will inevitably collapse in the cultural absorption of Quechua into Spanish, the internal colonialism model proposes that spatial differentiation will last only as long as it is useful to the urban center.

The colonial language debate is intelligible only in the context of spatial interpenetration of Spanish and Quechua Peru: on the one hand, Spanish Peru penetrated the remotest rural highland communities economically, administratively, and individually from the earliest years of the colonial period; on the other hand, Quechua took on new social and political meanings within colonial Peruvian culture, as a language of subordination or resistance, or as an expression of nascent nationalism, depending on the political circumstances.

3. " . . . siempre la lengua fue compañera del imperio." For a genealogy of Nebrija's association of language and empire, see Asensio (1960).

4. See Blas Valera, cited by Garcilaso (1609: VII, iii, 248) and Cieza (1550: ch. 24, p. 84), among others.

5. The term *Criollo* has been used since the late sixteenth century for native-born Americans of Spanish descent, for native-born Americans who speak Spanish as a first language, or—in Peru—for residents of the coastal regions of the country.

6. Heath's (1976) comparison of colonial language policy in New Spain, Peru, and the modern United States includes a lucid discussion of changing language policy in colonial Peru, as do Romero (1964), Konetzke (1965), Hartmann (1972), Heath and LaPrade (1982), and Rivarola (1985, 1989). I have drawn upon all of them in the present chapter.

7. The *Recopilación de leyes* (1681) is cited by the date of the law, *libro* in uppercase roman, *título* in lowercase roman, and law in arabic numerals, followed by the volume and page number of the reprint edition cited here.

8. Compare also Angulo (1925: 327–328, footnote 43) and Vargas Ugarte (1942: 110). On colonial translators in general, see Solano (1975).

9. Thus Guaman Poma (1615: 590) pointed out "q' los mismos le enpide a q' no sepa leer ni escriuir ni gusta q' ayga maystro de escuela por q' no sepa pleytos y hordenansas." Elsewhere he mentions a ladino who was expelled from his parish for being literate: "ci saue leer y escriuir le pondra capitulos" (1615: 595). For a representative debate on this point, see the seventeenth-century exchange of letters between the count of Chinchón and the Jesuit provincial, reproduced by Eguiguren (1940: 875–897). See also Duviols (1971: 327).

10. Viceroy Toledo followed a decree to that effect by King Philip II (1576), with a more specific order for Peru in 1577. The Toledan order was apparently very strictly enforced; whereas long runs of Nahuatl notary records have been located in Mexican archives (see Anderson, Berdan, and Lockhart 1976; Karttunen and Lockhart 1976), only two notebooks of fragments of Quechua notarial registers have yet been discovered (see chapter 6, source 5).

11. "se usa de inclusion o exclusion en las primeras personas plurales assi de pronõbres como de verbos. Inclusion es quando incluymos en la materia a la persona, o personas, con quien hablamos, como si hablando con gentiles dixessemos, nosotros los hombres somos criados para el cielo, diremos, *ñocanchic runacuna hanacpachapac camascam cãchic.* Exclusion es quando excluymos de la materia a la persona o personas con quien hablamos, como si hablando con los gentiles dixessemos nosotros los christianos adoramos a vn Dios, diremos, *ñocaycu christianocuna huc çapay Diosllactam muchaycu*" (Tercer Concilio Limense 1584: f. 75r).

12. "los q'se llama Chinchaysuyos." Because of a printer's error, the page on which this passage appears is numbered 83.

13. "de vocablos, y modos de dezir tan exquisitos, y obscuros, que salen de los limites del lenguaje . . ."

14. Royal decree 1578 (Angulo 1925: 325); *Recopilación de leyes* 1681: I, vi, 29 (1: 44–45); 1681 [1578]: I, vi, 30 (1: 45); 1681 [1580]: I, xxii, 56 (1: 206); 1681 [1603]: I, xv, 5 (1: 132); 1681 [1609]: I, vi, 24 (1: 43); 1681 [1619]: I, xiii, 4 (1: 95–96); 1681 [1621]: I, xv, 7 (1: 133).

15. I use the same conventions for citing Solorzano as for the *Recopilación de leyes.*

16. "semejanza y conformidad de las palabras casi siempre suelen reconciliar y traer a verdadera unión y amistad a los hombres."

17. Natural law or right (*ius naturae*) is a legal principle that cannot be modified by human action. The concept of natural law was critically important to the Spanish colonial project. Even though Spanish dominion over newly discovered pagan lands was authorized by Pope Alexander VI (1493), the papal bull had shaky legal status because it assumed that the church had authority over temporal matters. In order to justify Spanish dominion over the American colonies legally, Spanish jurists were forced to argue that Native Americans were not fully rational and did not possess a civil society and therefore—by natural law—did not have dominion over their own territory. Spanish dominion over the New World could then be justified as a kind of tutelage over less-than-rational beings (Pagden 1987b). In addition, since natural law could not be modified by human action, arguments based on natural law could be used to settle discrepancies between codified laws, of which there were many in Spanish colonial jurisprudence.

18. "hay entre ellos lengua ninguna que sea bastante para declararles los misterios de nuestra Sancta Fé Católica, por ser todas ellos muy faltas de vocablos . . ." In the sixteenth and seventeenth centuries, it was commonly believed that Native Andean languages were too impoverished lexically to express religious doctrine; see also Garcilaso (1616: I, xxiii, 48f.); *Recopilación de leyes* (1681: VI, i, 18, reprint 2: 193); Matienzo (1567: 21); Consejo de las Indias (1596); Solorzano (1647: II, xxvi, reprint 1: 399). For a discussion of the modern developmentalist versions of the same belief, see Ortíz (1970: 52) and Escobar (1972).

19. The Dominican grammarian Domingo de Santo Tomás (1560a: 74r–74v) observed that it was natural for languages to borrow terms for "the things they don't have" and included Spanish religious vocabulary in his grammar under the heading *barbarismo* or borrowing.

20. "pues es para tan sancto fin como es para encajar en ellos la fé católica de nuestro Señor Jesucristo." José de Acosta (1577a: IV, viii, 516) ridiculed proposals such as Zúñiga's as "pure fantasy."

21. "tener buena vida y costumbres y a aborrecer y olvidar sus vicios, ritos y gentilidades." Acosta (1577a: III, xxiv, 502–503) dissented on this point. Although he endorsed the general project of teaching the Indians "Christian customs and discipline," he suggested that local customs could be maintained as long as they did not violate Catholic doctrine or universal standards of justice.

22. "cerdos para pronunciarla y darle el significado apropiado a las palabras . . ." See also Colin (1966: 93) and Rivarola (1989).

23. Real y General Orden 30-v-1691, Archivo General de Indias, Lima 306, cited by Santisteban (1963).

24. The *Pequeño Larousse ilustrado* (Toro 1943) follows its definition of *culteranismo* with the grave statement that "el culteranismo ha sido uno de los factores más importantes de la decadencia del idioma castellano"!

25. The innovations used to establish a relative chronology of these texts are related in a linear implicational series (see chapters 6, 8, and 10). On structural grounds, they are all "later" than Juan de Aguilar's manuscript grammar of 1690.

The last in the series, the Justiniani codex of *Ollanta,* was written no later than the 1770s or 1780s. These dates are approximate: (1) either the first or the last of the manuscripts may be copies of a slightly earlier text; and (2) the linear diachronic sequence assumed by the method flattens stylistic variation. Rowe himself observes (1954: note 18) that *Ollanta* had phonological characteristics that demonstrated that it was written later than the sixteenth century.

26. In chapter 10, I observe that the Sahuaraura and Justiniani manuscripts of *Ollanta* both show a shift of ʃ > *s* in stems. This change was restricted in stems to the dialect area north of Cuzco or east of the Vilcanota River. Therefore the association of *Ollanta* with the village of Tinta, southwest of Cuzco (Markham 1912: 90; Lewin 1943), is not supported by the phonological properties of the manuscripts.

27. "Y para que estos indios se despeguen del odio que hen concebido contra los españoles . . . se vistan de nuestros costumbres españoles, y hablan la lengua castellana, se introducirá con más vigor que hasta aquí el uso de sus escuelas bajo las penas más rigorosas y justas contra los que no las usen."

28. "Si concideramos que el idioma permanece en los indios, sin alteración, y en algunas partes tan integro, que si no ha perdido vos alguna del dialecto con que se manejavan aquellas rusticas gentes, es otro asunto digno de lastima a la nacion española: Yo bien veo que se fatigan las prensas en darnos ordenanzas, y establecimientos para quitar de los indios el lenguaje, y que en conformidad de los Reales Rescriptos sobre esta materia, los Prelados celosos lo tienen mandado con graves aspercivimientos en las Visitas de sus Diocesia, prescriviendo se doctrinen en castellano a los jovenes. ¿Pero, qué aprovecha este connato? Quando siguen a los naturales en su idioma, y por la maior parte tan tenazes, que hay poblacion en que se hablan tres distintos totalmente opuestos entre si, como son la Quichua general, la Aymara, y Puquina? Mas de doscientos años hé dicho tenemos de conquista, y quando el cistema de todo conquistador és traher á su idioma la nacion conquistada, nuestros españoles en nada mas parece que han pensado que en mantenerles en el suyo, y aun es acomodarse con el, pues vemos le usan con mas frequencia que el propio. Los incombenientes que de ello se siguen son obvios al mas ceigo, y mucho es lo que padecen, Dios, el Rey, y la causa publica por esta reprobable practica."

29. "la extirpación de la lengua índica."

30. "no siendo fácil la total abolición."

31. In a few pioneering cases, rural schools were established in eighteenth-century southern Peru. A school was founded in Paucartambo in 1743 by Sebastián Márquez Escudero, the former *corregidor,* who arranged for the Jesuits to run it. It only briefly survived their expulsion in 1767 (Macera 1967: 225). Two indigenous schools were established during the 1790s, one in Aymaraes and the other in Colca, and proposals were tendered for regional schools (Macera 1967: 231).

32. For a coastal example, see Ramírez (1986: 151).

33. On the regulation of legal interpreters, see *Recopilación de leyes* (1681: II, xxix, 1: 477–480) and Solano (1975: 270 ff.).

34. On the other hand, the colonial government preferred to appoint pliant

caciques who could speak Spanish over nonbilingual people who had legitimate right by traditional principles, the better to rule with. The particularly abusive appointee was able to manipulate his language skills to the detriment of the community (Hopkins 1977, 1983; Archivo Departamental del Cuzco, Archivo notarial de Teofilo Puma, legajo 9, 1779–1780, "Juzgamiento de Miguel de Zúñiga, Cacique de Ayllo Anza . . .").

35. "los indios Puquinas, Collas, Urus, Yuncas y otras naciones que son rudos y torpes, y por su rudeza en sus propias lenguas hablan mal, cuando alcanzan a saber la lengua del Cozco, para que echan de sí la rudeza y torpeza que tenían y que aspiran a cosas politicas y cortesanas, y sus ingenios pretenden subir a cosas más altas . . ."

36. "Procuran ocultarse de cualquier español o mestizo que no les hable en su idioma, y los consideran, como nosotros a ellos por bárbaros."

4. Linguistic Hegemony and the Two Dimensions of Language Variation

1. My use of *hegemony* here is unorthodox from the perspective of modern political theorists, but, I would argue, well within the scope of Gramsci's multivocal use of the term. This is not the place to argue that point in detail, though.

2. For the notion that Quechua speakers live in multiple landscapes of power that are closely associated with languages, I am indebted to the work of Penelope Harvey (1987, 1990) and Deborah Poole (1989, 1990).

3. Hoggarth (1973: i) has recorded a version in Calca, Department of Cuzco. An Ecuadorian version appears in Carvalho-Neto (1966: 175–178).

4. In preparing the translation, I used the Quechua text published by Ortíz, which unfortunately contains numerous errors that were introduced in the production of the book. Some of the errors were easy to spot and correct, and some may have affected the translation. The line structure, which differs considerably from the published original, is designed to help the narrative scan well. The major subunits of the text are indicated by location expressions, by changes of location, and by embedded dialogue. Smaller subunits are indicated by the sentence connectives *chaysi, chayñataqsi, hinaspa,* and *hinaspanku.* I preserved the organization of the text into subunits in the English translation, which was done directly from the Quechua. I should add that Quechua narrative is normally conversational; the text was probably edited for publication.

5. The Quechua version is garbled here.

6. The Quechua text is truncated in mid-sentence; I used the author's Spanish translation for the remainder.

7. I am quoting from the published Spanish translation of an article originally written in English. The English translation is mine.

8. " . . . de España habían enviado a este Reino por unto de los indios, para sanar cierta enfermedad, que no se hallaba para ella medicina sino el unto; a cuya causa, en aquellos tiempos, andaban los indios muy recatados, y se extrañaban de los españoles en tanto grado, que la leña, yerba, y otras cosas no las querían llevar a casa de español; por decir no las matasen, allí dentro, para sacar el unto."

9. A similar notion is also expressed in Aymara (Palacios 1977). For further discussion of the role of reciprocity in Andean social life, see Núñez del Prado (1972), Alberti and Mayer (1974), Mayer (1974b: 86–213, 1974c), Isbell (1978: 167–177), and Allen (1988).

10. A zero-nominalized verb is a verb that has been made into a substantive (noun or adjective) without adding any morphological material to the verb stem. An English example is *a walk* from *to walk*.

11. All four of these verbal suffixes are coded for voice and so reshape the relationship between the subject of the verb and the action denoted by the verb. The suffixes *-paku-* and *-naku-* include the middle voice suffix, *-ku-*, which incorporates the subject within the dimensions of the action denoted by the verb. The suffix *-nachi-* is the causative counterpart to *-naku-*, which treats the subject as the cause of the reciprocal action denoted by the verb. It includes the causative suffix *-chi-*. For verbs marked with *-chi-*, *-nachi-*, and *-ysi-*, the subject of the verb is causing or helping someone else to perform the action. The logical agent of the action is demoted to grammatical direct object, and marked with the accusative case. Double accusatives are frequent in such constructions.

12. According to Roswith Hartmann (1979) and Ruth Moya (1981: 140–150) Ecuadorian Quichua represents a relatively late preinvasion and even colonial expansion of the Quechua family. Mercedes Niño-Murcia (1988) argues that syntactic features peculiar to Ecuadorian and Colombian Quichua and its local Spanish counterparts are the result of mutual accommodation between the two languages.

13. "Cierta dama española, linda y bien vestida, estaba al balcón de su casa con una rosa en la mano, y pasando a su vista un decidor de buenas palabras, quiso lisonjearla con el adagio español siguiente: 'Bien sabe la rosa en qué mano reposa'; a que respondió con mucha satisfacción: 'Qui rosa, qui no rosa, qui no te costó to plata.'" For additional examples from colonial-era parodies, see Rivarola (1987a).

5. Common Southern Peruvian Quechua

1. This book is concerned entirely with the linguistic history of Southern Peruvian Quechua and so discusses the other Quechua languages only tangentially. For an excellent language family-wide survey of Quechua, see Cerrón-Palomino (1987a).

2. Parker and Chávez (1976) translate the 'toad' cognate as 'to walk with difficulty'.

3. The overwhelming majority of epenthetic *h* initials in Cuzco-Collao do not have corresponding *h* initials in Ayacucho-Chanka. Cerrón-Palomino (1987a: 185–186) proposes that examples like those in figure 5.2 reflect dialect borrowing from Cuzco-Collao. He argues further that "si asumimos que la regla de prótesis es un fenómeno concomitante a la presencia de una consonante glotalizada, entonces lo lógico es suponer que cuando, por alguna razón, no se da la modificación eyectiva, tampoco aparece la [h] protética (el propio cuzqueño ilustra este hecho al ofrecernos alternancias de tipo *al̄pa* ~ *hal̄p'a* 'tierra', *irqi* ~ *hirq'i* 'criatura', *amawta* ~ *hamawt'a* 'sabio', etc.). Ahora bien, si en alguna mo-

mento de su historia el ayacuchano perdió *C'*, entonces dicha perdida debió acarrear automáticamente la eliminación de la regla de prótesis."

Cerrón-Palomino contends that if the words in figure 5.2 acquired the initial *h* because of the presence of glottalization elsewhere in the word, then the *h* should have been lost when glottalization was lost. The process of *h*-epenthesis is a synchronic rule in modern Cuzco-Collao. Thus if a word beginning with a vowel acquires glottalization, it automatically acquires an epenthetic *h* as well (chapter 8); this much explains the alternations from Cuzco-Collao. But it does not follow logically that if the ejective is lost, the epenthetic *h* should be lost as well. (Although some phonological rules are biunique and allow the input to the rule to be inferred from the output, *h*-epenthesis is not.) Phonological changes are commonly conditioned by factors that later disappear without the reversal of the changes. For example, "Verner's law" accounted for a set of exceptions to the first Germanic consonant shift by showing that the exceptions were conditioned by the Indo-European accentual system. When the accentual system changed, the effects of Verner's law were not erased.

My own position is that the question is not as open and shut as Cerrón-Palomino suggests. Given the ways in which glottalization has diffused through the lexicon in the other Southern Quechua dialects, it is possible that it was lost at an incipient stage in Ayacucho-Chanka. It is also possible that the examples were borrowed from Cuzco-Collao, although there is no independent evidence to support borrowing either. When dealing with etymological exceptions, "borrowing" is the null hypothesis. I therefore hesitate to attribute any exceptions to borrowing unless there is independent evidence.

4. There are significant differences between Parker's studies of 1963 and 1969–1971. I have based my discussion of Parker on his later, more detailed work.

5. Gonçález Holguín (1607, 1608) devised special symbols to account for the uvulars with a Spanish-based orthography. He used both {cc} and {k} at the ends of syllables. It is unclear whether his orthographic variation can be interpreted as evidence of a variable fricativization process (in which {cc} = [q] and {k} = [x̣]) or is simply an orthographic quirk. But it is worthy of note that orthographic {g} does not appear, and by the early seventeenth century it is the expected representation of a final [x̣].

6. Two exceptions are *qquiñua* [qiñ$ua] 'cinchona tree' and *quinua* 'quinoa' (a grain) (both citations, Gonçález Holguín 1608: 309). Both have etymological syllable-final *ñ* prior to a labial glide. The former has since undergone metathesis of the *ñw* sequence, and is now [qewña] (see Cusihuamán 1976b: 114; and Lira 1944: 457). The latter has a number of currently attested variants: in addition to a form that is parallel to the first [kiwña], [kinwa] is common. (It was possibly back-borrowed from Spanish.) Two variant forms have unique epenthetic vowels (raised in the phonetic transcriptions) that do not form syllabic domains for the purposes of stress assignment: [kin^{u}wa] and [kiw^{i}na] (attested by Lira, 1944: 326 as *kíwina*). The first might be treated as having an underlying /ñ^{u}/. There is no independent evidence for this analysis, though. The epenthetic vowel in the second is clearly a reflex of the palatal property of the nasal and

appears to be a variant of the [kiwña] pronunciation. I am indebted to Peter Landerman for pointing out the problem.

6. Reading Colonial Texts

1. The *Bibliographie* actually begins in 1540, but the first two references are secondary and refer to texts that have not been located.

2. I discuss this passage at greater length in Mannheim (1987).

3. The Quechua *annotations* to the *Doctrina christiana* of the Third Council of Lima state: "Yñini, creer, assentir, conseder, viene de, y, que significa si, y de ñini que significa dezir, y es lo mismo que en otras partes diz[e]n, ariñini, checan ñini, sullullmi ñini" (*Yñini* 'to believe, assent to, or concede' comes from *y*, which means 'yes', and from *ñini* which means 'to say', and is the same that is said elsewhere as *ariñini, checan ñini, sullullmi ñini*).

4. For a discussion of belief as a social transaction, see Pouillon (1979).

There are also exuberances in translating Pérez Bocanegra's seventeenth-century use of *creer* into modern English. Although in (ii) *Iñiy* is used for a false belief, it could not have had this meaning more generally, because Pérez also used it in the *Credo*. The second edition of the *Random House Dictionary of the English Language* (p. 190) defines *to believe* as "to have confidence in the truth, the existence, or the reliability of something, although without absolute proof that one is right in doing so," although in modern usage it also connotes false belief (de Certeau 1981). Another modern connotation of *believe* is that it involves belief in something that cannot be experienced. But that is certainly not true of Quechua dream interpretation (in the example), which is part of everyday experience. Needham (1972: ch. 4–7) explores the historical and cultural resonances of the English verb *believe* in the context of a study of the problems of translating *belief* cross-linguistically. He argues that any attempt to fix meanings cross-linguistically is "impaired by the relativity that must affect any linguistic means of representing them" (1972: 224).

5. For a detailed study of the festival narrative and song and a normalization of the song text, see Mannheim (1986). It needs to be mentioned that this passage is only part of a larger song, which in turn is part of a festival narrative. I have inserted diagonal lines to indicate where the lines end in the original manuscript.

6. See Urioste (1980: xxx) and Mannheim (1986: 45, 53; 1987: 139–140) for examples. Rivarola (1987b) discusses the morphological and syntactic traces of Guaman Poma's Quechua in his Spanish.

7. The enclitic *-chi* is not attested in contemporary Ayacucho Quechua. On the basis of comparative evidence from the Central Quechua languages (Parker 1976: 150–151 for Ancash; Escribens and Proulx 1970 for Huaylas; Solá 1958 for Huánuco), I assume that it marked supposition or conjecture.

8. " . . . *huaca* . . . pronunciada la última sílaba en lo alto del paladar, quiere decir ídolo . . . y es nombre que no permite que de él se deduzga verbo para decir idolatrar."

9. "Esta misma dicción *huaca*, pronunciada la última sílaba en lo más interior de la garganta, se hace verbo: quiere decir llorar. Por lo cual dos historiadores

españoles que no supieron esta diferencia dijeron: los indios entran llorando y guayando en sus templos a sus sacrificios, que *huaca* eso quiere decir. . . . Verdad es que la diferente significación consiste solamente en la diferente pronunciación sin mudar letra ni acento . . ." Garcilaso was apparently referring to Gómara's *Historia general de las Indias* (Porras 1955: 228–229).

10. Porras (1951) suggests that Garcilaso was referring to Santo Tomás. But Santo Tomás returned to South America the same year (1561) that Garcilaso arrived in Spain.

11. Santo Tomás (1560a, 1560b) worked with informants from both the Central and Peripheral branches.

12. Cisneros (1965) discusses problems in the phonological interpretation of Quechua words cited in colonial-era chronicles. See Beyersdorf (1986) for a survey of longer Quechua texts included in these sources.

13. Porras (1951) suggests that the *Lexicon* and grammar of Domingo de Santo Tomás represented an extinct coastal dialect of peripheral Quechua (cf. Torero 1964: 448, and Parker 1969b: 278, 1969f: 166–167). In contrast, Cerrón-Palomino (1987c: 78–79) identified the Quechua described by Santo Tomás with an Inka *lingua franca* (*la lengua general*) that was distinct from the Quechua spoken in the Inka capital, Cuzco (*la lengua del Cuzco* or *la lengua del ynga*). But Santo Tomás (1560a: 15) himself stated in the prologue of his *Lexicon* that he not only drew on the lingua franca for vocabulary, but culled terms indiscriminantly from among the Quechua languages. As Guaman Poma (1615: 1079) observed, the *Lexicon* contained "la lengua del Cuzco chinchaysuyo quichiua todo rrebuelto. . . ." Thus, the language of the *Lexicon* was neither an extinct coastal dialect nor the Inka *lingua franca*.

14. Molina of Cuzco is traditionally called "El Cuzqueño" to distinguish him from another sixteenth-century chronicler of the same name.

15. The term "inclusive" first appeared in the Aymara annotations (Mannheim 1982: 141).

16. It is not even clear whether the manuscripts are transcriptions of Huarochiriños speaking the Inka lingua franca or an indigenous translator's Quechua reworking of narratives that were performed in a non-Quechua language (Taylor 1980: 9). According to the Jesuit missionary linguist Alonso de Barzana, a language other than the Quechua lingua franca was spoken in Huarochirí; women spoke only the local language (Acosta 1577b: 268). Gerald Taylor (1985, 1987: 221) has noted evidence of Jaqi/Aru (non-Quechua) and local Quechua substrata alongside the Inka lingua franca in which the manuscript was written.

17. I plan to publish an edition of *Cay q[ui]quin llactapi* . . . in the near future.

18. There was also a "Gonzálo Holguín" who was named as "intérprete general de los indios en las lenguas Quichua, Puquina y Aimará" by Viceroy Toledo (1575b), but who is not to be confused with Diego de Gonçález Holguín, who did not arrive in America until 1581.

19. Garland Bills (personal communication, 1982) has observed the form [chiq] dialectally in Bolivia.

20. The genitive {cpa} in *aucacpa sutin* 'the name of the enemy' (line 507) is problematic. It is usually assumed that the present-day postvocalic genitive [x̣pa] was formed by double-marking, the postconsonantal form *-pa* following the

postvocalic *q*. But {-cpa} is attested here in a system in which the postvocalic genitive is still *-p*.

21. T. L. Meneses (1950) has published a careful transcription of the Sahuaraura codex of *Usca Paucar* that I have checked against the manuscript.

22. Compare *ccochincuna* [khuchinkuna] (line 125) 'their pigs'.

23. The single exception is the form *rafranta* [<rapra] (line 366) 'wing'. Meneses attributes the form to a copyist's error on the part of Sahuaraura (1950: 170). No other syllable-final *p* shows up as *f* including those in other tokens of *rapra* (line 860, for example); cf. *chapra* (lines 412 and 571) 'branch'. A poem roughly contemporary with the period in which the Sahuaraura codex was copied shows a [ɸ] reflex of syllable-final *p* in the same word, *raffra* (Basagoita in Rivero and Tschudi 1851: 85).

The only reason I have not also suggested that the *-cti* form of the subordinate clause marker is also a copyist's error is that it involves a merger as well as the lenition, and so one might expect greater care in maintaining the written form. The sporadic change of *s* > *x* in *wisch'u* 'throw' is first attested here (1.423), as it is in the Justiniani codex of *Ollanta* (p. 9).

24. Galante published a transcription of the Sahuaraura codex, which I have checked against the manuscript.

25. This is the manuscript described by Markham (1856: 170–172, 1912: 90f.). See Rivet and Créqui-Montfort (1951–1956: 1, xxviii) and Lara (1969: 64f.).

26. According to Angeles Caballero (1987: 83, 97, 116, 126), Aguilar borrowed occasionally from earlier grammars of Quechua, Spanish, and Latin, but not systematically. Aguilar used these sources for grammatical terminology, but did not copy Quechua forms verbatim.

27. In modern dialect variation, lenition of syllable-final *p* always precedes uvularization. It seems safe to assume that the implicational relationship uvularization ⊃ lenition also held for earlier stages of the language.

7. The Sibilants

1. The responsibility for any misinterpretation is mine, of course.

2. See Catalán (1957) and Landerman (1979, 1983) for the peninsular phonological background. This is a classic area of study in Spanish history and dialectology (Martinet 1951; Canfield 1952; Alonso 1955; and Harris 1969: ch. 7).

3. {ç}, {c} (before i and e), and {z} are alternative representations of the same segment in systems in which *z* > *ç*. Between vowels, {s} and {ss} are alternate representations of the same segment.

4. {c} is an orthographic variant of {z} before *i* and *e*.

5. Gonçález Holguín occasionally substituted *ç* for *z* syllable-finally, citing the same form differently in two different places, as *yzccon* ~ *içcon* 'nine' (1608: 270, 405). His grammar (1607), in contrast, used *z* both syllable-initially and syllable-finally.

6. The absence of {x} in Cuzco-Collao Quechua was mentioned explicitly by Anonymous (1970 [1586]: 19) and Garcilaso (1609, *advertencias* and VII, iv), along with Gonçález Holguín and Diego de Molina (see below). According to Landerman (1983: 209), Huerta (1616) and Torres Rubio (1619) also noted its absence.

7. Santo Tomás regularly described the syllable-final palatal stop as {x}. In one instance an epenthetic *i* shifted it to syllable-initial position where it remained a stop: *achica* (106 and 172) 'many' (< *achka*). In addition several instances of syllable-final *t* are written as *th*, perhaps to suggest fricativization as in *xuthquini* 'descalsarse' (179r) and *mithma* ~ *mithima* 'forastero, o estrangero que está de asiento' (152r).

8. I cite immediate sources for these forms, not reconstructed proto-Quechua expressions.

9. Gonçález Holguín (1842 [1607]: 215) stated: "Y aunqué esto es lo mas propio y natural á la lengua, mas ya cuanto toca á los concuñados tienen otro vocablo no tan confuso, que es, massa, y, massapura, los concuñados varones todos entre si sin distincion, y para las concuñadas, khachun, todas sin distincion. Y notense, que (massa) es otro vocablo diferente de (massani) que arriba ya puesto, que (massa) con posesivo dice (massay) y (massani) dice (massaniy)."

10. Cf. Menéndez Pidal (1925: 94, footnote 1). Landerman (1979: 13f., 1983: 218; based on Bertonio 1603 and 1612) suggests that velarization began as early as the beginning of the seventeenth century. Bertonio's data are consistent with an interpretation in which {j}, {g}, and {x} were distinct and {j} represented a velar before {x} did.

11. On restriction of the older of two competing forms, see Kuryłowicz (1966 [1949]: 169). Occasionally sheep are called *Luisa* as well.

12. Gonçález Holguín (1608: 359) cited it as *ussuta, calçado de indios.* Santo Tomás (1560b: 178r) cited the Northern-Central form *uxota,* which is just as likely as a source for the loan. But in a sense the question of whether the [ʂ] form or the [ʃ] form is the source of the loan is immaterial because there is no corresponding alternation in the Spanish form.

13. Santiago del Estero Quechua shows two sibilants, /s/ and /ʃ/, as the result of a split (de Reuse 1986). On the basis of a personal communication from Gabriel Escobar, Parker (1969f: 200, footnote 11) suggests that the distinction may have survived in some dialects of Cuzco-Collao. Parker does not cite any examples. I have not found any dialect evidence for the older distinction in the modern-day Department of Cuzco. There are modern dialects of Cuzco-Collao Quechua (generally to the southwest of the city of Cuzco) in which ʃ is distinguished from s̱, but these instances of ʃ are from more recent innovations: lenition of syllable-final č, and palatalization of s̱.

14. The Sahuaraura and Justiniani (p. 21) manuscripts of *Ollanta* are on opposite sides of the *haykuy* ~ *yaykuy* isogloss.

15. In order to avoid misunderstanding, I should point out that the reanalyses take place at a relatively shallow genetic level, entirely within Southern Quechua. There is some evidence that *ya-* is a weakly productive verb stem in Central Quechua languages (see Parker 1973: 22, among others). For Ancash Quechua *sha-*, other suffixes can intervene in the sequence *sha-mu-* (Parker and Chávez 1976: 159). Both are thus plausibly reconstructed as monosyllabic stems in proto-Quechua (cf. Parker 1969e: 13).

16. Corresponding citations in Anonymous 1951 [1586] are *canchis* (21); *yscon* (165); *masca-* (58); *cosni* (26); *casco* (23); *haspi-* (142); *mosco-* (61); *chasqui* (34); *asna-* (17).

17. Wanka and Cajamarca Quechua are exceptions to this areal feature (Cerrón-Palomino 1977: 87). The Central and Northern languages as a whole are often referred to as "Chinchaysuyu" in the colonial and ethnohistorical literature. But "Chinchaysuyu" was used very loosely in the colonial literature and refers to no known genetic subgrouping or structural isogloss.

18. It appears in four entries and in their corresponding cross-listings (Gonçález Holguín 1608: 87): "*çuclla huclla.* De vna vez, o de vn tiron; *çucñincalla.* Todos a vna, o *huctantalla,* o *çucllaña.* Agora desta hecha, o desta vez; *çucllana huanayari.* Acabate ya de enmendar de vna vez; *çuclla çucllana huanani.* Agora desta vez yame enmendare."

19. "*Ssecssehuanmi.* Tengo comezón. Vease *cec cec,* y *cec cihuan* con (ç) pocos lo dizen con *(ss).*"

20. Since the two sibilants have merged, the two terms have become partial homophones, despite the lack of any derivational relationship between them. And as such, they may be used today by Quechua speakers to comment on one another through folk etymology, as Billie Jean Isbell observed in Chuschi (Cangallo, Ayacucho).

21. Except by Santo Tomás, but there we come up against the problem of dialect provenience.

22. "una elevada proporción de las raices que en protoquechua poseían /c/ en posición interior se encuentran en cuzqueño-boliviano con glotalización sea en la africada (*/mica/ > /mich'a/ 'mezquino', */hicay/ > /hich'ay/ 'derramar', */sucu/ > /such'u/ 'tullido', */waci/ > /wach'i/ 'flecha, dardo', */saca/ > /sach'a/ 'arbol', etc.), sea en la oclusiva inicial del tema si la hay (*/qicuy/ > /q'ichuy/ 'despojar', */qica/ > /q'icha/ 'diarrea', */puncaw/ > /p'unchaw/ 'día')."

23. I am not proposing a formal subgrouping of Southern Quechua and Junín-Wanka Quechua at this point. A linguistic subgrouping can only be proposed on the basis of shared innovations, not on what are likely to be shared retentions. It may well be that the irregular word-initial shift of *s* > *h* could provide a basis for such a subgrouping. Consider three possible accounts of the point-for-point correspondence between Southern Peruvian Quechua and Wanka: (1) The ṣ : s̱ distinction is a shared retention, in which case the standard reconstruction of the proto-Quechua sibilant opposition as ʃ : s̱ (Parker 1963; Torero 1964: 455–456) is wrong. (2) The ṣ : s̱ distinction is a shared innovation, in which case the subgrouping is wrong, unless (3) the innovation diffused areally. (Wanka and Southern Peruvian Quechua are contiguous.) Cerrón-Palomino (1977: 87ff.) assumes that it is an innovation in Wanka; Landerman (1983: 225) proposes that it is a shared retention.

8. The Ejectives and Aspirates

1. Ladefoged (1971) distinguishes ejectives, aspirates, and plain plosives in terms of the glottal stricture and airstream mechanism used to produce them. Plain plosives are produced using lung air pushed out under the control of the respiratory muscles. Ejectives are produced using pharynx air compressed by the upward movement of the closed glottis. Aspirates use a pulmonic airstream (like plain plosives), but the glottis is slack at the posterior end between the arytenoid

cartilages. Voicing, on the other hand, requires a constricted glottis. There is therefore a brief period of voicelessness during and immediately after the release of an articulatory structure. I use the term *ejective* (after Ladefoged 1971) to describe the class of "glottalized" sounds to emphasize that they are not simply "plain plosives followed by something else," as the term *glottalized* might otherwise suggest. I use *glottalization* to mean "produced by a glottalic airstream."

For a detailed study of the laryngeal physiology of the different stop types, see Dent (1981), especially chapters 3 and 5. Dent directs her analysis toward explaining the articulatory differences among ejective, aspirate, and plain voiceless stops in Bolivian Quechua, but without observations of first-language speakers.

2. Since the glottal catch is predictable, it has not appeared in any orthography for Southern Peruvian Quechua except the one used by John Rowe (1950, 1953, and elsewhere). Rowe uses ' to indicate an initial glottal catch as in *'uspha* 'ash'.

3. "introduziendo vocablos que por vetura se vsauan antiguamente, y agora no, o aprouechando de los que vsauan los Ingas, y señores, o tomandolos de otras naciones con quien tratan."

4. The expressions "duality of patterning" and "double articulation" are used within different intellectual traditions to refer to the same phenomenon. Americans are most familiar with "duality of patterning," the phrase used in a series of well-known articles by Charles Hockett (e.g., 1960). "Double articulation" is the expression used in European traditions as early as the medieval scholastic grammarians and the notion of *articulatio prima et secunda* (Jakobson 1985 [1975]: 189; see Martinet 1957; Jakobson 1971 [1970]: 673). I use "double articulation" interchangeably with "duality of patterning."

5. Woodbury (1987) proposes that the principle of double articulation must be reformulated to refer to pragmatically meaningful but fully conventionalized phonological processes, which are found interspersed with nonmeaningful phonological processes in the phonological component of the grammar of Central Alaskan Yupik. The argument rests on identifying the second ("meaningless") set of conventions with the entire phonological component of the grammar, in place of the narrower claim made here, which concerns only the "sense discriminative" aspects of the sound system. My position is that only "sense discriminative" aspects of the sound system can change by means of regular, exceptionless sound changes (*Lautgesetze*). The difference between Woodbury's formulation and mine can be tested empirically with historical evidence from Central Alaskan Yupik. His formulation is correct if and only if pragmatically meaningful phonological processes change by means of *Lautgesetze.*

6. I reject the notion that language is ever grounded in a world that is unmediated linguistically and culturally, since no such world ever presents itself to our experience.

7. In a discussion about the nature of narrative writing attended by several prominent Peruvian novelists, Arguedas argues that, for him, word and object are consubstantial even in the novel: "linguistic reality is *reality* reality" (*lo que es realidad verbal es realidad realidad;* Alegría et al. 1969: 140; cf. Rama 1982: 235–236).

8. Similarly, Dimock (1957: 24) writes that Bengali expressives "are not terms of clarity, specificity, or directness; their aim is imagination, subtlety of suggestion." Michael Shapiro (1983: 92–93), who is concerned with motivating linguistic patterning semiotically, emphasizes the fluidity of all patterns: ". . . there is nothing obligatory, necessary, or inevitable about the coherence of language data *in the short run.* Whereas the overarching teleological thrust of language development tends to direct the cooccurrence of linguistic phenomena into patterns which are iconic, at any given point in the history of a language the process may not yet have run its full course, thereby presenting learner and analyst alike with a mottled picture characterized by variation . . ." (emphasis Shapiro's).

9. For a discussion of expressives from a Peircian viewpoint, see Anttila (1977a).

10. Compare the word stem for 'flutter' and related stems in Semai, a Central Asian language of Malaysia, as reported by Diffloth (1976: 260–261). Diffloth approaches Semai expressives as a problem for synchronic morphological analysis, but observes that expressives raise historical cross-cultural problems analogous to those posed here.

11. Greenberg (1970a: 16–17, 1970b) observes that glottalization seems to be the only nonprosodic feature that marks the word as a phonological domain. As I suggest below, the restrictions on aspiration may be a formal "mimic" of the restrictions on glottalization.

12. It is also possible that the use of *t'ipiy* with the meaning 'to stretch' involved a confusion of the two verbs that was later accepted by other speakers with the new meaning.

13. For the durative, however, there are no strictly phonological reasons that would prohibit it from appearing after a stem and series of suffixes without any stops. These would have occurred in a minority of cases, however: since Quechua has virtually no allomorphy, I suspect that they would have been leveled to their unaspirated counterparts.

14. Landerman (personal communication, 1981) observes that *h*-epenthesis is variable in the Bolivian dialect of Apolobamba, which is quite close to Cuzco Quechua. Apolo Quechua shows other archaic features including significant lag in the syllable-final lenitions.

9. Syllable-Final Weakenings

1. This is an effect of the word structure constraint that restricts ejectives and aspirates to the first stop in a word (chapter 8). The comparatively few occurrences of the durative immediately following a stem with no stops would presumably have been leveled out.

2. *mutki-* is attested by Gonçález Holguín (1608: 608) as *mutquini; mitka-* in Anonymous, *Ollanta* (Sahuaraura codex, 114) as *mitcasccaita;* and *utqay* in Anonymous, *Ollanta* (Sahuaraura codex, 114) as *utccaitan.* For these words, the sources of aspiration and glottalization and the time of their acquisition are not known.

3. In addition, the accusative case was leveled from *-kta* (/V___) ~ *-ta* (/C___)

to *-ta*. The change appeared variably in Aguilar's *Arte* and was completed by the time of Centeno.

10. Conditions on Sound Change

1. There is also a sociological reason for assuming that the implicational hierarchies are intrinsically, rather than extrinsically, governed. As we saw in chapter 4, speech variation within Southern Peruvian Quechua is not referred to as an overarching, intersubjective system of social evaluation, as it is in all of the cases in which sociolinguists have observed structurally heterogeneous implicational hierarchies.

2. Compare Lastra and Horcasitas (1978) on word-final "lead" of sound change over word-internal in Nahuatl.

3. I understand boundaries such as $ and # to be a linear shorthand for hierarchically organized phonological constituents.

4. "Discourse level morpheme" here refers to a class of suffixes that indicate the epistemic and evidential status of the utterance as well as question, negation, and affirmation and their respective discourse scopes.

5. See Lefebvre and Muysken (1988: 93–100) for justification of left-branching compositional structures as lexical representations in Southern Peruvian Quechua. Wölck (1987: 38–39) describes the Quechua word similarly, including a diagram of a left-branching compositional structure, but writes (inexplicably): "Como si fuera para compensar la estructura izquierdizante de la sintaxis, la morfología quechua, en el sentido de composición de palabras, se ramifica completamente hacia la derecha." What I believe Wölck is observing here is that, within the word, a modifier follows the constituent that it modifies, whereas in syntax (above the level of the word), a modifier precedes the constituent that it modifies. This arrangement is a consequence of a consistently left-branching morphology and syntax.

6. See Bybee (1985) for a compatible account of the principles governing the order of inflectional affixes on the verb. Bybee (1985: 11) proposes that the sequential order of affixes is determined cross-linguistically by "the extent to which their meanings directly affect the lexical content of the verb stem." The more directly (and the more) the affix modifies the verb, the closer it is to the stem; conversely, the more an affix affects or refers to other elements in a clause, the more distant it will be from the verb stem (cf. Wölck 1987: 39).

7. "Discourse-level suffix" here refers to a set of morphemes that can be identified on both formal and semantic grounds. Formally, they attach to the final member of any main clause constituent, regardless of the categorial status of the constituent. Semantically, they indicate and bound the domains of affirmation, status, and emphasis or indicate parataxis. (Although anaphora is a discourse phenomenon, it is handled by the derivational and inflectional machinery in Quechua. Recent claims have been made as to the discourse sensitivity of many grammatical phenomena, so it is important to keep in mind the narrow sense of "discourse level" used here.)

8. Compare Greenberg (1963: 93, universal 28) and Bybee (1985).

9. Phillips (1984) suggests that physiologically motivated sound changes

affect the most frequent forms first and conceptually motivated changes affect the least frequent. Her results, however, are based on diffusion through lexical morphemes and are therefore inapplicable to the present situation, in which phonological change is sensitive to the distinction between lexical morphemes and several classes of grammatical morphemes. Dressler (1982) observes that accounts of sound change based on frequency are at best correlations, rather than explanations, since they do not provide principled accounts of why frequency should affect sound change.

References Cited

Colonial

Acosta, José de, s.i. 1577a. *De procuranda indorum salute.* Spanish translation in Francisco Mateos (ed.). 1954. *Obras del P. José de Acosta.* Biblioteca de Autores Españoles 73. Madrid: Atlas, 387–608.

———. 1577b. "Carta anua de 1576, al P. Everardo Mercuriano, Préposito General de la Compañía de Jesús." In Francisco Mateos (ed.). 1954. *Obras del P. José de Acosta.* Biblioteca de Autores Españoles 73. Madrid: Atlas, 260–290.

———. 1583. "Declaración judicial." In Antonio de Egaña (ed.). 1961. *Monumenta peruana,* vol. 3, 1581–1585. Rome: Monumenta Historica Societatis Iesu, 270–274.

———. 1590. *Historia natural y moral de las Indias.* In Francisco Mateos (ed.). 1954. *Obras del P. José de Acosta.* Biblioteca de Autores Españoles 73. Madrid: Atlas, 1–247.

Acuña, Francisco de. 1586. "Relación fecha por el corregidor de los Chunbibilcas Don Francisco de Acuña por mandado de su Ex.[a] del Señor Don Fernando de Torres y Portugal, Vissorey destos Reynos, por la discrepción de las Indias que Su Magestad manda hacer." *Relaciones geográficas de Indias* 2: 310–325.

Aguilar M., Juan de. 1690. *Arte de la lengua quichua general de Indios del Perú.* Facsimile of holographic manuscript, 1939. Tucumán: Instituto de Antropología, Universidad Nacional de Tucumán.

Albornoz, Cristóbal. 1584. "Instrucción para descubrir todas las guacas del Pirú y sus camayos y haziendas." Transcription published in Pierre Duviols. 1984. "Albornoz y el espacio ritual andino prehispánico." *Revista Andina* 2: 194–222.

Almonte, Clemento. 1813. "Respuestas al interrogatorio al cura de Andahua (partido de Condesuyos) sobre las costumbres y organización de los poblados de su jurisdicción." Archivo General de Indias, Lima 1598. Transcription published in Luis Millones Gadea. 1971. "Pastores y tejedores de los Condesuyos de Arequipa: Un informe etnológico al Consejo de Regencia." *Quinto Congreso Internacional de Historia de América* 3: 302–317.

Alvarez y Jiménez, Antonio. 1792. "Memoria legalizada de la visita que en cumplimiento de las ordenanzas de intendentes hizo a la provincia de Arequipa su

Gobernador Intendente . . ." Archivo General de Indias, Intendencia de Arequipa, 2138 (old numeration). Transcription published by Victor M. Barriga (1942–1946), *Memorias para la historia de Arequipa.* 2 vols. Arequipa: La Colmena.

Anonymous. 1586. *Arte y vocabulario en la lengua general del Peru llamada Quichua y en la lengua Española.* Lima: Antonio Ricardo. Additional editions: 1603. *Grammatica y vocabulario en la lengua general del Peru llamada Quichua, y en la lengua Española.* Seville: Clemente Hidalgo; Juan Martínez (ed.). 1604. *Vocabulario en la lengua general del Peru llamada Quichua, y en la lengua española.* Lima: Antonio Ricardo; 1614. *Arte, y vocabulario en la lengua general del Peru llamada Quichua, y en la lengua española.* Lima: Francisco del Canto; Guillermo Escobar Risco (ed.). 1951. *Vocabulario y phrasis en la lengua general de los Indios del Perú, llamada Quichua* (dictionary only). Lima: Universidad Nacional de San Marcos; Rafael Aguilar Paez (ed.). 1970. *Gramática quechua y vocabularios.* Lima: Universidad Nacional de San Marcos. I used Escobar's reedition, which includes a word-by-word comparison of the four colonial texts. Aguilar revised the orthography in the 1970 edition.

Anonymous. 1600. *Historia general de la Compañia de Jesús en la Provincia del Perú.* Francisco Mateos (ed.). 1944. 2 vols. Madrid: Consejo Superior de Investigaciones Científicas, Instituto Gonzalo Fernández de Oviedo.

Anonymous, Huarochirí. Early 17th century. *Runa yn.° niscap machoncuna ñaupa pacha . . .* manuscript 3169, ff. 64R–114R, Biblioteca Nacional, Madrid. Editions: H. Galante. 1942. *De priscorum huaruchiriensium origene et institutis* (transcription, Latin translation, photocopy of most of the manuscript). Madrid: Instituto Gonzalo Fernández de Oviedo; Hermann Trimborn and Antje Kelm. 1967. *Francisco de Avila* (transcription, German translation). Berlin: Mann; José María Arguedas, Pierre Duviols, and Karen Spalding. 1966. *Dioses y hombres de Huarochirí* (transcription, Spanish translation). Lima: Instituto de Estudios Peruanos; Gerald Taylor. 1980. *Rites et traditions de Huarochirí: Manuscrit quéchua de début de 17e siècle* (transcription, French translation). Paris: L'Harmattan; George L. Urioste. 1983. *Hijos de Pariya Qaqa: La tradición oral de Waru Chiri (Mitología, ritual u costumbres).* 2 vols. (annotated transcription, Spanish translation). Syracuse: Syracuse University Foreign and Comparative Studies Program; Gerald Taylor. 1987. *Ritos y tradiciones de Huarochirí del siglo xvii* (annotated transcription, revised from Taylor [1980], Spanish translation). Lima: Instituto de Estudios Peruanos and the Institut Français d'Etudes Andines.

Anonymous, *Ollanta.* n.d.a. Justiniani: *Tragicomedia del Apu Ollantay y Cusi Coyllur: Rigores de un padre, y generosidad de un Rey.* Facsimile edition, Hyppolitus Galante (ed.). 1938. *Ollantay.* Lima: Universidad Nacional de San Marcos.

Anonymous, *Ollanta.* n.d.b. Sahuaraura: *Comedia trágica que intitula los rigores de un Padre y generosidad de un Rey.* Published in Hyppolitus Galante (ed.). 1938. *Ollantay.* Lima: Universidad Nacional de San Marcos.

Anonymous, *Usca Paucar.* n.d. *Auto sacramental: El Patrocinio de Nuestra*

Señora María Santicima en Copacabana (Sahuaraura codex). Biblioteca Nacional del Perú.

Aquaviva, Claudio, s.i. 1603. Letter [to Rodrigo de Cabredo, Jesuit Provincial], 7-iv. In Enrique Fernández (ed.). 1986. *Monumenta peruana,* vol. 8, 1603–1604. Rome: Institutum Historicum Societatis Iesu, 147–150.

Areche, José Antonio de. 1781. "Sentencia pronunciada en el Cuzco por el visitador José Antonio de Areche contra José Gabriel Tupac Amaro, su muger, hijos, y demas reos principales de la sublevación, 15-v-1781." In Carlos Daniel Valcarcel (ed.). 1971. *La rebelión de Túpac Amaru,* vol. 2. Colección documental de la independencia del Perú. Lima: Comisión Nacional de Sesquicentenario de la Independencia del Perú, 765–773.

Avendaño, Hernando de. 1649. *Sermones de los misterios de Nuestra Santa Fé Católica, en lengua castellana, y la general del Inca.* Lima: Herrera.

Avila, Francisco de. 1608. *Tratado y relación de los errores, falsos dioses y otras supersticiones y ritos diabólicos en que vivian antiguamente los Indios de las provincias de Huara Cheri, Mama y Chaclla . . .* Biblioteca Nacional de Madrid, manuscript 3169, ff. 115–130. Published in José María Arguedas, Pierre Duviols, and Karen Spalding (eds.). 1966. *Dioses y hombres de Huarochirí.* Lima: Instituto de Estudios Peruanos, 199–217.

———. 1648a. *Tratado de los Evangelios, que Nuestra Madre la Iglesia propone en todo el año desde la primera Dominica de Adviento . . .* Lima: n.p.

———. 1648b. *Segundo tomo de los sermones de todo el año en lengua indica y castellana para la enseñanza de los Indios y extirpación de sus idolatrías.* Lima: n.p.

Bertonio, Ludovico, s.i. 1603. *Arte y grammatica muy copiosa de la lengua aymara.* Rome: Luis Zannetti. Facsimile edition, Leipzig: Teubner, 1879.

———. 1612. *Vocabulario de la lengua aymara.* Juli: Francisco del Canto. Facsimile edition, La Paz: Don Bosco, 1956.

Betanzos, Juan de. 1551. *Suma y narración de los Incas.* María del Carmen Martín R. (ed.). Madrid: Atlas, 1987.

Cabello Valboa, Miguel. 1590. *Miscelánea antártica, donde se describe el orígen de nuestros Indios occidentales . . .* Modern edition: *Miscelánea antártica, una historia del Perú antiguo.* Lima: Universidad Nacional Mayor de San Marcos, 1951.

Cantos de Andrada, Rodrigo de, Garci Núñez Vela, Gaspar de Contreras, and Francisco Caballero. 1586. "Relación de la villa rica de Oropesa y minas de Guancavelica." *Relaciones geográficas de Indias* 2 (1965): 303–309.

Carabajal, Pedro. 1586. "Descripción fecha de la Provincia de Vilcas Guaman por el ilustre señor don Pedro de Carabajal, corregidor y justica mayor della." *Relaciones geográficas de Indias* 1 (1965): 205–219.

Centeno, Gabriel. n.d. *El pobre más rico.* José M. B. Farfán and Humberto Suárez Alvarez (eds.). 1939, including a facsimile of the manuscript. Lima: Universidad de San Marcos.

Cepeda, Juan de, s.i., and Francisco de Vera, s.i. 1585. Letter [to Felipe II, Rey de España] 14-ii. In Antonio de Egaña (ed.). 1961. *Monumenta peruana,* vol. 3, 1581–1585. Rome: Institutum Historicum Societatis Iesu., 551–555.

Cieza de Léon, Pedro. 1550. *Del señorio de los yngas yupangues (Segunda parte de la Crónica del Perú).* Reprinted 1967 (from the 1880 edition, ed. Jiménez de la Espada) with an introduction by Carlos Aranibar. Lima: Instituto de Estudios Peruanos.

Cisneros, Gregorio de, s.i. 1601. Letter [to Claudio Aquaviva, Jesuit General] 18-iii. In Antonio de Egaña and Enrique Fernández (eds.). 1981. *Monumenta peruana,* vol. 7, 1600–1602. Rome: Institutum Historicum Societatis Iesu., 283–293.

Cobo, Bernabe, s.i. 1956 [1653]. *Historia del nuevo mundo.* Published by M. Jiménez de la Espada (ed.). 1892. Seville: Rasca and Tuvera. Reprinted in Francisco Mateos (ed.). *Obras del P. Bernabe Cobo,* vol. 2. Biblioteca de Autores Españoles 92. Madrid: Atlas.

Concolorcorvo (Carrio de la Vandera y Acarette?). 1773?. *El lazarillo de ciegos caminantes.* Emilio Carilla (ed.). 1973. Barcelona: Labor.

Consejo de las Indias. 1596. "Consulto del Consejo de las Indias sobre las causas porque pareció se debia ordenar que los Indios hablasen la lengua castellana." Madrid, 20-vi-1596. Archivo General de Indias, Indiferente 744. In Richard Konetzke (ed.). 1958. *Colección de documentos para la historia de la formación social de hispanoamérica, 1493–1810,* vol. 2, part 1, 1593–1659. Madrid: Consejo Superior de Investigaciones Científicas, 38–40.

Diez de San Miguel, Garci. 1964 [1567]. *Visita hecha a la provincia de Chucuito.* Lima: Casa de la Cultura del Perú.

Espinoza Medrano, Juan. 1662. *Apologético en favor de D. Luis de Góngora, principe de los poeta lyricos de España. . . .* Lima: Quevedo y Zarate. Reprinted 1965. *Revista Universitaria* (Cuzco) 122/125 (separate pagination).

Esquivel y Navia, Diego de. 1753. *Noticias cronológicas de la gran ciudad del Cuzco.* Reprinted 1980. Félix Denegri Luna (ed.). 2 vols. Lima: Fundación Wiesse.

Fornee, Niculoso de. 1586. "Descripción de la tierra del Corregimiento de Abancay." *Relaciones geográficas de Indias* 2 (1965): 16–30.

Garcilaso de la Vega, El Inca. 1609. *Primera parte de los Commentarios reales que tratan del origen de los Yncas, reyes que fueron del Perv, de sv idolatria, leyes y gouierno en paz y en guerra: de svs vidas, y conquistas: y de todo lo que fue aquel Imperio y su Republica, antes que los Españoles passaran a el.* Lisbon: Crasbeeck. Reprinted in Carmelo Saenz de Santa María (ed.). 1960. *Obras completas del Inca Garcilaso de la Vega,* vol. 2. Biblioteca de Autores Españoles 133. Madrid: Atlas.

———. 1616. *Historia general del Perú, Trata del descubrimiento de el, y como lo ganaron los españoles.* Cordova. Reprinted in Carmelo Saenz de Santa María (ed.). 1960. *Obras completas del Inca Garcilaso de la Vega,* vol. 3. Biblioteca de Autores Españoles 134. Madrid: Atlas.

Gómara, Francisco López de. 1553. *Hispania victrix: Historia general de las Indias.* Reprinted 1947. Biblioteca de Autores Españoles. Madrid: Atlas.

Gonçález Holguín, Diego de, s.i. 1607. *Gramática y arte nueva de la lengua general de todo el Perú llamada lengua Qquichua o del Inca.* Los Reyes: del Canto. Reprinted Genoa, 1842.

———. 1608. *Vocabulario de la lengua general de todo el Perú llamada lengua*

Qquichua o del Inca. Los Reyes: del Canto. Reprinted 1952. Lima: Universidad Nacional Mayor de San Marcos. Page references are to the 1952 edition.

Guaman Poma de Ayala, Felipe. 1615. *El primer nueva corónica i buẽ gobierno.* Facsimile edition, 1936. Paris: Institut d'Ethnologie. Edition by A. Posnansky. 1944. *La obra de Phelipe Guaman Poma de Ayala, "Primer corónica y buen gobierno."* La Paz: Instituto de Antropología, Etnología y Prehistoria. Edition by Rolena Adorno, John V. Murra, and Jorge Urioste. 1980. *Nueva corónica y buen gobierno.* México (D.F.): Siglo XXI.

Huerta, Alonso de. 1616. *Arte de la lengva qvechva general delos Yndios de este Reyno del Pirú.* Lima: del Canto.

Jurado Palomino, Bartholomé. 1649. *Declaración copiosa de las quatro partes mas essenciales, y necessarias de la doctrina christiana.* Lima: López de Herrera. Reprinted in H. Galante (ed.). 1943. *Catechismus Quichvensis Bartholomaei Juradi Palomini.* Madrid: Consejo Superior de Investigaciones Científicas. An excerpt also appears in Rivero and Tschudi 1958 [1851]: 81–85.

Lira, Francisco de, o.p. 1689. "Relación de la doctrina de Quihuares." In Horacio Villanueva Urteaga (ed.). 1982. *Cuzco, 1689, Informes de los párrocos al Obispo Mollinedo.* Cuzco: Centro de Estudios Rurales Andinos "Bartolomé de las Casas," 127–141.

Matienzo, Juan de. 1567. *Gobierno del Perú con todas las cosas pertenecientes a su historia.* Guillermo Lohmann Villena (ed.). 1967. Paris and Lima: Institut Français d'Etudes Andines.

Mendoza, Diego de, o.f.m. 1665. *Chronica de la Provincia de S. Antonio de los Charcas del Orden de . . . San Francisco.* Madrid. Facsimile edition, 1976. La Paz: Casa Municipal de la Cultura.

Molina, Alonso de. 1571. *Vocabulario en lengua castellana y mexicana y mexicana y castellana.* México: de Spinosa. Facsimile edition, 1970. México (D.F.): Porrua.

Molina, Cristóbal de (el Cuzqueño). 1574. *Relación de las fábulas y ritos de los yngas . . .* Biblioteca Nacional de Madrid, Manuscript 3169, ff. 2–36. Reprinted in Carlos A. Romero and Horacio Urteaga. 1916. *Colección de libros y documentos referentes a la historia del Perú,* series 1, vol. 1. Lima: Sanmarti. And in F. A. Loayza. 1943. *Las crónicas de los Molinas.* Lima: n.p., second pagination, 3–84. Edition by Henrique Urbano in Henrique Urbano and Pierre Duviols (eds.). *Fábulas y mitos de los incas.* Madrid: Historia 16, 1989, 47–134.

Molina, Diego de. 1649. "Sermones dela quaresma en lengua quechua." Manuscript, Guánuco. The manuscript, held by the Biblioteca Nacional del Perú, was partially destroyed by fire. All margins and about two inches of the upper lefthand corner were destroyed. Ink was lightened by water damage. The preface and a few excerpts were published by C. A. Romero (1928) prior to the Biblioteca Nacional fire.

Mollinedo y Angulo, Manuel de. 1699. Letter to the King, 17-i-1699. Archivo General de Indias, Lima 306. Excerpted in Julian Santisteban Ochoa. 1963. "Documentos para la historia del Cuzco existentes en el Archivo General de Indias de Sevilla." *Revista del Archivo Histórico del Cuzco* 11: 63.

Monzón, Luis de. 1586a. "Descripción de la tierra del repartimiento de Atunsora . . ." *Relaciones geográficas de Indias* 1 (1965): 220–225.

———. 1586b. "Descripción de la tierra del repartimiento de San Francisco de Atunrucana y Laramati . . ." *Relaciones geográficas de Indias* 1 (1965): 226–236.

———. 1586c. "Descripción de la tierra del repartimiento de los Rucanas Antamarcas . . ." *Relaciones geográficas de Indias* 1 (1965): 237–248.

Moscoso, Juan Manuel. 1781. Letter [to Visitador General José Antonio Areche] 13-iv. In Comité Arquidiocesano del Bicentenario Tupac Amaru (eds.). 1983. *Tupac Amaru y la Iglesia: Antología.* Lima: Banco de los Andes, 270–278.

Nebrija, Antonio de. 1492. *Gramática castellana.* Facsimile edition with an introduction by E. Walberg, 1909. Halle: Niemeyer.

Ocón de Contreras, Rodrigo Antonio (*visitador general y juez eclesiástico*). 1649. [no title; inquest into church finances in Andahuaylillas]. Archivo Arzobispal del Cuzco (portions are published in Hopkins 1983).

Oré, Luis Jerónimo de. 1598. *Symbolo cathólico indiano, en el qual se declaran los mysterios dela Fé contenidos en los tres Symbolos Cathólicos Apostólico, Niceno, y de S. Athanasio.* Lima: Antonio Ricardo.

———. 1607. *Ritual seu manuale Peruanum et forma brevis administrandi . . .* Naples (see de la Grasserie 1894).

Pachacuti Yamqui (see Santa Cruz Pachacuti Yamqui).

Pérez [de] Bocanegra, Juan de. 1631. *Ritual formulario e institución de curas para administrar a los naturales de este Reyno los Santos Sacramentos . . . por el Bachiller J.P.B., presbíterio, en la lengua Quechua general.* Lima: Geronimo de Contreras.

Piñas, Baltasar, s.i. 1585. Letter [to Claudio Aquaviva] 14-iv. In Antonio de Egaña (ed.). 1961. *Monumenta peruana,* vol. 3, 1581–1585. Rome: Monumenta Historica Societatis Iesu., 605–630.

Ramírez, Balthasar. 1597. *Description del reyno del Piru del sitio temple, prouincias, obispados, y ciudades, de los Naturales de sus lenguas y trage.* In Hermann Trimborn (ed.). 1936. *Quellen zur Kulturgeschichte des präkolumbischen Amerika.* Stuttgart: Strecker and Schröder, 10–68.

Recopilación de leyes . . . 1681. *Recopilación de leyes de los Reynos de las Indias.* Madrid: Juan de Paredes. Reprint of the fourth edition of 1791 in 1943. Madrid: Consejo de la Hispanidad.

Relaciones geográficas de Indias. 1965 [1881–1897]. Marcos Jiménez de la Espada (ed.). 4 vols. in 3. Biblioteca de Autores Españoles vol. 183–185. Madrid: Atlas.

Ribera y Chaves, Pedro de. 1586. "Relación de la Ciudad de Guamanga y sus terminos." *Relaciones geográficas de Indias* 1 (1965): 181–204.

Santa Cruz Pachacuti Yamqui, Juan de. 1615. *Relación de antigüedades deste reyno del Pirú.* Manuscript 3169, ff. 132–169. Biblioteca Nacional, Madrid.

Santo Tomás, Domingo de, o.p. 1560a. *Grammatica o arte de la lengua general de los indios de los reynos del Peru.* Valladolid: Fernández de Cordova. Facsimile edition, 1951. Lima: Universidad Nacional de San Marcos.

———. 1560b. *Lexicon o vocabulario de la lengua general.* Valladolid: Fernández de Cordova. Facsimile edition, 1951. Lima: Universidad Nacional de San Marcos.

———. n.d. "Relación del P. Fr. Domingo de Santo Tomás, al reverendo obispo D. Fr. Bartolomé de las Casas." In Luis Torres de Mendoza (ed.). 1867. *Colección de documentos inéditos relativos al descubrimiento, conquista, y organización de las antiguas posesiones españolas de América y Oceanía sacados de los archivos del Reino, y muy especialmente de las Indias*, vol. 7. Madrid: Frias, 371–387.

Solorzano Pereira, Juan de. 1647. *Política indiana*. Madrid: Díaz de la Carrera. Reprinted 1930. Madrid: Compañía Ibero-Americana.

Tercer Concilio Limense. 1583. "Decretos del Concilio de Lima del año 1583, y sumario del concilio de 1567, remitidos con una carta original por el Arzobispo de Los Reyes, Toribio Alfonso Mogrovejo a S.M. Felipe II." In Roberto Levillier (ed.). 1919. *Organización de la Iglesia y órdenes religiosas en el Virreinato del Perú en el siglo XVI, Documentos del Archivo de Indias*, vol. 2. Madrid: Rivadeneyra, 154–233.

———. 1584. *Doctrina christiana y cathecismo para instrucción de los Indios, y de las demás personas que han de ser enseñados en nuestra sancta Fé*. Lima: Antonio Ricardo.

———. 1585. *Tercero cathecismo y exposición de la doctrina christiana, por sermones*. Lima: Antonio Ricardo.

Toledo, Francisco de. 1571. "Carta a Su Magestad." Cuzco, 25-iii-1571. In Luis Antonio Eguiguren (ed.). 1951. *La universidad en el siglo xvi*, vol. 2. Lima: Universidad Nacional Mayor de San Marcos, 536.

———. 1572. "Carta a Su Magestad sobre materias referentes al gobierno eclesiastico." Cuzco, 24-ix-1572. In Roberto Levillier (ed.). 1924. *Gobernantes del Perú*, vol. 4. Madrid: Pueyo for the Biblioteca del Congreso Argentino, 404–415.

———. 1573. "Carta a Su Majestad sobre asuntos tocantes a gobierno temporal . . ." Potosí, 20-iii-1573. In Roberto Levillier (ed.). 1925. *Gobernantes del Perú*, vol. 5. Madrid: Pueyo for the Biblioteca del Congreso Argentino, 47–75.

———. 1575a. "Ordenanzas para los indios de la provincia de Charcas." Arequipa, 6-i-1575. In Roberto Levillier (ed.). 1925. *Gobernantes del Perú*, vol. 8. Madrid: Pueyo for the Biblioteca del Congreso Argentino, 304–382.

———. 1575b. "Ordenanzas estableciendo las funciones del intérprete general de los indios en las lenguas Quichua, Puquina y Aimará." Arequipa, 10-ix-1575. In Roberto Levillier (ed.). 1925. *Gobernantes del Perú*, vol. 8. Madrid: Pueyo for the Biblioteca del Congreso Argentino, 299–303.

———. 1579a. "Carta a Su Majestad sobre cosas tocantes al gobierno eclesiastico." Lima, 27-xi-1579. In Roberto Levillier (ed.). 1924. *Gobernantes del Perú*, vol. 6. Madrid: Pueyo for the Biblioteca del Congreso Argentino, 184–201.

———. 1579b. "Ordenanzas e institucion de la Catedra de la lengua de los Indios." In Luis Antonio Eguiguren (ed.). 1951. *La universidad en el siglo xvi*, vol. 2. Lima: Universidad Nacional Mayor de San Marcos, 592–598.

———. 1582. "Memorial que Don Francisco de Toledo dio al Rey." In Marqués de Pidal and Miguel Salvá (eds.). 1855. *Colección de documentos inéditos para la historia de España*, vol. 16. Madrid: Vda. de Calero.

Torres Rubio, Diego de, s.i. 1619. *Arte de lengua quichua.* Lima: Francisco Lasso.

Ulloa Mogollon, Juan de. 1586. "Relación de la provincia de los Collaguas para la discrepción de las Yndias que Su Magestad manda hacer." *Relaciones geográficas de Indias* 2 (1965): 326–333.

Vázquez, Antonio, s.i. 1637. Letter, 22-iii-1637. In Luis Antonio Eguiguren. 1940. *Diccionario histórico cronológico de la Real y Pontificia Universidad de San Marcos y sus colegios.* Lima: Imp. Torres Aguirre, 876.

Vera, Fernando de, o.s.a. 1635. Letter to the King, 1-iii-1635. Archivo General de Indias, Lima 305. Summary in Julian Santisteban Ochoa. 1963. "Documentos para la historia del Cuzco existentes en el Archivo General de Indias de Sevilla." *Revista del Archivo Histórico del Cuzco* 11: 27–28.

Zúñiga, Antonio de, o.f.m. 1579. "Carta de Fray Antonio de Zúñiga al Rey Don Felipe II, 15-vii-1579." In Marqués de Pidal and Miguel Salvá (ed.). 1855. *Colección de documentos inéditos para la historia de España* 26. Madrid, Vda. de Calero, 87–121.

Modern and Theoretical

Acosta, Antonio. 1987. "Francisco de Avila, Cusco 1573(?)–Lima 1647." In Gerald Taylor (ed.). *Ritos y tradiciones de Huarochirí del siglo xvii.* Lima: Instituto de Estudios Peruanos and the Institut Français d'Etudes Andines, 551–616.

Adams, Stewart I. 1976. *The Emergence of a Quechua Subculture in the City of Arequipa as a Result of the Phenomenon of Internal Migration from Rural Areas within Peru.* Saint Andrews: Center for Latin American Studies, University of Saint Andrews, Working Paper 5.

———. 1979. "Los urbanizadores de Arequipa." Doctoral dissertation in Latin American Linguistic Studies, University of Saint Andrews.

Adamson, Walter. 1980. *Hegemony and Revolution, A Study of Antonio Gramsci's Political and Cultural Theory.* Berkeley: University of California Press.

Adelaar, Willem F. H. 1979. "De Dialectologie van het Quechua." *Forum der Lettern* 20: 477–496.

———. 1982. "Incidental Changes in the Suffix Part of Quechua Verbs." *Lingua* 56: 59–73.

———. 1984. "The Significance of Grammatical Processes Involving Vowel Lengthening for the Classification of Quechua Dialects." *International Journal of American Linguistics* 50: 25–47.

———. 1986. "La relación quechua-aru: Perspectivas para la separación del léxico." *Revista Andina* 4: 379–426.

———. 1987. "La relación quechua-aru en debate." *Revista Andina* 5: 83–91.

Adorno, Rolena. 1978. "Felipe Guaman Poma de Ayala: An Andean View of the Peruvian Viceroyalty." *Journal de la Société des Américanistes* 65: 121–143.

———. 1980. "The *Nueva corónica y buen gobierno:* A New Look at the Royal Library's Peruvian Treasure." *Fund og Forskning* (Copenhagen) 24: 7–28.

———. 1986. *Guaman Poma, Writing and Resistance in Colonial Peru.* Austin: University of Texas Press.

Alberti, Giorgio, and Enrique Mayer. 1974. "Reciprocidad andina: ayer y hoy." In

Reciprocidad e intercambio en los Andes peruanos. Lima: Instituto de Estudios Peruanos, 13–33.

Albó, Xavier, s.i. 1970. "Social Constraints on Cochabamba Quechua." Doctoral dissertation in anthropology, Cornell University.

———. 1973. *El futuro de los idiomas oprimidos en los Andes.* La Paz: Centro de Investigación y Promoción del Campesinado.

———. 1974. *Los mil rostros del quechua.* Lima: Instituto de Estudios Peruanos.

———. 1987. "Problemática lingüística y metalingüística de un alfabeto quechua: Una reciente experiencia boliviana." *Allpanchis Phuturinqa* 29/30: 431–468.

Alegría, Ciro, José María Arguedas, et al. 1969. *Primer encuentro de narradores peruanos, Arequipa 1965.* Lima: Casa de la Cultura.

Alencastre Gutiérrez, Andrés. n.d. *Yawar para.* Cuzco: Garcilaso.

Allen, Catherine J. [as Catherine A. Wagner]. 1976. "La coca y la estructura cultural en la sierra del Perú." *Allpanchis Phuturinqa* 9: 193–223.

——— [as Catherine A. Wagner]. 1978. "Coca, Chicha, and Trago." Doctoral dissertation, University of Illinois.

———. 1981. To Be Quechua: The Symbolism of Coca Chewing in Highland Peru." *American Ethnologist* 8: 157–171.

———. 1988. *The Hold Life Has.* Washington, D.C.: Smithsonian Institution Press.

Alonso, Amado. 1955. *De la pronunciación medieval a la moderna en español.* Madrid: Gredos.

Andersen, Henning. 1980. "Morphological Change: Towards a Typology." In Jacek Fisiak (ed.). *Historical Morphology.* The Hague: Mouton, 1–48.

Anderson, Arthur J. O., Frances Berdan, and James Lockhart. 1976. *Beyond the Codices.* Los Angeles: University of California Press.

Anderson, Perry. 1976. The Antinomies of Antonio Gramsci." *New Left Review* 100: 5–78.

Angeles Caballero, César Augusto. 1987. *La gramática quechua de Juan de Aguilar.* Lima: San Marcos.

Angulo, Domingo, o.p. 1925. "El cedulario arzobispal de la Arquidiocesis de Lima: 1533–1820" (part 2). *Revista del Archivo Nacional del Perú* 3: 219–254.

Anttila, Raimo. 1977a. "Toward a Semiotic Analysis of Expressive Vocabulary." *Semiosis* 5: 27–40.

———. 1977b. *Analogy.* The Hague: Mouton.

Arguedas, José María. 1941. *Yawar fiesta.* Buenos Aires: Losada. English translation (tr. Frances Horning Barraclough) 1986. *Yawar Fiesta.* Austin: University of Texas Press.

———. 1958. *Los ríos profundos.* In 1983. *Obras completas,* vol. 3. Lima: Horizante, 9–213; English translation (tr. Frances Horning Barraclough) 1982. *Deep Rivers.* Austin: University of Texas Press.

———. 1964. "Puquio, una cultura en proceso de cambio." In *Estudios sobre la cultura actual del Perú.* Lima: Universidad Nacional de San Marcos, 221–272.

———. 1966. "Introducción" to José María Arguedas, Pierre Duviols, and Karen Spalding (eds.). 1966. *Dioses y hombres de Huarochirí.* Lima: Instituto de Estudios Peruanos, 9–15.

———. 1967. "Mitos quechuas pos-hispánicos." *Amaru* 3: 14–18.
———. 1968. "No soy un aculturado." In *El zorro de arriba y el zorro de abajo.* Buenos Aires: Losada.
———. 1972. *Katatay huc jayllicunapas.* Reprinted in 1983. *Obras completas,* vol. 5. Lima: Horizonte.
Aristotle. n.d. *On the Art of Poetry* (tr. Ingram Bywater). Oxford: University Press.
Asensio, Eugenio. 1960. "La lengua compañera del imperio, historia de una idea de Nebrija en España y Portugal." *Revista de Filología Española* 43: 399–413.
Baciero, Carlos. 1986. "La promoción y evangelización del Indio en el plan de José de Acosta." In Luciano Pereña (ed.). *Doctrina cristiana y catecismo para instrucción de los Indios, Introducción del genocidio a la promoción del Indio.* Madrid: Consejo Superior de Investigaciones Científicas, 163–226.
Bareiro Saquier, Rubén. 1975. "Expresión de grupo dominante y dominado en el bilingüismo paraguayo." *Actas del 39 Congreso Internacional de Americanistas* 5: 289–295.
Barnadas, Josep M. 1973. *Charcas, orígenes históricos de una sociedad colonial.* La Paz: Centro de Investigación y Promoción del Campesinado.
Bartra, Enrique. 1967. "Los autores del catecismo del Tercer Concilio Limense." *Mercurio Peruano* 52(470): 359–372.
Becker, Alton L. 1982. "The Poetics and Noetics of a Javanese Poem." In Deborah Tannen (ed.). *Spoken and Written Language.* Norwood: Ablex, 217–238.
Bendezú Aibar, Edmundo. 1978. "El mito de wiraqocha en un himno de Sallqamaywa." *Actas del IV Congreso Internacional de la Associación de Lingüística y Filología de America Latina,* 221–228.
Benveniste, Emile. 1939. "Nature du signe linguistique." *Acta Linguistica Hafniensia* 1: 23–29. Reprinted in 1966. *Problèmes de linguistique générale.* Paris: Gallimard.
Beyersdorf, Margot. 1986. "La tradición oral quechua vista desde la perspectiva de la literatura." *Revista Andina* 4: 213–236.
Bird, Robert McK. 1984. "The Chupachu/Serrano Cultural Boundary—Multifaceted and Stable." In David L. Browman, Richard L. Burger, and Mario A. Rivera. *Social and Economic Organization in the Prehispanic Andes.* Oxford: BAR, 79–95.
Bird, Robert McK., David L. Browman, and Marshall Durbin. 1984. "Quechua and Maize: Mirrors of Andean Culture History." *Journal of the Steward Anthropological Society* 15: 187–240.
Bloomfield, Leonard. 1933a. *Language.* New York: Holt, Rinehart, and Winston.
———. 1933b. "The Structure of Learned Words." In *A Commemorative Volume Issued by the Institute for Research in English Teaching.* Tokyo: Institute for Research in English Teaching, 17–23.
———. 1946. "Algonquin." In Harry Hoijer (ed.). *Linguistic Structures of Native America.* New York: Wenner-Gren Foundation for Anthropological Research, Viking Fund Publications in Anthropology 6, 85–129.
Boas, Franz. 1938. "Language." In *General Anthropology.* Boston: Heath, 124–145.
Bolinger, Dwight. 1940. "Word Affinities." *American Speech* 15: 62–73.
Boothroyd, Margaret. 1979. "Patterns of Orthography Use in Community-based

Quechua Literature." Master's thesis in Latin American linguistic studies, University of Saint Andrews.

Borges Morán, Pedro. 1986. "Evangelización y civilización en América." In Luciano Pereña (ed.). *Doctrina cristiana y catecismo para instrucción de los Indios: Introducción del genocidio a la promoción del Indio.* Madrid: Consejo Superior de Investigaciones Científicas, 163–226.

Bourdieu, Pierre. 1982. *Ce que parler veut dire: L'économie des échanges linguistiques.* Paris: Fayard.

Bouysse-Cassagne, Thérèse. 1976. "Tributo y etnias en Charcas en la epoca del Virrey Toledo." *Historia y Cultura* (La Paz) 2: 97–114.

———. 1977. "Pertenencia étnica, status económico y lenguas en Charcas a fines del siglo xvii." In N. David Cook (ed.). *Tasa de la Visita General de Francisco de Toledo.* Lima: Universidad Nacional de San Marcos, 312–328.

———. [with Philipe Bouysse]. 1988. *Lluvias y cenizas, dos pachacuti en la historia.* La Paz: Hisbol.

Braudel, Fernand. 1958. "Histoire et sciences sociales: La longue durée." *Annales: Economies, Sociétés, Civilisations* 13: 725–753.

Briggs, Lucy. 1976. "Dialectal Variation in the Aymara Language of Bolivia and Peru." Doctoral dissertation in anthropology, University of Florida, Gainesville.

Bright, William. 1970. "On Linguistic Unrelatedness." *International Journal of American Linguistics* 36: 288–290.

Buchwald, Otto von. 1919. "Tiahuanaco y Cuzco." *Boletín de la Sociedad Ecuatoriana de Estudios Históricos Americanos* 1: 105–108.

Bybee, Joan. 1985. "Diagrammatic Iconicity in Stem-inflection Relations." In John Haiman (ed.). *Iconicity in Syntax.* Amsterdam: Benjamins, 11–47.

Cáceres, B. 1978. "La coca, el mundo andino y los extirpadores de idolatrías del siglo xx." *América Indígena* 38: 769–785.

Campbell, Lyle. 1976. "Language Contact and Sound Change." In William Christie (ed.). *Current Progress in Historical Linguistics.* Amsterdam: North Holland, 181–194.

Cancian, Frank. 1979. *The Innovator's Situation.* Stanford: Stanford University Press.

Canfield, D. Lincoln. 1952. "Spanish American Data for the Chronology of Sibilant Changes." *Hispania* 35: 25–30.

Cardenas Ayaipoma, Mario. 1977. "El Colegio de Caciques y el sometimiento ideológico de los residuos de la nobleza aborigen." *Revista del Archivo General de la Nación* 4/5: 5–24.

Carenko, E. I. 1972. "O laringalizačii v jazyke kečua." *Voprosy jazykoznanija* 6(1): 97–103. English translation 1975. "On Laryngealization in Quechua." *Linguistics* 146: 5–14.

Carvalho-Neto, Paulo de. 1966. *Cuentos folklóricos del Ecuador.* Quito: Editorial Universitaria.

Castillo Arroyo, J. 1966. *Catecismos peruanos en el siglo xvi.* Cuernavaca: Centro Intercultural de Documentación.

Castro, José Gregorio, o.f.m. 1906. *Texto y catecismo de la doctrina cristiana en*

Keshua. Cuzco: Americana. 3rd edition 1961. *Catecismo de la doctrina cristiana en Kechua*. Cuzco: Archdiocese of Cuzco.

Castro Pineda, Lucio. 1963. "La cátedra de lengua quechua en la Catedral de Lima." *Nueva Corónica* 1: 136–147.

Catalán, Diego. 1957. "The End of the Phoneme / z / in Spanish." *Word* 13: 283–322.

Cerrón-Palomino, Rodolfo M. 1969. "Wanka Kechua Morphology." Master's thesis in linguistics, Cornell University.

———. 1974. "Morphologically Conditioned Changes in Wanka-Quechua." *Studies in the Linguistic Sciences* 4(2): 40–75.

———. 1975. "La 'motosidad' y sus implicancias en el enseñanza del Castellano." In Martín Quintana Chaupín and Danilo Sánchez Lihón (eds.). *Aportes para la enseñanza del lenguaje*. Lima: Retablo de Papel, 125–165.

———. 1976a. *Gramática Quechua: Junín-Huanca*. Lima: Ministerio de Educación y Instituto de Estudios Peruanos.

———. 1976b. *Diccionario Quechua: Junín-Huanca*. Lima: Ministerio de Educación y Instituto de Estudios Peruanos.

———. 1977. "Huanca Quechua Dialectology." Doctoral dissertation in linguistics, University of Illinois, Urbana.

———. 1979. "La primera persona posesora-actora del protoquechua." *Lexis* 3: 1–40.

———. 1980. "El quechua: Una mirada de conjunto." Universidad Nacional de San Marcos, Centro de Investigación de Lingüística Aplicada, Documento de Trabajo No. 42.

———. 1981. "Aprender castellano en un contexto plurilingüe." *Lexis* 5: 39–51.

———. 1982. "El problema de la relación Quechua-Aru: Estado actual." *Lexis* 6: 213–242.

———. 1983. "La cuestión lingüística en el Perú." In *Aula quechua*. Lima: Ediciones Signo, 105–123.

———. 1984. "La reconstrucción del proto-Quechua." *Revista Andina* 2: 89–120.

———. 1986. "Comentario [on] Willem F. H. Adelaar, 'La relación quechua-aru: Perspectivas para la separación del léxico.'" *Revista Andina* 4: 403–408.

———. 1987a. *Lingüística quechua*. Cuzco: Centro de Estudios Rurales Andinos "Bartolomé de las Casas."

———. 1987b. "La flexión de persona y número en el Proto-Quechua." *Language Sciences* 9: 77–89.

———. 1987c. "Unidad y diferenciación lingüística en el mundo andino." *Lexis* 11: 71–104.

Certeau, Michel de. 1981. "Croire: Une pratique de la différence." Translated as "What We Do When We Believe." In Marshall Blonsky (ed.). 1985. *On Signs*. Baltimore: Johns Hopkins University Press, 192–202.

Chen, Matthew Y. 1972. "The Time Dimension: Contribution toward a Theory of Sound Change." *Foundations of Language* 8: 457–498.

Chen, Matthew Y., and William S.-Y. Wang. 1975. "Sound Change: Actuation and Implementation." *Language* 51: 255–281.

Cherry, E. Colin. 1957. *On Human Communication*. Cambridge: MIT Press.

Cisneros, Luis Jaime. 1951. "La primera gramática de la lengua general del Perú." *Boletín del Instituto Riva-Agüero* 1: 197–264.

———. 1965. "Datos fonéticos en los cronistas." *Documenta* (Lima) 4: 338–344.

Colin, Michele. 1966. *Le Cuzco à la fin du xvii*ᵉ *et au début du xviii*ᵉ *siècle.* Caen: Université de Caen.

Condero, Luis Agustín. 1979. *Incunables peruanos y estudios bibliográficos.* Lima: Seminario de Historia Rural Andina of the Universidad Nacional de San Marcos.

Condori Mamani, Gregorio. 1977. *Autobiografía* (ed. and tr. Ricardo Valderrama Fernández and Carmen Escalante Gutiérrez). Cuzco: Centro de Estudios Rurales Andinos "Bartolomé de las Casas."

Cook, N. David. 1977. "Introducción" [to] *Tasa de la Visita General de Francisco de Toledo.* Lima: Universidad Nacional de San Marcos, ix–xxvii.

Cosio, José Gabriel. 1941. "El drama quechua *Ollantay:* El manuscrito de Santo Domingo del Cuzco." *Revista Universitaria* 81: 3–26.

Cotler, Julio. 1968. "La mecánica de la dominación interna y el cambio social en el Perú." In José Matos Mar (ed.). 1970. *El Perú actual (sociedad y política).* México (D.F.): Universidad Nacional Autónoma de México, 47–87.

Créqui-Montfort, Georges de, and Paul Rivet. 1925. "La langue uru ou pukina." *Journal de la Société des Américanistes* 17: 217–244.

Cusihuamán Gutiérrez, Antonio. 1976a. *Gramática Quechua: Cuzco-Collao.* Lima: Instituto de Estudios Peruanos.

———. 1976b. *Diccionario Quechua: Cuzco-Collao.* Lima: Instituto de Estudios Peruanos.

Custred, Glynn. 1974. "Llameros y trueque de alimentos." In Giorgio Alberti and Enrique Mayer (eds.). *Reciprocidad e intercambio en los Andes peruanos.* Lima: Instituto de Estudios Peruanos, 252–289.

———. 1977a. "Peasant Kinship, Subsistence, and Economics in a High Altitude Andean Environment." In Ralph Bolton and Enrique Mayer (ed.). *Andean Kinship and Marriage.* Washington, D.C.: American Anthropological Association, 117–135.

———. 1977b. "Las punas de los Andes centrales." In Jorge A. Flores Ochoa (ed.). *Uywamichiq punarunakuna: Pastores de puna.* Lima: Instituto de Estudios Peruanos, 55–86.

———. 1979. "Symbols and Control in a High Altitude Andean Community." *Anthropos* 74: 379–392.

———. 1980. "The Place of Ritual in Andean Rural Society." In Benjamin S. Orlove and Glynn Custred (ed.). *Land and Power in Latin America.* New York: Holmes and Meier, 195–210.

Davidson, Joseph O. Jr. 1977. "A Contrastive Study of the Grammatical Structures of Aymara and Cuzco Quechua." Doctoral dissertation, University of California, Berkeley.

———. 1979. "On the Genetic Relationship of Aymara and Quechua." Unpublished paper presented to the 43rd International Congress of Americanists.

DeCamp, David. 1971. "Analysis of a Post-Creole Speech Continuum." In Dell Hymes (ed.). *Pidginization and Creolization of Language.* Cambridge: Cambridge University Press, 349–370.

———. 1972. "Hypercorrection and Rule Generalization." *Language in Society* 1: 87–90.
———. 1973. "What Do Implicational Scales Imply?" In Charles-James Bailey and Roger W. Shuy (eds.). *New Ways of Analyzing Variation in English.* Washington, D.C.: Georgetown University Press, 141–148.
Denegri Luna, Félix. 1980. "Prólogo" to Diego de Esquivel y Navia, *Noticias cronológicas de la gran ciudad del Cuzco (1753).* Lima: Fundación Wiesse, ix–lx.
Dent, Laurel Jane. 1981. "Laryngeal Control in the Production of Three Classes of Voiceless Stops, with Occasional Reference to Bolivian Quechua." Doctoral dissertation in linguistics, University of Pennsylvania.
Diebold, A. Richard. 1961. "Incipient Bilingualism." *Language* 37: 97–112. Reprinted in Dell Hymes (ed.). 1965. *Language in Culture and Society.* New York: Harper and Row, 495–508.
Diffloth, Gérard. 1976. "Expressives in Semai." In Philip N. Jenner, Laurence C. Thompson, and Stanley Starosta (eds.). *Austroasiatic studies* (part 1). Honolulu: University Press of Hawaii, 250–264.
Dimock, Edward C. 1957. "Symbolic Forms in Bengali." *Bulletin of the Deccan College Research Institute* 18: 22–29.
Dressler, Wolfgang U. 1982. "A Semiotic Model of Diachronic Process Phonology." In Winifred P. Lehmann and Yakov Malkiel (eds.). *Perspectives on Historical Linguistics.* Philadelphia: Benjamins, 93–131.
Dumézil, Georges. 1955. "Catégories et vocabulaire des échanges de service chez les Indiens quechua: Ayni et mink'a." *Journal de la Société des Américanistes* 44: 1–16.
———. 1957. "Le bon pasteur: Sermon de Francisco Davila aux Indians du Pérou (1646)." *Diogène* 20: 84–102.
Durán Jáuaregui, Juan Guillermo. 1982. *El catecismo del Tercer Concilio Provincial de Lima y sus complementos pastorales (1584–1585).* Buenos Aires: Facultad de Teología, Universidad Católica de Argentina.
Duviols, Pierre. 1966. "Estudio biobibliográfico de Francisco de Avila." In José María Arguedas, Pierre Duviols, and Karen Spalding (eds.). 1966. *Dioses y hombres de Huarochirí.* Lima: Instituto de Estudios Peruanos, 230–237.
———. 1971. *La lutte contre les religions autochtones dans le Pérou colonial, L'extirpation de l'idolatrie entre 1532 et 1660.* Lima: Institut Français d'Etudes Andines.
———. 1973. "Huari y llacuaz." *Revista del Museo Nacional* 39: 153–187.
Earls, John. 1969. "The Organisation of Power in Quechua Mythology." *Journal of the Steward Anthropological Society* 1: 63–82.
Earls, John, and Irene Silverblatt. 1977. "Ayllus y etnias de la region Pampas-Qaracha: El impacto del imperio Incaico." In *Tercer Congreso Peruano del Hombre y la Cultura Andina, Actas y Trabajos* 1, Lima, 157–177.
Eckert, Penelope. 1980. "The Structure of a Long-Term Phonological Process." In William A. Labov (ed.). *Locating Language in Time and Space.* New York: Academic Press, 179–220.
Eguiguren, Luis Antonio. 1940. *Diccionario histórico cronológico de la Real y Pontificia Universidad de San Marcos y sus colegios.* Lima: Imp. Torres Aguirre.

———. 1951. *La universidad en el siglo xvi.* 2 vols. Lima: Universidad Nacional Mayor de San Marcos.

Empson, William. 1930. *Seven Types of Ambiguity.* 3rd edition, 1947. New York: New Directions.

Escobar, Alberto. 1972. "Lingüística y política." In Alberto Escobar (ed.). *El reto del multilingüismo en el Perú.* Lima: Instituto de Estudios Peruanos, 15–34.

Escobar, Alberto, José Matos Mar, and Giorgio Alberti. 1975. *Perú: ¿País bilingüe?* Lima: Instituto de Estudios Peruanos.

Escobar, Gloria, and Gabriel Escobar. 1981. *Huaynos del Cusco.* Cuzco: Garcilaso.

Escribens, Augusto, and Paul Proulx. 1970. *Gramática del quechua de Huaylas.* Lima, Universidad Nacional de San Marcos.

Espinoza Soriano, Waldemar. 1974. "El habitat de la etnía pinagua, siglos xv y xvi." *Revista del Museo Nacional* 40: 157–220.

———. 1983. "Los fundamentos lingüísticos de la etnohistoria andina y comentarios en torno al anónimo de Charcas de 1604." In Rodolfo Cerrón-Palomino (ed.). *Aula quechua.* Lima: Signo Universitario, 163–202.

Esquivel Villafana, Jorge. 1979. "Procesos de asimilación fonética en las vocales del Quechua de Huancavelica." In Gustavo Solis Fonseca and Jorge Esquivel Villafana. "El fonema postvelar quechua y sus efectos coarticulatorios." Documento de Trabajo, Centro de Investigación de Lingüística Aplicada, Universidad Nacional de San Marcos, Lima.

Farfán Ayerbe, José M. B. 1954. "Cronología Quechua—Aymará según el cálculo estadístico." *Revista del Museo Nacional* 23: 50–55.

Favre, Henri. 1967. "Evolución y situación de la hacienda tradicional de la región de Huancavélica." *Revista del Museo Nacional* 33. Reprinted in José Matos Mar (ed.). 1976. *Hacienda, comunidad y campesinado en el Perú.* Lima: Instituto de Estudios Peruanos, 105–138.

———. 1987. Unpublished lecture on the *Pistaco* in Huancavélica, Peru. Annual Meeting of the Latin American Indian Literatures Association, Ithaca, New York, June.

Ferrario, Benigno. 1956. "La dialettologia ed i problemi interni della Runa-simi (vulgo Quéchua)." *Orbis* 5: 131–140.

Firth, J. R. 1935. "The Use and Distribution of Certain English Sounds." *English Studies* 17. Reprinted in 1957. *Papers in Linguistics, 1934–1951.* Oxford: Oxford University Press, 34–46.

Flores Ochoa, Jorge A. 1968. *Los pastores de Paratía.* México (D.F.): Instituto Indigenista Interamericana. Translated 1979. *Pastoralists of the Andes.* Philadelphia: ISHI.

———. 1974. "Mistis and Indians: Their Relations in a Microregion of Cuzco." *International Journal of Comparative Sociology* 5(3): 182–192.

Friedrich, Paul. 1971. "Dialectal Variation in Tarascan Phonology." *International Journal of American Linguistics* 37: 164–187.

———. 1979a. "The Symbol and Its Relative Non-arbitrariness." In *Language, Context, and the Imagination.* Stanford: Stanford University Press, 1–61.

———. 1979b. *Language, Context and the Imagination.* Stanford: Stanford University Press.

Galante, Hyppolitus (see Anonymous, Huarochirí; Anonymous, *Ollanta;* Jurado Palomino)

Galdo Gutiérrez, Virgilio. 1970. "Colegios de curacas: Frente a dos mundos." *Educación* (Lima) 3: 30–38.

Galdos Rodríguez, Guillermo. 1987. *Comunidades prehispánicas de Arequipa.* Arequipa: Fundación Bustamante de la Fuente.

García y García, Antonio. 1986. "La reforma del Concilio Tercero de Lima." In Luciano Pereña (ed.). *Doctrina cristiana y catecismo para instrucción de los Indios, Introducción: Del genocidio a la promoción del Indio.* Madrid: Consejo Superior de Investigaciones Científicas, 163–226.

Gelles H., Paul. 1988. *Los hijos de Hualca Hualca, historia de Cabanaconde.* Arequipa: Centro de Apoyo y Promoción al Desarrollo Agrario.

Ghersi, Humberto, and José Arquinio. 1966. "Taraco." In *Sociedad, cultura y economía en 10 areas andino-peruanas.* Lima: Ministerio de Trabajo y Comunidades.

Gibbs, Donald L. 1979. "Cuzco, 1680–1710: An Andean City Seen through Its Economic Activities." Doctoral dissertation in history, University of Texas at Austin.

Glave, Luis Miguel. 1987. "Comunidades campesinas en el sur andino, siglo xvii." In *Comunidades campesinos: Cambios y permanencias.* Lima: CONCYTEC and Chiclayo: Centro Solidaridad, 61–94.

Gobierno Revolucionario de las Fuerzas Armadas. 1975. "Kay qelqawanmi noqanchisman kutirinchis." *Cronicawan,* 3 June.

Goddard, Ives, III. 1975. "Algonquian, Wiyot and Yurok: Proving a Distant Genetic Relationship." In M. Dale Kinkade, Kenneth L. Hale, and Oswald Werner (eds.). *Linguistics and Anthropology: In Honor of Carl F. Voegelin.* Lisse: de Ridder, 249–262.

Golte, Jürgen. 1973. "El concepto de *sonqo* en el *runa simi* del siglo XVI." *Indiana* 1: 213–218.

Gose, Peter. 1986. "Sacrifice and the Commodity Form in the Andes." *Man* 21: 296–310.

Gramsci, Antonio. 1971 [1929–1935]. *Selections from the Prison Notebooks* (ed. and tr. Quintin Hoare and Geoffrey Nowell Smith). New York: International.

———. 1985 [1929–1935]. *Selections from Cultural Writings* (ed. David Forgacs and Geoffrey Nowell Smith; tr. William Boelhower). Cambridge: Harvard University Press.

Grasserie, Raoul de la. 1894. *Langues américaines, Langue puquina, Textes puquina contenues dans le* Rituale seu Manuele Peruanum *de Geronimo de Oré.* Paris: Maisonneuve.

Greenberg, Joseph H. 1963. "Some Universals of Grammar with Particular Reference to the Order of Meaningful Elements." In Joseph Greenberg (ed.). *Universals of Language.* Cambridge: MIT Press, 73–113.

———. 1970a. "The Role of Typology in the Development of a Scientific Linguistics." In L. Dezsö and P. Hajdú (eds.). *Theoretical Problems of Typology and the Northern Eurasian Languages.* Budapest: Akadémiai Kiadó, 11–24.

———. 1970b. "Some Generalizations concerning Glottalic Consonants Es-

pecially Implosives." *International Journal of American Linguistics* 36: 123–146.
———. 1987. *Language in the Americas.* Stanford: Stanford University Press.
Grimm, Juan M. 1897. *La lengua quichua (dialectos de la República del Ecuador).* Freiburg: Herder.
Guillet, David. 1979. *Agrarian Reform and Peasant Economy in Southern Peru.* Columbia: University of Missouri Press.
Gumperz, John. 1958. "Dialect Differences and Social Stratification in a North Indian Village." *American Anthropologist* 60: 668–681.
———. 1967. "On the Linguistic Markers of Bilingual Communication." *Journal of Social Issues* 23(2): 48–57.
Gumperz, John, and Robert Wilson. 1971. "Convergence and Creolization." In Dell Hymes (ed.). *Pidginization and Creolization of Languages.* Cambridge: Cambridge University Press, 151–167.
Haas, Mary R. 1966. "Historical Linguistics and the Genetic Relationship of Languages." *Current Trends in Linguistics* 3: 113–154. Reprinted in 1978. *Language, Culture, and History.* Stanford: Stanford University Press, 220–281.
Haiman, John. 1985. *Natural Syntax: Iconicity and Erosion.* Cambridge: Cambridge University Press.
Hardman-de-Bautista, Martha J. 1964. "Discussion." *Proceedings of the Ninth International Congress of Linguists,* 391.
———. 1966a. *Jaqaru: Outline of Phonological and Morphological Structure.* The Hague: Mouton.
———. 1966b. "El Jaqaru, el Kawki y el Aymara." *El simposio de Montevideo* (= *ALFAL* 1: 186–192) (appeared in 1975).
———. 1976. "Proto-Jaqi: Reconstrucción del sistema de personas gramaticales." *Revista de Museo Nacional* 41: 433–456.
———. 1978. "Jaqi: The Linguistic Family." *International Journal of American Linguistics* 44: 146–153.
———. 1985. "Quechua and Aymara: Languages in Contact." In Harriet E. Manelis Klein and Louisa R. Stark (eds.). *South American Indian Languages: Retrospect and Prospect.* Austin: University of Texas Press, 617–643.
Hardman-de-Bautista, Martha J., Juana Vásquez, and Juan de Dios Yapita Moya. 1974. *Outline of Aymara Phonological and Grammatical Structure.* Gainesville: Department of Anthropology, University of Florida. [Available from University Microfilms, Ann Arbor, MI 48106, as LD00175.]
Harrell, Richard S. 1957. *The Phonology of Colloquial Egyptian Arabic.* New York: American Council of Learned Societies.
Harrington, John P. 1943. "Hokan Discovered in South America." *Journal of the Washington Academy of Sciences* 33 (11): 334–344.
Harris, James W. 1969. *Spanish Phonology.* Cambridge: MIT Press.
Harrison, Regina. 1982. "Modes of Discourse: The *Relación de antigüedades deste reyno del Piru,* by Joan de Santacruz Pachacuti Yamqui Salcamaygua." In Rolena Adorno (ed.). *From Oral to Written Expression: Native Andean Chronicles of the Early Colonial Period.* Syracuse: Syracuse University Foreign and Comparative Studies Program, 65–99.

Hartmann, Roswith. 1972. "Linguistik im Andengebiet: Geschichte und Stand der Quechuaforschung." *Zeitschrift fur Lateinamerika* (Wien) 4: 97–131.

———. 1975. "En torno a las ediciones más recientes de los textos quechuas recogidos por Francisco de Avila." *Atti del XL Congresso Internazionale degli Americanisti* 3: 31–42.

———. 1979. "¿'Quechuismo preincaico' en Ecuador?" *Ibero-Amerikanisches Archiv* (n.s.) 5 (3): 267–299.

———. 1981. "El texto quechua de Huarochirí—Una evaluación crítica de las ediciones a disposición." *Histórica* 5: 167–208.

Harvey, Penelope. 1987. "Lenguaje y relaciones de poder: Consecuencias para una política lingüística." *Allpanchis Phuturinqa* 29/30: 105–131.

———. 1990. "Drunken Speech and the Construction of Meaning." *Language in Society* (forthcoming).

Haugen, Einar. 1971. "The Ecology of Language." In 1972. *The Ecology of Language, Essays by Einar Haugen.* Stanford: Stanford University Press, 325–339.

Heath, Shirley Brice. 1972. *Telling Tongues.* New York: Teachers College Press.

———. 1976. "Colonial Language Status Achievement: Mexico, Peru, and the United States." In A. Verdoodt and R. Kjolseth (eds.). *Language in Sociology.* Louvain: Peeters, 49–91.

Heath, Shirley Brice, and Richard LaPrade. 1982. "Castilian Colonization and Indigenous Languages: The Cases of Quechua and Aymara." In R. L. Cooper (ed.). *Language Spread.* Bloomington: Indiana University Press.

Hock, Hans Heinrich. 1986. *Principles of Historical Linguistics.* Berlin: Mouton de Gruyter.

Hockett, Charles F. 1960. "Logical Considerations in the Study of Animal Communication." In W. E. Lanyon and W. N. Tavolga (eds.). *Animal Sounds and Communications.* Washington, D.C.: American Institute of Biological Sciences, 392–430.

———. 1965. "Sound Change." *Language* 41: 185–204.

Hoenigswald, Henry M. 1964. "Graduality, Sporadicity, and the Minor Sound Change Processes." *Phonetica* 11: 202–215.

———. 1978. "The *Annus Mirabilis* of 1876 and Posterity." *Transactions of the Philological Society:* 17–35.

Hoggarth, Pauline. 1973. "Bilingualism in Calca, Department of Cuzco, Peru." Doctoral dissertation in Latin American linguistic studies, University of Saint Andrews.

Hopkins, Diane E. 1977. "'No estemos entre perros y gatos en un ayllo solo': El común del ayllu de Lurucachi contra su Cacique, Don Santos Mamani, 1779–1780." Manuscript.

———. 1982. "The Inka of Andahuaylillas: Power and Authority in Quechua Culture." Paper presented to the 44th International Congress of Americanists, Manchester, U.K.

———. 1983. "The Colonial History of the Hacienda System in a Southern Peruvian Highland District." Doctoral dissertation in development sociology, Cornell University.

———. 1985. "The Peruvian Agrarian Reform: Dissent from Below." *Human Organization* 44: 18–32.

———. 1988. "Ritual, Sodality, and Cargo among Indigenous Andean Women, A Diachronic Perspective." In Diane E. Hopkins and Albert Meyers (eds.). *Manipulating the Saints: Religious Sodalities and Social Integration in Post-conquest Latin America.* Hamburg: Wayasbah, 175–195.

Hornberger, Nancy. 1987. "Bilingual Education Success, But Policy Failure." *Language in Society* 16: 205–226.

Husson, Jean-Philippe. 1985. *La poesie quechua dans la chronique de Felipe Waman Puma de Ayala: de l'art lyrique de cour aux chants et danses populaires.* Paris: L'Harmattan.

Hymes, Dell H. 1955. "Positional Analysis of Categories: A Frame for Reconstruction." *Word* 11: 10–23.

———. 1970. "Linguistic Method in Ethnography." In 1983. *Essays in the History of Linguistic Anthropology.* Philadelphia: Benjamins.

———. 1973. "Speech and Language: On the Origins and Foundations of Inequality among Speakers." *Daedelus* 102 (3): 59–85.

———. 1974. "Ways of Speaking." In Richard Bauman and Joel Sherzer (eds.). *Explorations in the Ethnography of Speaking.* Cambridge: Cambridge University Press, 433–451.

Isbell, Billie Jean. 1978. *To Defend Ourselves.* Austin: University of Texas Press.

Isbell, William H. 1974. "Ecología de la expansión de los quechua hablantes." *Revista del Museo Nacional* 40: 141–155.

Jackson, Jean. 1974. "Language Identity of the Colombian Vaupés Indians." In Richard Bauman and Joel Sherzer (eds.). *Explorations in the Ethnography of Speaking.* Cambridge: Cambridge University Press, pp. 50–64.

Jakobson, Roman. 1929. *Remarques sur l'évolution phonologique du russe comparée à celle des autres langues slaves.* Travaux du Cercle Linguistique de Prague 2. Prague: Cercle Linguistique.

———. 1941. *Kindersprache, Aphasie und allgemeine Lautgesetze.* Uppsala. Reprinted in 1962. *Selected Writings, Volume 1: Phonological Studies.* The Hague: Mouton, 328–401; English translation (tr. A. R. Keiler). 1968. *Child Language, Aphasia and Phonological Universals.* The Hague: Mouton.

———. 1959. "Boas' View of Grammatical Meaning." In W. Goldschmidt (ed.). *The Anthropology of Franz Boas.* Memoirs of the American Anthropological Association 80. Washington, D.C.: American Anthropological Association, 139–145.

———. 1963. "Implications of Language Universals for Linguistics." In Joseph Greenberg (ed.). *Universals of Language.* Cambridge: MIT Press, 208–219.

———. 1965. "Quest for the Essence of Language." *Diogenes* 51: 21–37. Reprinted in 1987. *Language in Literature.* Cambridge: Harvard University Press, 409–427.

———. 1970. "Linguistics in Relation to Other Sciences." In 1971. *Selected Writings, Volume 2: Word and Language.* The Hague: Mouton, 655–696.

———. 1975. "Glosses on the Medieval Insight into the Science of Language." In 1985. *Selected Writings, Volume 7: Contributions to Comparative Mythology, Studies in Linguistics and Philology, 1972–1982.* The Hague: Mouton, 185–198.

Jakobson, Roman, E. Colin Cherry, and Morris Halle. 1953. "Toward a Logical Description of Languages in Their Phonemic Aspect." *Language* 29: 34–46.

Jakobson, Roman, and Morris Halle. 1956. *Fundamentals of Language.* The Hague: Mouton.

Jakobson, Roman, and Linda R. Waugh. 1979. *The Sound Shape of Language.* Bloomington: Indiana University Press.

Jammes, Robert. 1966. "Juan de Espinosa Medrano et la poésie de Góngora." *Cahiers du Monde Hispanique et Luso-Brésilien* (Caravelle) 7: 127–142.

Jijón y Caamaño, Jacinto. 1941–1947. *El Ecuador interandino y occidental antes de la conquista castellana.* 4 vols. Quito: Editorial Ecuatoriana.

Jones, William. 1786. "The Third Anniversary Discourse, on the Hindus." In Winifred P. Lehmann (ed.). 1967. *A Reader in Nineteenth-Century Historical Indo-European Linguistics.* Bloomington: Indiana University Press, 7–20.

Joos, Martin. 1952. "The Medieval Sibilants." *Language* 28: 222–231. Reprinted with revisions in 1966. *Readings in Linguistics.* 4th edition. Chicago, University of Chicago Press, 372–378.

Jung, Ingrid, and Luís Enrique López. 1987. "Las dimensiones políticas de una escritura: El caso del quechua en el Perú." *Allpanchis* 29/30: 483–510.

Kamen, Henry A. F. 1985. *Inquisition and Society in Spain in the Sixteenth and Seventeenth Centuries.* Bloomington: Indiana University Press.

Karttunen, Frances. 1981. "Nahuatl Lexicography." In *Nahuatl Studies in Memory of Fernando Horcasitas.* Texas Linguistic Forum (Austin) 18. Austin: Department of Linguistics, University of Texas, 105–118.

Karttunen, Frances, and James Lockhart. 1976. *Nahuatl in the Middle Years, Language Contact Phenomena in Texts of the Colonial Period.* University of California Publications in Linguistics 85. Berkeley: University of California Press.

Keleman, Pál. 1967 [1951]. *Baroque and Rococo in Latin America.* 2nd edition, 2 vols. New York: Dover.

King, Robert D. 1967. "Functional Load and Sound Change." *Language* 43: 831–852.

Klein, Harriet E. Manelis. 1973. "Los uros: Extraño pueblo del Altiplano." *Estudios Andinos* 7: 129–150.

Konetzke, Richard. 1958. *Colección de documentos para la historia de la formación social de hispanoamérica, 1493–1810,* vol. 2, part 1, 1593–1659. Madrid: Consejo Superior de Investigaciones Científicas.

———. 1965. *Die Indianerkulturen Altamerikas und die spanisch-portugiesische Kolonialherrschaft.* Frankfurt: Taschenbuch. Spanish translation (tr. Pedro Scaron) 1972. *América Latina II: La época colonial.* Madrid: Siglo XXI.

Krishnamurti, Bh. 1978. "Areal and Lexical Diffusion of Sound Change." *Language* 54: 1–20.

Kubler, George. 1946. "The Quechua in the Colonial World." *Handbook of South American Indians* 2: 331–410. Washington, D.C.: Smithsonian Institution, Bureau of American Ethnology Bulletin 143.

Kuryłowicz, Jerzy. 1949. "La nature des procès dits 'analogiques.'" *Acta Linguistica* 5: 121–138. Reprinted in Eric Hamp, Fred Householder, and Robert

Austerlitz (eds.). 1966. *Readings in Linguistics II.* Chicago: University of Chicago Press, 158–174.
———. 1973. "Internal Reconstruction." *Current Trends in Linguistics* 11: 63–92.
LaBarre, Weston. 1947. "Potato Taxonomy among the Aymara Indians of Bolivia." *Acta Americana* 5: 83–103.
Labov, William A. 1965. "On the Mechanism of Linguistic Change." In 1972. *Sociolinguistic Patterns.* Philadelphia: University of Pennsylvania Press, 160–182.
———. 1966a. *The Social Stratification of English in New York City.* Washington, D.C.: Center for Applied Linguistics.
———. 1966b. "Hypercorrection by the Lower Middle Class as a Factor in Linguistic Change." In 1972. *Sociolinguistic Patterns.* Philadelphia: University of Pennsylvania Press, 122–142.
———. 1970. "The Study of Language in Its Social Context." In 1972. *Sociolinguistic Patterns.* Philadelphia: University of Pennsylvania Press, 183–259.
———. 1980. "The Social Origins of Sound Change." In *Locating Language in Time and Space.* New York: Academic, 251–265.
———. 1981. "Resolving the Neo-grammarian Controversy." *Language* 57: 267–308.
———. 1982. "Objectivity and Commitment in Linguistic Science: The Case of the Black English Trial in Ann Arbor." *Language in Society* 11: 165–201.
Ladefoged, Peter. 1971. *Preliminaries to Linguistic Phonetics.* Chicago: University of Chicago Press.
Lakoff, Robin. 1972. "Another Look at Drift." In Robert P. Stockwell and Ronald K. S. Macaulay (eds.). *Linguistic Change and Generative Theory.* Bloomington: Indiana University Press, 172–198.
Landerman, Peter. 1978. "The Proto-Quechua First Person Marker and the Classification of Quechua Dialects." Paper presented to the Workshop on Andean Linguistics, Urbana.
———. 1979. "Sixteenth Century Sibilants in Spanish, Quechua and Aymara: A Three-Sided Puzzle." Paper presented to the 43rd International Congress of Americanists, Vancouver.
———. 1982. "Ollantay Manuscripts and Editions." Manuscript.
———. 1983. "La sibilantes castellanas, quechua y aimaras en el siglo xvi: Un enigma tridimensional" (translation of 1979). In Rodolfo Cerrón-Palomino (ed.). *Aula quechua.* Lima: Ediciones Signo, 203–234.
Lara, Jesús. 1957. *Tragedia del fin de Atawallpa.* Cochabamba: Universitaria.
———. 1969. *La literatura de los Quechuas.* La Paz: Juventud.
———. 1975. *Qheshwataki.* Cochabamba: Los Amigos del Libro.
Lass, Roger. 1980. *On Explaining Language Change.* Cambridge: Cambridge University Press.
Lastra de Suárez, Yolanda. 1970. "Categorías posicionales en Quechua y Aymara." *Anales de Antropología* (México, D.F.) 7: 263–284.
Lastra de Suárez, Yolanda, and Fernando Horcasitas. 1978. "El Náhuatl en el norte y el occidente del Estado de México." *Anales de Antropología* 15: 185–250.

Lathrap, Donald W. 1970. *The Upper Amazon.* New York: Praeger.
Lavallé, Bernard. 1987. *Le marquis et la marchand, les luttes de pouvoir au Cuzco (1700–1730).* Paris: Maison des Pays Ibériques, CNRS.
Lawler, John. 1989. "Women, Men, and Bristly Things: The Phonosemantics of the *br*-Assonance in English." In G. Larson, D. Brentari, and L. MacLeod (eds.). *The Joy of Grammar: A Festschrift for James D. McCawley.* Chicago: University of Chicago Press.
Lefebvre, Claire, and Pieter Muysken. 1988. *Mixed Categories: Nominalizations in Quechua.* Dordrecht: Kluwer.
Lewin, Boleslow. 1943. *La rebelión de Túpac Amaru.* 3rd edition, 1967. Buenos Aires: Sociedad Editora Latino Americana.
Liffman, Paul. 1977. "Vampires of the Andes." *Michigan Discussions in Anthropology* 2: 205–226.
Lira, Jorge A. 1944. *Diccionario Kkéchuwa-Español.* Tucumán (Argentina): Universidad Nacional de Tucumán.
———. 1973. *Breve diccionario Kkéchuwa-Español.* Cuzco: Dario León.
Lockhart, James, 1981. "Toward Assessing the Phoneticity of Older Nahuatl Texts: Analysis of a Document from the Valley of Toluca, 18th Century." In Frances Karttunen (ed.). *Nahuatl Studies in Memory of Fernando Horcasitas.* Texas Linguistic Forum (Austin) 18. Austin: Department of Linguistics, University of Texas, 151–170.
Longacre, Robert. 1968a. "Comparative Reconstruction of Indigenous Languages." *Current Trends in Linguistics* 4: 320–360.
———. 1968b. "Proto-Quechuamaran: An Ethnolinguistic Note." *Ethnohistory* 15: 403–414.
López, Luis Enrique. 1987. "Balance y perspectivas de la educación bilingüe en Puno." *Allpanchis* 29/30: 347–382.
López-Baralt, Mercedes. 1988. *Icono y conquista: Guamán Poma de Ayala.* Madrid: Hiperión.
Lukács, Georg. 1922. *Geschichte und Klassenbewusstsein.* Berlin. Translated 1971 (tr. R. Livingstone). *History and Class Consciousness.* Cambridge: MIT Press.
Macera, Pablo. 1967. "Noticias sobre la enseñanza elemental en el Perú durante el siglo xviii." *Revista Histórica* 29. Reprinted in 1971. *Trabajos de historia,* vol. 2. Lima: Instituto Nacional de Cultural, 215–301.
———. 1975. "El arte mural cuzqueño, siglos xvi–xx." *Apuntes* (Lima) 4: 59–112.
McQuown, Norman A. 1956. "Evidence for a Synthetic Trend in Totonacan." *Language* 32: 78–80.
Malkiel, Yakov. 1962. "Etymology and General Linguistics." *Word* 18: 198–219.
———. 1964. "Weak Phonetic Change, Spontaneous Sound Change, Lexical Contamination." *Lingua* 11: 263–275.
———. 1968a. "The Inflectional Paradigm as an Occasional Determinant of Sound Change." In Winifred P. Lehmann and Yakov Malkiel (eds.). *Directions for Historical Linguistics.* Austin: University of Texas Press, 25–64.
———. 1968b. "Genetic Linguistics." In *Essays on Linguistic Themes.* Berkeley: University of California Press, 1–19.
———. 1982. "Semantically-marked Root Morphemes in Diachronic Morphol-

ogy." In Winifred P. Lehmann and Yakov Malkiel (eds.). *Perspectives on Historical Linguistics.* Amsterdam: Benjamins, 133–243.

———. 1985. "Studies in Secondary Phonosymbolism." *Archivio Glottologico Italiano* 69: 1–25.

Mannheim, Bruce. 1982. "Person, Number and Inclusivity in Two Andean Languages." *Acta Linguistica Hafniensia* 17: 138–154.

———. 1985. "Southern Peruvian Quechua." In Harriet E. Manelis Klein and Louisa R. Stark (eds.). *South American Indian Languages, Retrospect and Prospect.* Austin: University of Texas Press, 481–515.

———. 1986. "Poetic Form in Guaman Poma's *Wariqsa arawi.*" *Amerindia* 11: 41–67.

———. 1987. "A Semiotic of Andean Dreams." In Barbara Tedlock (ed.). *Dreaming: Anthropological and Psychological Approaches.* Cambridge: Cambridge University Press, 132–153.

Mannheim, Bruce, and Madeleine Newfield. 1982. "Iconicity in Phonological Change." In Anders Ahlqvist (ed.). *Papers from the Fifth International Conference of Historical Linguistics.* Amsterdam: John Benjamins B.V., 211–222.

Manrique, Nelson. 1985. *Colonialismo y pobreza campesina: Caylloma y el Valle del Colca, siglos xvi–xx.* Lima: Centro de Estudios y Promoción del Desarrollo.

Markham, Clements. 1856. *Cuzco: A Journey to the Ancient Capital of Peru and Lima: A Visit to the Capital and Provinces of Modern Peru.* London: Chapman and Hall.

———. 1864. *Contributions toward a Grammar and Dictionary of Quichua, the Language of the Incas of Peru.* London: Trübner.

———. 1871a. "On the Geographical Positions of the Tribes Which Formed the Empire of the Yncas, with an Appendix on the Name 'Aymara.'" *Journal of the Royal Geographical Society* (London) 41: 281–338.

———. 1871b. *Ollanta: An Ancient Ynca Drama, Translated from the Original Quichua.* London: Trübner.

———. 1912. *The Incas of Peru.* London: Trübner.

Martin, Luis. 1968. *The Intellectual Conquest of Peru: The Jesuit College of San Pablo, 1568–1767.* New York: Fordham University Press.

Martinet, André. 1938. "Role de la corrélation dans la phonologie diachronique." *Travaux du Cercle Linguistique de Prague* 8: 273–288.

———. 1951. "The Unvoicing of the Old Spanish Sibilants." *Romance Philology* 5: 133–156.

———. 1955. *Economie des changements phonetiques.* Berne: Francke.

———. 1957. "Arbitraire linguistique et double articulation." *Cahiers Ferdinand de Saussure* 15: 105–116. Reprinted in Eric Hamp et al. (eds.). 1966. *Readings in Linguistics II.* Chicago: University of Chicago Press, 371–378.

———. 1960. *Eléments de linguistique générale.* Paris: Colin. English translation (tr. Elisabeth Palmer) 1964. *Elements of General Linguistics.* Chicago: University of Chicago Press.

Marx, Karl. 1957 [1852]. *The Eighteenth Brumaire of Louis Bonaparte.* Translation of the 3rd German edition of 1883. New York: International Publishers.

Mateos, Francisco, s.i. 1944. "Introducción" [to] Anonymous. 1600. *Historia general de la Compañia de Jesús en la Provincia del Peru*, vol. 1. Madrid: Consejo Superior de Investigaciones Científicas, Instituto Gonzalo Fernández de Oviedo.

Matos Mar, Jose. 1956. "Yauyos, Tupe y el idioma Kauke." *Revista del Museo Nacional* 25: 140–183.

———. 1970. "El indigenismo en el Perú." In *El indio y el poder en el Perú*. Perú Problema 4. Lima: Instituto de Estudios Peruanos. Reprinted in Julio Ortega (ed.). 1974. *Realidad nacional*, vol. 1. Lima: Retablo de Papel, 100–111.

Mauss, Marcel. 1925. "Essai sur le don." *Année sociologique* (n.s.) 1: 30–186.

Mayer, Enrique. 1974a. "El trueque y los mercados en el imperio Incaico." In *Los campesinos y el mercado*. Lima: Pontificia Universidad Católica del Perú, 13–50.

———. 1974b. "Reciprocity, Self-sufficiency and Market Relations in a Contemporary Community in the Central Andes of Peru." Cornell University Latin American Studies Program Dissertation Series No. 72.

———. 1974c. "Las reglas del juego en la reciprocidad andina." In Giorgio Alberti and Enrique Mayer (eds.). *Reciprocidad e intercambio en los Andes peruanos*. Lima: Instituto de Estudios Peruanos, 37–65.

———. 1978. "El uso social de la coca en el mundo andino: Contribución a un debate y toma de posición." *América Indígena* 38: 849–865.

———. 1982. "Los alcances de una política de educación bicultural y bilingüe." *América Indígena* 42: 269–280.

Medina, José Toribio. 1904. *La imprenta en Lima, 1584–1824*, vol. 1. Santiago de Chile: private publication.

Meillet, Antoine. 1924. *La méthode comparative en linguistique historique*. Oslo: Aschehoug. Translated (tr. G. B. Ford) 1967. *The Comparative Method in Historical Linguistics*. Paris: Champion.

———. 1931. *Esquisse d'une histoire de la langue latine*. Reprint of 3rd edition. 1966. Paris: Klincksieck.

Mendiburu, Manuel de. 1933. *Diccionario histórico-biográfico del Perú*, vol. 6. Lima: Gil.

———. 1934. *Diccionario histórico-biográfico del Peru*, vol. 10. Lima: Gil.

Menéndez Pidal, Ramon. 1925. *Manual de gramática histórica española*. 5th edition. Madrid: Suárez.

Meneses, Teodoro. 1950. "El *Usca Paucar*, drama religioso en Quechua del siglo xviii." *Documenta* (Lima) 2: 1–178.

———. 1962. "En pos de una nueva traducción de los himnos quechuas del cronista Cristóbal de Molina, el Cusqueño." *Sphinx* (Lima) 15.

———. 1965. "Nueva traducción de preces o himnos quechuas del cronista Cristóbal de Molina, el Cusqueño." *Documenta* (Lima) 4: 80–111.

———. 1976. "Datación y paternidad del drama *Apu Ollantay*." *San Marcos* 17: 49–82.

Mesa, José de, and Teresa Gisbert. 1962. *Historia de la pintura cuzqueña*. Buenos Aires: Universidad de Buenos Aires, Facultad de Arquitectura y Urbanismo.

Middendorf, Ernest W. 1890a. *Die einheimischen Sprachen Perus, I: Das Runa-Simi oder die Keshua-Sprache wie sie gegenwärtig in der Provinz Cuzco gesprochen wird*. Leipzig: Brockhaus. Spanish translation (tr. E. More) 1970. *Gramática keshua*. Madrid: Aguilar.

———. 1890b. *Die einheimischen Sprachen Perus, II: Wörterbuch des Runa-Simi oder der Keshua-Sprache*. Leipzig: Brockhaus.

———. 1890c. *Die einheimischen Sprachen Perus, III: Ollanta, ein Drama der Keshua-Sprache*. Leipzig: Brockhaus.

———. 1891. *Die einheimischen Sprachen Perus, IV: Dramatische und Lyrische Dichtungen der Keshua-Sprache*. Leipzig: Brockhaus.

Millé, Andrés. 1968. *Derrotero de la Compañía de Jesús en la conquista de Perú, Tucumán y Paraguay*. Buenos Aires: Emecé.

Millones Gadea, Luis. 1967. *Introducción al proceso de aculturación religiosa indígena*. Lima: Instituto Indigenista Peruano.

———. 1971. "Pastores y tejedores de los Condesuyos de Arequipa: Un informe etnológico al Consejo de Regencia." *Quinto Congreso Internacional de Historia de América* 3: 302–317.

Mitchell, W. J. Thomas. 1984. "What Is an Image?" In 1986. *Iconology*. Chicago: University of Chicago Press, 7–46.

Molinié Fioravanti, Antoinette. 1982. *La Vallée Sacrée des Andes*. Paris: Société d'Ethnographie.

Montoya, Rodrigo. 1980. *Capitalismo y no-capitalismo en el Perú*. Lima: Mosca Azul.

———. 1987. *La cultura quechua hoy*. Lima: Mosca Azul.

Montoya, Rodrigo, Edwin Montoya, and Luis Montoya. 1987. *La sangre de los cerros/Urqukunapa yawarnin*. Lima: Centro Peruano de Estudios Sociales, Mosca Azul, and Universidad Nacional Mayor de San Marcos.

Montoya, Rodrigo, Maria José Silveira, and Felipe Lindoso. 1979. *Producción parcelaria y universo ideológico: El caso de Puquio*. Lima: Mosca Azul.

Morote Best, Efraín. 1952. "El degollador (Nakaq)." *Tradición* 11: 67–91.

Morris, Craig. 1985. "From Principles of Economic Complementarity to the Organization and Administration of Tawantinsuyu." In Shozo Masuda, Izumi Shimada, and Craig Morris (eds.). *Andean Ecology and Civilization*. Tokyo: University of Tokyo Press, 477–490.

Moscoso, Maximiliano. 1965. "Apuntes para la historia de la industria textil en el Cuzco colonial." *Revista Universitaria* (Cuzco) 122/125: 67–94.

Mosonyi, E. E. 1982. "Responsabilidad del lingüista frente a los pueblos indígenas americanos." *América Indígena* 42: 289–300.

Mouffe, Chontal. 1979. "Hegemony and Ideology in Gramsci." In *Gramsci and Marxist Theory*. London: RKP.

Moya, Ruth. 1981. *Simbolismo y ritual en el Ecuador andino* [and] *El quichua en el español de Quito*. Otavalo: Instituto Otavaleño de Antropología.

Murra, John V. 1980 [1956]. *The Economic Organization of the Inca State*. Hartford: JAI.

———. 1967. "La visita de Los Chupachu como fuente etnológica." Commentary on Iñigo Ortíz de Zúñiga. 1967 [1562]. *Visita de la provincia de León de Huánuco 1*. Huánuco: Universidad Nacional Hermilio Valdizán, 383–406.

———. 1968. "An Aymara Kingdom in 1567." *Ethnohistory* 15: 115–151.

———. 1970. "Current Research and Prospects in Andean Ethnohistory." *Latin American Research Review* 5 (1): 3–36.

———. 1972. "El 'control vertical' de un máximo de pisos ecológicos en las sociedades andinas." Commentary on Iñigo Ortíz de Zúñiga. 1972 [1562]. *Visita de la provincia de León de Huánuco* 2. Huánuco: Universidad Nacional Hermilio Valdizán, 429–462.

———. 1975. *Formaciones económicas y políticas del mundo andino.* Lima: Instituto de Estudios Peruanos.

———. 1980. "Waman Puma, etnógrafo del mundo andino." In Rolena Adorno, John V. Murra, and Jorge Urioste (eds.). 1980. Felipe Guaman Poma de Ayala, *Nueva corónica y buen gobierno.* México (D.F.): Siglo XXI, xiii–xix.

Murra, John V., Nathan Wachtel, and Jacques Revel (eds.). 1986. *Anthropological History of Andean Polities.* Cambridge: Cambridge University Press.

Muysken, Pieter. 1979. "La mezcla de quechua y castellano: El caso de la 'media lengua' en el Ecuador." *Lexis* 3: 41–56.

———. 1981. "Halfway between Quechua and Spanish: The Case for Relexification." In Arnold Highfield and Albert Valdeman (eds.). *Historicity and Variation in Creole Studies.* Ann Arbor: Karoma, 52–78.

Needham, Rodney. 1972. *Belief, Language, and Experience.* Chicago: University of Chicago Press.

Niño-Murcia, Mercedes. 1988. "Construcciones verbales del Español andino: Interacción quechua-española en la frontera colombiana-ecuatoriana." Doctoral dissertation in Romance linguistics, University of Michigan.

Núñez del Prado, Daisy. 1972. "La reciprocidad como ethos de la cultura indígena." Bachelor's thesis, Universidad Nacional San Antonio Abad del Cuzco.

Núñez del Prado, Juan Victor. 1970. "El mundo sobrenatural de los quechuas del sur del Perú a través de la comunidad de Qotobamba." *Allpanchis Phuturinqa* 2: 56–119.

Oblitas Poblete, Enrique. 1968. *El idioma secreto de los Incas.* La Paz: Los Amigos del Libro.

Ohala, John. 1981. "The Listener as a Source of Sound Change." In Carrie S. Masek, Roberta A. Hendrick, and Mary Frances Miller (eds.). *Papers from the Parasession on Language and Behavior.* Chicago: Chicago Linguistic Society, 178–203.

O'Phelan Godoy, Scarlet. 1976. "Túpac Amaru y las sublevaciones del siglo xviii." In A. Flores Galindo (ed.). *Sociedad colonial y sublevaciones populares: Tupac Amaru II, 1780.* Lima: Retablo de Papel, 67–81.

———. 1985. *Rebellions and Revolts in Eighteenth Century Peru and Upper Peru.* Cologne: Böhlau.

Orent, Wendy. 1988. "Out of the Panther's Skin." Manuscript, Department of Anthropology, University of Michigan.

Orlove, Benjamin S. 1977. *Alpacas, Sheep, and Men: The Wool Export Economy and Regional Society in Southern Peru.* New York: Academic.

Orr, Carolyn, and Robert Longacre. 1968. "Proto-Quechuamaran." *Language* 44: 528–555.

Ortíz Rescaniere, Alejandro. 1970. "Lenguas aborigenes y educación nacional." *Educación* (Lima) 2: 50–52.

———. 1973. *De Adaneva a Inkarrí.* Lima: Retablo de Papel.

Ossio A., Juan M. 1977. "Myth and History: The Seventeenth Century Chronicle of Guaman Poma de Ayala." In R. K. Jain (ed.). *Text and Context* (ASA Essays 2). Philadelphia: ISHI, 51–93.

———. 1978. "Guamán Poma y la historiografía indianista de los siglos XVI y XVII." *Historia y Cultura* 10: 181–206.

Osthoff, Hermann, and Brugmann, Karl. 1878. "Einleitung" to *Morphologische Untersuchungen auf dem Gebiete der indogermanischen Sprachen I.* Leipzig: Hirzel, iii–xx; English translation in Winifred P. Lehmann (ed.). 1967. *A Reader in Nineteenth-Century Historical Indo-European Linguistics.* Bloomington: Indiana University Press, 197–209.

Pacheco Zegarra, Gavino. 1878. *Ollantai, drame en vers Quechuas du temps des Incas.* Paris: Maisonneuve.

Pagden, Anthony. 1982. *The Fall of Natural Man: The American Indian and the Origins of Comparative Ethnology.* Cambridge: Cambridge University Press.

———. 1987a. "Identity Formation in Spanish America." In Nicholas Canny and Anthony Pagden (eds.). *Colonial Identity in the Atlantic World, 1500–1800.* Princeton: Princeton University Press, 51–93.

———. 1987b. "Dispossessing the Barbarian: The Language of Spanish Thomism and the Debate over Property Rights of the American Indians." In *The Languages of Political Theory in Early-Modern Europe.* Cambridge: Cambridge University Press, 79–98.

———. 1990. "Old Constitutions and Ancient Indian Empires: Juan Pablo Viscardo and the Languages of Revolution in Spanish America." In *Spanish Imperialism and the Political Imagination.* New Haven: Yale University Press, 117–132.

Palacios, Felix. 1977. "' . . . hiwasaha uywa uywatana, uka uywaha hiwasaru uyusiyu': Los pastores aymara de Chichillapi." Master's thesis, Pontificia Universidad Católica del Perú.

Palacios, José. 1837. "Tradición de la rebelión de Ollantay." *Museo Erudito o periodico político histórico literario y moral* (Cuzco) 1 (6): 9–12; (7): 1–4; (8): 1–3.

Palomino Flores, Salvador. 1970. "El sistema de oposiciones en la comunidad de Sarhua (Ayacucho)." Bachelor's thesis in anthropology, Universidad de Huamanga.

Parker, Gary J. 1963. "La clasificación genética de los dialectos quechuas." *Revista del Museo Nacional* 32: 241–252.

———. 1969a. *Ayacucho Quechua Grammar and Dictionary.* The Hague: Mouton.

———. 1969b. "Bosquejo de una teoría de la evolución del Quechua *A.*" *Programa interamericano de lingüística y enseñanza de idiomas, El simposio de México.* México: Universidad Nacional Autónoma de México, 270–281.

———. 1969c. "Comparative Quechua Phonology and Grammar I: Classification." *University of Hawaii Working Papers in Linguistics* 1 (1): 65–87.

———. 1969d. "Comparative Quechua Phonology and Grammar II: Proto-Quechua Phonology and Morphology." *University of Hawaii Working Papers in Linguistics* 1 (2): 123–147.

———. 1969e. "Comparative Quechua Phonology and Grammar III: Proto-Quechua Lexicon." *University of Hawaii Working Papers in Linguistics* 1 (4): 1–61.

———. 1969f. "Comparative Quechua Phonology and Grammar IV: The Evolution of Quechua A." *University of Hawaii Working Papers in Linguistics* 1 (9): 149–204.

———. 1971. "Comparative Quechua Phonology and Grammar V: The Evolution of Quechua B." *University of Hawaii Working Papers in Linguistics* 3 (3): 45–109.

———. 1973. "Derivación verbal en el quechua de Ancash." Universidad Nacional de San Marcos, Centro de Investigación de Lingüística Aplicada, Documento de Trabajo 25.

———. 1976. *Gramática quechua, Ancash-Huailas.* Lima: Ministerio de Educación and Instituto de Estudios Peruanos.

Parker, Gary J., and Amancio Chávez. 1976. *Diccionario Quechua: Ancash-Huailas.* Lima: Ministerio de Educación and Instituto de Estudios Peruanos.

Parker, Gary J., Antonio Cusihuamán, Gloria Escobar, Alicia Ibañez, Yolanda Lastra, Alfredo Olarte, and Donald Solá. 1964. *English-Quechua Dictionary: Cuzco, Ayacucho, Cochabamba.* Ithaca, N.Y.: Cornell University Quechua Language Materials Project.

Paul, Hermann. 1880. *Prinzipien der Sprachgeschichte.* Halle: Niemeyer. English translation of the 2nd edition (tr. H. A. Strong). 1889. *Principles of the History of Language.* New York: Macmillan.

Paulston, Christina Bratt. 1973. "Del dilema moral de una especialista en sociolingüística." *América Indígena* 33: 97–105.

Pease G. Y., Franklin. 1977. "Collaguas: Una etnía del siglo xvi, problemas iniciales." In *Collaguas, I.* Lima: Pontificia Universidad Católica del Perú, 131–168.

Peirce, Charles Sanders. 1902. "Logic as Semiotic." In Justus Buchler (ed.). 1940. *The Philosophy of Peirce.* London: Routledge and Kegan Paul, 98–115.

Phillips, Betty S. 1984. "Word Frequency and the Actuation of Sound Change." *Language* 60: 320–342.

Polivanov, E. D. 1928. "Faktory fonetičeskoj èvoljucii jazyka kak trudovogo processa." *Učenye zapiski Instituta jazyka i literatury Rossijskoj associacii naučnoissledovatel'skix institutov obščestvennyx nauk* 3: 20–42. English translation, "Factors in the Evolution of Language as a Work Process." In A. A. Leont'ev et al. (eds.). *Selected Works* (tr. Daniel Armstrong). The Hague: Mouton, 65–80.

Poole, Deborah. 1987. "Qorilazos, abigeos y comunidades campesinas en la provincia de Chumbivilcas." In Fernando Oshige (ed.). *Comunidades campesinos: Cambios y permanencias.* Lima: CONCYTEC and Chiclayo: Centro Solidaridad, 257–295.

———. 1989. "Landscapes of Power in a Cattle-Rustling Culture of Southern Andean Peru." *Dialectical Anthropology* 12: 367–398.

———. 1990. "The Choreography of History in Andean Dance." In B. J. Isbell (ed.). *An Andean Kaleidoscope* (forthcoming).

Pope, Alexander. 1711. "An Essay on Criticism." In Howard Foster Lowry and

Willard Thorp (eds.). 1935. *An Oxford Anthology of English Poetry.* New York: Oxford University Press, 413–422.

Porras Barrenechea, Raúl. 1943. "El Padre Cristóbal de Molina (el Cuzqueño)." In F. A. Loayza. 1943. *Las crónicas de los Molinas.* Lima: n.p., second pagination, 94–98.

———. 1951. "Prólogo" to Domingo de Santo Tomás. *Lexicon o vocabulario de la lengua general.* Lima: Universidad Nacional de San Marcos.

———. 1952. "Prólogo" to Diego de Gonçález Holguín. *Vocabulario de la lengua general de todo el Perú llamada lengua Qquichua o del Inca.* Lima: Universidad Nacional de San Marcos.

———. 1955. *El Inca Garcilaso en Montilla.* Lima: Universidad Nacional de San Marcos.

———. 1962. *Los cronistas del Perú.* In 1986. *Los cronistas del Perú y otros ensayos* (ed. Franklin Pease G. Y., Oswaldo Holguín Callo, Félix Alvarez Brun, and Graciela Sánchez Cerro). Lima: Banco del Credito del Perú.

Pouillon, Jean. 1979. "Remarques sur le verbe *croire.*" In Michel Izard and Pierre Smith (eds.). *La fonction symbolique.* Paris: Gallimard, 43–51. English translation (tr. John Leavitt), "Remarks on the Verb 'to believe'." In 1981. *Between Belief and Transgression.* Chicago: University of Chicago Press, 1–8.

Proulx, Paul. 1972. "Proto-quechua / ph /." *International Journal of American Linguistics* 38: 142–145.

Pullum, Geoffrey, and William Ladusaw. 1986. *Phonetic Symbol Guide.* Chicago: University of Chicago Press.

Purizaga Vega, Medardo. 1972. *El estado regional en Ayacucho, Período intermedio temprano, 1200–1470.* Lima: Yachayhuasi.

Quispe M., Ulpiano. 1969. *La herranza en Choque Huarcaya y Huancasancos, Ayacucho.* Instituto Indigenista Peruano Monografía 20. Lima: Ministerio de Trabajo.

Rama, Angel. 1982. *Transculturación narrativa en américa latina.* Mexico (D.F.): Siglo XXI.

Ramanujan, A. K. 1968. "The Structure of Variation: A Study in Caste Dialects." In Milton Singer and Bernard S. Cohn (eds.). *Structure and Change in Indian Society.* Chicago: Aldine, 461–474.

Ramírez, Susan E. 1986. *Provincial Patriarchs: Land Tenure and the Economics of Power in Colonial Peru.* Albuquerque: University of New Mexico Press.

Reuse, William J. de. 1986. "The Lexicalization of Sound Symbolism in Santiago del Estero Quechua." *International Journal of American Linguistics* 52: 54–64.

Rhodes, Richard A., and John M. Lawler. 1981. "Athematic Metaphors." *Papers from the Seventeenth Regional Meeting of the Chicago Linguistic Society,* 318–342.

Rivarola, José Luis. 1985. *Lengua, comunicación e historia del Perú.* Lima: Lumen.

———. 1987a. "Para la historia del español de América: Parodias de la 'lengua de indio' en el Perú (ss. XVII–XIX)." *Lexis* 11: 137–164.

———. 1987b. "La formación del español andino, aspectos morfo-sintácticos."

Actas del Primer Congreso Internacional de Historia de la Lengua Española, 209–225.
———. 1989. "Contactos y conflictos de lenguas en el Perú colonial." In *Cultural Identity in Colonial Latin America, Problems and Repercussions.* Leiden: n.p.
Rivera Serna, Raúl. 1949. "Los cuatro Cristóbal de Molina." *Fenix* 6: 590–594.
Rivero y Ustariz, Mariano E. de, and Johann Jakob von Tschudi. 1851. *Antigüedades peruanas.* Vienna: Kaiserlich, Königlichen Hof- und Staatsdruckerei. Reprinted 1958. Lima: Mejía Baca.
Rivet, Paul. 1924. "Langues américaines." In Antoine Meillet and Marcel Cohen (eds.). *Les langues du monde.* Paris: Champion, 596–707.
Rivet, Paul, and Georges de Créqui-Montfort. 1951–1956. *Bibliographie des langues aymará et kičua.* 4 vols. Paris: Institut d'Ethnologie.
Robertson, John. 1977. "A Phonological Reconstruction of the Ergative Third-Person Singular Pronoun of Common Mayan." *International Journal of American Linguistics* 43 (3): 210–219.
Roel Pineda, Josefat. 1959. "El wayno del Cuzco." *Folklore Americano* 6/7: 129–246.
Rojas, Ricardo. 1939. *Un titán de los Andes.* Buenos Aires: Losada.
Rojas Rojas, Ibico. 1980. *Expansión del quechua.* Lima: Ediciones Signo.
———. 1983. "En torno a la oficialización de las lenguas quechua y aimara." In Rodolfo Cerrón-Palomino (ed.). *Aula quechua.* Lima: Ediciones Signo, 139–159.
Romaine, Suzanne. 1982. *Socio-historical Linguistics, Its Status and Methodology.* Cambridge: Cambridge University Press.
Romero, Carlos A. 1916. "Los dos Cristóbal de Molina." In F. A. Loayza. 1943. *Las crónicas de los Molinas.* Lima: n.p., v–xxvi.
———. 1928. "Un libro interesante." *Revista Histórica* 9: 51–87.
Romero, Oswaldo. 1964. "Introducción" to Juan de Velasco. *Vocabulario de la lengua índica.* Quito: Instituto Ecuatoriano de Antropología y Geografía (= *Llacta* 6 (20): iii–xxxv).
Root, Deborah. 1988. "Speaking Christian: Orthodoxy and Difference in Sixteenth-Century Spain." *Representations* 23: 118–134.
Rostworowski de Diez Canseco, María. 1970a. "Los Ayarmaca." *Revista del Museo Nacional* 36: 58–101.
———. 1970b. "Mercaderes del valle de Chincha en la época prehispánica." In 1977. *Etnía y sociedad.* Lima: Instituto de Estudios Peruanos, 97–140.
Rouse, Roger. 1988. "Mexicano, Chicano, Pocho." *Página Uno* (Suplemento político de *Uno más Uno*, México) 578: 1–2.
Rowe, John Howland. 1946. "Inca Culture at the Time of the Spanish Conquest." In Julian H. Steward (ed.). *Handbook of South American Indians*, vol. 2. Washington, D.C.: Smithsonian Institution, Bureau of American Ethnology, Bulletin No. 143, 183–330.
———. 1950. "Sound Patterns in Three Inca Dialects." *International Journal of American Linguistics* 16: 137–148.
———. 1953. "Eleven Inca Prayers from the Zithuwa Ritual." *Papers of the Kroeber Anthropological Society* 8/9: 82–99.

———. 1954. "El movimiento nacional inca del siglo xviii." *Revista Universitaria* (Cuzco) 107: 17–47.

Roze, Marie-Augustin, o.p. 1878. *Les dominicains en amérique ou, Aperçu historique sur la fondation des diverses provinces de l'ordre des frères prêcheurs.* Paris: Poussielgue Frères.

Salas de Coloma, Miriam. 1979. *De los obrajes de Canaria y Chincheros a las comunidades indígenas de Vilcashuamán, siglo xvi.* Lima: Sesator.

Salomon, Frank. 1978. "Vertical Politics on the Inka Frontier." In John V. Murra, Nathan Wachtel, and Jacques Revel (eds.). 1986. *Anthropological History of Andean Polities.* Cambridge: Cambridge University Press, 89–117.

———. 1982. "Chronicles of the Impossible." In Rolena Adorno (ed.). *From Oral to Written Expression: Native Andean Chronicles of the Early Colonial Period.* Syracuse: Syracuse University Foreign and Comparative Studies Program, 9–39.

———. 1984. "El culto a los ancestros y la resistencia al estado en un pueblo arequipeño, 174(8?)–1754." Manuscript presented to the seminar on Resistance and Rebellion in the Andean World, University of Wisconsin, Madison, 26 April.

———. 1985. "The Dynamic Potential of the Complementarity Concept." In Shozo Masuda, Izumi Shimada, and Craig Morris (eds.). *Andean Ecology and Civilization.* Tokyo: University of Tokyo Press, 511–531.

———. 1987. "Ancestor Cults and Resistance to the State in Arequipa, ca. 1748–1754." In Steve J. Stern (ed.). *Resistance, Rebellion, and Consciousness in the Andean Peasant World, 18th to 20th Centuries.* Madison: University of Wisconsin Press, 148–165.

Samuels, M. L. 1972. *Linguistic Evolution, with Special Reference to English.* Cambridge: Cambridge University Press.

Santisteban Ochoa, Julián. 1963. "Documentos para la historia del Cuzco existentes en el Archivo General de Indias de Sevilla." *Revista del Archivo Histórico del Cuzco* 11: 1–118.

Sapir, Edward. 1921. *Language.* New York: Harcourt Brace and World.

———. 1924. "The Grammarian and His Language." Reprinted in David G. Mandelbaum (ed.). 1949. *Selected Writings of Edward Sapir.* Berkeley: University of California Press, 150–159.

———. 1925. "Sound Patterns in Language." Reprinted in D. Mandelbaum (ed.). 1949. *Selected Writings of Edward Sapir.* Berkeley: University of California Press, 33–45.

———. 1929. "The Status of Linguistics as a Science." Reprinted in David G. Mandelbaum (ed.). 1949. *Selected Writings of Edward Sapir.* Berkeley: University of California Press, 160–166.

———. 1933. "Language." Reprinted in D. Mandelbaum (ed.). 1949. *Selected Writings of Edward Sapir.* Berkeley: University of California Press, 7–32.

Saussure, Ferdinand de. 1971 [1915]. *Cours de linguistique générale.* Ed. C. Bally, A. Sechehaye, and A. Reidlinger. Paris: Payot.

Scott, James. 1977. "Hegemony and the Peasantry." *Politics and Society* 7: 267–296.

Shapiro, Michael. 1983. *The Sense of Grammar: Language as Semeiotic*. Bloomington: Indiana University Press.
Sherbondy, Jeanette. 1986. "Organización hidráulica y poder en el Cuzco de los incas." *Revista Española de Antropología Americana* 17: 117–153.
Silverblatt, Irene. 1980. "Andean Women under Spanish Rule." In Mona Etienne and Eleanor Leacock (eds.). *Women and Colonization*. Brooklyn: Bergin, 149–185.
Skar, Harald O. 1982. *The Warm Valley People, Duality and Land Reform among the Quechua Indians of Highland Peru*. Oslo: Universitetforlaget.
Solá, Donald F. 1958. "Huanuco Kechua, The Grammar of Words and Phrases." Doctoral dissertation in linguistics, Cornell University.
Solá, Donald F., and Antonio Cusihuamán Gutiérrez. 1967a. *Spoken Cuzco Quechua*. Ithaca, N.Y.: Cornell University Quechua Language Materials Project.
———. 1967b. *The Structure of Cuzco Quechua*. Ithaca, N.Y.: Cornell University Quechua Language Materials Project.
Solano, Francisco de. 1975. "El interprete, uno de los ejes de la aculturación." In *Estudios sobre la política indigenista española en américa, Terceras Jornadas Americanistas de la Universidad de Valladolid*. Valladolid: University of Valladolid, 265–276.
Solís F., Gustavo. 1987. "Revitalización de lenguas en su contexto social." *América Indígena* 47: 648–651.
Soto Ruíz, Clodoaldo. 1976a. *Gramática quechua: Ayacucho-Chanca*. Lima: Instituto de Estudios Peruanos.
———. 1976b. *Diccionario quechua: Ayacucho-Chanca*. Lima: Instituto de Estudios Peruanos.
Stark, Louisa R. 1969. "The Lexical Structure of Quechua Body Parts." *Anthropological Linguistics* 11: 1–15.
———. 1972. "Machaj-Juyai: Secret Language of the Callahuayas." *Papers in Andean Linguistics* 2: 199–227.
———. 1975. "A Reconsideration of Proto-Quechua Phonology." *Actas del 39 Congreso Internacional de Americanistas* 5: 209–219.
———. 1985. "The Quechua Language in Bolivia." In Harriet E. Manelis Klein and Louisa R. Stark (eds.). *South American Indian Languages, Retrospect and Prospect*. Austin: University of Texas Press, 516–545.
Steinthal, Heymann. 1890. "Das verhaltniss, das zwischen dem Keschua und Aymara besteht." 7 *Congrès Internacional des Américanistes* (Berlin, 1888), 462–465.
Stern, Gustav. 1964 [1931]. *Meaning and the Change of Meaning*. Bloomington: Indiana University Press.
Stevenson, Robert M. 1968. *Music in Aztec and Inca Territory*. Berkeley and Los Angeles: University of California Press.
Stockwell, Robert P. 1979. "Perseverance in the English Vowel Shift." In Jacek Fisiak (ed.). *Historical Phonology*. The Hague: Mouton, 337–348.
Swadesh, Morris (Mauricio). 1969. "Un nexo prehistórico entre Quechua y Tarasco." *Anales del Instituto Nacional de Antropología e Historia* (México, D.F.) 7: 127–138.
Szemiński, Jan. 1987. *Un kuraca, un dios y una historia: "Relación de anti-*

guëdades de este reyno del Pirú" por don Juan de Santacruz Pachacuti Yamqui Salca Maygua. Jujuy: Instituto de Ciencias Antropológicas.
Tamayo Herrera, José. 1980. *Historia del indigenismo cuzqueño.* Lima: Instituto Nacional de Cultura.
Taussig, Michael T. 1987. *Shamanism, Colonialism, and the Wild Man: A Study in Terror and Healing.* Chicago: University of Chicago Press.
Taylor, Gerald. 1978. "Langue de prestige et parlers d'opprimés: Le statut du Quechua dans la société péruvienne." *Actes du 42e Congrès International des Américanistes,* 4: 521–526.
———. 1980. "Avant-propos" to *Rites et traditions de Huarochirí: Manuscrit quechua du début de 17e siècle.* Paris: L'Harmattan, 5–23.
———. 1982. *Aspectos de la dialectología quechua I: Introducción al quechua de Ferreñafe.* Paris: Chantiers Amerindia.
———. 1984. "Yauyos: Un microcosmo dialectal quechua." *Revista Andina* 2: 121–146.
———. 1985. "Un documento quechua de Huarochirí—1608." *Revista Andina* 3: 157–186; 4: 211–212.
———. 1987. "Introducción" [to] *Ritos y tradiciones de Huarochirí del siglo xvii.* Lima: Instituto de Estudios Peruanos and the Institut Français d'Etudes Andines, 15–37.
Thieme, Paul. 1964. "The Comparative Method for Reconstruction in Linguistics." In Dell Hymes (ed.). *Language in Culture and Society.* New York: Harper and Row, 585–598.
Thomason, Sarah Grey, and Terrence S. Kaufman. 1976. "Contact-induced Language Change: Loanwords and the Borrowing Language's Pre-borrowing Phonology." In William M. Christie, Jr. (ed.). *Current Progress in Historical Linguistics.* Amsterdam: North-Holland, 168–179.
Toon, Thomas E. 1976. "The Variationist Analysis of Early Old English Manuscript Data." In William M. Christie, Jr. (ed.). *Current Progress in Historical Linguistics.* Amsterdam: North-Holland, 71–81.
Torero Fernández de Cordova, Alfredo. 1964. "Los dialectos quechuas." *Anales Científicos de la Universidad Agraria* 2: 446–478.
———. 1965. "Le puquina, la troisième langue générale de pérou." Thèse pour le doctorat de troisième cycle, Université de Paris, Sorbonne.
———. 1968. "Procedencia geográfica de los dialectos quechuas de Ferreñafe y Cajamarca." *Anales Científicos de la Universidad Agraria* 6: 168–197.
———. 1970. "Lingüística e historia de la sociedad andina." *Anales Científicos de la Universidad Agraria* 8: 231–264. Reprinted in Alberto Escobar (ed.). 1972. *El reto del multilingüísmo en el Perú.* Lima: Instituto de Estudios Peruanos, 46–106. And 1975. *Actas del 39 Congreso Internacional de Americanistas* 5: 221–259.
———. 1974. *El quechua y la historia social andina.* Lima: Universidad Ricardo Palma.
———. 1983. "La familia lingüística quechua." In Bernard Pottier (ed.). *América Latina en sus lenguas indígenas.* Caracas: Monte Avila, 61–92.
———. 1987. "Lenguas y pueblos altiplánicos en torno al siglo xvi." *Revista Andina* 5: 330–405.

Toro y Gisbert, Miguel de. 1943. *Pequeño Larousse ilustrado* (adaptation of the French edition ed. Claude Auge). Buenos Aires: Babel.

Torres Saldamando, Enrique. 1882. *Los antiguos Jesuitas del Perú.* Lima: Liberal.

Trimborn, Hermann (see Anonymous, Huarochirí.)

Tschudi, Johann Jakob von. 1853. *Die Kechuasprache,* vol. 2. Vienna: Kaiserlich-königlichen Hof- und Staatsdruckerei.

———. 1876. "Ollanta: Ein altperuanisches Drama aus der Kechuasprache." *Denkschriften der Kaiserlichen Akademie der Wissenschaften, Philosophisch-Historiche Classe* 24: 167–384.

Turner, Ralph Lilley. 1924. "Cerebralization in Sindhi." *Journal of the Royal Asiatic Society* 3: 555–584.

———. 1927. "The Phonetic Weakness of Terminational Elements in Indo-Aryan." *Journal of the Royal Asiatic Society* 2: 227–239.

———. 1937. "Anticipation of Normal Sound Changes in Indo-Aryan." *Transactions of the Philological Society:* 1–14.

Ugarte, Marco A. 1978. "La coca, instrumento de dominación." *Crítica Andina* 2: 69–102.

Uhle, Max. 1912. "Los origines de los Incas." *Actas del 17 Congreso Internacional de Americanistas* (Sesión de Buenos Aires), 301–353.

Urbain, Jean-Didier. 1980. "Le système quechua de l'échange: Développements métaphoriques et adaptation d'un 'vocabulaire de base.'" *L'Homme* 20: 71–90.

Urbano, Henrique. 1989. "Introducción" [to] Cristóbal de Molina (el Cuzqueño). *Relación de las fábulas y ritos de los yngas. . . .* In Henrique Urbano and Pierre Duviols (eds.). 1989. *Fábulas y mitos de los incas.* Madrid: Historia 16, 9–46.

Urioste, Jorge. 1973. "Chay simire caymi: The Language of the Manuscript of Huarochirí." Doctoral dissertation in linguistics, Cornell University.

———. 1980. "Estudio analítico del Quechua en la *Nueva corónica.*" In Rolena Adorno, John V. Murra, and Jorge Urioste (eds.). Felipe Guaman Poma de Ayala. *Nueva corónica y buen gobierno.* México (D.F.): Siglo XXI, xx–xxxi.

———. 1982. "The Editing of Oral Tradition in the Huarochirí Manuscript." In Rolena Adorno (ed.). *From Oral to Written Expression: Native Andean Chronicles of the Early Colonial Period.* Syracuse: Syracuse University Foreign and Comparative Studies Program, 101–108.

Urton, Gary. 1981. *At the Crossroads of the Earth and the Sky.* Austin: University of Texas Press.

Valcárcel, Carlos Daniel. 1947. *La rebelión de Túpac Amaru.* 3rd edition, 1970. Lima: Universo.

Valcárcel, Luis E. 1936–1941. *Mirador indio.* 2 vols. Lima. Reprinted 1958. Cuzco: Primer Festival del Libro Sur-peruano.

Valderrama Fernández, Ricardo, and Carmen Escalante Gutiérrez (see Condori).

Vallée, Lionel, and Salvador Palomino Flores. 1973. "Quelques elements d'ethnographie du 'nakaq.'" *Bulletin de l'Institut Français d'Etudes Andines* 2: 9–19.

Varèse, Stefano. 1972. "Considerations d'anthropologie utopique." *Les Temps Modernes* 29 (316): 760–769.

Vargas, José María, o.p. 1947. "Noticias biográficas de fray Domingo de Santo

Tomás." In *La primera gramática quechua*. Quito: Instituto Histórico Dominicano, xxiii–xxxvi.

Vargas Ugarte, Rubén, s.i. 1938. *Manuscritos peruanos del Archivo de Indias*. Biblioteca peruana vol. 2. Lima: La Prensa.

———. 1941. *Los jesuitas del Perú*. Lima: n.p.

———. 1942. *Historia del Perú, Virreynato (1551–1590)*. Lima: La Prensa.

———. 1947. *Manuscritos peruanos en las bibliotecas y archivos de Europa y América*. Biblioteca peruana vol. 5. Buenos Aires: n.p.

———. 1951–1954. *Concilios Limenses*. Lima: Tip. Peruana.

———. 1953. *Historia de la iglesia en el Perú*, vol. 1. Lima: Imprenta Santa María.

———. 1960. *Historia de la iglesia en el Perú*, vol. 3. Burgos: Aldecoa.

———. 1963. *Los jesuitas del Perú y el arte*. Lima: n.p.

Villanueva, Horacio. 1983. "Diego Cristóbal Tupac Amaru y Antonio Valdés." In Comité Arquidiocesano del Bicentenario Tupac Amaru (eds.). *Tupac Amaru y la iglesia: Antología*. Lima: Banco de los Andes, 301–323.

Villar, Leonardo. 1890. *Lingüística nacional, Estudios sobre la Keshua*. Lima: El Comercio.

Voegelin, Carl, Florence Voegelin, and Noel W. Schultz Jr. 1967. "The Language Situation in Arizona as Part of the Southwest Culture Area." In Dell Hymes and William Bittle (eds.). *Studies in Southwest Ethnolinguistics*. The Hague: Mouton, 403–451.

Wachtel, Nathan. 1971. *La vision des vaincus*. Paris: Gallimard. Translated (tr. Ben and Siân Reynolds) 1977. *The Vision of the Vanquished*. Hassocks: Harvester.

———. 1987. "Comentario" [on] Alfredo Torero. "Lenguas y pueblos altiplánicos en torno al siglo xvi." *Revista Andina* 5: 392–394.

Wang, William S-Y. 1969. "Competing Changes as a Cause of Residue." *Language* 45: 9–25.

Watkins, Calvert. 1962. *Indo-European Origins of the Celtic Verb*. Dublin: Institute for Advanced Study.

———. 1973. "Language and Its History." *Daedelus* 102 (3): 99–111.

Waugh, Linda R. 1984. "Some Remarks on the Nature of the Linguistic Sign." In Jerzy Pelc, Thomas Sebeok, Edward Stankiewicz, and Thomas Winner (eds.). *Sign, System, and Function: Papers of the First and Second Polish-American Semiotics Colloquia*. Berlin: Mouton, 389–438.

———. 1990. "Iconicity in the Lexicon and Its Relevance for a Theory of Morphology." In Marge Landsberg (ed.). *Syntactic Iconicity and Freezes*. Berlin: Mouton de Gruyter.

Waugh, Linda R. and Madeleine Newfield. 1989. "Iconicity and the Morpheme: Toward a Model of the Lexicon." Manuscript, Department of Modern Languages and Linguistics, Cornell University.

Weber, David. 1976. *Suffix-as-Operator Analysis and the Grammar of Successive Encoding in Llacón Quechua*. Yarinacocha: Instituto Lingüístico de Verano.

Whitney, William Dwight. 1875. Φύσει or Θέσει—Natural or Conventional?"

Transactions of the American Philological Association for 1874: 95–116. Reprinted in Michael Silverstein (ed.). 1971. *Whitney on Language*. Cambridge: MIT Press, 111–132.

Wijk, Nicolaas van. 1938. "L'étude diachronique des phénomènes phonologiques et extra-phonologiques." *Travaux du Cercle Linguistique de Prague* 8: 297–318.

Williams, Clyde E. 1968. "Quechua Phonology." Doctoral dissertation in linguistics, Indiana University.

Williams, Raymond. 1977. *Marxism and Literature*. London: Oxford.

Wölck, Wolfgang. 1987. *Pequeño brevario quechua*. Lima: Instituto de Estudios Peruanos.

Wood, Robert D., s.m. 1986. *"Teach Them Good Customs": Colonial Indian Education and Acculturation in the Andes*. Culver City: Labyrinthos.

Woodbury, Anthony C. 1987. "Meaningful Phonological Processes." *Language* 63: 685–740.

Woolard, Kathryn. 1985. "Language Variation and Cultural Hegemony." *American Ethnologist* 12: 738–748.

Yepez Miranda, Alfredo. 1946. *Signos del Cuzco*. Lima: Miranda.

Yokoyama, Masako. 1951. "Outline of Kechua Structure I: Morphology." *Language* 27: 38–67.

Zonneveld, Wim. 1980. "The Looking Glass War: On the Role of Hypercorrection in Phonological Change." In Wim Zonneveld, Frans van Coetsem, and Orrin W. Robinson (eds.). *Studies in Dutch Phonology*. The Hague: Nijhoff, 293–325.

Zuidema, R. Tom. 1966. "Algunos problemas etnohistóricos del departamento de Ayacucho." *Wamani* (Ayacucho) 1: 68–75.

———. 1968. "El estudio arqueológico, etnohistórico y antropológico social en unas comunidades del Rio Pampas." *Verhandlungen des 38 Internationalen Amerikanistenkongressen* 2: 503–505.

———. 1970. "Social versus Structural Change in Quechua Society of Southern Peru." In *Anniversary Contributions to Anthropology*. Leiden: E. J. Brill, 153–158.

———. 1971. "What Are Asymmetric Alliance Systems?" Manuscript.

———. 1973. "The Origin of the Inca Empire." *Les grandes empires, Recueils de la Société Jean Bodin pour l'Histoire Comparative des Institutions* 31: 733–757.

———. 1977. "The Inca Kinship System." In Ralph Bolton and Enrique Mayer (eds.). *Andean Kinship and Marriage*. Washington, D.C.: American Anthropology Association, 240–281.

———. 1980. "El *ushnu*." *Revista de la Universidad Complutense* (Madrid) 117: 317–362.

———. 1982a. "Myth and History in Ancient Peru." In Ino Rossi (ed.). *The Logic of Culture*. Brooklyn: Bergin, 150–175.

———. 1982b. "Catachillay: The Role of the Pleiades and of the Southern Cross and α- and β-Centauri in the Calendar of the Incas." In Anthony F. Aveni and Gary Urton, (eds.). *Ethnoastronomy and Archaeoastronomy in the American Tropics*. New York: New York Academy of Sciences.

———. 1982c. "The Sidereal Lunar Calendar of the Incas." In A. F. Aveni (ed.). *New World Archaeo-astronomy.* Cambridge: Cambridge University Press, 59–107.

———. 1986. *La civilisation inca au Cusco.* Paris: PUF.

Zúñiga, Madeleine. 1979. "Programa experimental de Quinua, Informe de 1964–1968." Documento de Trabajo, Centro de Investigación de Lingüística Aplicada, Universidad Nacional de San Marcos, Lima.

———. 1987. "Sobre los alfabetos oficiales del Quechua y el Aymara." *Allpanchis* 29/30: 469–482.

Zúñiga, Madeleine, M. Lozada, and L. Cano de Gálvez. 1977. "Diseño de un programa experimental de educación bilingüe quechua-castellano." Documento de Trabajo 34, Centro de Investigación de Lingüística Aplicada, Universidad Nacional de San Marcos, Lima.

Index

Lightning Source UK Ltd.
Milton Keynes UK
UKHW040825020819
347268UK00011B/49/P